Counsels from the Holy Mountain

Selected from the
Letters and Homilies of
Geronda Ephraim of Arizona

A translation of "Πατρικαὶ Νουθεσίαι"
("Fatherly Counsels"), Third Edition

.

©1999, 2020 St. Anthony's Greek Orthodox Monastery
4784 N. Saint Joseph's Way
Florence, Arizona 85132 USA

Second Editon 2020

Contents

Introduction

Years ago, we began an undertaking to collect letters of our venerable Elder addressed to his spiritual children—monks, nuns, and laymen—which they eagerly sent to us at our request. From these letters we selected the paragraphs concerning spiritual subjects. We arranged those paragraphs by theme, and in this way ten booklets were made, each containing views, opinions, counsels, and in general everything that a spiritual father offers—with God's enlightenment—to his spiritual children. These writings are the fruit of his many years of laboring to practice all that the Holy Fathers have given us as a spiritual "heritage" (cf. 2 Tim. 1:14).

These booklets were distributed to a very limited number of the Elder's spiritual children as an aid in their spiritual struggle. Following their exhortations and encouragement, we proceeded to publish the present book by combining these booklets and including a few excerpts from the Elder's homilies. [Since the Greek edition had several paragraphs that merely repeated ideas stated elsewhere in the book, they were omitted in this translation, with the Elder's blessing.] We pray that all who read this with good intentions and pious zeal will be greatly benefited and will delight to drink the spiritual water of our venerable Elder.

It is our duty to thank everyone who in various ways contributed to the completion of this publication, praying that they be rewarded abundantly by God.

This book is dedicated to all who are traveling along the narrow and difficult way which leads to eternal life.

The Fathers of the Holy Monastery of Philotheou

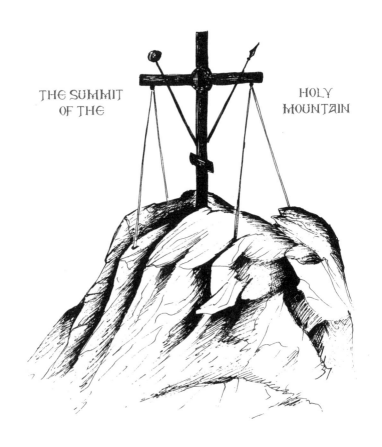

THE SUMMIT
OF THE

HOLY
MOUNTAIN

Prologue for the English Edition

by His Eminence Hierotheos Vlachos,
Metropolitan of Nafpaktos and St. Vlasios

I consider it to be my special honor that the Very Reverend Archimandrite Paisios, abbot of Saint Anthony's Greek Orthodox Monastery, asked me to write a prologue for the book of the Elder and Father of this holy monastery, Archimandrite Ephraim, the former abbot of the Holy Monastery of Philotheou on Mount *Athos*.* I thank God that this book is now translated into English, because I believe that it will give another perspective to those who desire their rebirth in Christ and want to overcome the great problems that torment man today: death and the duality between pleasure and pain.

I have met Father Ephraim in the past and I am able to appreciate his words. In the 1960's, when I was a student at the Theological School of Thessalonica, I heard about the presence of an extraordinary monk who lived in *hesychia** at New *Skete** of the *Holy Mountain** and occupied himself with *noetic prayer*.* At that time I had an intense desire to become acquainted with this Elder. I went to see him in his hut at New Skete and waited patiently to meet with him, since he was resting after his all-night vigil of noetic prayer which concluded

---

*Terms found in the Glossary are marked with an asterisk and written in italics the first time they appear.

with the Divine Liturgy. After a few hours I was able to meet with Father Ephraim, and I remember the sweet words that came out of his mouth. For the first time, I heard a word that he would often repeat: "occupy" *(adolescho).*† I realized that I had before me a *hieromonk** who unceasingly occupied himself with God and lived the insatiable profusion of divine mercy.

Later I met him again on the Holy Mountain when he was the abbot of the Holy Monastery of Philotheou. I visited him with a group of young people, and again I experienced the same sensation. His words were very compunctious, sweet, penetrating, revealing, clairvoyant, renewing, healing, and extracted from *patristic** wisdom. He was exactly the same person whom one meets in the book *Counsels from the Holy Mountain,* for it contains words full of grace, words of a spiritual father to his spiritual children. And we know clearly that a spiritual father is he who gives birth to spiritual children, who brings them out of the maelstrom of the *passions** and leads them into the glorious liberty of the children of God[1]—he gives them another perspective and meaning in life.

Father Ephraim, as I remember him very well from my youth and as one encounters him in this book, is a genuine teacher of the spiritual life and a reliable guide for the Christian's journey towards rebirth, since he himself has experienced and learned the divine, which is why his words are "full of grace and truth."[2] And in this case the saying of St. John of Sinai, the author of *The Ladder,* applies: "A genuine teacher is he who has received the spiritual tablet of *knowledge** from God inscribed by His finger—that is, by the operation of *illumination**—and who has no need of other books."

The content of this book is in harmony with the hesychastic way of life, which is antithetical to the rationalistic and sensual way of life. And we know very well that hesychia is the apos-

---

† "Adolescho" means to occupy oneself in prayer or *contemplation.**

[1] cf. Rom. 8:21

[2] Jn. 1:14

tolic and patristic lifestyle. In other words, it is the true life that Christ taught and the Apostles and Holy Fathers of the Church lived; it is the prerequisite for the prophetic, apostolic, martyric, and ascetical grace. *Noetic** hesychia, in its true anthropological dimension, is the basis of theology, the foundation of all the dogmas of the faith.

The Holy Fathers dogmatized that Christ is perfect God and perfect man, that in His person the divine nature was united with the human nature "without confusion, without undergoing change, indivisibly, inseparably," that Christ is one of the Trinity. They developed all the Christological and Trinitarian teachings precisely because they had personal experience of this truth—that is, they saw the glory of the Divinity in the human nature of the Logos. And this existential knowledge was a fruit and result of noetic hesychia. First came *praxis,** which is the *purification** of the *heart,** and then followed *theoria,** which is illumination and *theosis.**

The council that was held during the times of St. Gregory Palamas (which bears all the characteristics of an Ecumenical Council) is, in fact, the cornerstone of all the Ecumenical Councils, from the viewpoint that it dogmatized on the true way and the true method which one can and must use to reach the vision of God, which is crucial since the dogmas are a fruit of this vision of God. In other words, God-seeing Fathers are the ones who make a council Ecumenical/Orthodox. What was stated in the Synodal Tome of 1347 is very characteristic: "We hereby pronounce the aforementioned most honorable hieromonk Gregory Palamas and the monks in agreement with him . . . to be most reliable defenders and champions and aids of the Church and of the Orthodox faith," and whoever speaks against St. Gregory and the monks with him, "we pass the same judgment of excommunication upon, whether they be clergy or laymen." In other words, whoever denies Orthodox hesychasm is excommunicated by this Council, and whoever cannot understand the hesychastic life shows that he does not have the mind-set of the Church.

Consequently, a theology that is not linked with hesychasm—in the Orthodox sense of the word—a theology that is not the fruit of Orthodox noetic hesychia and that does not lead to it, by which one is not healed and does not see the divine, is a worldly, intellectualistic theology created by the mind, and it offers absolutely nothing to man—or rather creates more confusion and trouble. According to the inspired words of the God-seer St. Gregory Palamas, Orthodox noetic hesychia is "true praxis, the entrance to true theoria, or vision of God—or, to put it more simply, is the only proof that a soul is truly healthy."

I am in a position to know that the following chapters are an outcome and a fruit of obedience and noetic hesychia, a result of divine ascents, and they are certainly words coming from a paternal heart, words that help a person be healed in the atmosphere of spiritual love. They are texts that inspire the person who reads them with faith and hope; they give another dimension to the spiritual life; they open new horizons and help him overcome the frightful dual relationship between pleasure and pain; they present another language that is different from the language of intellectual and academic theology—a theology that operates either within the limits of rational thinking or within the framework of the spiritually void and spineless social work. His words arouse the heart to prayer, precisely because they proceed from prayer.

It is a well-known fact that when a person is genuine, when he truly loves, when he has tasted the gift of the goodness of the Lord, then, even if his wording is deficient, he nevertheless helps his fellow man effectively, more than one who employs elaborate words and elegant theological expressions. This is so because it is one thing to come across a spring in the woods, which is not ornamented but provides cool and fresh water that quenches man's thirst, and another thing to make a wonderful drawing of a fountain, which, however, has no water and cannot quench man's thirst, or even to find a fountain which is very beautiful but unsuitable for quenching man's thirst, since its water is recycled and dirty.

It is significant that the spiritual words contained in this book, which emanate from the vigils and stillness of the Holy Mountain, are presented to America where, on the one hand, a great disillusionment with the rationalistic and sensualistic atmosphere prevails, and on the other hand, a search for authentic life is being observed—a search that extends beyond Vaticanized ecclesiology, academic and intellectualistic theology, Protestantizing sociology and ethicology, spiritually void and deluded *meditation*,* atheistic social activism, etc. And I believe that this book will be of great help to those who seek to taste in their personal life—in proportion to their struggle, of course—the true scriptural and patristic food that gives meaning to the life of man and constitutes the true bread of life.

Papa-Ephraim* (as we call him here in Greece), in the words of St. Symeon the New Theologian, "received fire," and he has imparted this fire to many monks of the Holy Mountain and in turn to the Church in America that has great need of it. Now, with the English edition of this book, he will spread this fire to all who seek genuine Orthodox life.

October 30, 1998
Sts. Cleopas and Artemas
the Holy Apostles

The Holy Mountain

St. Anthony's Monastery, Arizona

St. Anthony the Great

The Panagia of Arizona

St. Joseph the Hesychast
(1897~1959)

Geronda Ephraim
(1928~2019)

The Chapel of St. Menas at St. Anthony's Monastery

The Tomb of Geronda Ephraim in the Chapel of St. Menas

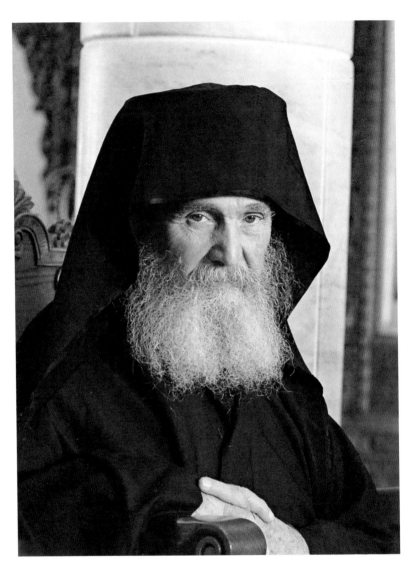

Geronda Ephraim

Chapter One

On Salvation and Paradise

Now in the springtime, when nature is wearing its most beautiful apparel, one feels inexpressible joy when this natural beauty is accompanied by a sublime spiritual state. Truly, our holy God has made all things in wisdom![1] The soul cannot get enough of beholding the beauty of nature. Oh, if man would only lift his mind above this earthly realm to the heavenly Jerusalem, to the inconceivable beauty of paradise, where the finite, earthly mind ceases to operate!

If here in exile, in this accursed land of weeping, our holy God has given us so much beauty to enjoy, I wonder how much there will be in the place where God Himself dwells! Truly, "the sufferings of this present time are not worthy to be compared with the coming glory and bliss."[2]

*Theosis***** in the Heavens, my child! There the Lord our God will remove every tear from our eyes, and do away with all sorrow and pain and sighing, for there the angelic way of life reigns, and the only work is to chant hymns and spiritual odes! An eternal Sabbath is prepared for us where we shall live in joy

---

[1] cf. Ps. 103:26 (All quotations from the Old Testament are from the Septuagint.)
[2] cf. Rom. 8:18

with our Father, God, Who is waiting for us to be ready so that He may call us to Him forever! There every saved soul will live in an ocean of love, sweetness, joy, amazement, and wonder!

2. A time will come, the hour will strike, the moment will arrive for these eyes to close and for the soul's eyes to open. Then we shall see a new world, new beings, a new creation, a new life without end. Its title is "Infinite Immortality," the great homeland, incorruptible and everlasting—the heavenly Jerusalem, the mother of the firstborn, where redeemed souls, which have been washed of their impurity by the Blood of the innocent Lamb, will dwell!

Who is able to express in words or with a pen the joy, the exaltation, the bliss of those blessed saved souls? Blessed are they who have died in the Lord, for the riches of God's goodness await them. Blessed is he who wins the "lottery" for the heavenly festival, for riches that cannot be taken away, for the glory that God Himself has described: "sons of the Most High, children of God, heirs of God, and joint heirs with Christ."[3]

Before the Passion, the Lord entreated His Heavenly Father on behalf of His disciples and those who would believe through them: "Father, I desire that they also whom Thou hast given Me may be with Me where I am, that they may behold My glory which Thou hast given Me; for Thou didst love Me before the foundation of the world."[4]

How great is Jesus' love for us! He took on human nature and was hanged upon the Cross, freeing us from the tyranny of sin and death. And as a dear brother, He makes us worthy of jointly inheriting the infinite wealth of His Heavenly Father! Oh, what love for us! Oh, how cold we are to Him! Oh, how ungrateful I am towards my Benefactor! My God, my God, have pity on me, and do not condemn me as I deserve because of my deeds!

---

[3] cf. Rom. 8:16-17
[4] Jn. 17:24

3. Just as God has spiritually united us with an unbreakable bond, likewise may He count us worthy to be together in His Heavenly Kingdom, so that we may dine at the spiritual table and delight in His divine fare, united with the Heavenly Father, in Whom the everlasting rivers of His divine waters flow. Oh, what a great calling! Oh, how rich are the fruits of transitory afflictions!

The children of God will be adorned with heavenly garments; the divine features in their faces will appear radiant; they will enter into the paternal legacy—the eternal repose! They will go about those heavenly dwellings, and beholding those boundless riches, they will remain in *ecstasy** without realizing that eons are passing! Oh, what a great calling for man! But two distressing thoughts blemish this good *meditation.** The first one is that I shall not participate in all of this glorious blessedness—this is just a meditation now, but later it will take on flesh and bones, in other words, it will materialize. The second one is that people live their lives in ignorance of this great calling, and consequently this ignorance gives rise to separation from God, and spiritual death.

O my God, Lord of Sabaoth, enlighten the darkness of our hearts that we may see Thee, the true light, the blessed light that enlightens and gladdens the hearts of Thy friends. Enlighten us that we may follow Thee until the eternal rest.

4. Everything will pass and will end as if it had never existed, whereas works done in God will remain with the soul that worked them so that the worker may reap eternal life from them. Blessed are the spiritual philosophers of God, Who give away transient things and store up eternal things, so that when they depart, they will find their treasures in God's treasury with accrued interest. Blessed are they who clean their hearts from the weeds of sin and cultivate the good seed, for the time will come for them to reap sheaves of eternal life! Blessed are they who sow tears with spiritual fasting, that is, always hungering and thirsting for good works, for they will reap eternal joy!

5. All the labor, toil, and temptations in this life, my blessed child, cannot be compared with that blessed life. Even if we had thousands of lives and sacrificed them all, we would not have done anything significant in comparison with the future glory in which Christ the Master longs to establish us through His precious and life-giving Blood! This is why the Apostle Paul says, "The sufferings of this present time are not worthy to be compared with the glory which shall be revealed in us."[5]

Furthermore, reflect that man "withers like a flower and passes like a dream,"[6] and that "when the trumpet sounds, all the dead will rise as if in an earthquake"[7] to meet Christ. When the door of the age to come opens, and when the present world is destroyed, then our nature will be restored to its original state. The Lord "will transform our lowly body that it may be conformed to His glorious body."[8] Our nature, which groans and travails together with all of creation,[9] awaits the glorious revealing of the children of God with an intense yearning. "For the earnest expectation of the creation eagerly waits for the revealing of the sons of God."[10]

The grandeur of man, whom God raises to such heights and glory, is unrivaled! Yet we *passionate** sinners are unaware of and indifferent to these great riches, and our way of thinking is completely earthly. Just think: this body which is fetid dirt is counted worthy to be conformed to God's glory, to become angelic![11]

Now, men are material in comparison to the angels, which are purely spiritual beings. Angels in comparison to God are somewhat "material." They are not purely spiritual as God is, Who is unapproachable light. In this manner men will also

---

5 Rom. 8:18   9 cf. Rom. 8:22
6 cf. Is. 40:6-8   10 Rom. 8:19
7 cf. 2 Thes. 4:16   11 cf. Phil. 3:21
8 Phil. 3:21

become angelic then. Then, a single unity of the fullness of the Church, of the faithful with Christ will occur. How tenderly and paternally our Lord puts it: "Father," He said to His Father, "I desire that they also whom Thou hast given Me may be with Me where I am, that they may behold My glory which Thou hast given Me."[12]

Can worldly riches compare with these words of God? If only we were there where our Lord is—where angels shudder and tremble to approach! O hidden wisdom and infinite wealth of God!

6. Do not forget your goal, my child. Look into Heaven and see the beauty that awaits us. What are the present, earthly things? Aren't they but ashes and dust and a dream? Don't we see that everything here is subject to decay? Whereas things above are everlasting, the Kingdom of God is endless, and blessed is he who will dwell in it, for he will behold the glory of His divine face!

My child, do not forget that we are in this world only temporarily and that our life dangles by a thread and that all the desirable things in the world are vain. So, whoever despises the vain things of the world—in other words, does not passionately desire them—will participate in the eternal good things.

So, when we have this knowledge of the truth, naturally we shall turn the eyes of our soul at every moment towards the eternal life, towards the heavenly Jerusalem, where the choirs of angels chant godly canticles of ineffable sweetness and wisdom. Oh, my children, how much glory your souls will have when after death they ascend to the Heavens and are numbered with the angels in Heaven!

7. Let us glorify the risen Lord, Who counted us worthy to celebrate His holy Resurrection. Let us pray that He will also count us worthy to celebrate the eternal Sabbath in the Heav-

---

[12] Jn. 17:24

ens, in the new Jerusalem, in the eternal joy. "And no one will take this joy away from you."[13] Indeed, my child, for earthly joy is followed by sorrows which can annihilate it, whereas heavenly joy is not, because it flows continuously as if from an inexhaustible and life-giving spring.

Let us compel ourselves in our Christian duties in order to be able to celebrate the eternal *Pascha** close to our Christ and see Him face to face for our blessed enjoyment, without it being interrupted anymore by trials and despair.

8. Ah, if you could only see a little bit of paradise, if you could only hear for a few seconds the chanting of the sweet angels who shine with heavenly light and emit paradisiacal fragrance! Oh, what beauty! Unfortunately, we are in the dark about all these things.

There everything shines with limitless bliss. And what does the throne of Christ tell you? Christ the Master sits upon a throne, and due to His light no one can discern His sacred and most sweet face. Oh, what sweetness and beauty! What is more beautiful than this? This is truly paradise: to behold the face of our Jesus! Glory to Thy Cross, O Lord, and to Thy Resurrection!

O depth of the wisdom of God! O Mysteries of the three-sun Deity! Blessed is he who humbles himself like a child, obeying all commands with a guileless soul for the love of God! And woe to him who will hold on to his egotism, like me; how many divine gifts does he deprive himself of!

My children, run with humility to reach the Lord Who humbled Himself for our sake—our sweetest, beloved Christ, the light of our poor souls.

See what beauty awaits us! If you could only see how beautiful it is! You would disregard everything; you would even become like trash to be stepped on, just as long as you

---

[13] cf. Jn. 16:22

would not be deprived of everything that the sweet love of Jesus has prepared! These are the kinds of things my Elder used to tell me, and I am conveying them to you so that you may be sweetened. I am done—forgive me!

9. The Apostle Paul speaks to us about paradise very beautifully. He was caught up to the third heaven[14] and to the beauty of the Kingdom of Heaven and cried out in ecstasy, "How lovely and exquisitely beautiful the Kingdom of God is, which cannot be compared with any earthly beauty!" Paradise is so beautiful that the eye of man has never been able to see such beauty. Likewise, a human ear has never heard sweeter chanting, since in Heaven angelic choirs chant incomparably more sweetly than the most sweet-voiced nightingales!

The Apostle Paul goes on to say that man has never conceived what God has prepared in Heaven, in paradise, for His children. Indeed, it is the truth that if we knew the spiritual pleasures of paradise, we would be patient in every situation in order to gain it. Whereas now, because of our ignorance, we do the opposite and thus go far away from it!

Oh, if we only knew what paradise is! The human mind is unable to conceive the magnitude of its beauty! There the choirs of angels and holy souls chant incessantly—an eternal Pascha! There, souls converse with exultation. They talk about how they passed this vain life and how much God helped them to escape hell and to repose in this blissful place of God! They offer endless thanks to God for this tremendous mercy of His, that He gave them paradise! I, however, am not fit for paradise, because my works notify me in advance that I am only fit for hell.

What is paradise? It is a place full of unfading flowers, replete with divine aromas, the delight of angels, Paschal life,

---

[14] vid. 1 Cor. 12:2

divine *eros,** ceaseless doxology of God, and an eternal life! So then, it is worth struggling for—but how insignificant our struggle is in light of this "fantastic," so to speak, paradise!

Oh, paradise, how beautiful you are! Your beauty allures me and changes me into a different person. Why shouldn't I endeavor and struggle properly to obtain you? My God, our Lord, deliver us from accursed pride, so that guided by holy humility we may become inhabitants of sweetest paradise. Amen; so be it.

THE PRAYER OF ANNA

THE GARDEN

Chapter Two

On Afflictions, Pain, and Labors

May the love of our Heavenly Father be with your souls, so that being invigorated by it you may bear the fruit of obedience to His life-giving commandments. "Those who desire to live piously in Christ Jesus will suffer persecution."[1] Since you follow the Savior Christ through your devotion to the angelic way of life, your greatest duty is to bear all suffering, whether it comes from nature, indolence, sins, or people. Since we desire to live a Christ-like life, we are obligated to submit to God's will, because all things come from God. And since they are from God—and thus are the divine will—the Heavenly Father commands them. Shall we not obey? Shall we not cry out with the blessed Job, "As it seemed good to the Lord, so it has come to pass. Blessed be the name of the Lord"?[2]

Through patience and thanksgiving to God, then, we show obedience to the divine will. Won't the obedient one be counted worthy to acquire even here eternal life in himself? Yes, he will live unto the ages of ages! Therefore, let us struggle; let us make our souls keen by working them over the whetstone of patience, in order to carry out a work pleasing to God. Afflictions, illnesses, distresses, trials—none of these will separate us from the love of Christ. For we have already been taught that narrow and difficult is the way which leads

[1] 2 Tim. 3:12
[2] Job 1:21

those who walk along it into the life without sorrow.[3] Thorns and thistles are placed to the right and left along the way; therefore, we need much caution.

Along the difficult way—that is, in the trial of sickness and so forth—the thorn of doubt, of impatience, of cowardice comes to rend the garment of the soul. What is needed, therefore, is to pull out this thorn through faith, hope, and patience, having Jesus Christ as a model. Throughout His life on earth He had many afflictions, and His all-holy soul was oppressed by many thorns, and so He exclaimed, "In your patience you will gain your souls."[4]

Through illnesses and through grievous things in general, God bestows gifts upon us as a Father, for He seeks ways to impart His holiness: "What son is there whom his father does not discipline? If you are without discipline, you are illegitimate children and not sons."[5] Oh! Whenever we suffer, then it becomes manifest that we are children of God. And who would not like to be a child of God? Therefore, if you want to be a child of God, endure the afflictions and trials sent by God with thanksgiving, faith, and hope.

Even trials coming from people are really sent from God so that we may acquire tolerance, forbearance, compassion, and patience, for all these are divine characteristics, as the Lord says to us: "He makes His sun rise on the evil and the good, and sends rain on the just and the unjust."[6] For this reason we are obliged to love all people. May no trace of hatred or evil be found in our souls, so that we may be called children of God.

The sufferings of our whole life are not worthy to be compared with the inconceivable good things that God has prepared for those souls which carry their cross, whether it comes from the devil, other people, or one's own nature.

---

[3] vid. Mt. 7:14   [5] Heb. 12:7-8
[4] Lk. 21:19   [6] Mt. 5:45

Because whatever passion or weakness may fight us, when we fight back against it, it causes us to be counted worthy of the blessing: "Blessed is the man who endures trial, for when he has stood the test, he will receive the crown of life."[7]

For this reason, my child, endure everything, for a crown is being woven invisibly for the head of each one of us. Winter is bitter, but paradise is sweet. Endure the frost of trials, that your feet may joyfully dance in Heaven.

2. Many things afflict us, my child, but blessed is he who passes through the grievous things of this present life with patience and thanksgiving. Yes, we ought to thank God, Who through such grievous things prepares our immortal soul to inherit the eternal blessings of the Kingdom of Heaven!

"The Lord disciplines us for our good, that we may share His holiness."[8] Through various afflictions He works in us an eternal glory that far outweighs them all![9] For this reason it is neither necessary nor beneficial to be indignant when the Lord disciplines us. Rather, it is beneficial for everyone's soul to have perfect obedience to the Physician of our souls and bodies, Who during various afflictions operates on the invisible wounds of the soul of each one of us, with the holy aim of giving us health—that is, the purification of the *heart** from vile passions. To such an omniscient spiritual Physician, we have the indispensable obligation to offer unceasing thanks by our actions, so that we do not grieve Him by any offense.

All the saints passed their lives in afflictions and manifold sufferings, in spite of the fact that sin did not have any power over them to afflict them. Nevertheless, many times their life was a true martyrdom. Now, what justification will we give— we who have fallen into and occupy ourselves with many sins—to claim the right to pass our lives without afflictions and sufferings? Most certainly we are accountable for sin, and

---

[7] Jam. 1:12

[8] cf. Heb. 12:10

[9] cf. 2 Cor. 4:17

consequently we need the whip of the salvific discipline of the Lord, that we may have the good fortune of being saved into the Kingdom of Heaven, by grace of the mercies of our God Who loves mankind.

3. Why are you sorrowful and glum while walking along the way of God? Those who have forgotten God, Who have no hope in the living and eternal fountain of God, should grieve. But we, who believe in the living God and whose hopes depend upon Him, ought to rejoice that we have such a Father in the Heavens, Who loves us more than all fathers and mothers and Who takes infinite care to render us worthy of Him.

But, you say, we fall every moment! Yes, I do not deny it—but we know that our nature is from clay and that it desires the earth and seeks what is base, for "the mind of man is inclined to evil from his youth."[10] And we see within us a law which seeks to capture our free will, to subjugate it and render it a slave of sin.[11]

In all this, however, our good intention triumphs. God has given us spiritual weapons to fight against every satanic attack: the glorious banner of the Cross of hope—living hope in Him Who said, "I will never leave you nor forsake you"[12]—hope in our Christ, Who was hanged on the Cross, and all who look upon Him and hope in Him will not be put to shame. The all-immaculate Blood which was poured out on the Cross pardoned the sins of mankind and poured forth life. "Blessed is the man who hopes in Him."[13]

Take courage, my child; this grief of yours will turn into joy. This grief produces great good for you; it surrounds you as with a breastplate of iron, so that the evil darts of attachment to earthly things do not tear your mind away from the concern for heavenly things and for your immortal soul.

---

[10] cf. Gen. 8:21   [12] Heb. 13:5
[11] cf. Rom. 7:23   [13] cf. Ps. 33:8

Grief will succeed joy, and joy, grief, just as night follows day. This is how the Father of lights has established the path of those who are being saved. Just have patience and hope: engrave these in the depths of your heart—with these, all adversities will be faced.

Cling to our sweet Jesus; cry out to Him in your afflictions. Entrust to Him the care of grievous things and He will do good to you, as to Hannah, the mother of the Prophet Samuel, who, out of extreme grief because of her barrenness, fell down before the Lord and poured out her soul as if beside herself. And her petition did not fail.[14]

Who ever hoped in God and was put to shame? Of course, this does not mean blameworthy hope but active hope—that is, hope along with spiritual works according to our strength; otherwise, it is not hope but mockery. Save us from such deceitful hope, O God.

4. How much loss a person suffers when he forgets his sonship and does not reflect that he is disciplined as a child of God! Love imposes, on genuine parents, an absolute and indispensable duty to exercise discipline on their children. Therefore, since God is our Father, He disciplines His own children to educate them and make them partakers of His holiness.

"My son, do not despise the Lord's discipline or be weary of His reproof."[15] So the Christians' forgetfulness of their own Father, God, is a great evil; for when the paternal rod strikes them (sufferings, afflictions, trials, etc.), they despair; ten thousand *thoughts** overcome them and their discipline becomes very toilsome, without any consolation. How beautifully the Apostle Paul says to us, "You have forgotten," he says, "the exhortation which addresses you as sons."[16] We have forgotten, he says, the consoling counsel which God addresses to us as His children.

---

[14] vid. 1 Kings (1 Sam.) 1:1-18

[15] Prov. 3:11

[16] Heb. 12:5

The discipline of the Lord is inevitable towards His own children, whom He knows. God does not practice favoritism; God, being dispassionate and holy, is not overcome by unhealthy love—which many foolish parents practice on their children and which afterwards causes the destruction and eternal punishment of their loved ones. He does not overlook His beloved children's misconduct and lack of discipline so that He would not upset them. No, a thousand times, no! He is God, possessing genuine love towards His children. He will discipline them; He will admonish them; He will bind their freedom and will rebuke them in various ways in order to transform evil characters into His own holy characters, unto glory and praise in Christ Jesus.

Even Christ, when He was on earth, the beloved Child of the Father, was tried in the discipline of the Lord; not that He, the sinless God, needed it, but for the salvation of man and for our admonition and example, so that we would follow His footsteps: "If it be possible, let this cup pass from me; nevertheless, not as I will, but as Thou dost will; Thy will be done."[17]

How then will we justify ourselves, when our Christ, without having committed any sin—for He was God—went through such fearful sufferings? Reflect on the stupendous condescension of the infinite God: He became Man and suffered such a shameful Passion for the sake of us, the sinful, guilty, and condemned; He was slapped in the face; they scourged Him, reviled Him, crucified Him; He died the most evil death: "Cursed is everyone who hangs on a tree"![18] He, as God, suffered so much for us sinners; what excuse do we have if we do not endure one trial out of love for Him, or at least for our sins?

5. In all circumstances have the *noetic** eye of the soul

---

[17] Mt. 26:39, 6:10
[18] Deut. 21:23, Gal. 3:13

turned upwards, whence help will come. Do not despair, whatever may happen. According to the trial, the way out follows. God never allows, or rather, He does not give a person a load beyond his strength. If men have the discernment to do this with animals, how much more does the good God, Who shed His All-holy Blood for man on the Cross!

The truth is that Christians who endure temporary afflictions acquire through them future eternal joy and repose. We should never envy those who have constant joy and peace here on earth—rather we should pity them, for temporary joy will become for them an obstacle to the future life.

God is merciful but also just—merciful in the present life, but after death a just Judge. It is not possible for Him to give afflicted Christians—that is, true Christians, not just Christians in name—eternal distress as well. But there He will give them constant joy, which no one will be able to take from them. God cannot cast a person from punishment to punishment. Therefore, rejoice instead of grieving, because God counted you worthy to suffer temporarily in order to give you eternal repose.

Eternal joy is reserved only for suffering Christians. In the holy Gospel, the Lord says about the rich man and Lazarus: "Abraham said, 'Son, remember that in your lifetime you received your good things, and likewise Lazarus evil things; but now he is comforted and you are tormented.'"[19]

God never shows favoritism, but He acts according to righteous principles. If you glance through the lives of the saints, you will see continuous trials, afflictions, and distress. This is how they passed their lives. No pleasure-lover will enter into the eternal habitation which is full of ineffable joy, but rather those who were afflicted and endured for God, for the sake of keeping His commandments.

---

[19] Lk. 16:25

The Lord says, "In the world you will have tribulation; but be of good cheer, I have overcome the world."[20] This was said by the God Who came to the earth and labored and suffered throughout His life, and then finally, where did He end up? Hanging on the Cross as accursed, in order to throw down the barrier of the curse.

Terrible anguish wrung the heart of the God-Man, and He cried out, "My God, My God, why hast Thou forsaken Me?" The earth shook and the veil of the Temple was torn in the middle, as could be seen perceptibly. But also on the spiritual plane, the impregnable wall of the curse between God and man shook and utterly crumbled. And as Jesus expired, what had formerly been divided was united, and man became, not simply a friend of God, but God's own kin; man received the grace of adoption into sonship: "heirs of God, and joint heirs with Christ."[21] For mankind gave the All-holy Virgin as a Mother to the Son, and Christ took flesh from Her pure blood. This deified human flesh sat at the right hand of God the Father. Henceforth, God was seen in the Heavens and was worshipped also in human nature by the angels.

Do you see where the human race has ascended? We shall become gods by grace![22] But without afflictions, is anyone able to reach there? We shall be distressed, we shall be afflicted, but one day all will come to an end and will be forgotten; suddenly, the eternal Joy will open wide His tender arms and will call out, "Come to Me, all you who labor and are heavy laden (with afflictions), and I shall give you rest."[23]

In each of your deeds and actions, whether in word or in thought, remember that God is present and He sees them and one day will judge them. From this saving meditation arises godly fear, which produces the greatest benefit: "I beheld the Lord ever before me, for He is at my right hand, that I might

---

[20] Jn. 16:33
[21] Rom. 8:17
[22] cf. Jn. 10:34
[23] Mt. 11:28

not be shaken,"[24] said the Prophet David. "Thy law is a lamp unto my feet and a light unto my paths."[25] It even produces humility. So humble-mindedness does not arise only from trials and tests but also from spiritual meditation and from realizing our weakness.

One reflects on how weak man is, that he is not able to do good, even though it is sown within his nature. Evil, on the contrary, he does very easily, even though it is alien to him. Man wants to please God, but if the grace of God does not work together with him, the good he does is not good; and even if he wants to labor, if God does not help, his desire and labor are in vain.

When a person considers his past—when he did not know God, how much he sinned—he feels contrition, humbles himself, weeps, seeks forgiveness, and reflects: "Even now, if the grace of God leaves me, I am capable of doing worse things." Then a certain fear mingled with humility protects the soul as with a wall. This meditation is called awareness of man's weakness, and it bears the fruits of humility and benefit, without toil and afflictions.

Yes, trials come, but most of them are sent because of our pride. When someone is found in a state of humility, the trials will be fewer and light. But one must be ready, as a captain who expects a storm after the calm. When someone anticipates something, it does not seem strange to him when it comes, because he expected it. Thus one must always be prepared, so that when it comes he will not be distressed. But is it possible, my child, that we not experience distress? For it is from distress, from this affliction, that we shall inherit the eternal, unceasing good things which "eye has not seen, nor ear heard, nor have entered into the heart of man the things which God has prepared for those who love Him."[26]

---

[24] Ps. 15:8
[25] Ps. 118:105
[26] 1 Cor. 2:9

6. Let us not forget, my child, that all the saints passed through this furnace of afflictions in different forms, each one according to the vocation to which he was called. If we take a look at the famous life and conduct of the Empress Saint Theophano, we shall see afflictions heaped up one after the other, throughout her life full of suffering. She suffered greatly; she endeavored in every way—through admonitions, prayers, tears, and examples—to reform her lawful spouse, the Emperor Leo the Wise, who was straying into sin. Her holy soul bore this cross throughout her life. And these sufferings, along with her good works, made her holy.

This is how the life of man is mapped out on this earth; since he has fallen from immortality, he gathers the fruit which disobedience has brought forth. No matter how much he wants to, and no matter how much he strives to live without afflictions and thinks that he will reach this goal, he will not be able to achieve this, because the tempter is going to and fro on the earth and walking around it,[27] sifting everyone and watering them with the poison of afflictions as a result of the curse of the law.[28] Wherever you look, whomever you ask, all as with one mouth will confess that some thorn pricks them and they suffer.

However, there are different kinds of affliction. Some are afflicted because they are not able to revel in illicit deeds; this is blameworthy affliction. Others are afflicted lawfully and for good reason; this is a natural outcome. But when there is also spiritual knowledge, then afflictions are engrafted into the one who endures patiently for his sanctification.

This is precisely what happened with Saint Theophano as well; she suffered lawfully, because her spouse was unfaithful to her. But she, with spiritual knowledge, admonition, and a Christian example, enduring, weeping, and praying, placed all her trust in God. Because of all this, holiness was grafted onto

---

[27] cf. Job 1:7
[28] cf. Gal. 3:10

what was lawful. For this reason, bear all these things; become holy through afflictions. Give thanks to God, Who disciplines you temporally in order to give you repose eternally!

When I see or hear that someone lives without afflictions and prospers according to all his desires, I consider this to be abandonment by God! As for us, may God count us with the sufferers, so that He may write our names in the book of life, so that we not remain outside His divine bridal chamber. No matter how much we may suffer, one day all will come to an end and be forgotten; only deeds, whether evil or good, will remain to follow the soul to the tribunal, where it will hear the great verdict. This thought often moves me and I weep: what will I, the unworthy priest, speak in my defense at the judgment seat of Christ? Pray for me that I not be condemned.

7. My beloved brother in Christ, may the grace of our Lady *Theotokos** preserve you from everything which would soil your dear little soul. Amen.

"Tribulations and necessities have found me, Thy commandments are my meditation."[29] Afflictions succeed one another; we need patience. By meditating on the divine law, we are enlightened as to how to bear them, why they come, and what purpose they have. They come in order to teach us to become bearers of hardship, practiced fighters, followers of Him Who was crucified for us, brothers of all the saints who walked the thorny road of the Cross: the martyrs by martyrdom, the monastics by *asceticism,** the faithful by keeping the holy commandments and through the various trials caused by the world, the devil, and the *flesh.**

No one has ever been saved in comfort and without trials. Thus it follows that if we also bear trials, we should rejoice, for thus walked all those who were saved. And since we want to be saved, too, there is no other road but afflictions!

---

[29] Ps. 118:143

Afflictions come in order to bring us closer to God, for afflictions grieve and oppress the heart, softening and humbling it. And when it is humbled, God looks upon it: "A heart that is broken and humbled God will not despise."[30] "Upon whom shall I look, if not upon him who is humble and meek, and trembles at my words?"[31]

He who bears his sorrows with joy and knowledge will be freed from his sins and their penance. A spiritual character is also created in him: the person becomes merciful, humble, meek, etc. The one who does not have true knowledge of trials is distressed and grieved at a time when he should rejoice, for he walks the road of holy Golgotha and of the saints.

May the grace of God, which heals infirmities and makes up for deficiencies, help all of us to be patient in all things, that we be counted worthy of the Kingdom of God. Amen.

8. It is very consoling, my child, that each one of us will receive his reward based on how much he has labored for the love of Christ. It involves much labor to bear the burden of souls in the present era, which is ruled by egotism and self-will.

Let us not lose our courage; for invisibly present is Jesus, Who will rebuke the stormy sea of trials and bring the calm of grace. Struggle upon the raging waves; call upon the only all-powerful God: "Lord, Lord, look down from Heaven and behold my trials and perfect my soul to do Thy will, for Thou art my God."[32]

9. Glory to the only wise God, Who knows how to extract the sweet out of the bitter and thus enrich our knowledge out of His boundless love toward us. He scourges us with afflictions and trials, so that He can draw us near Him; for He knows that through the sorrowful things of this present life, man remains near Him and is saved.

---

30 Ps. 50:17
31 Is. 66:2
32 cf. Ps. 79:15-16

The comfortable life is very hazardous for eternal salvation. It is not the Spirit of God that dwells in those living in comfort, but rather the spirit of the devil, according to the saying of the Fathers. For this reason, in this life's sorrows we need to have patience and thanksgiving, for God is well pleased with both of these virtues. May the Lord give us much patience in our life's sorrows, so that in everything we may thank the Giver of good things Who provides for us.

10. About the grief that torments you, I have told you many times that it is your cross which our Jesus has given to you so that you may become an imitator of Him and not be a stranger to His love. For whoever loves Him sincerely not only follows Him to Mount Tabor, where the glory of His divinity appeared (in other words, not only at the time of His visitation through His sweet grace and joy), but follows Him also on the uphill climb to Golgotha and His Crucifixion (in other words, also in the absence of His grace and in sorrowful occurrences, which produce distress, pain, despair, perplexity, labor, and sweat). Precisely then is the inner man tested and it is revealed what he is: counterfeit or true, skilled or unskilled, captain or sailor. Precisely then are our intentions tested, and he who is courageous and patient is rewarded internally by the visitation of God through the increase of grace. In this manner, the Christian is trained in the spiritual struggle until he reaches the end and finds rest.

Struggle philosophically; carry your cross with patience and joy until you bring it to the Place of the Skull, to the tomb, so that our Jesus may give you the resurrection! He who bears his cross for the love of Christ will be raised by the Lord on the last day. How long will our life be? The time of our death is unknown, whereas patience will be rewarded eternally.

This cross of grief you are bearing has already given you very much, and how much more it will give you! And yet you do not see this, for God wisely hides it from you for your benefit. Entreat God continuously to give you patience, and thank Him with knowledge; then you will be able to endure joyfully, awaiting your salvation through these afflictions.

11. Man's life is a martyrdom. Ever since we fell from true happiness we gather the fruit of disobedience: "Thorns and thistles will the earth bring forth to you"[33]—the earth of the heart will, too. How will we know that we are exiles, if not through afflictions and torments?

There is no person who does not have something that afflicts him. Pious Christians are afflicted, too, but in the depths of their souls they also have the hope that one day the many afflictions will result in blessed repose for them. Without afflictions and sufferings let no one expect repose in the life beyond the grave. That life is for those who have labored and were heavy laden by the weight of this present life.

Of course, the saints had much grace and spiritual strength, and they rejoiced in suffering. But we, and I first of all, suffer and sometimes our patience breaks. But glory be to God, Who enlightens us to repent and correct ourselves. "The spirit indeed is willing, but the flesh is weak."[34]

12. Concerning the sorrow which you have in your soul because of your sins, it is good and beneficial. Only when it leads you to despair, then it is clearly demonic. Immediately turn toward hope and say: "Since I repent for everything, I hope that everything I have done is forgiven. There is no sin which surpasses the compassion of God. However great the sins may be, when they come to *repentance** they are dissolved. Oh, the depth of the humility, forbearance, and compassion of the Lord!"

---

[33] Gen. 3:18
[34] Mt. 26:41

May all those who are laden with a heavy sentence take courage, for there is a God Who does not consider whatever evil we may have done to Him. He forgives all sins, if only we sincerely repent. Endure the trials, my child, and it will turn out well for you. Patience—yes, patience: this will open the gates of paradise for us.

13. In the tragic ordeal that my Elder went through, how tangibly he felt Christ! While to others the approach of death causes trembling and fear, he remained in the eros of Christ. What a wonder this is! "Christ is the same yesterday, today, and forever."[35]

14. Affliction is an instrument, a tool, which God holds in His hand. He alone uses it as His infinite wisdom dictates. He uses it differently for each person, according to the need of each.

Affliction in its various forms purifies and sanctifies the one who accepts it with wisdom and knowledge. That is, each affliction a Christian has is a divine visitation for his salvation, sent by the most sweet right hand of our Heavenly Father, even though our nature dislikes such things, just as bitter medicines are unpleasant to the sick.

Besides, if we had no afflictions, certainly we would have the fate of Lucifer. For he, at the height of glory and repose, forgot the greatness of God and his own puniness and weakness, and said, "I shall set my throne upon the clouds, and I shall be like the Highest."[36] After he thought these things, God cast him down; the former dawning star and most luminous angel became a demon, Satan, the devil, the filthiest of God's creatures, not by nature—for God made everything very good—but by his own choice to be evil and rebellious.

The devil sows within families grumbling, dislike, envy, obstinacy, etc., and thus in many families there is one person

---

[35] Heb. 13:8
[36] cf. Is. 14:13

who will disturb their peace, serenity, and joy. This evil seed was not absent even from the midst of the sacred family of the Lord, which He had created on earth for the coming salvation—that is, in the midst of His sacred disciples: Judas Iscariot, a God-slaying seed!

The devil sows his seed in the midst of the wheat; even in the *synodias** of monastics such people exist. Not that the person himself is evil, but with his weaknesses of grumbling, envy, etc., he becomes an instrument of the devil that disturbs the peace and quiet of the others.

All these things bear witness to the fact that we are exiles from our true fatherland and are now in the reformatories where the discipline of the Lord is practiced. And all who accept the discipline are led back into the heavenly paternal inheritance and recover their lost sonship, as ones worthy to receive God as their inheritance. But all who remain undisciplined, like me, and do not acknowledge the discipline, but instead through their works are shown to be illegitimate, are driven away and condemned as unworthy of the adoption to which the discipline of the Lord aimed. May our good God and Father count us worthy to be among the successful who have received adoption as sons, unto the ages of ages. Amen.

15. My child, be patient in everything, for the reward is great. Do not look at the weight of afflictions, but consider the payment: your light afflictions reserve eternal glory for you in the Heavens that far outweighs them all.[37] For this reason you should rejoice instead of grieving. Thank our good God in everything and do not let our enemy see you lose your patience, because then he will attack you even more in order to demolish the wall of patience completely.

16. Concerning your question, whether or not your heartfelt sorrow and *mourning** are beneficial, I tell you that they

---

[37] cf. 2 Cor. 4:17

are very beneficial, for they hold you back from sin, especially from the attachment and pleasure of the world, which are alien to God.

Yes, but even here *discernment** is necessary, that sorrow and mourning are not done inordinately, for then they become harmful. Behold a sign: when you mourn reflecting on your old sins and the mourning becomes inordinate, it ends up in despair; and then you regard God as a merciless punisher, which is absurd. For He disciplines as a Father, and this is how the Christian understands it when he does not mourn inordinately. This is why discernment is most important, for it delivers us from excesses and deficiencies.

When despair overcomes you, think about something else: If God commanded men to forgive the faults of their fellow men seventy times seven each day, how much more will an infinitely compassionate God forgive? Who has ever repented and not been saved? Who has ever said, "I have sinned" and was not forgiven? Who has fallen and sought help and was not raised up? Who has wept and was not comforted by God? "If you then," says the Lord, "being evil, know how to give good gifts to your children, how much more will your Father who is in Heaven give good things to those who ask Him?"[38]

Our Heavenly Father disciplines us, not to make us despair, but rather to make us repent and correct ourselves. When we misunderstand the meaning of discipline, we end up in despair. Under the sway of such an influence, it is impossible for the soul to be consoled. But when we retain a healthy understanding of the meaning of discipline and afflictions, much divine comfort follows. Behold, my child, under what circumstances mourning and grief are beneficial.

17. In this world, my child, people are divided into good and bad, rich and poor, educated and uneducated, noble and

---

[38] Mt. 7:11

lowborn, smart and not so smart. All, however, have one thing in common: suffering. For without exception all people will suffer in their life. As the maxim says: "It is a wonder if anyone has been happy throughout his life." So then, all people live in the kingdom of suffering.

We know that suffering is something personal, which one must face alone. It is his cross, which he must carry, just as the Savior of the world, Jesus, carried His Cross for our sake.

So be at ease, my child, in the paternal hand, which at this time performs surgery on you by means of suffering, and be calm. Accept that God sends it to you, reconcile yourself with suffering, so that you will be able to face it. I know how difficult this is, but also how beneficial for your salvation. The saints rejoiced in their afflictions; let us at least accept ours with patience, and God will not forget even this minuscule, voluntary patient acceptance of His will, which is represented by suffering.

My child, muster the powers of your soul when you suffer, and try to understand the purpose of suffering, through which God opens Heaven for you. Do you think that He Who numbers the hairs of your head does not know the measure of your suffering? Yes, He knows it. Therefore be at rest, trusting in our Heavenly Father.

Do not grow weary; with our Christ's help you will pass through everything, and will also become His heir in the boundless fortune of our common Father. Amen.

18. Are you able to enumerate the mercies of God? The sins of the worst person, before the compassion of God, are like a handful of sand in the ocean. There is no sin which overcomes the compassion of God. God may be portrayed as our mother: is it possible for the sin of a child to overcome his mother's love? If a mother loves her child so much, how infinitely does God love us, Who clearly proved this by being crucified on the Cross? The Apostle Peter denied the Lord three times, yet through repentance he was restored. The great persecutor of Christians, the Apostle Paul, through repentance became the chief of the Apostles. Prostitutes, thieves, tax collectors, and innumerable other guilty people were sanctified by repentance. For this reason, cast away your distress and excessive remorse; be hopeful; take courage, and drive away every thought of despair.

19. No matter how much we may suffer, the time will come when all will end and each one of us will be given repose in accordance with his labors. Are you afflicted? Are you in pain? Do you weep from the pressure of sorrowful events? Are you weary? Take courage, for through such things the Kingdom of God is acquired. But if you have it easy in everything and do not remember God, then grieve, for you are not walking the path that leads to God.

Afflictions, sicknesses, and torments weary us continually so that we abhor this world and desire the world there, where Cherubim and Seraphim hymn God, where there is the real and true repose, the day without evening, the blessed light; while things here, in comparison with the eternal things, are dark and abominable. May our holy God grant us spiritual understanding, so that we always prefer the everlasting things, the highest good, our sweet God.

20. Oh, how beneficently our God and Father intervenes by means of pain in the life of man, His child! If man knew the spiritual benefit that pain brings, he would pray to bear all kinds of pain throughout his life in order to deposit spiritual "money," the money of pain, in the bank of God, in the city above, and to receive the money of blessedness at the time when all souls will receive the wages for labors, pain, and afflictions.

21. Have patience, my child, in the trial which the goodness of God is sending you for the greater benefit of your soul. You should rejoice, because this shows God's concern for your greater spiritual progress, primarily in humility. Many times, man's pride becomes a cause for God to give us a fatherly "slap" so that we walk more securely in humility. This is the best sign of how greatly God is concerned for our souls.

So be patient, my child. This is also a cross; take it up for the love of the Lord. Resemble Him, so that He may give you His love; for He says, "He who has My commandments and keeps them, it is he who loves Me."[39] One of His commandments is obedience until Golgotha, with the cross on our shoulder. Blessed is he who endures trials, for as one tried he will receive the crown of eternal life.[40]

22. We are disciplined that we may become worthy of the Heavens. The Heavenly Father disciplines us in every way in order to form a spiritual character within us, so that we may resemble our Heavenly Father as His children. We must nurture in ourselves characteristics which clearly reflect that we are legitimate sons of God. Let us be distinguished in patience, in meekness, in love, in brotherly affection, and so forth—characteristics of God's children, who are about to inherit, along with Christ, the boundless spiritual riches of the Heavenly Father.

Be courageous, my child, in the struggle; through many tribulations we shall ascend to Heaven. The path of our salvation is strewn with thorns, and we shall have pain and shed blood; but be patient. The blessed hour will come when all the pain and blood will inscribe our names in the book of life! Then we shall bless God, Who with unfathomable wisdom devised pain and affliction as a means of great salvation.

---

[39] Jn. 14:21
[40] cf. Jam. 1:12

Do not grow tired of crying out to Christ, if you want your mouth to be sanctified. As for the temptations which you see in your sleep, do not think about them, but disregard them, for they themselves do not have any substance. When you disregard them, they will not bother you.

23. My blessed child, may joy and peace be upon your dear little soul. Trials are always beneficial when we bear them patiently. When the trials have passed, they leave behind experience for the one tried by them, and fruit in proportion to the patience and skill which he showed in the struggle. Since there is no road which saves other than trials, what should we do? Have patience to the point of shedding blood. This is also how our fathers struggled, and they became holy. Trials befit us also in order that we be humbled, even though we are humble by nature—that is, we are made of earth and even our works are like rubbish and chaff.

Do not forget, my child, what the sweet-scented mouth of Jesus said: "In the world you will have tribulation; but be of good cheer; I have overcome the world."[41] Therefore, whoever has Christ with him will also overcome the world of his passions. Do not let the magnitude of the trials terrify you, but be attentive lest the enemy craftily rob you with thoughts without your realizing it, lest you continue yielding to the point that evil thoughts coerce you.

Anyway, the truth is one: most holy humility is the most salvific medicine. Be humble in everything, and without the least doubt you will by all means obtain perfect—or at least satisfactory—freedom from the passions.

24. I pray, my child, that you have peace in both soul and body, for what is more beautiful than peace of soul and health of body! Both make man's life pleasant; in their absence, however, a harsh tempest rises and the little boat of one's soul

---

[41] Jn. 16:33

is tossed about in the midst of raging waves. How many prayers are offered then! But the Lord, when He was on earth, met a similar storm: "and He rebuked the wind and the sea and there was a great calm."[42] Let us call on this peacemaking Lord and Master whenever spiritual storms overcome us, my child, and I believe that when we call on Him with faith, He will hasten to our aid and say, "Behold, I am here."

25. Blessed daughter. . . , the Lord be with you. I received your little letter; do not grieve so much, my child. Moderation is necessary in all things, for by weeping excessively you will get worse, because the nervous system does not endure great grief and distress.

See to it that you be humble and careful, and that you not grieve the Eldress, but do whatever she tells you with faith, and you will miraculously see the hand of God caressing you!

Do not stray off the straight path, so that you are not tormented by remorse. Make an effort, my good child, to correct yourself a little, cutting off your own will entirely, and be careful not to do things without a *blessing*,* but ask the Eldress for whatever you want. And if she does not allow some of the things you want, be patient, for it is then that your genuine love for Christ is demonstrated. For if our elders fulfill our every wish, then where is that virtue which is called cutting off of the will?

Yes, my child, compel yourself. I know what you are suffering from and how much you suffer, but it takes patience. For even our Christ was patient, when we were sinning in front of Him and He was waiting for us to repent. I pray that our *Panagia** may always console you and refresh your dear little soul. Amen.

26. My blessed child, may the God of love be with you.

Be patient in everything, for it is in this way that you will reap benefit from everything. Our Christ loves you, and for

---

[42] cf. Mk. 4:39

this reason He continually visits you so much. If He did not love you, He would have abandoned you and you would have been lost, whereas now you are alive and are struggling. It is irrelevant if you suffer temporally; consider and meditate on what is eternal, and this will relieve and refresh you in the burning heat of harsh trials. You are passing through the furnace that refines those souls which have dedicated their lives to God. So take courage and rejoice, for through this your soul will be purified to receive the most pure Lord. Be humble and love everyone for the love of Christ, and in this way you will be saved.

I leave you with the peace and love of God.

With fatherly love, *Geronda*.*

27. My blessed child, I pray that the Heavenly Father grants you discernment so that you can discern the truth from the devil's lie.

Concerning the first thought that you wrote about, I reply: Didn't God declare that Job was blameless? Then why did He permit trials so severe that he reached such a difficult situation that he cursed the day of his birth? All this was permitted in order to teach him, of course; for this is what the Lord usually does: first He tests and then He shows His love. The love of God is manifested not only when He caresses, but also when He slaps. If the Heavenly Father slaps us, He reveals through this that He loves us.

If God did not consider us His children, He would not have sent us trials but would have abandoned us as we are: spiritually uneducated, without any solicitude. In the other world, the ones nearest the Lord will be those who have been educated in soul and wise in spiritual struggles. And because He loves us wretched ones and wants to honor us, He educates us spiritually here, in the University of Monasticism. But since we are inexperienced as to how divine providence works, we blame God, asking why He should send us trials, and thus we jeopardize our eternal happiness through our ignorance. Spiritual education consists of deliverance from the passions and especially from egotism.

So, my child, let us struggle not to condemn; let us say, "*Bless*,"* and, "May it be blessed." Let us have genuine love. And when do we have genuine love? When we do not condemn the others, but justify them.

28. Do not lose your courage, my child. The deprivations we bear are meant to prepare for us the eternal enjoyment of Heaven! We knowingly deprive ourselves of the pleasurable things of this life for the love of our Christ. If we wanted to, we could enjoy them freely, but voluntarily we do not accept them so that we may be given the affectionate love of our exceedingly sweet Jesus.

My daughter, we have an immortal and eternal Bridegroom, Who preserves the glory of virginity forever. We have been called to become angels, my beloved daughter, so shouldn't we deprive ourselves of things pleasurable and sinful? Isn't it worth depriving ourselves of foul things for Jesus' divine love? So struggle worthily of your calling with fortitude. The martyrs shed their blood for the love of our Christ, so can't we resist one loathsome, counterfeit pleasure? Glorify God in your body and in your soul.

> Struggle to the end.
> Farewell, my daughter.
> Your father.

29. Here in this vain world, my child, we shall be afflicted, we shall be embittered, we shall feel pain. But all this is for a limited time; it is temporary—let us pray that God does not abandon us to an eternal degree and measure, for then we would not bear it.

Whenever you are in pain and are afflicted, call to mind Him Who was crucified and then you will find much relief. For who could gaze at the Crucified One and reflect on His Passion which He suffered for us, and not find balm for his wounds, whether spiritual or physical? Look up, my child, there on Golgotha, there where the holy Lamb triumphed victoriously in order to wash the wounds of our sins and passions with His Blood. His compassion is great; never lose your confidence in Him Who was crucified for you.

I pray that you pass Great Lent with flourishing health of both soul and body. Amen.

30. A physician torments a sick person with operations, bitter medicines, amputation of body parts, etc. with the purpose, of course, of curing him and not of torturing him out of wickedness. Likewise God, as the Physician of our souls and bodies, heals us with all kinds of medicines, afflictions, and sufferings to give us our spiritual health, which is the greatest good that exists. But those who are indignant and do not bear it patiently—like me—lose the spiritual benefit and thus gain only pain.

So since God saves us in such a miraculous way, we have the necessary obligation to thank Him unceasingly and to bless His all-holy name. We should do so not only with our mouth, but primarily with our works, so that no deed of ours may offend God's grandeur. For if we bless Him with our lips and revile Him with our works, then we are mocking Him. Let us make an effort not to grieve our Christ by any offense, so that the Holy Spirit may rest in our souls. Amen.

On Illness

The truth is that the illnesses, afflictions, and tribulations of Christians bring about the cleansing of their soul and the forgiveness of their sins. Every Christian has the sacred obligation to accept with a guileless and simple heart whatever kind of cross God has placed upon him, and to carry it up to glorious Golgotha. Sometimes he may fall to his knees under the toil and burden, but God will send another good Simon of Cyrene[1]—that is, the grace of patience—who will lift the cross to Golgotha.

When we visit a cemetery, we see a cross on every grave—some wooden, others stone, others iron, etc. Likewise, God gives a cross to every Christian soul. To one He gives an iron cross, to another a wooden cross, to another a stone cross; each person is given one as the wisdom of God deems best. The main purpose of the Lord is to save our precious soul, regardless of whether or not it suffers in the process. He Himself provides us with the patience and enlightenment to be able to bear the cross to the end.

The afflictions felt in illnesses are sent by the holy hand of our good God. The most effective medicine for spiritual health is bodily illness. Illnesses are the reveille for the soul that has become drowsy with the narcotic drink of ignorance, of forgetfulness of God. Illnesses force the soul that has become careless, because of its spiritually harmful physical health, to get back to the right way of life. "In affliction I remembered Thee."[2] "In my affliction Thou hast made me prosper."[3] "We must through many tribulations enter into life."[4] "By your patience possess your souls."[5]

The slaps of pure love are absolutely never occasioned without a holy and saving purpose foreseen! The Lord tells us

---

[1] vid. Mt. 27:32

[2] Is. 26:16

[3] Ps. 4:1

[4] cf. Acts 14:22

[5] Lk. 21:19

in the Holy Gospel that without the will of our Heavenly Father, not even a sparrow falls dead, and that the very hairs of our head are numbered.[6] How assuring these words are, that all our deeds, words, and thoughts are known to God, and that our afflictions occur with His knowledge, are from His providence, and aim at some salvific goal!

What great corruption, both physical and spiritual, did mankind have before the coming of the Lord! Which medicine brought about spiritual rebirth to the souls of men? Was it not the gigantic Cross of our Lord Jesus? If the Lord had not died on the Cross, man could not have been saved in any other way.

Jesus became a model for us by bearing His Cross. He showed thus that whoever wants to be saved must follow Him, endure the cross which the Lord will lay upon him according to his strength, ascend to Golgotha, be crucified together with Jesus, and then be glorified together with the Lord in the Kingdom of God.

When the soul sees that the glory and repose in the bliss of Heaven are given in proportion to the cross it carried, it will regret that it did not carry a heavier cross in order to receive greater glory and repose. It will say, "The labor then lasted only a short time, whereas now I am deprived of eternal blessings!" Even the Patriarch Abraham, when he sees blessings being distributed, will regret not having struggled more!

One young girl was continuously sick with a nasty illness, which finally killed her. One night she appeared to her sister, who asked her, "How are you doing, my sister, in the place where you are?" And she answered, "What can I say, my sister? Christ gave me much glory and repose because of my illness. Oh, if only I could return to the earth to suffer a greater illness, so that I would receive more glory here!"

---

[6] cf. Mt. 10:29-30

If the Lord Himself—the omnipotent and sinless One—carried a cross for the sake of man, for his salvation, how much more so do we sinners, who sin every hour, need a cross for our salvation?

"I made ready and was not troubled,"[7] says the Prophet David. We must always be ready to endure without grumbling every trial that the holy hand of the Physician will send us. Since this trial comes from and is permitted by Him Who loves us boundlessly, the trial will absolutely never be for our harm, for after it is over we shall see its good result; we shall see God's main purpose.

The Lord Jesus, foreseeing the future trials of His followers, gave them support by saying, "By your patience possess your souls. He who endures to the end will be saved."[8] By enduring your illness with patience, you are also counted among the beloved children of God. Your burden will one day become your resurrection; your sorrows, joy; your patience, eternal life! Cry out with thankfulness to the Lord: "Blessed be the name of the Lord. As it seemed good to the Lord, so has it come to pass. Glory to God for everything."[9] As you cry out like this, your soul will be filled with joy and peace, and at the same time you will strengthen yourself in patience.

What is a Christian? What must he have? Certainly, he must have much patience in everything.

The road that takes wayfarers to the city of paradise is completely strewn with thorns; those who travel along it will bleed. But the hope of enjoying paradise overcomes everything and provides the wayfarers with patience—as the holy Forty Martyrs said when they were thrown onto the frozen lake: "Winter is bitter, but paradise is sweet; the frost is painful, but the enjoyment will be sweet."

May the all-good God also count us the lowly along with

---

[7] Ps. 118:60

[8] Lk. 21:19, Mt. 10:22

[9] cf. Job 1:21

those who labor and are heavy laden in order to give us eternal repose. Amen.

2. From the time our sweet Jesus lifted the life-giving wood of the precious Cross on His immaculate shoulders and was hanged upon it, from that time and throughout the ages, lifting the cross is continued by His followers in the form of various afflictions and trials, through which the Christian triumphs over the many forms of destructive self-love.

Through Luke the Evangelist, the Savior stresses that "whoever does not bear his cross and come after Me cannot be My disciple."[10] And again: "If anyone desires to come after Me, let him deny himself, take up his cross daily, and follow Me."[11]

Abba Isaac, the *hesychast** philosopher, says, "Man changes at every moment." Indeed, the dispositions of both the soul and body never stop changing, sometimes bringing about distress, at other times pain, sometimes expectation of sad news, at other times an undefined disorder and distress of soul and body. All of these are due to either bodily or spiritual causes, which confirm God's curse that burdened the race of man due to the disobedience of Adam and Eve. But the good Jesus, the Tree of life, on the one hand by His holy example, and on the other by His divine teachings, pours out the balsam of consolation upon the cross of afflictions along with many life-giving assurances that it is through many tribulations that we shall be able to enter His Kingdom.[12]

In the Old Testament, in the Book of Numbers, among other things the following distinctive event is narrated: "When the Israelites had disobeyed God in the wilderness, as a punishment for their disobedience He sent serpents to them which bit and killed them. But God heard the prayer of Moses, who was fervently praying for this wrath to abate, and

---

[10] Lk. 14:27
[11] Lk. 9:23
[12] cf. Acts 14:22

ordered him to make a bronze serpent and lift it up on a pole. And all who were bitten by the serpents were immediately healed when they looked at the bronze serpent."[13] And in the Holy Gospel, our Jesus likened the elevation of the bronze serpent to His own life-giving elevation on the Cross by saying: "And as Moses lifted up the serpent in the wilderness, even so must the Son of Man be lifted up."[14]

So sin—which is the meaning of the poisonous serpent— bites man, poisoning the entire being of his poor soul through culpable and passionate pleasure, which brings about the soul's death and separation from God. But our Christ, the noetic bronze serpent, Who was hanged on the life-giving wood of the precious Cross, through the lofty truths of the Gospel heals the souls that have been bitten by various sins, giving them a living hope of a life beyond comprehension. "O Death, where is thy sting? O Hades, where is thy victory?"[15] The powers of your horrible tyranny were abolished, annihilated, enfeebled, and completely put to death by the death and resurrection of Jesus, our God, Who saves our souls.

The heart is poisoned and darkened by pleasure and sensuality. Then, since it is darkened, it does the works of darkness, grieving the Holy Spirit, Whom it had received through rebirth in the sacred baptismal font. Conversely, pain and affliction expel culpable sensuality from the heart. As it is cleansed by pain, it becomes capable of receiving the comforting Spirit. Once the good Comforter comes, He consoles, encourages, and enlightens the heart, and as a nurturer He gives it life with the divine teachings and the aids of joy and hope.

So look upon the noetic bronze serpent, Jesus, Who heals through pain all souls that suffer from the bites of poisonous sin in its many forms.

---

[13] cf. Num. 21:6-9
[14] Jn. 3:14
[15] 1 Cor. 15:55

From the unshakeable truths derived from experience, it follows that pain and affliction are the most essential medicine for the soul which is ill with sin. At the same time, they are also excellent teachers for the spiritual uplifting of the soul which has sullied its beauty in sin and moral darkness and has thereby acquired morally evil habits.

Pain, in the various meanings of the word, becomes the skillful cultivator that takes a sinful soul that is like a wild olive tree and grafts it onto a good olive tree. Sin hardens the heart of the sinner and renders him unfeeling; nothing moves him, because God, Who has feeling and sympathy for people, is missing. However, what does God do—He Who loves mankind, Who "came to seek and to save that which was lost"?[16] He draws up a plan of salvation through pain, and especially through illness, for the soul which has gone astray.

You see, for example, a youth in his prime, puffed up because of his strength and behaving arrogantly, forgetting about God and his soul—then suddenly he lies prostrate on a bed of pain. Then, as a most experienced and skillful doctor, pain begins its surgery. First, it operates on the heart by removing its hardness little by little, and thus it softens the soul. He who was formerly hard of heart becomes soft and calm in his feelings. He commiserates with his fellow patients, and he who was formerly unsympathetic speaks with sympathy. And once his heart has been prepared through these and various other feelings brought about by the instructive rod of pain, then the ears of his previously deaf soul open, and he accepts, retains, and attentively listens to the word of truth, the Gospel of salvation.

Then he who was formerly indifferent to God and to his soul becomes zealous in reading various religious books and periodicals. He begins to recall his sinfulness with genuine

---

[16] cf. Lk. 19:10

contrition and feeling. Thus he learns to pray with compunction and soon becomes an eloquent preacher of the benefactions of the excellent doctor, pain, proclaiming that it alone cures the illness of being far from God.

Pain cures not only the person who is far from God; it also heals souls that are healthy, but partially ill with a "sickness not unto death,"[17] such as occasional indifference, criticism, self-love, cowardice, doubts, and so on. Pain exercises its activity even in the saints so that through their patience their glory may be increased. However, the saints often suffer also to give an example to others, as happened with long-suffering Job, St. Syncletiki, and so many other saints.

When we have a beautiful piece of furniture and leave it unattended for a period of time, we see that a layer of fine dust settles upon it. True—it is not ruined, but it has lost some of its shine and beauty. This also happens to a healthy soul when it does not have afflictions now and then. For example, indifference, if one does not attend to it in time, little by little without anyone realizing it, settles in the soul like dust on the furniture, and the soul loses its original zeal towards God. It does pray, it does fulfill its duties, but not as it should. But if pain comes, if affliction visits, then the wind blows and the flame—that is, the zeal to fulfill its duties to God—is kindled again.

Just as it happens with indifference, so it happens also with every other illness of the soul. Pain is the divine medicine which the infinite wisdom of God devised for the ailing soul, and He uses it with absolute authority and no reserve so that through such an effective medicine, we may come to our senses and be watchful and vigilant in executing His holy will. Thus at the time of repayment we may receive, as a reward for vigilantly cleaving to His will, entrance into the

---

[17] Jn. 11:4

eternal delight of the Lord, rejoicing and exulting in it together with those who have been called from all ages.
There, together with the Lady Theotokos, the angels, and
all the saints, we shall praise with endless, joyful hymns
the blessed name of our Lord and God and Savior Jesus
Christ, to Whom belong all glory, honor, and dominion
unto the endless ages of ages.

3. God chastens and then heals; He raises up and casts
down—who is able to withstand the will of the Lord? If
God wills that we suffer, He has some salvific purpose in
mind which we earthly ones are unable to foresee.
Patience, forbearance, and the humble acceptance of trials
will always—yes, always—bring certain benefit later.

My child, bear your cross, and know that all that we suffer is known to God, and as a true Father He tries in every
way to form Jesus Christ within us.[18] He wants us to suffer
because He knows what He has prepared in the Heavens
for His suffering children. But if He did not send them afflictions, He would do them injustice, because they would
be deprived of the ineffable blessings of Heaven. The more
we suffer, the more beautifully our crown of glory is woven!

Never believe that you are possessed; never let any such
thought deceive you. Such things happen to many monks
when they become ill. This is how God has arranged
things: when the body is ill, the soul follows accordingly,
and when the soul suffers, the body also wastes away and
sulks. The tempter was envious of you, my child, but let us
be patient so that he may be foiled and God may be glorified.

Who does not feel pain when he undergoes surgery, and
who does not feel pain when he loses the grace of God and is

---

[18] cf. Gal. 4:19

swarmed by thousands of warped thoughts? This is how God's wisdom has arranged things to bring about the soul's correction.

All things will pass, as well as the winter of our passions, and the sweet spring of health will blossom again, and you will rejoice and say, "It is good for me that Thou hast humbled me, that I may learn Thy statutes."[19]

As nature's seasons—winter, spring, summer, and autumn—follow one another, likewise the spiritual seasons follow one another. One goes, another comes—and thus the soul becomes accustomed to all spiritual changes and becomes wise and experienced. This experience is grace, which supports the soul in times of terrible changes, so that from past trials it will know well that only patience and forbearance can provide a peaceful state and beneficial thoughts. In this manner, we emerge from trials with benefit, and we become wiser and more experienced.

4. My child, although much of your illness is due to disobedience, the love of God is evident in you. God loves you very much, which is why He chastens you. God is working out your precious salvation through the trials you are undergoing. He wants to lighten your burden and fill the vessel of your soul with the gift of the great hope of obtaining Heaven and dwelling eternally near Christ, Whom you have ardently loved in this life!

So what remains for you to do? Maintain utmost patience, exercise courage in the trial you are undergoing, and give boundless thanks to the excellent Guide of our souls, coupled also with grace-filled humility. My child, walk up the path to Golgotha with the cross you have been given by the greatly beneficent hand of Him Who loves and chastens you so that you may partake of His holiness.

---

[19] Ps. 118:71

5. My child, I pray that the God of patience and consolation[20] will strengthen you in your illness, which you have fallen into by the will of God. When I heard that you were seriously ill, I felt much pain for you and begged our Panagia to make you well, first in soul and then in body.

My child, think of the holy martyrs—how much they endured for the love of our Christ! Therefore, you should also say to yourself, "Lowly one, patiently endure the torments of illness so that you may avoid the eternal torments of hell!" Those martyrs voluntarily submitted to the tortures of martyrdom, whereas you are in pain involuntarily. But even this is good; it will benefit you significantly—just bear the chastisement of the Lord with joy and thankfulness.

Tell yourself these and other such things to strengthen yourself and to give yourself fortitude and consolation.

6. Entrust your health to God. If your illness or the doctor imposes something on you, accept it with the hope that through it God will accomplish what He wants. Of course, our self-denial should not lead us to death (which would be suicide), nor should we have so much attentive care that it leads to self-love, but we should walk the middle road—that is, in faith we should do what is prescribed so that it is not considered suicide. But as to whether or not we shall get well through the means we use, in faith we leave this up to God.

My child, have patience in all your sufferings. Illnesses provide great benefit to the soul when we endure them, as long as we blame ourselves for them, since we suffer from them primarily on account of our sins, and especially on account of our pride of heart.

7. I pray that you will always be healthy. But when you are ill, bear patiently the chastening of the Lord, which is sent from His affectionate and immense heart. The chastening pro-

---

[20] Rom. 15:5

ceeding from such a heart will never be fruitless, harmful, or undiscerning. Rather, it chastens us for our own good, for the forgiveness of our sins, for our protection, and for our eternal salvation!

The heart that chastens us is the heart of God Himself, our Heavenly Father. He sees all, especially the purpose of every act. He sees how you are suffering and are afflicted. Know that He will not try you beyond your strength. Through afflictions, He brings about the cleansing of your soul and its eternal salvation.

"We glory in tribulations, knowing that tribulation produces perseverance."[21] Since we are His children, God disciplines us so that His features may be formed in us. It is when children bear the features of their parents that their legitimacy shows. So this is the purpose of the Lord's chastening. Your afflictions are salvific; always have hope and you will by no means be put to shame.

8. Ignorance, my child, is known as the soul's death. Ignorance does not enlighten a sick person; it does not say to him: "Your illness is the will of God, and you ought to pass through it with patience and thankfulness, so that you will not become a transgressor before God with your impatience!" To the enlightened Christian, however, knowledge of God's will not only makes him bear everything with thankfulness, but also helps him acquire a strong spiritual constitution and at the same time obtain the refreshment of consolation. He reflects: "By undergoing these pains and afflictions I am doing God's will, and this will bring about the forgiveness of my previous offenses. By paying here the debt of my sentence, I shall receive my freedom there in the life to come, where I shall live eternally—whereas here, no matter how much suffering I may undergo, it is temporary and short-lived."

---

[21] Rom. 5:3

So, my child, we need patience so as not to be condemned with the unrepentant world. Regardless of what might happen to us, through patience everything is put right, and the inner man will find peace, bearing patiently what God has allowed.

Bear your cross, and I shall bear mine, as we follow the heavenly Bridegroom, Christ, Who for us ungrateful sinners bore a Cross of disgrace. What do we bear that is equal in worth to such good things that we enjoy from God? If I were to enumerate the blessings of God and the ingratitude of man, I think my mind would stop; for how can the finite mind comprehend the infinite benefactions of God towards man?

9. May the God of patience and consolation[22] grant you patience and His caress of consolation to strengthen you to continue the struggle.

My child, do not look only at the present pains, but raise your eyes "as one weaned from his mother"[23] and behold: "The sufferings of this present time are not worthy to be compared with the glory which shall be revealed in us,"[24] who long for the manifestation of our Christ.

Do not measure only the pains, but philosophically consider the reward, for isn't God just? God deprived you of the comfort of having healthy feet in order to count you worthy to celebrate the great resurrection of your soul "with a joyful step"[25] there in the Jerusalem on high. Yes, indeed, all of Scripture proclaims this.

My child, walk in Christ bearing in mind the eternal joy to come. Do not grow weary of contending; do not imagine that you are beating the air, for truly there is a fight going on as there was with Job. He patiently bore a martyrdom of a variety of pains, and his wife pushed him towards eternal death

---

22 Rom. 15:5

23 Ps. 130:3

24 Rom. 8:18

25 Paschal Canon, Ode Five

through her evil advice; whereas you are being advised through these pains to obtain eternal life. He sat on a dung heap, was covered with sores, and was ridiculed as a sinner, but you rest at home upon a bed and are considered to be a virtuous Christian. Do you see how inferior we are? Therefore, endure patiently and thank God Who gave you such a gift, so that He might make you, as a grateful servant, an heir of His boundless Kingdom! Amen; so be it.

10. You say that your brother was hungry, thirsty, and so on when he was sick, and he blasphemed. You also said that your brother was committing a mortal sin. God, though, Who is very compassionate, wanted to bring him to a realization of his guilt so that he would repent, so He gave him this illness out of paternal love as a spiritual medication to cure his soul of its illness.

If you had looked after your brother and offered him every bodily comfort, what pains would he have suffered for God to see and have pity on him? You should realize that the more he was tormented, the more his penalty was lightened! God gave him the illness and allowed the brethren to neglect their duty towards him so that his conscience would make him feel remorse and repent. He is like a patient who is given medicine by a doctor, but lacks the necessary patience. Thus, he curses and grumbles at the doctor, which only leads to his own demise.

11. When you are in pain, gather the powers of your soul and try to understand what Heaven is trying to tell you in this trial of yours. If perhaps you cry from the pain, the tears will cleanse your vision, as they did for Job the much-suffering, and then you, too, will be able to say along with him, "Now mine eye hath seen Thee."[26]

Don't forget that God sees you and watches you when you

are in pain; He perceives even the beating of your heart. Consequently, He will not leave you without consolation and His fatherly protection. Naturally, the saints rejoiced in their afflictions; as for us, let us at least manage to accept affliction or pain patiently.

My child, pray within your heart, and the name of Jesus will become for you a comforting balm so that you can bear this trial of yours in a way which benefits you. You will greatly benefit from this trial if you submit yourself to it patiently. So again I say to you, with the almighty armor of prayer continually approach the omnipotent Lord, and you will come to know how He wondrously lifts the burden of pain and marvellously gives rest to sufferers.

12. I pray that you will get fully well. What can we do? The Lord chastens us so that we may have an eternal reward. Since we have no asceticism, the Lord gives us illnesses and afflictions to count it as asceticism for us so that we may have some small consolation when we are judged before Him.

What can we do, my child? This is how God wants things: that we suffer here in order to find repose in the world to come. Everything here is transient; there, eternal. Winter is bitter, but paradise is sweet. Let our feet freeze here so that they may dance there eternally! Glory to Thee, O God.

13. My blessed child in Christ, I am praying that the great Physician of souls and bodies grant you your full health, in accordance with His holy will.

There were holy men, my child, who were gravely ill, yet in their illness they healed others. Oh, how much God loved them! An exceptional sign of God's love for a soul is when He saddles it with illnesses or afflictions. Pain of body or soul purifies, cleanses, and brightens the garment of the soul from every stain of sin.

---

26 Job 42:5

There was one holy monastic father who was always ill. It happened once that he was not ill for a period of time, and he complained, saying: "Ah, my God, why didst Thou forget me and not consider me worthy of Thy visitation?" This blessed man yearned for illnesses because he knew from his experience how much the soul benefits from them.

Pain brings the unrepentant sinner to repentance, whereas for the righteous, it fortifies the strength of his soul and becomes a mighty wall around him so that he does not stray into sin. Just as a sick person gladly submits himself to the painful treatment of the doctor because he knows his aim, similarly we should endure with gratitude and knowledge all things that befall us involuntarily as sent from the kind hand of God for our salvation. "The athlete is tested by the stadium, the captain by the storm and tempest, the general by the battle, the magnanimous by misfortune, and the Christian by temptation," says St. Basil the Great.

Just as the earth becomes productive when the plow tills it deeply, likewise the soul becomes fruitful in virtues when pain and illness visit it frequently and intensely! The more pain and affliction a person has, the more beautiful his crown becomes. And if there are many and various pains that oppress him, then the crown of glory is adorned with many flowers and pearls.

Gold has to pass through the furnace to become purified, and the soul of a Christian has to pass through the furnace of temptations to receive the seal of eternal glory in the royal treasury of Christ the King. If holy and blessed people passed through the furnace of pain and were benefited, how much more pain suits us and how much benefit we will derive from it when we endure it with knowledge and gratitude! It is when we see pain oppressing us, physically or spiritually, that we should consider that we are loved by God and that he has placed us in the ranks of His chosen.

O blessed chastening of the Lord, I love you. But I am unworthy of such a gift, for I live in comfort and shall become a victim of the eternal fire. So, my child, I envy you because you are suffering and will obtain eternal repose! Your crown is decorated and beautified for your eternal glory! Endure for the Lord's sake until the end. Bear your cross well lest you drop it, and you can be sure that you will be glorified with Christ eternally! Pray for me, too, lest I be shut out of paradise as one who does not practice what he preaches.

14. My child, I pray that the good Comforter, the good and true Spirit, the Holy Spirit, will overshadow you, console you, and ignite in you the love of Christ.

I pray with all my soul that our Christ will grant you your health. I see and know from my experience, my child, that if one suffers various afflictions, whether bodily or spiritual, and patiently endures them with knowledge, and thanks God, then God is definitely obliged to send consolation to refresh his soul. But if we do not endure pain and labor, God does not console—He does not give His grace.

Do you see after you recover from pain how much the love of Christ ignites within you? Yes, it is the reward for your labor, your patience. If you didn't have this illness, you wouldn't have so much love and consolation. Do you see that when you recover, you feel like a child? This is a sign that God forgives your sins and that you are free from blame. All this is caused by the patience you have when you are ill. When God deigns for you to get well, then you will see in practice what I am telling you. The more one suffers, the more grace one is given.

One monk was ill, and he had such a horrible disease that

the brethren were disgusted by him and drove him away. He blamed himself by saying that he deserved such treatment. Because of his humility, God made him well. But afterwards, this holy monk kept saying, "Ah, my Christ, I was unworthy to suffer more for Thy love!" He knew from experience how much he gained during his illness.

Therefore, do not grieve at all. Only thank our Christ, Who loves you so much that He has given you temporary afflictions here in order to give you everlasting joy there. When you are ill and unable to fulfill your spiritual duties with exactitude, do not be sad, because it is not a sin since your will does not exercise authority over your health. Nevertheless, a monk must compel himself. But if he is ill, it is not a sin not to fulfill his duties—God is just. Obedience with humility and thanksgiving to God replace the asceticism of fasting. Great is the benefit of self-reproach when one is unable to fast due to illness.

15. I pray, my child, that a drop of the infinite patience of God may drip into your soul, where it will build a tower of patience so that you may find the unfailing treasure of eternal life.

You wrote that at times when grace was afire, you asked our Christ to grant you illness or even something worse so that you could suffer out of love for Him. He did not overlook you but sent you an illness, as you had asked. So you have to be patient now, and you will learn discernment from experience, that is, not to seek things from God that we have not tried through experience. Therefore, we should always pray that the Lord's will be done. Now pray like this: "My God, make me well, but let not my will be done, but Thine."

Like naïve children, we often seek things that are not to our benefit. But God, as our Father, fulfills our requests in order to teach us through experience how we should pray to Him. Afterwards, we see that we did not pray properly, and we suffer. Nevertheless, God is forbearing and delivers us, so that the lesson of giving up our own will becomes deeply rooted within us.

Moreover, at times when we suffer from our lack of discernment, God does not abandon us, but sends His grace and comforts us so that we may bear the burden. This is what is happening with you, my child. What you saw and felt was the grace of God, which nurses you until you grow in experience. The fact that God lets you suffer shows that you still need such chastening.

Leave it all to God and say: "My God, I leave my illness in Your holy hands, and whenever You—Who love me so much—want to heal me, I also will want it then. I only ask Your infinite goodness that You not overlook me, but always give me the patience to bear this cross of mine, until Your will is done again."

16. I am sick with the flu and feel sharp pains in my appendix. I don't know what will happen. In any case, glory to Thee, O God.

God loves us and through involuntary pain seeks to count us worthy to participate in His most perfect blessings. Unfortunately, we—and I—do not love our soul in a spiritual way. If we loved it, we would endure trials of both soul and body without complaining, in order to attain the eternal blessings.

Pain softens the heart and removes its hardness. As the heart is softened in this manner, the ground is prepared for the sowing of genuine repentance and correction. We who are cowardly in every affliction chase away, so to speak, the grace of God.

When man is prospering, he cannot remember God, and if he remembers Him, it is only faintly. When affliction or pain approaches, he remembers Him vividly and with fervor. When sorrow oppresses him or when he expects tribulations, then he prays most ardently. And our holy God is pleased with this, just as a mother is pleased when her child seeks her with heartfelt pain, for in this she discerns love.

No matter how man is tried, he always benefits when he shows the corresponding patience and gratitude during the trial. This is revealed at the end of the trial, when he sees the lightness of his soul, the clarity of his mind, and the sweetness that comes to his inner self.

Let us pray to be granted knowledge and patience in life's miseries, so that we may gain our salvation. Amen.

SAINT MAXIMOS
KAFSOKALYVIS
BURNING HIS HUT

Chapter Three

On Sin, Repentance, Mourning, and Tears

To fall and be injured is human, since—even if a man's life lasted for only one day—his mind is inclined to evil from his youth.[1] But to fall and remain fallen is not human. Repentance recreates man; it was given to us to cure the soul after Baptism. If it did not exist, rarely would a person be saved. That is why the virtue of repentance is unending as long as man is alive, for only the perfect do not err. My children, every time you see your thoughts reproaching you for some sin, immediately take the medicine: repent, weep, go to confession, and behold, you return to your former and better state.

2. After Judas the traitor dedicated himself to the Lord and became a partaker of grace, he performed miracles along with the rest of the Apostles, yet in the end he shipwrecked; whereas the thief who had done impious, evil, immoral deeds, by crying out for mercy, was granted repose in the calm haven of eternal bliss. The Jewish nation, which had received the promises of God and was called by Him special, chosen, and holy,[2] was blinded and lost Him forever. The barbaric nations, on the other hand, which were like the harlot in their works, received the Gospel and inherited what Israel had rejected: God. Therefore, away with despair and hope-

---

[1] cf. Gen. 8:21

[2] vid. Ex. 19:5, 1 Pet. 2:9

lessness! No matter how sinful we may be, we should always turn the eyes of our soul to God and entrust ourselves to Him as servants entrust themselves to the hands of their master. In this manner let our eyes be fixed on the Lord, always trusting in His mercy until He has mercy on us.[3]

3. The fall of man into physical mortality and the consequences of exile and alienation from our good Heavenly Father brought about the law of sin, which wars against the law of God.[4] From his youth, man is subject to the law of sin as a tendency, as an inclination, and as wickedness.[5] And this tendency towards evil—as an ancestral inheritance and as a mark, product, and remnant of the ancient severance from the fountain of happiness—naturally took on substantial proportions in human nature, thus drawing it to evil. Thereafter, it was only natural for grievous calamities to befall the children of Adam and Eve.

The restoration to the sonship of old by means of the Lord Jesus' death on the Cross led to eternal salvation. However, this did not remove the law of sin existing within man: not that God was unable to—for just one drop of the awesome and Holy Blood of Jesus Christ could transform everything— but providentially He let it coexist in man so that by means of it He could not only instruct him, but also make manifest the intentions of each person. The Scriptures say that God did not permit Joshua the son of Nun to destroy all the surrounding idolatrous nations, but he left some so that through them He could teach the art of war to the sons of Israel.[6]

So when this law of sin does not find a brave adversary (that is, one with good intentions and with the divine commandments and precepts as weapons), then it vanquishes and captures the spiritual struggler; it strips him of his divine weapons and then drags him to the life of sin.

---

[3] cf. Ps. 122:2
[4] cf. Rom. 7:23
[5] cf. Gen. 8:21
[6] vid. Josh. 17:13

From all these and many other things, we reach the truthful conclusion that all the distressing events and things in human nature are a consequence of its fall from its original immortality to mortality. Furthermore, we see that the salvific sacrifice of the God-Man Jesus providentially did not remove the law of sin existing within man in order to instruct him, as well as for many other reasons pertaining to our salvation, so that by them He may make him a wise heir of His eternal blessings.

4. "As I find you, I will judge you."[7] Behold, the value of a moment. Did He find you in repentance? Did He meet you in confession? Did He reach you saying, "I have sinned against Heaven and before you"?[8] Did He approach you when you had tears of genuine repentance and self-reproach in your eyes? Behold, it is in one moment that God makes his decision. "The Lord is faithful in all His words."[9]

However, if He finds you otherwise, O man, then the eyes of your soul will open, and you will see what you have lost—but what is the use? If God condemns a person, repentance is futile; when the "fair" of life ends, words are pointless. It is all over!

Oh, what a great mystery this is! O my God, my Sweet Jesus, open the eyes of my soul that I may see very clearly this great mystery of my eternal salvation, so that, helped by Thy grace, I may prepare provisions and not repent at the end of my life to no avail. As Thou dost see, I do absolutely nothing and am entirely leprous with passions. Grant me tears and complete repentance before the last hour comes, when I shall hear Thy voice, "Set thy house in order, for thou shalt die and not live."[10]

5. Repentance is endless. All the virtues, by the grace of God, may be perfected by man, but no one can perfect repen-

---

[7] cf. Ez. 33:12-16

[8] Lk. 15:18

[9] Ps. 144:13

[10] Is. 38:1

tance, since we need repentance until our last breath, for we err in the twinkling of an eye. Therefore, repentance is interminable.

Oh, how good God is! Justly will my fellow sinners be punished, for they have ignored the infinite compassion of the Heavenly Father. Although we err as humans, we are sluggish to say, "I have sinned!" But how can we say this, since we (and I, above all) are forgetful and lazy and proud, too—mighty obstacles on the road to humility! Christ showed this road to us through His Cross, but unfortunately we voluntarily turn a deaf ear to Him, to our great regret.

Time flies, the years roll by, and we are drawing nearer and nearer to eternity. We see this, yet a mental numbness has bound us until we (and I, first) are thrown into hell!

My God, Who has delivered the human race from the enemy's slavery, deliver us also from the future condemnation when You come to judge the world and render to each according to his works.[11]

Through your prayers, may I find mercy when my wretched soul is judged, for I am afraid to meet the fearsome Judge because my conscience reproaches me.

6. Obedience, cutting off one's will, self-reproach, and patience in general are what lay the foundations of the soul, while fervor and zeal preserve one's tears. If you want to be zealous until the end of your life, diligently pursue constant tears. If you have such tears, do not be afraid; the zeal of yearning for your salvation will remain. Water normally quenches fire; the water of God, however, which streams from the eyes of the repentant, lights not a physical fire—as we know—but a divine fire burning up the enemy's weeds!

7. Let us sincerely repent; let us confess frankly and in detail. Let the tribunal of God and His decision preoccupy us

---

[11] cf. Rev. 22:12

continuously, and let us say, "I wonder, shall I be saved or shall I face the torments of hell?" Now is the time we must shed tears of repentance—in fact, constantly. Ah, how much we should be preoccupied by the question of how white and clean our soul is! We must purify it; otherwise, we shall be unable to present ourselves before Christ as we are now. Meditation on death should not escape us at all during our monastic routine.

8. How precious is the time of this life! Every minute has great worth, for within one minute we can think so many things, either good or evil. One godly thought raises us to Heaven, and one diabolical thought lowers us to hell. So then, behold how valuable every minute in this present life is. Unfortunately, though, we do not think about this, and hours, days, and years pass with no profit—but is it merely with no profit? How much damage we have all suffered—and I, first—without realizing it! But someday, when our soul is about to depart from our body, we shall realize it. But alas, it will be too late; there is no room for correction then.

We must realize this now when we can still make a start. We should take advantage of the precious time of our life. Truly blessed is he who compels himself and makes a start, because some day he will become spiritually rich. It is never too late, for the Lord waits for each one of us to awaken so that He may give us work. He waits until the eleventh hour.[12] He tries with every means to awaken us.

I pray that all of us will awaken, light our lamps, and with a vigilant eye wait patiently for the Lord to come, so that we may enter the resplendent bridal chamber of eternal bliss, the festival of the bright angels, to chant with them the resurrectional canticles, which will elevate us from *theoria** to theoria and to divine ascents! Then—oh, then!—we shall fully realize

---

[12] cf. Mt. 20:6

what a great work it is to compel ourselves in everything and that our superiors did well to push us and grieve us, for we shall say, "Behold what we see now!" Then our thanks to God will have no limits. Then we shall really render thanks worthily to God!

9. Let us not lose our time in vain. The Kingdom of Heaven belongs to those who force themselves.[13] Bear in mind the departure of our souls, the final hour and moment of that difficult separation. Keep in mind how the demons seek to snatch the poor soul at this final hour and lead it to Hades. Oh, what grief! What pain of soul! How the soul sighs then! Alas, what a sorrowful situation it is in at that moment! How many promises a person will make to God that he will change his life, that he will walk the path of repentance and hardship, as long as he does not die!

All of us shall reach this hour and encounter the above and much more, and we shall then promise much more earnestly that we shall take the path of repentance and spiritual warfare. Let us imagine that this has already happened and that God has heard our request. Now what is left for us to do? To fulfill our promises by showing true repentance and to struggle to correct our soul. Behold the appropriate time for repentance and spiritual warfare! Little by little the time of our life is cut short, and without even realizing it, we are led to the end and to the grave!

A tribunal and a Judge await us, as well as entire books in which the deeds of each one of us are written. Who is able to escape these things? No one. We shall all stand before the judgment seat of Christ "naked and open"[14] for each of us to give an account of his deeds, words, and thoughts. Let us bear in mind these and many more such things night and day, so that we may bring our souls to mourning and tears!

---

[13] cf. Mt. 11:12
[14] Heb. 4:13

10. Sin, as a hook camouflaged with the suitable pleasure, comes craftily as something sweet and charming to the tongue in order to attack the soul. However, he who has been lured by the momentary pleasure and its comfort will find it more bitter than poison and more destructive than a pestilent disease in his soul.

11. No matter what happened with your parents, confession forgives and erases everything, my dear brother in the Lord. Recall how much the prodigal son sinned,[15] and how much he grieved his father with his reckless life. But when he repented, at once his father's arms opened and the past was wiped out as if it had never happened.

So the cure for your sad parents has already occurred, for the change of your life to a spiritual life has rectified everything. Now that they are in the true life, they are informed by God about the change of your lifestyle and your repentance, as well as your alms and the memorial services you have done for them.

If, when we sin against our true Father, God, He forgives us no matter what we have done, how much more so will our parents be pleased, there in the true life, where they see things clearly. They know human weakness and how easily youth slips, and they are aware of the great master of evil, the devil, who was the cause of all the troubles. They will even be thankful to you that through you they receive aid from God.

Remain fully at peace, my brother. Walk the path of repentance with a peaceful mind, and do not let the past trouble you. "Forgetting those things which are behind, and reaching forward to those things which are ahead,"[16] we should look to the goal of our salvation.

As soon as man says, "I have sinned!" God forgives him immediately and overlooks his sins. How much did Blessed

---

[15] vid. Lk. 16:19-31

Augustine grieve that holy mother of his! Nevertheless, what sanctity and eros of God he attained later! With repentance everything is corrected. There is nothing that overcomes the compassion of God. "He is merciful to the last and provides for the first; to this one He gives, and to that one He shows kindness."[17] The love of God covers and corrects everything. No one is sinless except for one—God.

12. *(The Elder writes to one of his spiritual daughters in the world:)*[†]

All that you suffered, my daughter, was because of your self-reliance. Didn't I advise you to have humility and self-reproach? What did you trust in? Don't you know that if one boldly leans on a bamboo rod, it will break and pierce his hands? So what did you trust in? Don't you know the saying "Without Me you can do nothing"?[18] Don't you know that many Fathers fell by trusting in themselves?

Humble yourself, blame yourself, weep, my daughter, wash your wedding garment. Your Bridegroom, Who is more beautiful than the sons of men, is calling you, is seeking you, and has prepared an abode for you in the Heavens. The spiritual bridal chamber is extremely luxurious! Angels are serving; do not be sluggish. Arise; get some water and wash your wedding gown well, for you do not know when He will come. The time of death is unknown; it comes to us all. We do not know at what moment it will come.

Repent. See how the harlot washed the immaculate feet of the Master. She shed tears more precious than myrrh, and they attracted God's mercy and forgiveness. Then she heard, "Your sins are forgiven; go in peace."[19] Repent, my daughter. Fall before the fearsome feet of the Master with mourning. Weep; cry out, "I have sinned, my Jesus. Accept me in repentance and save me. Overlook not my tears, O joy of the angels. Abhor me

---

[16] Phil. 3:13

[17] Paschal Homily of St. John Chrysostom

[†] "In the world" means not in a monastery.

[18] Jn. 15:5

not, cast me not away, Thou Who hast bent the Heavens by Thine ineffable abasement." With these and many other such words importune Christ, resting assured that you will find His love three times as strong.

Your repentance will give limitless joy to the angels, and exuberantly they will exclaim, "She stopped! She stopped! She stopped!" That is, she stopped short of falling. You were caught out of the flow, and now you are ascending again.

13. Pray for me, my brother, so that the Lord may grant me repentance before I depart on the great journey from this world—for we were not created for this earth, but for Heaven. There, God has prepared a place for His children who are obedient to Him in everything He tells them. On the contrary, for all who are deaf to His divine commandments, He has prepared a place of eternal imprisonment—may God keep us from going there.

Now God cries out through the Holy Scriptures, the preachers, the spiritual fathers: "Repent, for the Kingdom of Heaven is at hand."[20] Unfortunately, though, those who think they are smart and strong turn a deaf ear to Him with various excuses. But the all-good God, wanting to distribute His riches to man, calls "all the feeble, the weak, the things that are not."[21] "Go out quickly into the streets and lanes of the city, and bring in here the poor and the maimed and the lame and the blind, that my house may be filled,"[22] says God through the Holy Gospel. By calling the useless, His compassion is glorified more, and man is led to gratitude, for what leper counted worthy of purification would not render thanks to his benefactor? What person condemned to an eternal imprisonment would not be grateful to his Savior? Unfortunately, my brother, I do not thank God, because forgetfulness—the offspring of pride—has made me lose my head.

---

[19] Lk. 7:48, 50
[20] Mt. 3:2
[21] cf. 1 Cor. 1:27, 28
[22] Lk. 14:21, 23

14. Beloved brother, may God, Who has visited our humbleness, grant us genuine repentance, through which God's tribunal is propitiated. Sincere repentance is repentance that displays regret for sins committed, mourning, burning tears that break down the strongholds of sin, and sincere and frank confession. Repentance leaves nothing unhealed. If man had not been given repentance, no one would be saved. Triumph and victory are given to man through the weapon of repentance. Glory to the only wise God, Who gave man such an effective medicine that cures every kind of illness, as long as it is taken properly.

Let us struggle, my brother; let us live in simplicity and innocence of heart like small children, as the Savior said: "Unless you become as little children, you will by no means enter the Kingdom of Heaven."[23] With simplicity and faith we are freed from evil daydreaming, which destroys the good seeds of the Holy Spirit. Things will happen according to our faith. What you sow is what you reap.

Let us ask God for compunction and mourning, and He will grant them to us, so that a stream of life-giving tears may follow. Then our heart will produce the fruits of the Holy Spirit.

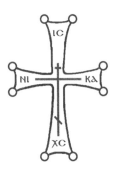

---

[23] Mt. 18:3

On Confession and Spiritual Accounting

This confession of yours gave my soul much joy, because God and the angels, who were awaiting it, rejoiced. You succeeded in putting the devil to shame, who greatly rejoices when someone hides his thoughts from his spiritual father.

When a snake leaves its lair, it rushes to hide somewhere because it feels as if it will be struck. The same thing happens with a diabolical thought, which is like a poisonous snake. When such a thought leaves a person's mouth, it disperses and disappears, because confession is humility, and since Satan cannot even bear the smell of humility, how could he possibly remain after a humble, sincere confession?

My child, I wish you a good beginning and cautious progress. Don't be ashamed before me. Don't see me as a man, but as a representative of God. Tell me everything, even if you have a bad thought about me, because I am experienced with demonic influences, and I know how the devil fights man. I know that spiritual children have simple hearts and that if evil thoughts come to them, it is due to the devil's malice and the spiritual child's ego, who is permitted to fall and have such thoughts against his Elder, so that the spiritual child may be humbled more. Therefore, don't worry. I will always rejoice when you speak freely and sincerely to me, for without frank confession, there will be no spiritual progress.

2. My child, have no worries. I have taken up your burden. I only beg you to be at peace. Your words may be just on paper, but I feel the power, the meaning, and the essence of what you write; I enter into the spirit of your words. I entreat you to be at peace from now on. You are forgiven everything with the confession you made. Satan perceived your character and torments you, but without anything serious having occurred. Everything you write (that is, the thoughts that torture you) is a trick of the evil one to make you despair, be distressed, and so forth. Throw everything that happened to you into the depths of the sea. Map out a new course in your life.

If you keep thinking the same way, know that you will become the laughingstock of the demons. I beg you, just be obedient to me. After your confession, everything has been forgiven, so let bygones be bygones. Don't scratch a wound that made you suffer so much. Don't be deceived by the thought that it is your fault. If you hadn't taken him to the doctors, etc., then such thoughts would rightfully fight you. Whereas, as things are now, you have fulfilled your duty. God wanted to take him, for a reason that only His infinite wisdom knows, while you are thinking you killed him! Be careful with this thought, or else it might lurk in your heart. It is a ruse of the devil to harm you, as he knows how. This skilled trickster has drowned in the depths of hell countless multitudes with despair.

When something happens and the devil sees that a person is upset by it, his trick is to pile on a multitude of supposedly legitimate thoughts in order to lead the poor person to a great storm and drown him. (As the saying goes, a fox loves a scuffle.) And when the storm passes, he sees that he was in danger of drowning in just a spoonful of water.

3. Humble yourself, and from now on confess, for confession contains most holy humility, without which no one is saved. The devil greatly rejoices when he manages to persuade a person to hide diabolical thoughts. This is because he will achieve his premeditated, soul-destroying goal.

4. I have written to you about the conscience, that we must be careful not to do something that will make it reproach and condemn us. Bear in mind that God sees everything and that nothing is hidden from His eyes. So how could I tell lies before God? Don't you know that lies are from the devil, and that by not being careful, it becomes a practice, then a habit, and then a passion, and don't you know that liars will not inherit the Kingdom of God?[1]

Fear God. God is not pleased with material offerings when we neglect attending to our inner heart. But it is necessary to do these also without leaving the others undone.[2]

Attend to your conscience, for we do not know the hour of our death. And if we do not repay our creditor (our conscience, that is) everything we owe him, he will accuse us vehemently, without holding back. Then—alas!—our mouth will be silenced, not having any answer to give.

5. Every night, review how you passed the day, and in the morning review how the night passed, so that you know how your soul's accounts are doing. If you see a loss, try to regain it through caution and forcefulness. If you see a profit, glorify God, your invisible helper.

Do not let your conscience prick you for long, but quickly give it whatever it wants, lest it take you to the judge and the prison.[3] Does your conscience want you to attend to your *prayer rule** and regain prayer? Give it these things, and behold, you are delivered from going to the judge. Do not weaken the saving voice of your conscience by disregarding it, because later you will regret it to no avail.

6. See to it that you are sincere in your deeds as well as in your words, and especially in confession. For God searches out the hearts and reins,[4] and nothing remains obscure in the sight of His sleepless eye.

Fear God; God is not mocked;[5] He is not fooled. He chastises severely when He does not see sincerity; so be careful.

---

[1] cf. Rev. 21:8
[2] cf. Mt. 23:23
[3] cf. Mt. 5:25
[4] Ps. 7:9
[5] Gal. 6:7

When you are disobedient and commit a secret sin, counteract it by openly revealing it in confession. Do not let your ego overcome you and make you hide the truth and remain uncorrected and passionate. Correct everything now if you want to see good days of *dispassion** and peace.

Saint Kosmas

equal to the apostles

Chapter Four

On Monasticism, Virginity, and Purity

There is nothing more choice than monasticism. Monasticism means theosis, sanctification of soul and body, communion with God. Monasticism is consciousness, awareness, and discovery of the Kingdom of God within man. Who is wise and will understand these things?[1] Who is truly prudent and has recognized that within monasticism lies the extraordinary grace of God, as theosis and sanctification? Who left the world, his desires, and freedom, went to live this life, and by constant digging and struggling found Jesus and became a king ruling with dispassion?

Without monasticism no one reaches dispassion. No one obtains a pure *nous** without vigils, abstinence, and unceasing prayer. No one attains theoria without a monastic lifestyle. No one acquires such a close relationship and contact with Jesus as he who stays near Him and does not abandon Him. Then he will be worthy of the beatitude: "Blessed are those who hear the word of God."[2]

If the heart is not purified, our pure Jesus will not come to make an "abode"[3] in it. But how is it possible for someone to purify his heart while living in the midst of the world? The Fathers realized the difficulty of this, and for this reason they

---

[1] cf. Ps. 106:43
[2] Lk. 11:28
[3] cf. Jn. 14:23

abandoned the world and dwelt in the wilderness. They set up their arena there and won the crowns of victory.

So, man is called to begin the struggle and the spiritual contest with God as an ally and the Elder as a helper. But the enemies—the devil, the world, and the flesh—will offer strong resistance to intimidate the fighter. But if he firmly holds on to the counsels and advice of his spiritual guide, by all means he will obtain victory and will receive the crowns of eternal glory.

Monasticism is supernatural. The life of a monk is supernatural because he renounces nature in the full sense of the word. For behold: he breaks the natural bonds with his parents and relatives and abandons them for his entire life—not for selfish purposes, but exclusively for the sake of serving God with complete dedication.

The goal of his new life is to mortify his carnal mentality and through the struggle to obtain angelic purity. It is natural to sleep at night, but monasticism prescribes vigil so that a monk becomes "like a sparrow sitting alone upon the housetop."[4] It is natural for an individual to have freedom, but as soon as one begins the monastic life, he forces himself to mortify his self-will for the sake of the love of God. And in general, the life of a monk is completely different from worldly life, which is why it is called angelic, because of its supernatural course.

It is a great gift from God to be called to monasticism and an even greater gift to find a spiritual guide in it. To leave the world is easy, but to find a competent guide is a special gift from God, because whether or not he makes progress will depend on his guide.

When the remembrance of death is diligently meditated upon, it provides great strength in the beginning when one in-

---

4 Ps. 102:7

tends to renounce the world, as well as throughout one's monastic life. This remembrance will become an all-powerful spiritual philosophy for him, from which he will draw forth the truth of things to supplant everything transitory.

Visit the frigid tombs and listen carefully, and hear what those dwelling in them will tell you: "For what will it profit a man if he gains the whole world, and loses his own soul?"[5] "Vanity of vanities; all is vanity."[6]

At the extremely difficult and exceedingly grievous hour of death, there is no one to help a person except for his works. In fact, no one except God. If we serve Him, we shall have an almighty helper and protector at the fearful and deadly separation of our soul and body. What a struggle the soul has as it is separated from the body! Keep this struggle constantly in mind; think and note that we also have to pass the aerial *toll-houses,** which impede souls from ascending as they present the deeds of our life in order to obstruct our souls' ascent and drag them down into Hades. Then we must bear in mind that we also have to face a tribunal. And alas, what a tribunal! Saying, "I have sinned" and "forgive me, the sinner," is not effective then, for every mouth shall be silenced with no excuse.

We should ponder these things and other such things so that we can trace out more clearly what kind of goal we have and so that we can run as quickly as possible to obtain it, for we do not know what tomorrow holds. The time of death is unknown. Only good deeds done for God will remain and will follow man beyond death.

And what is better than working for God all one's life so that one takes the profit of this work with him when he goes to God! Truly this person is the wise merchant who found the pearl of great price. If you hear the voice of the Lord your

---

5 Mk. 8:36

6 Eccl. 1:2

God, do not harden your heart, but listen to what He will tell you: "He will speak peace to His saints and to them that turn their heart unto Him."[7]

I pray with all my heart that through divine eros you acquire a ceaseless yearning for God, and that by soaring with it you attain beauty equal to the angels, through the intercessions of the Abbess of the Holy Mountain, the Lady Theotokos. Amen; so be it.

2. Oh, what bliss is hidden within monasticism! O luxuriousness of Heaven, how you captivate the monk who practices *hesychia** and is far from the vain world! How much the nous in a quiet place is drawn above and passes from knowledge to knowledge, from theoria to theoria, ascending in his heart, beholding only God with divine eros! Oh, the depth of the knowledge of God! Indeed, the obscure monks who wandered around in the wilderness were divine philosophers; they walked on earth, but they resided in Heaven through theoria and eros.

O monasticism, how great is your glory! When a person settles down from all the tumult and becomes a monk under the guidance and supervision of a precise guide, he is led to the internal glory of monasticism.

We wrestle against powers, against principalities, against dark and very sly authorities,[8] against legions very experienced in warfare, against the flesh and the world of passions, which are like dreadfully painful wounds that take time, patience, diligence, and a correct approach to be healed.

Take a look at the Holy Fathers in their initial years; they endured droughts, terrible times of discouragement, and many deadly temptations. But they held on tightly to patience and forcefulness, and then grace visited them in proportion to whatever they endured beforehand.

---

[7] cf. Ps. 84:8

[8] cf. Eph. 6:12

3. *(The Elder writes to nuns about the life of virginity.)*

The life of virginity resembles a small boat that is constantly struggling with the relentless harsh storm, with no haven in sight, and is continuously tossed about by the waves. For a virgin bears within her the flame of carnality and for this reason there can be no cease-fire, but rather a constant war, keeping one's weapons always in hand.

When a storm breaks out, a married woman takes shelter in the harbor, which is conjugal union, and thus escapes the danger. A virgin, however, braves the storms and proceeds in the open sea while firmly holding the helm of the boat of her soul. She is not alone, though, but protected by perfect obedience to her spiritual parents and strengthened by the grace of the angelic schema, she courageously struggles with the rough waves of the flesh while incessantly calling upon Jesus until He comes and rebukes the sea, saying to it: "Peace, be still."[9]

Oh, how lofty is chastity! How much its resplendent garment shines, and how immense is its boldness towards God, for it not only equates man with the angels, but it even raises him above them! The angels effortlessly remain in chastity, because they are living in accordance with their nature, whereas a virgin has set her course above nature. Not only does she have the struggle to turn her nature in another direction, but she also has a constant battle and lifelong endeavor against the dreadful demons, who gnash their malicious teeth to make the straight paths of the Lord crooked—that is, to tear the pure bride of Christ away from His love and turn her into a beast, like a pig that devours the muck of passionate pleasure.

Let us labor, my children, let us struggle. Let us run that we may obtain the prize of the high calling,[10] for Christ the Judge

---

[9] cf. Mk. 4:39
[10] cf. Phil. 3:14

of the contest is present, compassionately observing each person's struggle, so that we may enjoy His likeness when He appears. As Paul the Apostle of the Gentiles wrote: "When Christ Who is our life appears, then you also will appear with Him in glory."[11]

Girls desert their beloved parents and brothers and relatives, and through marriage cleave to a mortal man and bear with his weaknesses, his bad manners, his passions, and sometimes (if he has a bad character) even with his beatings and curses. Nevertheless, they do not leave their husband because they respect the bond of the sacrament of marriage, or because they want financial support and security.

But you, on the contrary, have married the incorruptible Bridegroom Christ and have deserted parents and all the good things of this vain world in order to be united with Christ through a spiritual marriage. You lovingly follow Jesus, Who for our sake endured the Cross and death and gave you an immense dowry: the Kingdom of Heaven. Although you were poor and dirty, He made you into queens to enjoy in Heaven more glory and delight than emperors.

How incomparably the grace of virginity surpasses marriage, and how much loftier is the gift of the mystery of the mystical spiritual wedding with the Bridegroom Christ than a carnal wedding! And this is because the Bridegroom is heavenly, spotless, eternal—God!

We see that the wife in common marriages becomes a heroine of patience by enduring the sorrows, the worries and difficulties of married life, the passions, the beatings from her husband, and the difficulties beyond her strength in raising and fostering her children. So then—alas!—how reprehensible we are when we don't have patience, forcefulness, obedience, and everything that the easy yoke[12] of the sweetest

---

[11] Col. 3:4
[12] cf. Mt. 11:30

Jesus calls for, to a greater degree than a married woman does! Therefore, we ought to demonstrate a way of life that corresponds to the excellence of our calling and to the impending trophies and eternal rewards of Heaven.

Let us humble ourselves and cry out to Christ the Bridegroom: "O Bridegroom of my poor soul, close not Thy heavenly bridal chamber as Thou didst unto the foolish virgins, but count us worthy to have lamps filled with the oil of good works, love, patience, chastity, discernment, and the rest of the virtues, so that they will be sufficient to keep the light lit until Thou comest, so that our entire synodia may enter with Thee into the eternal wedding with a bright garment, radiant with the light of Thy grace, while celebrating and rejoicing with Thee, unto the endless ages of ages. Amen; so be it."

4. *(To a novice nun)*

Love Christ your Bridegroom more than your mother, and you will be called blessed in Heaven. Care for nothing earthly except for how to please your most beautiful Bridegroom Christ. The spiritual wedding with Him will last eternally, whereas worldly weddings last only a little while, and then the torments, the toil, and the labor begin.

In the monastic life, any labor one puts in will be rewarded richly and eternally—and even here on earth we shall receive a hundredfold what we give by leaving our parents, brothers, etc. Our Christ gives us the sisterhood in Christ, where the love is spiritual and aims to contribute towards our spiritual progress, whereas carnal love loves only physical and vain things. In the worldly life the toil and torments are vain, whereas in the monastic life they help us to acquire God.

Oh, how wonderful it is when there is love in a sisterhood, when a sisterhood is one soul with many bodies! Truly, they live a heavenly life. But God allows things to happen from time to time that will cause vexation and coolness. This happens, however, for our benefit so that we may be trained and so that our virtue or weakness may be revealed. That is why the spiritual law tells us: sometimes joy, sometimes mourning; sometimes winter, sometimes summer; sometimes war, sometimes peace. This is how the spiritual road has been mapped out by the omniscient God.

5. *(To a spiritual daughter)*

"I heard a voice . . . like the sound of harpists playing their harps. And they sang a new song before the throne . . . and no one could learn that song. . . . These are the ones who did not defile themselves with women, for they are virgins . . . following the Lamb wherever He goes."[13]

My daughter, may the grace of the Lord grant you His ardent love so that you become all afire with it and thus walk with exultation the blessed path of monastic life. This path is angelic, and when someone walks it worthily, his soul becomes a bride of Christ, and it shines more than the angels, for the soul of man is created in the image and likeness of God.

Yes, my daughter, never exchange your heavenly Bridegroom for a carnal man, your Creator for an earthly creature, the divine heavenly nature for human nature. Is there a more glorious achievement for a person than to have as the bridegroom of his soul the Son of God, Who will keep his angelic virginity forever and will give him eternal life in Heaven within the divine dwellings of angelic heavenly pleasure?

What more do the girls do who leave their parents and siblings to get married? Those who become nuns do the same thing, too. Therefore, those who become nuns do not sacrifice anything more than those who get married, with the only difference that the latter obtain an earthly man with passions and

---

[13] Rev. 14:2-4

weaknesses, while the former marry a Bridegroom Who is heavenly, dispassionate, and God. So how much more successful are those girls who become nuns with Christ, both here in this world and there in Heaven forever!

The devil creates many impediments for someone who wants to become a monk or nun. He wants him to stay in the world so that he can hurl him into sins more easily. Therefore, my daughter, keep in mind the wiles of the devil and be wise regarding the thoughts or temptations that come to you. When I am not nearby, reveal them clearly to the Eldress, and she, with the enlightenment she has, will help you very much.

Say *the prayer** constantly, for it will help you in everything and will dissipate everything that prevents you from achieving your holy goal. Be careful; keep yourself pure from every carnal defilement, for the heavenly Bridegroom loves above all a person's chastity of soul and body. I pray, my daughter, that you love and be loved by our Lord Jesus, and that He becomes to you the beloved Bridegroom of your soul forever.

6. *(To another spiritual daughter)*

My good little child, I send you my fatherly greetings from the garden of our Panagia, the Holy Mountain. I am also sending you a bouquet of beautiful little prayers to strengthen you in the path of virginity.

Each person will face the fearsome hour of death all by himself, and works done with humility will be his true aid. What is more humble than the robe of a recluse nun? A nun sits far away from worldly joys and weeps for her sins in order to find the genuine joy of the soul which comes from a clear conscience.

The monastic life is very beautiful and sweet. But unfortunately, our passions and weaknesses sometimes make it seem difficult. The more one comes to the knowledge of God with understanding, the more beautiful he perceives the monastic life to be, because he perceives and tastes the heavenly grace and sweet love of God.

The world is ignorant of Him Who gives these divine and heavenly gifts, and this is why it is miserable and leprous with sin. The angels, though, see Him—how greatly they love and worship Him! But even a nun who senses Him is not left out of such a divine vision and love. However, the world "knew Him not and for this reason its heart is full of sorrow and distress.

The more a nun approaches, lives with, and beholds—as far as possible—the Bridegroom of her soul, the more beautiful she becomes on the inside. She sees this with the eyes of her soul, and she lives it with spiritual perception—how wonderful she feels then! She deplores the joys and delights of the vain and seductive world and feels sorry for the miserable people who rely and depend on them and who in the end will be hopelessly embittered because of them.

7. *(To a spiritual daughter)*

My child, I received the confession you sent me. I thank our good God that the rays of divine illumination again and again enlighten souls to inherit the paternal authority, with regard to the essential issue of the soul—the communication, I mean, of the soul with God by means of *noetic prayer.**

God is an infinite Nous, whereas the human nous is limited. When the small nous of man is united through noetic prayer with the infinite Nous—God—he naturally partakes of His divine and blessed energies and becomes blessed. Perceiving the unspeakable joy, the sweetness, and the exultation, the sweetest tears comfort his soul and fill it with divine consolation.

Prayer is the mighty weapon of the Christian and especially of the monk, who bears the title of a soldier of the divine army, who with an oath has raised the glorious banner of
an unequal, lifelong war against the world, the flesh, and the
devil. We have been called to become unknown heroes, visible only to the unsleeping eye of God.

"If you want to be perfect, go, sell what you have and give
to the poor, and you will have treasure in Heaven; and come,
follow Me."[14] Become my follower along the steep ascent to
Golgotha. Let us be crucified together, let us breathe our last
together, so that we may also be risen together and live together.

"If anyone desires to come after Me, let him deny himself,
and take up his cross every day."[15] If anyone loves Me, let
him follow Me, for everything is rubbish, more illusory than
dreams. "Riches do not remain; glory does not accompany
one to the other world; for when death strikes, it obliterates
them all."[16]

Theology—true theology—is not gained in universities,
but rather by despising the world and by living in a quiet and
peaceful place far from the world's noise and turmoil, with a
program of prayer and asceticism. Then, once a person has
thus purified his *intellect** and been delivered from the surges
of the flesh, he will obtain the light of true theology, of knowing himself. "If you are a theologian, you pray well; if you
pray well, you are a theologian."[17]

In stillness the nous quiets down. Furthermore, once the
nous is stripped of earthly thoughts, it naturally returns to itself and through itself to God, by means of the *single-
phrased** prayer "Lord Jesus Christ, have mercy on me."

If a person withdraws from the world, then he will discover
its stench, whereas one who wanders about in it clothes him-

---

[14] Mt. 19:21
[15] cf. Mt. 16:24
[16] from the funeral service

[17] *The Philokalia,* Vol. I, (Faber and
Faber: NY, 1983), p. 62.

self with the rags of worldly delights and pleasures as if with a glorious garment. There is nothing sweeter than to be an outcast in the house of God rather than to dwell in the tents of the sinful world[18] with all the seductions of sensuality, by which Hades obtains most of its booty.

My child, love of the world is enmity with God. If you love God and want to serve Him completely and effectively, forget about the vanity of the big city's worldly concerns, and come to the beloved and desired dwellings of the Lord, wherein you will study the science of sciences: the art of how to conquer the devil, the world, and your own self. This is the science of fighting bravely for eternal rewards and positions!

8. *(To a spiritual daughter)*

"Oh, the depth of the riches of the wisdom and knowledge of God,"[19] cried out the Apostle Paul when he was overwhelmed by the visions of divine light and the burning of his heart with divine eros! What is sweeter than God? Are not all human things vanity? Doesn't the grave cover everything? Where is one's youth, where is one's beauty, where are one's glory and riches? Isn't everything dust and ashes? Who was a king and who was a soldier? Who was rich and who was poor? Don't we see just bones? Where are the palaces of the kings, the luxuries of the wealthy, the lavish tables and banquets of the pleasure-loving? Where are the sensual pleasures of the immoral? Don't worms and an unbearable stench cover them all? Truly vanity of vanities; all is vanity![20]

While philosophizing about these things, let us exert ourselves and love with great longing the pure and holy path of glorious virginity, so that when we leave our body on the earth and our soul ascends to Heaven, the beauty and loveliness of virginity will adorn it, so that the Bridegroom of pure souls, our Christ, will love it.

---

[18] cf. Ps. 83:11

[19] Rom. 11:33

[20] Eccl 1:2

Fight the good fight, my child. Continuously remember the holy name of our Jesus. Lower your head while you walk and say in a whisper or mentally, "Lord Jesus Christ, have mercy on me." Bear in mind the uncertainty of the time of your death; sigh and say: "Ah, in what state will death find me? Ah, will I be ready? Will I have served Christ enough to expiate my sins?" And always bear in mind the lives of holy monastics so that your yearning for monasticism is kindled even more.

9. *(To another spiritual daughter)*

I am praying that God may guide you aright in everything. When one goes to a monastery, he brings with him his virtues and passions. He is called to monasticism to increase his virtues and to eradicate his passions. The difficulty he encounters in uprooting his passions corresponds to the roughness or the multitude of them, and he needs the corresponding self-denial to achieve his goal, which is the liberation from the dishonorable, sinful passions.

As time passes in the monastic life and as spiritual knowledge grows, the laboriousness of Golgotha is lessened because the good Cyrenian[21]—the consolation of luminous knowledge—comes and lifts the burden of the passions. Thereafter the follower of Jesus walks as light as air towards the complete mortification of the passions, and then his resurrection will follow. And oh, my child, what a resurrection! A taste of the Kingdom of Heaven! An heir of God and joint heir with Christ! Then the soul receives its betrothal promise: that it will become a bride of Christ after death in an undefiled bridal chamber with eternal delight! Then it will see itself sailing in oceans of joy and theorias. And all these spiritual good things are won when one struggles well to eradicate his passions with patience and humility. I pray, my child, that you will excel in your future struggle.

---

[21] vid. Mk. 15:21

10. *(Another letter to the same spiritual daughter)*

I pray with all my soul that our good God will preserve you under His mighty protection and guide you like an unerring compass to the pole of your pure destination, to a holy dedication at the feet of Jesus, like St. Mary, the sister of St. Martha,[22] to hear the words of grace spoken in your heart.

Fear no one but God, Who examines hearts and rewards each according to his works. Fight the fight of salvation; meditate upon the uncertainty of life; reflect that we are passersby, strangers, and sojourners, as were all our fathers;[23] and that we came, we saw, and we departed. When death strikes, it obliterates everything. Struggle so that you hate with all your soul the temporal good things, and as a wise merchant trade and buy the field in which the treasure, the precious pearl, is hidden, and dig and find it, and then you will become rich in grace.

The field is monasticism, and he who sells all his self-will, pleasures in general, and his freedom, buys it. And he who digs—in other words, toils in monasticism—finds the grace of the Comforter and becomes rich in love and hope in God.

There is nothing more beautiful than monasticism, when it is lived along the lines that the Holy Monastic Fathers have mapped out. One acquires the luxury of true joy and rejoices in God with the blessed hope that he will live with God forever in blessedness and ineffable joy!

Oh, the depth of God! Oh, what sweet and inexpressible riches! If even the Apostle Paul in spite of all his eloquence could not present a simple image of everything he saw and felt when he was caught up into paradise, how will I, the wretch, be able to speak of the magnificence of the bliss of communion with God?

Taste and see that the Lord is good.[24] O child of mine and of Jesus, be wary lest any of the worldly things that are con-

---

[22] vid. Lk. 10:39

[23] 1 Chron. 29:15

[24] cf. Ps. 33:9

sidered to be good separate you from Him. Instead, transfer all your longing to the things of Heaven, for our citizenship is in Heaven.[25] Despise all worldly things; consider them dirt and ash. Nothing is certain in the present age. Flee from sin as from a fire and a poisonous snake, and with the prayer take refuge in Jesus, and He will rescue you miraculously. Sacrifice everything for Jesus because He deserves every sacrificial act of love.

11. *(To those desiring the monastic life)*

Oh, how can I appraise the inconceivable riches of virginity! What tongue of clay is able to extol its glory beside our Christ! Virginity is equality with the angels. It is that which makes an earthly human similar to our Christ and our Panagia, for both of them were virgins. Before Adam and Eve sinned, they were virgins; only after the Fall did they have marital relations. That is, virginity was dictated first, whereas marriage is a result of the Fall. Consequently, whoever wishes to attain the virtue that Adam and Eve had when they were in Paradise must live in virginity and chastity.[25a]

Virginity and chastity have great boldness before God. Therefore, sacrifice even your lives; just guard your virginity as the apple of your eye. But, in order to keep it, you must say the prayer constantly and make sure that you avoid occasions of sin; be especially careful with your eyes.

12. My child, we must attend to chastity, for this is how a monastic soul is kindled. It is chastity that best characterizes the monastic way of life as angelic. The Holy Spirit looks favorably upon chastity and visits the chaste. Then a monk feels as if he were in paradise. The devil attacks chastity in order to prevent the visitation of the Holy Spirit. This is why, my

---

[25] Phil. 3:20

[25a] On the superiority of virginity according to the Holy Fathers, see *The Life of St. Makrina & On Virginity*, by St. Gregory of Nyssa; *An Exhortation to Theodore after His Fall*, by St. John Chrysostom (both: SAGOM Press, 2019); *Concerning Viginity*, by St. Ambrose of Milan (NPNF 2 vol. 10, pp. 361–390); and Migne, PG 63:210; PG 48:540, 546; and PG 78:436–440.

child, he troubles us with bad thoughts: so that we will not become useful vessels of the Holy Spirit, and so that we will not feel that the monastic life is angelic. So let us struggle to acquire, by the grace of God, chastity of soul and body.

13. When people are *tonsured*,* grace visits some greatly, while others less. This, however, does not foretell the monk's future spiritual life. Some do not feel the grace of the angelic *schema** at all, and yet they make much progress thereafter; whereas the opposite happens with others. But the goal of monasticism is purity of heart, from which perfect love is attained. This is what should preoccupy us and what we should attend to: whether or not we have patience and bravery in our battles with the devil, pure love, a tongue free of criticism and backbiting, etc.

A monk has two joys: one when he becomes a monk, and one when he approaches death. What is the life of a monk but a continuous martyrdom? This is why death is joyful, because he ponders that he will escape the torments and battles of the tempter.

Heal yourself now that you are young and your passions are just sprouting, so that you find repose in old age. For a life with a good struggle will bring us much spiritual wealth in our old age and a good end.

14. I entreat you, pay attention to yourselves and do not forget the goal for which you left the world and which we should fight to achieve. For what good is it if we accomplish something worldly and harm our immortal soul, to which nothing is equivalent?

Our goal as monks is to ascend to the things above and dwell in the Heavens. We set our minds on the things above, on the purity of the angels. It is unbefitting to succumb to any indecent thought and to abandon the almighty weapon—the prayer.

The body of a monk is a temple of God, and we ought to beautify this sacred temple with every kind of cleanliness, so that it is pleasing to God. Whoever defiles this temple grieves the Lord, so be careful in regard to chastity.

Virginity is a distinctive trait of devoted souls, as well as of the angels. The devil absolutely hates virginity, since he is filthy and alienated from God. He brings us so many filthy thoughts in order to defile the beauty of chastity and make it thus lose its angelic radiance.

15. *(From Mt. Athos, October 1957)*

My beloved brother in Christ . . . , may God bless and enlighten you along the unerring path of salvation. You asked me in your letter if you have the calling from the Lord to become a monk, lest you do something without Him having called you to monasticism and thus desert your responsibilities, etc.

My brother, "He who is able to accept it, let him accept it. Not everyone can accept this saying."[26] The characteristics of a calling are when a person sees within himself a keen desire, zeal, yearning, and a kind of eros towards monasticism. When he sees such things in himself, he is assured that God is definitely calling him to become a monk. Yet he is left completely free to choose by himself one or the other, but with the conviction that he has been given the aptitude and the calling, and if he wants, he may voluntarily, without coercion, embrace monasticism, which is also called the life of virginity.

This calling is due to the grace of God, which a person must not lay aside and quench. For if he lays it aside by remaining in the world for two or three years, it will surely be quenched, and then one's desire can no longer be kindled for such a lofty goal.

While such a person is still in the world, he needs to fast in accordance with his physical strength and with discernment, to

---

[26] Mt. 19:12,11

keep vigil, to pray, to give alms, to guard himself from the things that defile his chaste disposition, to avoid bad company and talking with members of the opposite sex, to find time for stillness, to read, etc. All these things help to increase his desire for monasticism and keep it warm until the appropriate time comes to fulfill his desire, if, of course, he decides to; because as we said, a person is left completely free to choose, even though he has evidence of his calling from the characteristic signs.

Of course, when one has made a vow to God to become a monk, he is in a sense obligated to do so, just as the great Church Fathers say. When one is about to take a vow, one must think it over well, because breaking it will not have good results, since it is considered scorning God, to Whom he made the vow.

The life of virginity is lofty, for a person completely allows himself to please God without any obstacles, so that, in time, by working fully in the service of God, he may become holy in soul and body; he will be reborn; he will become a new man dedicated to Christ with the characteristics of the life in Christ.

My brother, whenever you want, you may come to the Holy Mountain, even as a pilgrim, and see things up close. If you like, you may stay as long as you want with us, or anywhere else. Our little house has two small cells: one for me, one for you. This way you will see better what you should do. You will also hear spiritual words from experience, from my Elder, and—in a word—you will be enlightened to know what to do.

In the beginning, the life in Christ has much toil and various temptations. But with time they abate and the spiritual consolation begins, such that when the grace of God visits, you will find yourself in a state of spiritual pleasure and delight.

16. *(From Mt. Athos, November 1957)*

My dearest brother in Christ, may the grace of the Holy Spirit always protect you. I received your letter yesterday and greatly rejoiced to see that you have grasped the true essence of monasticism and that you are well. My health is poor, as God wills.

What I meant about quenching grace is that if a person remains and lingers for two or three years in the world, his zeal is cooled and then he loses his vigor towards monasticism, for the grace of this fervency withdraws because of his negligence to fulfill his goal.

"Thorns and thistles will the earth bring forth to you,"[27] say the Scriptures. Thorns and thistles: that is, passions and bad habits arise in the earth of the heart. With much toil and sweat and tears the thorny roots of the passions and bad habits are plucked out in order to clear the earth of the heart, where the seed, the word of God, will be sown.

"Lord Jesus Christ, have mercy on me." According to the *Watchful Fathers,** the prayer is the seed which is sown in the heart of the novice with much labor and struggling in the beginning until it sprouts, grows, is reaped, and made into bread, the bread of life—in other words, so that he may eat the fruit of his labor which is the sweetness of the prayer, the love of Christ. This is the living water that waters the heart, refreshes it, and makes it flourish, things which I, the indolent one, lack. "The hour is coming when the true worshippers will worship the Father in Spirit and truth."[28] How beautifully the Lord clarifies noetic prayer!

While you remain in the world, struggle, read, pray, and say the prayer as much as you can, for its power is enormous. Pursue almsgiving; great is the power of almsgiving. I, too, when I was in the world, gave alms as much as I could, even

---

[27] Gen. 3:18

[28] cf. Jn. 4:23

though I was poor, so that God would help me achieve my goal.

Have you noticed how God glorifies the merciful? An angel of the Lord appeared to Cornelius the centurion and said to him: "Your alms and your prayers have come up for a memorial before God."[29] Likewise the Prophet Daniel said to the King: "O King, atone for your sins by alms and for your iniquities by compassion on the poor."[30]

Brother, let us—and first of all me, the senseless one—bear in mind the fearful reckoning before the dreadful tribunal of God, just as the holy ascetics did.

Abba Agathon wept when he was about to die, and his monks asked him: "Are you also weeping, Abba?"

"Believe me, my children, I strove to please God with all my strength, but I do not know if my deeds are pleasing to God!"

Saint Anthony the Great also wept when he approached death.

"Are you also weeping, Abba?"

"Believe me, my children, ever since I became a monk, the fear of death has never left me!"

So I think about myself as well; what defense shall I give to God?—I, the indolent and filthy one, whose passions have stripped me of my wedding garment!

You will encounter, my brother, many obstacles along your path, but do not lose your courage. Avoid everything that hinders you on the path of God. Cut off all friendships with worldly youths. Do not fear; when God is with us, no one is against us.

My little cell is very hesychastic. When you come, you will be very pleased. I live in profound stillness and freedom from care. My Elder gave me a blessing to eat something in the morning by myself in peace. Rarely does someone pass by. I

---

[29] Acts 10:4
[30] Dan. 4:24

eat my meager food by myself. I strive with the help of God to keep saying the prayer. I wake up by myself; I keep vigil by myself. So anyone who longs to live in stillness, prayer, and freedom from care will love it here.

I await you with much joy, and I beg that you do not hesitate to write. I am praying for you with love in Christ.

—Lowly Papa-Ephraim of Joseph.

17. Abstinence, fasting, keeping vigil, renouncing worldly things, etc. are the means, my child, by which we attain purity of heart. The primary property that characterizes purity of heart is love.

So our goal is purity of heart. Without purity, God is not beheld; He is not revealed. So how can we tell whether we have achieved our goal, whether we have drawn near to it, if we do not have a pure heart? The Apostle Paul says, "Love does not envy; love does not parade itself, is not puffed up; it does not behave rudely, does not seek its own, is not provoked, thinks no evil; it does not rejoice in iniquity, but rejoices in the truth; it bears all things, believes all things, hopes all things, endures all things. Love never fails."[31] All these characteristics which the Apostle Paul proclaims with a thundering voice indicate how much a person has progressed in purity.

The farmer starts by clearing his field. He clears it of rocks and thorns; he plows it; he sows and waits for God to send rain, sunshine, and wind, with one objective: to reap wheat and enjoy the fruit of his toils. The sailor and the merchant travel afar, risk facing storms and various dangers with the aim of increasing and enjoying their wealth. The monk endures the deprivation of his parents, siblings, relatives; he deprives himself of pleasure; he keeps vigil, prays, is obedient, battles with

---

[31] 1 Cor. 13:4-8

thoughts, etc.—with what goal? To achieve purity of heart, to see God! If it is not purified, he will not see God.

What is God? God is love. Therefore, he who lacks true love, love that is spiritual and unadulterated, is unable to know the Divine.

18. My daughter, may the sweetest Crucified Lord bestow thousands of blessings upon you, for He adores virginity, which is the spiritual sister of the virginity of the angels.

The Heavenly Father is a virgin; His Son, our Lord Jesus, is a virgin; the beloved disciple of Christ, John, was a virgin; but where shall I place the Virgin Mary, our Panagia, who is a wall of protection for struggling virgins? This most holy virtue of virginity, the adornment of the angels, I pray that you, my daughter, will choose in your life.

Everything that a person loses can be regained, except for virginity, which is a most pure life free of presumptuous and shameful sins. The angelic hosts rejoice when even just one more fellow combatant is added to their ranks. This is an enviable post. Wouldn't you like to occupy it, my daughter? I hope that the work of grace will be gloriously completed in you, for the glory of the Crucified Lord.

O daughter, love our Jesus and worship only Him in your life. May Jesus be the spiritual delight of your heart. Never exchange this holy love for deceitful worldly pleasures, no matter how hard the vain world tries to force you. Become a disciple of Jesus, like another myrrh-bearer offering as a precious myrrh your virginal purity to your Teacher.

All earthly things pass like a dream, and nothing in this world remains stable and unchangeable. So then, why should we love transitory and ephemeral things instead of the eternal and everlasting ones?

At every moment death threatens to send us to the other

world and in particular to the tribunal of God. So what are we to do? What else other than to prepare ourselves to give a good defense to God for everything in which we have sinned against Him!

Drive away every thought of yours that is sinful and not good as soon as it appears. Constantly call to mind the name of our Jesus, for this most holy name will give you victory against sin in all its forms.

19. Sometimes externally a monk may seem to be gloomy, whereas in reality he has joyful mourning, which is so beneficial and necessary. He appears sullen when he is fighting against evil thoughts or when he is being tempted by his ego, by disturbing words, or by some reproach, and he is struggling to crush his ego's uprising with thoughts of self-reproach. The seeming gloominess is not due to thoughts of despair, since he blesses the hour in which God took him out of the misery of the world and brought him to the saving life of monasticism. Instead of gloominess, we should call it joyful mourning, which means a deep joy and satisfaction that come from the systematic cultivation of the heart. Such mourning is unknown to worldly people, who pay attention only to externals and let their heart remain dangerously ill with egotism, pride, and vainglory!

External Christian works—without *watchfulness*,* unceasing prayer, and vigils in solitude in a dark cell—lead the Christian to vainglory, since he bases everything on his works that are so cheap! To clean the heart requires labor: the labor of self-reproach, prayer, self-denial, obedience, godly labors, many tears, etc. If the heart has not been cleansed in this manner, how can one's works be pleasing to God? Only monasticism strikes passions at their root like an ax, while without a monastic struggle one cuts only branches and leaves!

20. The supernatural miracles of the monks and their spiritual state, which is the fruit of their ascetical struggles, show what monasticism is. Although struggling to live the Christian life in the world is a godly pursuit, it does not even come close to monasticism in its yield of spiritual wealth and in its closeness to God. "A tree is known by its fruit."[32] An entire army of monastics has filled Heaven. How many Righteous[†] saints do we have? You can count them on your fingers.

Saint Peter   Saint Athanasios

Athos

---

[32] Mt. 12:33
[†] The Righteous are the saints who attained sanctity while living in the world and were not clergy, monastics, or martyrs.

On the World and Family

May an angel of God, my child, follow you and show you the path of God and of your salvation. Amen; so be it. I pray that God gives you health of soul, for this is a special gift of sonship which is bestowed only upon those souls that have been completely devoted to the worship and love of God.

The world attracts the youth like a magnet; worldly things have great power over the newly enlightened soul that has just started to find its bearings and see its purpose in life and the duty calling him. "Friendship with the world is enmity with God. Whoever, therefore, wants to be a friend of the world makes himself an enemy of God."[1] God has stored up pleasures for eternity, for both He and our soul are eternal. There is no comparison between the pleasures of the world and the pure pleasures of God.

The pleasures of the world are obtained with toil and expenses, and after their momentary enjoyment, they are followed by various consequences, so that they are incorrectly called pleasures. The pleasures of God, however, do not have such consequences, because spiritual pleasures down here on earth are the firstfruits of an eternal series of pleasures and delights in the Kingdom of God. Whereas on the contrary, one who has been corrupted by the pleasures of the world is compelled to undergo eternal damnation along with the first instigator of corruption, the devil.

The time of our life, my child, has been given to us as a sum of money so that each of us may trade for his salvation, and depending on the trade we deal in, we shall become either rich or poor. If we take advantage of the "money" of time by trading to increase our spiritual wealth, then we shall truly be

---

[1] Jam. 4:4

skilled traders, and we shall hear the blessed voice: "Well done, good and faithful servant! You were faithful over a few things; I will make you ruler over many things. Enter into the joy of your Lord."[2]

At the end of our life, an exact account will be demanded of each one of us—how and where we spent the money of time; and woe to us if we have squandered it in movie theaters, in entertainments, in debauchery, in futile dreams, in carnal pleasures. Then what defense will our tied tongue be able to utter, and how will we be able to lift up our eyes and see our Christ when He enumerates the countless benefactions which His boundless love profusely poured upon us?

Now that we have time, now that the money of time has not yet been spent completely and we still have it at our disposal, let us reflect sensibly on the vagrant world, which seeks to rob us. Let us push it away like a putrid dead dog, and with that money let us run to buy precious works which, when tried by fire, will become very bright—gifts worthy of our holy God, fit to be used as a decoration in the holy Jerusalem of Heaven. We should not purchase chaff, that is, punishable works of darkness, for we shall go down with them into the eternal fire of damnation, where the multitude of people who embezzled God's gifts will reap whatever they sowed! Sow good works with tears, and then in a time of visitation you will reap the sheaves of enjoying eternal life!

2. It is from God that you are being tested, because He is training you for battle; He is drilling you, just like the soldiers who are trained through severe labors in their drills. There, first they learn the theory of warfare, and then at the sound of the trumpet in the real war, since they have already been trained, they rush into the battle with the inner assur-

---

[2] Mt. 25:23

ance that they know how to fight, and they are ready to sacrifice themselves for their cause and ideology.

You are also in a similar situation: since you have been called to become soldiers of Christ and to fight against His enemy, He trains you in order to ascertain your love towards Him: "Who is it that loves me, but he who keeps my commandments?"[3] Take courage, my children; remain loyal and dedicated to Him Who has loved you with perfect love.

Before a battle begins, the generals boost the soldiers' spirits by singing various battle hymns and relating various stories of heroic deeds to kindle their sense of self-sacrifice. This tactic gives them great strength and bravery in the battle about to be fought.

Likewise, we too should contemplate, as the saints did, the struggles of the martyrs and of the holy monks: how they lived ascetically, how they renounced the world and everyone, and how nothing prevented them from following the path that leads to Jesus. This *contemplation** will greatly strengthen your good disposition and intention, for there have been many who were unaware of the concealed traps, with the result that their souls succumbed to temptation and thus they fell from the hope of eternal life.

Contemplate the love of our Jesus; the love of Jesus will overpower every other natural love. The more we renounce, the more love of God we shall enjoy.

Let us attend on high, where Jesus sits at the right hand of God. Let our eyes look on high, for the eternal and everlasting things are above, not below; for everything here is dust and ashes. Reflect on the luxuriousness of Heaven: the infinite wisdom of God is there; inconceivable beauty is there; the angelic melodies are there; the riches of divine love are there; the life free from pain is there; the tears and sighs will be

---

[3] cf. Jn. 14:21

taken away there; only joy, love, peace, an eternal Pascha, and an unending festival are there. "Oh, the depth of the riches and knowledge of God!"[4] "Eye has not seen, nor ear heard, nor have entered into the heart of man the things which God has prepared for those who love Him."[5]

Attend to the prayer; persevere in prayer, and it will put everything in order. Do not yield at all; remain firm in your holy goal. Remain beside Jesus to live with spiritual happiness. There is no happiness anywhere except in Christ. So-called "happiness" outside of Christ is incorrectly called happiness, since it is obtained with reprehensible means and since it ends quickly and leads man to the eternal unhappiness.

Struggle, my children; the angels are weaving crowns with flowers of paradise. Our Christ regards the struggle as a martyrdom—what is more excellent than to be a martyr for Christ!

3. I received your letter, my child, and we all rejoiced at your firm desire and wonderful aspiration for monasticism. "I have chosen to be an outcast in the house of my God rather than to dwell in the tents of sinners."[6]

May no other love separate you from the love of Christ; consider everything rubbish so that you may gain Christ. The sufferings of this present life are not worthy to be compared with the future glory which will be given to those who struggle.[7] Now is the time for struggles, afflictions, and labors for God; whereas the future is the time for crowns of eternal glory, rewards, praises, and dwelling together with the holy angels beside the supreme throne of God.

Youth passes by silently; the years roll by quietly, imperceptibly, like the water in a creek; hours disappear like smoke in the wind. This is how the present life passes and vanishes. God's strugglers advance toward eternal prizes of glory,

---

[4] cf. Rom. 11:33

[5] 1 Cor 2:9

[6] Ps. 83:11

[7] cf. Rom. 8:18

whereas the indolent and lovers of the world proceed towards an eternal damnation with the demons.

The allurements of the world and its pleasures will transform into eternal affliction and pain for those who delight in them, if they do not repent. While on the contrary, for the people of God a little deprivation will be recompensed by an eternal felicity and blessedness of God.

Do not let familial affection hinder you; reflect that you will be alone in the hour of death, and then you will need to have God as a helper. So if you love Him more than them, you will have Him. But if you succumb, you will reap the crops of bitter remorse all on your own. So for the love of our Christ, make the decision and begin your new life.

4. *(To a spiritual daughter)*

Everything depends on your will. Entreat our Panagia very fervently to warm your holy desire, so that you decide with self-denial to renounce the vain world along with that dream which is called life, and to follow Christ the Bridegroom, Who will give you Himself and His sweetest love, and will count you worthy to become an heir of His Kingdom. Entreat the Panagia to help you make the holy decision, and when she does, make the sign of the cross and follow the salvific voice of Jesus, saying: "If anyone desires to come after Me, let him deny himself, and take up his cross, and follow Me."[8]

In the dreadful hour of death, no one will help us; only the good works that we have done for God and our soul will help us. Therefore, since the monastic life in general consists of works of God which are very conducive to our soul's salvation, why shouldn't we sacrifice everything to live such a life which will make us rich in the Kingdom of God? "For what will it profit a man if he gains the whole world, and loses his own soul?"[9]

---

[8] Mt. 16:24
[9] Mk. 8:36

The life of man hangs by a hair; at every step, our life hangs in the balance. How many millions of people woke up in the morning, never to see the evening? How many millions of people fell asleep, never to wake up? Indeed, the life of man is a dream. In a dream, one sees things that do not exist: he might see that he is crowned a king, but when he wakes up, he sees that in reality he is just a pauper.

In this life that we live, man labors to become rich, to become educated, to have an easy life, to become great; but unfortunately, death comes and foils everything. Then what he labored for all his life is taken by others, while he leaves life with a guilty conscience and a soiled soul. Who is wise and will understand these things and will renounce them and follow Christ the Bridegroom, so that all the works he will do will be recompensed infinitely in His Kingdom?

Always, my daughter, remember death and the judgment of God which we will unavoidably undergo. Bear them in mind to have more fear of God, and weep for your sins, because tears console the soul of him who weeps.

5. My spiritual daughter, I pray that peace and divine joy may accompany your life. Amen.

I received your letter and saw your joy. I pray that this joy will be the firstfruits of a continual spiritual harvest, of a new life totally dedicated to the unrivaled love of God. Now you have experienced the fruits of the Spirit. If you were so invigorated by experiencing a little, how much more will you be invigorated when you find yourself in a completely spiritual environment!

Everywhere and until the end of our life we shall undergo temptations—even in a monastery, even in the wilderness, if we happen to be there. However, if we are far from the world we shall have the freedom to fight the battle in an open place, where we shall be able to gather spiritual reinforcements to help us, with high hopes of eternally winning the prize for which we have been called heavenward.[10] Here we have no continuing city, but we seek a future, eternal, glorious one![11] The form of this world is passing away,[12] whereas he who does good works abides unto the ages.

Struggle, my child, with all your strength. Do not give joy to Satan by neglecting your duties, but give him bitterness by performing them with precision and eagerness. Satan will not stop shooting poisoned arrows at you with various thoughts, and especially with filthy thoughts. But prepare yourself to battle valiantly to obtain the unfading crown. As soon as a bad thought appears, immediately destroy the *fantasy** and say the prayer at once, and behold, your deliverance will come!

Do not be afraid when you see the battle, lest you lose your morale; but invoke the Almighty God and humble yourself very much. Rebuke yourself with the worst names and convince yourself that this is how you really are. And then from this point begin the battle with the prayer. Be careful, for the battle we conduct is not slight; we have to fight with principalities and powers, and it takes prudence and caution to fight well, for something good is not good if it is not done properly.

I pray that you have a good fight, and be careful with the people you keep company with. . . .

> With many prayers and blessings,
> Your lowly Elder

---

10 cf. Phil. 3:14
11 cf. Heb. 13:14
12 1 Cor. 7:31

Chapter Five

On Obedience, Disobedience, and Cutting off of the Will

I always pray to our good God that you walk the true path of the monastic life. Do not forget against what enemy we are conducting the war and the battles, for salvation should not be pursued superficially. Compel yourselves; think about the reason why we became monks. We abandoned parents, brothers, sisters; if, however, we do not also abandon our own will and are not obedient, then we shall not find mercy when our souls are judged. Reflect on eternal punishment and do not forget paradise; for we shall earn one of the two.

For the sake of us unworthy ones, Christ showed perfect obedience to His Heavenly Father, as well as to His Mother according to the flesh—our Panagia—and to Joseph the Betrothed; how much more should we cut off our will and have obedience to our spiritual father on account of our sins!

The martyrs will present, as a fruit of their piety, their terrible martyrdoms; the confessors, their holy confession; the holy hierarchs, their labors against heresies; the monastics, their ascetic struggles. What will we (and first of all, I) present? If, we are obedient and cut off our will for the love of our Christ, we have also borne fruit; we will also offer something, so that we will not go empty-handed like the slothful servant.[1]

---

[1] vid. Mt. 25:24-30

2. Pay close attention to your obedience. If you carry it out well, you will gain eternal life through it; if not, punishment will be your end. So wake up from forgetfulness and indolence. It is time for us to rise from the sleep of negligence—for the end of our life is unknown. When will we wake up? When the Archangel comes to take our soul? Waking up then is of no use. The future life is the time for crowns; now is the time for struggling, laboring, and wrestling.

Compel yourselves; say the prayer; stop idle talk; close your mouths to criticism; place doors and locks against unnecessary words. Time passes and does not come back, and woe to us if time goes by without spiritual profit. This is what I write to you; this is what you should meditate on; this is what you should do. May the God of love be with you, and may our sweet Panagia strengthen and enlighten you and make you eager for the struggle.

3. Become last if you want to become first. When one disobeys and distresses his spiritual father, then God is also grieved. Our Christ showed us through His deeds the greatness of holy obedience, for He sacrificed Himself for the sake of obedience to His Father, "Therefore He has given Him the name which is above every name."[2] Indeed, he who has perfect obedience will be counted worthy to receive a great name in Heaven, a name of sonship, which will be revered even by the angels—a double crown in the heavenly glory.

St. Palamon said, "He who submits himself well has no need to pay attention to the commandments of Christ." Why? Because through perfect obedience he has fulfilled all of Christ's commandments, and therefore it is unnecessary to ask if he has carried them out. Obedience has genuine humility in its bosom. Wherever there is humility, there is the scent of Christ, the fragrance of God.

---

[2] Phil. 2:9

4. A struggle that has as its driving force absolute obedience which lacks curious inquiry and is "blind" is considered very lawful by the Holy Fathers. This struggle is the safest and most perfect because obedience includes humility, and wherever there is humility, there is lawfulness and safety.

Espouse perfect obedience and humility, my child, and then you will know that you are struggling lawfully. Obedience does not merely mean carrying out your assigned task, but it primarily signifies submitting readily to the advice that your Elder gives—that is, obeying whatever he advises you regarding your spiritual struggle. Do not undertake any struggle without your Elder's knowledge. In the old days, *disciples** would even tell their Elder how many cups of water they drank, so that their Elder would know everything in order that they would not be deluded and lose the reward for all their labors.

5. What is more blessed than obedience for the sake of God! What spiritual course is safer than this! Therefore, run with joy in order to gain possession of the unfading crown of obedience with which the Champion of lofty obedience, Jesus, will adorn the head of each disciple who has contested. Be obedient to the Elder as if obeying the Lord.

Compel yourselves in your spiritual struggle, and above all in obedience, which is the disciple's adornment. A disciple without obedience is a barren womb, whereas when he is adorned with obedience and cuts off every bit of self-will, he is a fruitful womb.

The disciple has the advantage of finding the will of God easily through his Elder. Oh, what a great advantage this is! Other people are completely at a loss and ask themselves, "Should I do this, or that?" They literally suffer, remain irresolute, and lose time—for today, due to our poor prayer, we rarely find the will of God precisely, and this is why we ship-wreck constantly. Therefore, my children, since the love of God has had so much mercy on you, in that without labor you can find His will, hasten to the haven of obedience with faith and confidence, and it will continuously show you His will, which is eternal life and blessed repose for souls.

Continuously, night and day, I hear confessions. What don't I hear, and what don't I learn! Problems without end, without a solution. And I know what a triumph is accomplished through obedience with confidence in one's guide, and what tempests and shipwrecks are suffered by those who rely on themselves because of their egotism. The result is that they pass from darkness to darkness, and from smaller errors to greater, going astray because of their arrogance.

6. O thrice-blessed obedience, what grandeur you conceal! Whoever has loved you has become rich from your beauty, has become childlike in Christ, and has humbled himself like a child. Therefore, he will also enter into the Kingdom of Heaven rejoicing—exactly as the Lord said: "If you do not turn and become as little children, you will by no means enter the Kingdom of Heaven."[3] A little child is characterized mainly by simplicity, innocence, and obedience to his dear mommy. So obedience makes spiritual babes—babes in mal-ice, but mature in the wisdom of God.

7. My child, follow faithfully behind me and do not fear. Tend to obedience, especially spiritual obedience. He who has obedience has eternal life, for all the virtues are contained within perfect obedience, and especially the soul's freedom from having to give an account.

My child, a disciple must show perfect obedience to his El-der with self-sacrifice and eagerness, as if seeing Christ before him. See to it, my child, that your obedience is sincere and

---

[3] Mt. 18:3

complete. Hate self-will as the death of your immortal soul. Take Adam and Eve as an example, who were disobedient to the divine will and suffered the penance of banishment. Do not contradict the Elder; reflect that he represents the divine will. Every transgression and disobedience is punished in proportion to the sin.

A disciple ought to keep his place steadfastly, so that he cannot be shaken. He should be obedient wherever he is placed and die fulfilling his duty; this is called obedience unto death, even death on a cross.

8. My beloved children in Christ, may the grace of our Christ be with you and may the holy prayers of my Holy Father Joseph guard you powerfully in my absence, since the spiritual union in Christ of a good disciple with his Elder is never broken.

My dear children, who fill my wretched soul with fragrance, remember the words which I spoke to you when I was with you, for when you remember my words and keep them, you are under spiritual obedience, the best type of obedience. And one who has such obedience becomes like Christ Jesus, because Christ became obedient unto death, even death on a cross, wherefore His Father has exalted Him and given Him the name Jesus, and at the name of Jesus all the powers of darkness shudder and tremble.[4]

He who has obedience already in this life lives the life of the Spirit, which will be continued even after death, unto the ages of ages. Let us reflect that we were not crucified for our Christ, our Savior, but He for us monsters suffered the Cross, the Cross for the sake of obedience.

9. There is no better path than obedience, for it gives to the one who loves it happiness, repose, freedom from responsibility, forgiveness, and a multitude of other good things—but

---

[4] cf. Phil. 2:8

first and foremost, protection from the snares of Satan, because he is safely guided by the experience of his spiritual father, and thus he walks the path of the spiritual life without many obstacles.

10. All disciples who cut off their own will and please their Elder in everything are considered martyrs by intention, without undergoing various bodily tortures. The majority of martyrs finished their life in a very brief time of martyric torture, whereas the martyrdom of monastic obedience is worked out for life, and consequently, it is considered a martyrdom of conscience. For this reason, I entreat all of you to be attentive to your obedience. This obedience of yours is offered to God through your Elder.

What will it benefit us if we have left the world and relatives, yet do not fulfill everything that we have promised to God? Is it to men that we have promised to live according to God? What account will we give? Let us, therefore, walk the path of absolute obedience wholeheartedly and thus our souls will gain the grace of God.

11. Whoever puts into practice everything his spiritual father advises has his blessing; whoever does not do what he is advised does not have the blessing of his Elder here or in the other world. Whoever disregards whatever he is commanded, whoever does not regard as law the things which he is advised and does not strive to apply them out of disdain, must realize that damnation will befall him!

My child, fear the righteous Judge and be obedient to your spiritual father's advice, for your Elder desires the salvation of your soul, whereas the devil desires to make you his own through egotism and disobedience.

12. Be obedient, I entreat you; without hesitation or surliness endeavor to please your father according to the spirit.

With him you live and will live; why do you grieve him? It is not advantageous to your soul that he sighs for you. You cannot be edified like that. You will be in ruins until the end if you do not correct your disobedience.

Look at how the disciples of old shone: they sacrificed everything on the altar of obedience and pleased the heart of their spiritual guides with perfect faith and love towards them. You, however, first examine whether the Elder's words will work, and then you are obedient or disobedient, accordingly. Such obedience is good for nothing! Not thoughts—but deeds! Not objections—but death! Death through obedience! Only thus will we be justified before God when we carry out our duties.

13. Obedience is the "panagia"[†] of the disciple: just as a panagia distinguishes the bishop from the priest, so also obedience reveals the good disciple from the unsubmissive. Love your spiritual father and be obedient to him as to God, for it is he who has the next position in the hierarchy. You will find great grace when you obey your Elder for God's sake. Do not grieve him in order not to grieve the Holy Spirit, Who anointed him a successor to the Apostles. Elders are their final successors and occupy this position hierarchically through the Holy Spirit. Consequently, those who grieve them grieve the Holy Spirit.

14. You, my children, take care to guard what you have received unadulterated and pure. Be attentive to observe the whole rule, just as I gave it to you. For every transgression and disobedience receives, according to the Apostle Paul, a "just reward."[5]

Fear the punishment of disobedience. Whoever disobeys resembles the disobedient Adam and Lucifer who rebelled against God, Who both miserably fell away from God. Abba

---

[†] A "panagia" is the medallion a bishop wears around his neck that has an icon of the Panagia.

[5] Heb. 2:2

Barsanuphius says that a disciple who disobeys his Elder is a "son of the devil."

I pray for you from my heart that you become perfect disciples, so that you shine like angels in the midst of the angels of God, so that you sing hymns and pray for me, too, your wretched and unworthy Elder, who teaches without practicing anything at all of what is taught.

15. It is characteristic that one who does not have obedience does not have humility either, and he is secretly robbed by pride. And how is it possible for pride to result in correct judgment and decisions beneficial for the soul? Therefore, we must be humble for divine enlightenment to come, for the humble gain wisdom and discernment, while the proud acquire an evil and warped conscience. For this reason they also misunderstand the texts of the sacred Scriptures and of the Holy Fathers, since humility, with a pure and enlightened conscience, is absent.

"A self-advised man is his own enemy." That is, one who listens to what his thoughts tell him and does not listen to the advice of his superiors becomes his own foe. Therefore, be careful, my children, and do nothing at all without the advice of your Elder, if you desire to walk the monastic path successfully. For if you do your own will, you should know that you will walk crookedly, and the more time passes, the more the crookedness will be strengthened. Eventually a time will come when you will want to "straighten out" and you will not be able to.

16. I pray that all of you who are obedient to your Elder may have the blessing and grace of the Holy Spirit, behold the face of God, and dwell with the angels of Heaven eternally. But as for all of you who disobey and contradict and quarrel and disregard your conscience, may God slap you so that you reform and come to yourselves, for "wherever words do not work, a rod does."

My great paternal love, my suffering for your correction, and my longing for your salvation compel me to behave strictly whenever some stray, for if the evil remains uncontrolled and unpunished, the responsibility falls upon both those in charge and those in submission.

Homilies on Obedience

Stories of Obedience and Disobedience

I n Katounakia on the Holy Mountain there was an elder by the name of Father Cyril, and he had a disciple named Father John. This disciple grieved and saddened his elder by his frequent disobedience.

As time passed, this disciple began to feel physically ill. Before he became completely possessed by the demon, he behaved like an irrational person. He used to go with our fathers, Father Athanasios and Father Joseph, to gather hazelnuts, but he couldn't. This person smelled like sulfur—I know this from my own personal experience. He had deranged thoughts, and his face showed his whole condition. Now and then he would come to our elder, Elder Joseph, to reveal his thoughts and seek advice, but he would not be obedient in anything.

Before his elder, Father Cyril, died, he told him, "My child, when I die, bury me here." When his elder died, however, he buried him elsewhere. The other fathers advised him not to disobey—be it even now—but to fulfill the last wish of his elder. But he replied, "No! I want to bury him here."

Once he buried him, the devil appeared before him and said to him, "Fool! I was the one who did all this to you. I was the one who incited you to grieve your elder with all your disobedience."

And as he opened his mouth, the devil entered inside him. From then on, he did crazy things. . . . When they chanted the Cherubic Hymn, he ridiculed them and acted like a wolf, like a wild beast. He took an axe and hacked at the *icon** of

St. John the Theologian. He would wander around all over the place. Now and then he would come to his senses.

One day at noon we heard the cries of a fox. Father Joseph the Cypriot said to me, "Just look how audacious that fox is! Isn't it afraid to howl in broad daylight?"

I said to him, "That's not a fox; it's that possessed man, Father John."

"I don't believe it," he replied.

"Then wait and see," I told him. And sure enough, in a little while Father John passed by in front of our house!

I am telling you all these things so that you understand the importance of obedience, and also as a warning, because it will be very useful to you in the future.

Another time, when Father John was in his right mind, he came to see my Elder. According to the *typikon** we had there, and according to the rule of our Elder, I had to leave. As soon as I saw a visitor, I disappeared. So as soon as he came, I went to the adjacent cell and sat down there.

Elder Joseph was sitting on a little stool. Father John came and sat down beside him. I knew from my Elder that he was possessed, because my Elder frequently told me about him for my instruction and experience. While I was sitting in the adjacent cell, I could hear what Father John said and how my Elder advised him.

"Geronda," Father John began, "when the demon seizes me, he lifts me up, he hits me, I speak incoherently, I do irrational things, and I find myself a mere spectator of what my body does and what my mouth says! I am a spectator, and I am unable to do anything, while all my members obey the devil!"

After Elder Joseph's repose when we were still at New *Skete,** we had a lot of work and trouble fixing up our cell.

The tempter made one of the fathers upset me with something. I kept telling him, "Don't act like that; it is not to your advantage." Finally, God gave him the personal experience to see that he should not behave like that. So one day during Great Compline—it was Lent—while he was reading at the lectern, he stopped reading for a moment, came over to me, and, terrified, he said to me, "Geronda, I am being possessed!"

"Why do you say that?" I asked him.

"Look," he answered, "each one of my fingers is becoming as big as my arm. My hand is swelling and is becoming three, four times its normal size by demonic activity! I am perishing, Geronda; cross me before I am possessed!"

Then I crossed him and said, "All right, now go and read Compline, and next time be careful not to talk back and not to have a different opinion than the elder, because it is not to your advantage."

So after being crossed, he was delivered from it and came to himself, and, trembling, went back to read.

The feats of an obedient disciple are great. Those who obey and do not sadden their elder achieve angelic feats. Through obedience, a disciple receives much grace.

The Apostle Paul, even though he was teaching Christians, stressed the basic virtue, obedience—that we must give joy to the spiritual fathers with our spiritual progress, for they watch out for our souls, as he said.[1] It is not to our benefit to sadden and grieve those who struggle for the good of our soul. When we do not find rest or benefit in obedience, something is not going well; we are missing something.

When a disciple is counseled by his elder about this or that, he should not take it merely as advice. In essence it is a

---

[1] cf. Heb. 13:17

command, even if it is not explicitly stated as such. For example, the elder counsels: "My child, be obedient, say the prayer, drive away evil thoughts as soon as they come, because the longer they stay and settle down, the more they defile the soul. But even if they leave after a long time, they will still leave spots and blemishes behind!" Or when he says: "As soon as the talanton† is struck, go down to church at once." Or: "In church, don't move around easily, but be patient in your seat, and only move when there is some great need."

When a monk does not obey every counsel and exhortation his elder gives him, he is being disobedient. Does the elder have to say explicitly, "I command you to do this and that," so that the monk is afraid and obeys? Of course not. Commands are given only in particular circumstances.

When someone comes to the monastery to become a disciple, it is very clear that he does not come for the abbot's sake or for the monastery's sake. It is clear—crystal clear—that he comes for the love of Christ and for the salvation of his soul. But since he does not see Christ, in order to be obedient to Him, Christ has left His representative (the abbot of the monastery) so that a disciple can show him the obedience he desires to show to Christ.

Every spiritual father is an icon of Christ. So corresponding to how one obeys his spiritual father, he obeys Christ. It is a terrible sin to act impiously towards an icon of Christ, the Panagia, or the saints. Nothing is considered to be worse than this. In this case, it is an icon that depicts a divine person—we venerate and kiss it, and the veneration is transferred to that person himself.

The spiritual father bears the living image of Christ, and the disciple is commanded to obey him and respect him

---

† A "talanton" is a specially shaped wooden plank that is struck in monasteries before services begin.

solely for the love of Christ—not for the person of the elder, because he might be a sinful person; he might be on his way to hell, as I am. However, obedience has another meaning: it is passed on directly to Christ. Since the love of Christ has called us to come here to struggle and save our souls, we must employ every means to acquire this basic virtue of obedience, which also has a universal quality: when you see a good disciple, you know that he has not only obedience, but many other virtues and achievements as well.

Another one of the many examples my holy Elder told us in order to strengthen our obedience and faith and love towards the person of the elder is the following, which happened in Katounakia.

There was a disciple who used to love his elder very much and was very obedient to him. Once they went up to Karyes. His elder became seriously ill there and wanted to return to his cell. So the disciple took him on his shoulders, and after walking for hours along the mountain ridge, he brought him back to Katounakia where they lived.

Later, this monk affiliated himself with a synodia at St. Basil's, where the fathers received Communion without fasting. He wanted to leave his elder and go there to continue his monastic life. Even though he was a great schema monk, he wanted to leave his elder and go there.

His elder told him, "You shall not go."

He answered, "Yes I will!"

"My child," the elder replied, "don't go. Pascha is coming; stay here so that we can celebrate the Resurrection together."

"No, I'm going," he repeated.

One day the elder lost his patience and said, "May an evil angel pursue you." The following day, a large pimple appeared on his nose and began to swell. Finally, he ended up going to Father Artemios, a self-taught doctor who had healed both Elder Joseph and me. He showed him the pimple, but he couldn't cure him.

In three or four days the swelling increased. The pimple burst and ran with pus, and he was approaching death. The fathers told him, "For the love of Christ, be reconciled with your elder so that he may forgive you and so that you may take his blessing with you." "No!" he kept saying. He had become fierce as if he were possessed! But in the end, when he was about to breathe his last, he beat his breast, saying these words: "I lost! I lost! I lost my salvation!!!"

My Elder used to tell us very many stories, because he knew many monks of the past.

In the *patristic** writings is written the story of a good disciple whose elder counseled him every day after Compline. He would advise him regarding obedience and what he must do in order to be saved.

One day the elder dozed off as he was talking. Then the devil began to disturb the disciple with thoughts, saying: "Leave, since your elder has fallen asleep. Why are you just sitting around? You should also go rest now; you are tired," and so on.

"But how can I go?" he thought. "I have to get Geronda's blessing first."

"But he's sleeping now," his thoughts told him.

"It doesn't matter; I'll be patient."

These thoughts of leaving fought against him seven times, but he wouldn't leave. Hours later, when it was almost time for Matins, the elder woke up and said to him, "Didn't you go rest yet?"

"I couldn't, Geronda, without your blessing."

"Then why didn't you wake me up?"

"It doesn't matter, Geronda. I wanted to be obedient and patient."

"Fine. Let's do Matins now, and then go rest well." And that is what happened.

When the elder went back to sleep again after Matins, he saw that he was in a chamber full of light, and in it was a resplendent throne, and on the seat of the throne were seven crowns with much grace. The elder wondered and said, "Who knows what great saint and holy man this throne belongs to, and what struggles he must have done to win these crowns!" And as he was standing there, lo and behold, a venerable person approached and said to him, "What are you marveling at, Geronda?"

"I'm marveling at the throne's splendor and thinking that it must be the throne of some great saint."

"No," he said, "it doesn't belong to some great saint, but to your disciple."

"But that's impossible," the elder said. "He is still very young, and he came just recently—and he has a throne and crowns already?"

"He certainly does! He was given the throne from the moment he did his metanoia of obedience,[†] and he received the seven crowns last night by opposing thoughts."

Then he came to himself and called his disciple and asked him, "My child, what thoughts did you have yesterday?"

"I didn't have any in particular, Geronda. I don't remember having any bad thoughts."

"Try thinking a little harder; review the day step by step."

And then, as he was examining himself, he said, "Yes, yes, Geronda, last night after Compline after you fell asleep, the thought to leave you and go rest fought against me seven times, but I resisted it, and, as you saw, I waited for you."

---

† Once a person has chosen his spiritual father and is accepted by him, he does a *metanoia** symbolizing his submission.

"Fine, my child; go." And the elder understood that his disciple had won the seven crowns the previous night by opposing thoughts.

Saint John the Forerunner

Behold the Lamb of God

Even now the ax is laid to the root of the trees. Therefore every tree which does not bear good fruit is cut down and thrown into the fire.

Monastic Obedience

By the example of our Jesus, Who humbled Himself so much, we are taught the grandeur that is hidden within obedience. Obedience is not merely obeying the elder, but it is also obeying every commandment of God. Here the elder gives commands, but above all, it is God Who does so with His commandments: "Thou shalt. . ." If a person is obedient, he will later enjoy the fruits of this obedience.

Christ humbled Himself out of obedience to His Heavenly Father. He obeyed as a man in order to teach us the lofty virtue of obedience, for without humility, one cannot approach God.

We see that Adam and Eve in Paradise were happy as long as they were obedient and kept the commandment of God—that is, not to eat the forbidden fruit. They were the king and queen of all creation; they ruled over all; they were happy, and they felt and saw God. The life they lived was the most blessed life. They had the protection of God; no one troubled them; no one condemned them. They were free to walk within Paradise without fear, without a remorseful conscience. Why? Because they had not fallen into any sin against God.

Later, when they misused their freedom and wanted, as free beings, to transgress the commandment, they did so and sinned against God. Right after their sin, remorse leaped up. Immediately after their fall, their consciences began to disturb and oppress their souls. It is clear that the reproof of the conscience was a result of transgression, of sin.

After the Fall, Adam and Eve found themselves at an impasse. "They heard God walking in Paradise," say the Scriptures, "and they were afraid and hid themselves"![2] Previously, however, when they had not sinned against God, why weren't they afraid of Him? Was this, perhaps, the only time God walked in Paradise? Was this the only time He approached them as transgressors? Since they were His genuine children, didn't He visit them and walk in Paradise? But they were not afraid of Him then because their conscience did not reprehend them; it was full of tranquillity and peace, and so they also remained at peace.

So, "As God was walking in Paradise, they both hid themselves, for they were afraid of God." God said to them, "Adam and Eve, where are you? Where have you hidden?"

What could they say to God now?

"Adam, why did you hide?"

"I was afraid," said Adam. "I heard You walking in Paradise, and I was afraid."

"But why should you be afraid? Are you afraid of your Father, your Creator, your Benefactor? Are you afraid of Me approaching, Who out of boundless divine love gave you an entire Paradise? Happiness Itself, the Fountain of life, joy, and peace approaches and you are afraid?"

"Yes," replied Adam. "I am afraid because I made a mistake. But it's not my fault; it's Eve's, that woman You gave me. She's the one who pushed me, who urged me to, and then I transgressed Your commandment and ate the forbidden fruit."

"Eve," said God, "why did you deceive your husband? Why did you eat it?"

"It's not my fault," said Eve. "The serpent—which You, of course, created and put here in Paradise—is the one that told me to eat. And he told me that if I ate this fruit I would become equal to God and would know good and evil."

---

[2] cf. Gen. 3:9

One sees here outright egotism and back talk. Egotism results in back talk in the mind and heart. It rises up against God and indirectly throws the responsibility on Him.

So, since God did not see repentance or hear an apology, He immediately ordered their exile. This dialogue between God and Adam and Eve gives us the precious advice and teaching that God does not abandon man when he transgresses His commandment. He does not condemn him immediately, but He approaches him. But how does He approach him? Man doesn't hear Him walking, as Adam did! I, however, hear Him very distinctly reproving me and saying to me, "You did badly here. There you did not do well. Why are you doing this?" Through our conscience God cries out, "Repent; you are human."

Man is easily corrupted; he falls easily; he is changeable, mutable, prone to fall. God knows this because He formed us. He made us human. But He also gave us the grace to repent; He has given us the power to arise. Why don't you do this? When He reproves you through your conscience and exhorts you through the Scriptures to repent, and you do not do so, then the condemnation and punishment begin.

Let us change the subject now to our way of life. Again, we see here that as long as one practices obedience, he lives happily. His conscience does not reprove him; it does not trouble him; it does not disturb him at all. When he does not obey well, his conscience reproves him and says, "You did badly here." Again egotism shouts, "No!" The conscience repeats, "You ought to repent." And thus there is a disturbance, a war begins, and a state of reproof is created in the soul. Such a state of reproof and disturbance, however, does not exist in a good disciple, but he lives in peace and tranquillity with the good hope of the future eternal *restoration** in God.

Now we are in a *cenobitic** monastery, which operates under a certain order, law, regulation, discipline, admonition, and obedience. When a disciple does not properly apply the order, admonitions, and commands of both God and the elder, then he feels reproof within himself.

The Fathers kept obedience with such exactitude that it is written that they would even ask, "Is it good that I drink ten sips of water a day?" What are they trying to tell us with this teaching and counsel and exhortation? They are trying to teach us how much exactitude we should have in obeying the counsels and orders of the elder.

Furthermore, the Fathers tell us that we make fools of ourselves when we have given up our parents, the world, freedom, and then we make a spectacle of ourselves before God, the angels, men, and the demons when they see us quarrel over a needle, a thread, or the merest trifle.

We have promised to God to have self-denial. What does self-denial mean? It means denying our passions and all our will. But when we do our own will and do things without a blessing to please and serve ourselves, do you think we are practicing obedience? If we shall give an account to God for one idle word,[3] won't we give an account for one act of self-will?

When we became monks, we promised self-denial and obedience till death. How, then, shall we justify ourselves when we stand before the humble Jesus, the utterly obedient One, when He shows us the wounds of the nails and the crucifixion? When He says to us, "Behold how much I obeyed the Heavenly Father and cut off My will. I did not cut off My will with regard to a needle, a thread, or some very minor command, but I cut off My will to the point of death, even death on a cross."[4]

---

[3] cf. Mt. 12:36

[4] cf. Phil. 2:8

But when, for example, we are reproved for an act of self-will, at once we get upset and there is a war within us. When something clashes with the desire of our self-will, we find an enormous upheaval of everything within us.

We see our Christ receiving an order and saying, "If it is possible, let this hour, this cup pass from Me, and let man be saved differently."[5] But the Father's answer was, "No. You will proceed the way of the Cross and of Golgotha." "May Thy will be done."

Therefore, we should be attentive to our conscience and not do anything without the elder's knowledge. For although now we are happy doing our own will and are pleased with it and are fulfilling our hearts' desire, the hour will certainly come when we shall find ourselves in a very difficult situation. Then we shall recall our former life and seek time for repentance and correction, but it will be too late! Now that we are able to correct things, let us do so. Let us not do anything without a blessing.

In *The Sayings of the Desert Fathers* it is written that a certain nun went to the garden and, without a blessing, took some lettuce and ate it, and a demon entered inside her. She then started behaving like a possessed person. So they called the elder to make her well. He rebuked the demon and asked it, "Why did you enter inside the sister?" "It's not my fault," said the demon. "I was just sitting on the lettuce and she ate me!"

The demon entered this nun physically, whereas when we do similar deeds and acts of self-will, the demon enters us differently: through our guilt. This is worse, because that demon was apparent, and in the end came to the attention of the elder, and the nun was healed. But when we transgress, the demon remains within and this is worse.

---

[5] cf. Mt. 26:39

The Fathers say: "It is not such a great thing for a demon to be cast out of a person. It is a far greater achievement to be able to cast out a demonic passion." A saint can cast out a demon, but to cast out a passion requires a personal struggle.

It is precisely for this reason that we should not labor in vain and lose our time and be deceived, thinking that we are on the right path of the monastic life and practice obedience, being content and self-complacent, when in fact we are transgressors. Perhaps we are being fooled by our thoughts—or rather our conceit—saying: "This is nothing, that doesn't matter. It's no big deal if I do this, too." Yet in reality it is a transgression of the divine law. And let us not forget that although we may modify it, the law of God is immutable, unchangeable, and constant, and one day it will be fully applied—when we are judged by it!

the scale
of justice

Patristic Obedience

Through humility the Holy Fathers attained great degrees of grace. But can't a disciple achieve such success? Of course he can. If he keeps silence, attends to his spiritual duties, and keeps himself free from cares, if he maintains introspection and regularly takes account of himself, he will definitely make progress.

When we were with Elder Joseph, we were disciples. We had our *diakonema*,* the daily labor, etc. With our Elder as an experienced guide in these divine paths of the spiritual life, some of the fathers were able to come to know those things that the Watchful Fathers have left us as a sacred heritage.

We should avoid saying unnecessary things. Let us be consistent in doing our prayer rule. Likewise, let us be punctual in going to church. We should be in church to hear the service, the Liturgy, Vespers. We should be all together in the refectory; we should have order in everything. "Wherever there is order, there is peace; wherever there is peace, there is God. Wherever there is disorder, there is confusion; wherever there is confusion, there is the devil." "Let all things be done decently and in order."[6]

As disciples, let us practice our obedience. Let us not do our own will. Self-will cast Adam and Eve out of Paradise. Christ's submission of His will to His Father brought Adam and Eve back into Paradise again, and thus obedience triumphed.

Lucifer disobeyed God. He proudly fantasized about equality with God, and God sent him far from Himself, and he became the devil who fights against us. The other ranks of the angels remained loyal and obedient to God and still remain in the presence of His glory. Though they used to be angels

---

[6] 1 Cor. 14:40

changeable by nature, they became incapable of falling by grace, for they learned so much from the falls of Lucifer and man that now they are unshakeable in their obedience to God.

How evil is the will of man, for concealed within it are pride, self-love, and so many other passions. That is why a disciple who has been freed from self-will is freed from the passions.

Christ was obedient to the point of death on the Cross, that is, a complete mortification of self-will. If Christ as Man had not been obedient, if He had not cut off His own will, man would not have been saved! In exactly the same way, a person who holds on to his own will and does what he wants is not saved.

What does denying one's will mean? It means putting it away from oneself, renouncing it, not having anything to do with it. Only when a disciple does away with his will in this manner is he delivered from the passions. The more he renounces his own will, the more he is relieved from the passions.

If a disciple knows in practice how to say "Bless" and "May it be blessed," this disciple will be crowned with an unfading crown in the heavenly world. Wherever a disciple has put forth his own will, he has injected poison, and with this poison he poisons himself. Even if the command he is given is wrong, God will bless it anyway for obedience's sake.

There was a disciple who had such unquestioning obedience that his elder would tell him to go steal various things from the brethren's cells, and he would go and do so! The elder would then take them and give them back to the brethren. He was never bothered when thoughts told him, "Hey, what is the elder doing to me? Is he inciting me, is he teaching me how to steal? And later I'll have the habit of stealing!" Instead, he thought about it and said, "I am being obedient. Now, what it is that I am doing, I don't know. I know only one thing—that I am being obedient."

Someone went and became a disciple of an elder who had a synodia. The elder told him, "Since you want to live in my synodia, I order you never to say a single word—to become mute for the sake of Christ!" He replied, "May it be blessed."

After he had spent some time in this synodia, the elder saw that it was not to his benefit to continue living there. So one day he told him, "I am going to send you to another elder, to another monastery." And he gave him a note and said, "Go to such-and-such monastery, and give this to the abbot and stay there." The abbot received the letter—it was a letter of recommendation that said, "Geronda, please keep this brother. He is a good monk," and so forth. So he kept him.

After a while, this monk died, without ever breaking his silence. After his death, the second elder wrote to the first elder, "Even though the brother you sent me was mute, he was a real angel!" Then the first elder answered, "He wasn't born mute, but he remained silent out of obedience!" And the second elder marveled at the strength of this brother and how well he adhered to the command of his first elder!

What I am trying to say is that complete renunciation of self-will sanctifies us. Many times I think to myself, "How much a perfectly obedient disciple will be honored by Christ, Who is first in obedience! And how is it possible for Christ not to take the perfectly obedient disciples in His synodia, where they will see His face eternally, as St. John the Theologian writes in the Book of Revelation?[7]

We monks of today hold on to our self-will very tightly, and thus we are unable to progress further. We do not say, "Bless" and "May it be blessed," but we say, "No, not like

---

[7] vid. Rev. 22:4

that. This is how it should be done," etc., and in this way we pour poison on ourselves and on our lives. And this is why we do not have the progress that good monks do.

We read in the books, in the Fathers, about some holy disciples. Just think, there was an abbot who put an ox in the cell of one of his disciples, and for so many years it kept ruining his yarn and his loom! And, of course, the ox must have done many other things to him in there. He wouldn't have had any quiet at all! In spite of all this, he never had any resentful thoughts—as he told Abba Paphnoutios: "Never, Abba, did a bad thought about my Elder cross my mind, questioning why he put the ox in my cell. But since he put it here, he knows what he is doing, and I am at rest with that."

He did not have his own way of thinking. His elder's way of thinking was also his. This is why we say, "If we don't have spiritual obedience, we haven't achieved anything at all." When we do not want what the elder wants, we are not in essence disciples—we do not have spiritual obedience. Even if we are obedient in our actions, it is as if we were humans with a body but no soul (as if it were at all possible for someone with only a body to be considered a real person), which is something logically unacceptable.

In exactly the same way, it is logically unacceptable from a spiritual point of view for one to be called a disciple if he has obedience only in his actions and at his diakonema. Above all, one must have a soul: one must have spiritual obedience. One should say, "Whatever the elder believes, thinks, and decides, I also believe, think, and decide in exactly the same way."

St. Symeon the New Theologian received the blessing from above solely for his obedience. He is a very strong and clear example for us.

St. Paisios told his disciple one day: "My child, go drink water from that wash basin." The disciple thought to himself, "Instead of the Elder telling me to go drink from the pitcher or from the fountain—since I have come from my diakonema tired and sweaty—he tells me to drink from this dirty water in the basin!" He trusted his own thoughts and missed out on a great blessing! Later he thought, "Why don't I go drink it?" But he didn't find any water. Then Abba Paisios said to him, "You poor fellow! Do you know what that rinse water was? It was water that had washed the feet of Christ!"

From then on, a spirit of grief came upon him, and Abba Paisios tried to console him, but how could he? He reached the point of having no peace at all. Then one day the saint told him (since he couldn't be at peace and remain beside him), "Go to such and such a place. There are three tombs there, and in front of one of them (he indicated which) say a prayer and pay attention to what you will hear." He did so, and heard a voice saying, "Go back to your Elder and be obedient."

But he had already shipwrecked internally. The house of his soul had been damaged beyond repair. This is why he passed the rest of his life vacillating and storm-tossed in his obedience to Abba Paisios.

While St. Symeon the New Theologian triumphed against his own will and received the theology from above for his perfect obedience, the other monk, by doing his own will, remained outside obedience and grace.

Of course, these are just a few examples. For if everything done by those Fathers—those excellent disciples—were written down, entire volumes could have been compiled. These examples are like mirrors in which we can see ourselves and how we are doing.

May God help each one of us to come to our senses, to see ourselves, to see how much we have renounced our own will. Let us struggle to rid ourselves of this poison so that we can live as God wills and as the monastic profession requires of us.

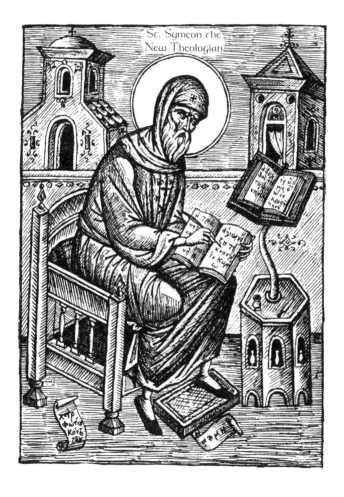

Homily on Conscience and Obedience

hen a person remains completely obedient to his conscience and implements whatever it tells him, he is not reproved by it anymore—not that its voice has weakened, but rather because of his good obedience, his conscience has nothing to reprove. The Apostle John says that when a man's conscience does not condemn him, he has confidence toward God.[8]

It is impossible for a person to proceed without ever stumbling somewhere, because from all sides the devil, the world, and the flesh are continuously inserting obstacles into his life, and he stumbles in proportion to his carelessness. Therefore, when he falls, he should arise at once and seek forgiveness. When one repents in proportion to the gravity of his fall, his conscience, which used to bother him, stops reproving him.

We must guard our conscience on three points—with respect to God, with respect to our neighbor, and with respect to things. One guards his conscience with respect to God when he avoids the various sins. He guards his conscience with respect to his neighbor when he does not grieve him, judge him, slander him, scandalize him, or push him towards evil deeds. He guards his conscience with respect to things when he does not cause destruction or damage to material things through carelessness, negligence, or unscrupulousness.

St. Theodore the Studite tells us many things about this "unscrupulousness." When you see something burning or being damaged and you don't pick it up and protect it, this is unscrupulousness. When your clothes get torn and you neglect them, and then they get completely ruined, this is unscrupulousness. When you are able to work but instead of working you wander around here and there, this is also unscrupulous-

---

[8] cf. 1 Jn. 3:21

ness. When you leave your food out and it goes bad and you throw it away, this is unscrupulousness because you should have taken care to eat it before it went bad. Therefore, unscrupulousness is when one errs in any way with respect to material things, and also when one offends God in any way.

The greatest wealth is obtained when one strives to preserve his conscience unburdened. But in the event that he senses that something has wounded him, he should correct it immediately, and thus he will return to his prior state.

How many times has our conscience reproved us! The more a person listens to his conscience, and the more he attends to it, the more precisely it guides him. And the more discreetly it guides and reproves him, the more he ascends in purity.

There is also the so-called "evil conscience," which often comes with the pretense and shape and form of the good conscience, yet in essence it is the evil, perverted conscience, the conscience which is opposed to God. The evil conscience is that voice which teaches things deceitful, perverted, and contrary. The good conscience has humility and obedience as its starting point, source, and foundation. The evil conscience has pride and disobedience as its source.

When one does not obey the Elder, when one resists, when one is deceitful, when one does not listen, then one has what is called self-reliance; such self-reliance is the evil conscience.

Humble-mindedness gives birth to the good conscience. Since the two consciences are entangled, one often asks himself, "Is this the evil conscience or the good one? Should I believe this thought or that one?" So to learn—or rather to be taught—what is the good conscience, one needs to have humility; but above all, he needs to place himself under the guidance of another, his superior, his leader, his spiritual father, and to obey whatever he says. Then little by little he will begin to perceive which thoughts are evil and which are good, what is the hue of the good conscience and what is the hue of the evil conscience. Thus, on the one hand, through the teaching and guidance of his spiritual father he avoids falling, and on the other hand, in time he is taught what the hue and appearance of the two consciences are and becomes a perfect man.

It is those who are without obedience who have suffered harm. For man is pressed by both consciences; the one works to save him and the other to destroy him, and many times he does not know which one to listen to. He who is under obedience avoids this danger and little by little becomes experienced and skilled in discerning the evil conscience from the good conscience.

Abba Poimen had two thoughts, and he went to tell them to his spiritual father, who lived very far away—he set out in the morning and arrived in the evening. He forgot one thought, however, and told him only the other one. When he returned to his cell, as soon as he put the key in the door, he remembered the second thought. So without even opening the door, he went back again to tell him his other thought. When his spiritual father saw his labor and his exactitude, he exclaimed, "Poimen,[†] Poimen, shepherd of angels! Your virtue will make your name known in all the world."

For one to become experienced enough to distinguish the voice of the good conscience from the voice of the evil conscience, he must pass through obedience. If he does not pass through obedience, he is deficient. He may have gifts; he may be a good soul; he may do various good works—but you will see that he always hobbles in discernment and humility. The virtue that submission to an Elder gives is, first and foremost, discernment, which comes through humble-mindedness. That

---

[†] "Poimen" in Greek means shepherd.

is to say, obedience forges a man's character and gives him, above all, discernment and humility.

"Ask your father," says the Scripture, "and he will tell you."[9] We see this in the patristic path the saints walked. We read in the *Lives of the Desert Fathers* that a certain Zacharias saw a vision, but his spiritual father was not in a position to elucidate whether it was from God or from the demons. So he rebuked his disciple, telling him not to pay attention to visions. The disciple went to a discerning Elder who told him, "The vision is from God, but go and submit yourself to your spiritual father," thus showing that being obedient is more important than seeing visions.

How much the Fathers have left us for our instruction! The best road, the most correct, the safest, the most free from responsibility, is the road of submission to an Elder. "He who practices obedience," says Abba Palamon, "has fulfilled all the commandments of Christ."

"The disciple has chosen the best road," says Abba Moses. "Run, children, to wherever obedience is. There lie joy, peace, brotherly love, unity, vigilance, consolation, crowns, and wages." But when we want to put forth our own will as disciples, then the road becomes difficult, rough, and dangerous. When one practices obedience, he finds himself in love, in forcefulness, in brotherly affection, in crowns, in sanctification, in salvation.

Self-will is a great barrier, a great obstacle—it is a wall between the soul and God. Just as when a wall is in front of us and blocks the sun, the place is damp and unhealthful and does not bear fruit because the sun does not shine there, the same thing happens with the wall of self-will. When it stands in front of the soul, the soul is darkened and remains without fruit. The Sun of Righteousness is Christ; when the soul is not

---

[9] Deut. 32:7

obstructed, the rays of Christ come and illuminate it, and man bears fruit and is sanctified.

Only the one who has tasted the fruit of obedience can speak about it. Obedience is the most grace-filled road. Above all, one who is obedient casts out the evil demon of selfishness and pride—which causes all evils—and brings humility and freedom from care.

We read in *The Sayings of the Desert Fathers* about two brothers who decided to become monks and left the world. One became a disciple in a cenobitic monastery; the other became a hermit. After two or three years the hermit said, "Let me go and see my brother who is in the monastery, living in the midst of cares and worries. Who knows how the poor thing is doing in the midst of so much bustle." He was confident that through his asceticism he had reached a high spiritual level. He went to the monastery, and with the excuse that he supposedly needed his brother, he said to the abbot, "I would like to see my brother a little." His brother came, and the abbot, who was a holy man, blessed them to go off by themselves and talk.

When they had gone some distance from the monastery, they saw on the path a dead man who was almost naked. The hermit said, "Don't we have any clothes to cover the man with?" The monk from the monastery, in his simplicity said, "Wouldn't it be better to pray for him to be resurrected?" "Let's pray," said the hermit. They both prayed, and the dead man arose. The monk from the monastery didn't attach much importance to the miracle; he believed it came about through the prayers of his Elder. The hermit, however, said within himself that the miracle occurred because of his own virtues—because of his asceticism and fasting, his nightly vigils and the hardship he endured, his sleeping on the ground and all his other achievements.

When they returned, before they had a chance to speak, the abbot said to the hermit, "Brother, do not think that it was because of *your* prayers that God raised the dead man—no! God did it because of the obedience of your brother!" When the hermit saw that the abbot immediately read his thoughts, that he had the gift of clairvoyance and was a holy man, he believed that in reality he himself was deluded, and that his brother, who he thought was anxious and worried about many things within the monastery, was actually above him.

Think with what confidence the disciple said, "Let's pray for him to be resurrected!" Here you see simplicity, guilelessness, faith. The hermit considered it impossible, but the monk from the monastery considered it natural; he trusted in the prayers of his Elder. What a struggle he must have undergone to reach such humility! How his egotism and pride must have been smashed in the monastery! What person coming from the world does not have egotism and pride? How many disciples were sanctified and gave forth myrrh after death!

On the Holy Mountain, in the region of St. Anne's Skete, there was a monk who hauled sacks of wheat up from the harbor with much labor and sweat. At one point he began to say in his thoughts, "I wonder if we will have a reward for all the sweat and labor we endure in order to obey our Elders." As he reflected on these things, he sat down to rest a little. A light sleep came upon him, and as he was half asleep, he saw the Panagia before him. "Do not be dismayed, my child," she said to him. "This sweat which you shed to haul your provisions for the sake of obedience is counted as the blood of a martyr before my Son." Then he came to himself, and his thoughts and distress left him. The fathers inscribed that event on the stone wall there, and whoever passes by there reads it.

Near the main church of St. Anne's Skete, there is a little

house called "The Patriarch's." A patriarch by the name of Cyril lived there in asceticism; he had abandoned the patriarchal throne and come to live as a simple monk. The fathers hauled their things on their backs, but they said to the Patriarch, "You are old, your All-Holiness, and not accustomed to our way of life. We will get you a little donkey to load your provisions on." So they got him a little donkey, and he went up and down the mountainside with it.

One day, as the Patriarch climbed up with the animal and the other fathers had their provisions on their backs, they sat down to rest a little. And as the Patriarch was half awake, he suddenly saw the Panagia together with the angels. The Panagia was holding a vessel and was giving a drink to the fathers who were carrying their things on their backs; the angels were holding handkerchiefs and wiping away their sweat.

He saw with surprise that they even wiped the sweat from the donkey, and he begged them, "Wipe me also, please." Then the Panagia said to him, "Father, you have not sweated; we will wipe the donkey because it has." Then he woke up and came to himself. He said to the fathers, "Take away the donkey, because I am missing out on many blessings. The Panagia and the angels wiped the donkey and not me!" From then on, he also carried his things on his back.

How very many such things have happened in the lives of the Fathers! If only we were there to see them! Now such things are rarely encountered; they have all been lost.

So let us be attentive to our conscience. Let us acquire a good conscience through obedience, contrition, confession, and humble-mindedness. Let us avoid self-will, which begets self-reliance and the evil conscience.

Selections on Obedience

What is a more beautiful example than that of the Lord Jesus! Didn't obedience towards His Father lead Him to the Cross and death? Couldn't He, being of one essence with the Father, have opposed this? But no, He walked with sweat; He fell to His knees with pain beneath the weight of cutting off His will as He ascended Golgotha. But He had to ascend it, reach the top, be lifted up on the glorious—and to the demons, dreadful—Cross, and there on it show perfect and absolute obedience, and receive the unfading crown of eternal glory.

This is how the resurrection of our soul is gained, and not by vacillating between obedience and disobedience with self-will. The crown is not acquired like that, but by a willingness to sacrifice. All obstacles are surmounted by the strong thought of preferring to die rather than betray the obedience of doing one's duty.

2. Through the obedience of Christ we were saved, whereas through the disobedience of Adam we were drawn into the abyss of hell. The road of obedience does indeed lead to Golgotha. It is uphill, and the ascent is a little laborious, and we shall sweat and be fatigued, but let us reflect that after the resurrection we shall gain purity of soul and sonship, and this wealth cannot be matched by any worldly enjoyments. What am I saying, worldly things? If one gives the entire world, he cannot buy even one drop of spiritual joy from that soul which has ascended Golgotha and seen its own resurrection.

3. Christ said to His disciples, "He who hears you hears Me, he who rejects you rejects Me, and he who rejects Me rejects Him Who sent Me."[1] The successors of the Apostles

---

[1] Lk. 10:16

are the hierarchs, the priests, the abbots, and the elders of small synodias. So whoever obeys the successors of the Apostles obeys Christ Himself, and whoever disobeys them, rejects Christ.

For this reason, since we want to place ourselves under obedience to Christ, we ought to show obedience—not merely obeying what we like and disobeying what we do not want. For in Gethsemane, Christ asked that the salvation of mankind happen differently from what the Heavenly Father desired. But since the Heavenly Father decided upon the Cross, Christ then replied, "Not My will, but Thy will be done, my Father."[2]

4. Theology emanates from prayer, and prayer from perfect obedience. Without obedience, a monk will soon lose whatever talent or gift he might have, whereas a true disciple is fertile and fruitful with all the gifts of the Comforter and is rich now and unto the ages.

5. For the grace of God to visit us, we must apply ourselves with absolute obedience to whatever we are taught. Let us not add our will to the will of the Elder, for this is called spiritual adultery. We must work at obedience with much sincerity, otherwise we shall not make any progress in our monastic journey.

Humility is the virtue which helps wonderfully to apply perfect Christ-like obedience. On the contrary, egotism and pride are opposed to its acquisition.

6. It is extremely terrible, very dreadful, to press and compel your Elder to do something that you want but that his soul does not want. It is frightful. Only someone with personal experience knows this.

Your spiritual Father and Elder is worth much more to you than all the people of the earth, even more than the whole uni-

---

[2] cf. Mt. 26:29

verse! The devil knows better than anyone else what it means to have an Elder and to have perfect obedience to him.

7. Never examine what your Elder does or why he does this or that. Do not judge him, for you will become an antichrist! Never in your life tolerate others who speak against your Elder, but oppose them immediately; shield him; defend him. Christ makes straight the "crookedness" of the Elder's human shortcomings and mistakes, on account of uncritical and guileless obedience.

8. It is a great achievement for Satan to persuade a disciple to hide his thoughts, to do anything without the permission and blessing of his Elder, and not to confess everything clearly to his spiritual father. Such a disciple will never make a good beginning and will never make progress in the grace of God, but will be dragged here and there until the wretched end of his life comes.

9. Obedience is of value only when the will is cut off with pain and labor; for passionate habits resemble thorny roots, and whoever wants to pull up such roots will naturally feel pain and be pricked, and his hands will bleed. The same thing also happens when uprooting evil habits for the sake of obedience to one's spiritual father.

10. Do not grieve your Elder or your brother monk, for immediately your peace of soul stops, the *Jesus prayer** ceases, and you are full of thoughts. The cure is confession, burning tears, and sincerely forgiving others. Be careful; if you have something against your Elder, be careful, for the devil will crush you and mislead you easily. Put your thoughts in order, so that nothing will trouble you with regard to him.

11. The obedient person bears the fruit of meekness, for the Elder will cut off his will, rebuke him, and criticize him, and when the disciple is obedient, he acquires precious meekness.

In a word, a good disciple acquires all the virtues when he is blindly obedient. If, however, he objects, quarrels, disobeys, is proud, etc., then he seriously injures his soul, for he grieves God, Who humbled Himself, whereas he, an earthly and wretched man, is proud.

12. The perfect disciple does not have to give an account when he passes through the toll-houses! He does not fear death, nor the demons, nor God, for he worships Him with burning zeal. The genuine disciple only fears disobedience to his Elder, who acts as a visible Christ for him. Disobedience to the Elder immediately exiles him from the paradise of the grace of the Holy Spirit, Who sweetens to the utmost the humble, dear soul of the disciple who is equal to the angels. The perfect disciple is an exact copy of our Christ, the God-Man.

13. When a disciple obeys his own Elder for the sake of Christ, he fulfills all the commandments of Christ. Perfect obedience, without murmuring and thoughts of objection, may properly be compared to all the various struggles of applying all the Master's commandments.

The one who obeys for the love of God is loved by God, and the entire Holy Trinity dwells within this good disciple. What grandeur this thrice-blessed obedience hides! It enables the humble, insignificant, little, obscure disciple, to become the abode of the Holy Trinity; it renders him a fulfiller of all of Christ's commandments and leads him into paradise, so that he walks about in the midst of the saints with a double crown and with a divine necklace around his neck.

14. What wondrous freedom is granted to one who completely cuts off his own self-will! How much rest the soul of the struggling combatant (i.e., the disciple) finds when he does not have his own will, but only that of his Elder! This blessed disciple leads a spiritually comfortable life, full of joy and hope. He lives most peacefully, wonderfully, with the assurance that since he gives rest to his Elder, he himself will also be given rest in paradise, through his prayers.

Blessed and thrice-blessed is the disciple who has cut off his ruinous self-will in everything and confesses everything to his spiritual father. Such a person becomes completely healthy spiritually here, and will shine among the angels as an angel of God before the dread throne of God.

15. Rejoice, therefore, O warrior disciple, imitator of the Great Disciple, "Who became obedient unto death, even the death of the Cross. Therefore God also has highly exalted Him and given Him the name which is above every name."[3] As for you, He will exalt you above the passions and will honor you with dispassion and with His love. Struggle, therefore, through denial of your self-will, fulfilling for the sake of Christ the counsels of him who sponsored you in the Lord when you promised to God perfect obedience unto death.

O obedience, salvation of all the faithful! O obedience, mother of all the virtues! O obedience, which opens Heaven and raises men up from earth! O obedience, nurturer of all the saints, by which they were suckled and through which they were perfected! O obedience, companion of angels!

---

3 Phil. 2:8-9

On Reverence and Love for the Elder

Skillfully and diligently maintain your faith and love for your spiritual guide, for herein lies the life and death of the soul. Do not grieve your father in Christ, if you desire to behold the face of God. He who grieves him should know that he grieves Christ. So then, how will he behold Christ when he dies?

2. Never permit the enemy to attack you with evil thoughts against your Elder, for such thoughts are serpents filled with venom. Be as one with your Elder. Listen to him as though his words were spoken by Christ. Love, reverence, and perfect obedience to the Elder please him. By pleasing the Elder, you please God; whatever you do to the Elder, you do to God.

3. It injures a disciple fatally when he does not reveal all his thoughts frankly and sincerely to his Elder. Just as a sick person is not healed when he does not disclose to the physician how his wound or sickness is, but the pain and fever continue, in the same way also a disciple is not healed when he does not reveal the wounds of his soul to his spiritual physician. It is his ego that prevents him from revealing to his Elder his ailments.

Therefore, my children, let us trample this dragon underfoot and slay it with the sword of sacred confession and by taking the spiritual medicines which the spiritual physician, the Elder, gives us for our healing.

4. Let us be vigilant, my children, and let us compel ourselves—what are we waiting for? The end is approaching and we shall be troubled. What will help us then? Forcefulness in our duties now, the acquisition of virtues, and especially spiritual unity with our spiritual parents by a life which is pleasing to them are what will help us in that great need. If we are spiritually separated from our spiritual father because we disobey and criticize him, how will we be fortified against the demons at the hour of death? Without the protection of his holy prayers, how will we stand in the presence of Jesus Christ Himself? When we ascend and meet the aerial toll-houses, whose prayers will deliver us? The elder's? But they have departed from us because we grieved him in this life and so they have no power in our hour of need. Therefore, my children, let us take care to live according to the will of God in order to please Him, so that He may give us repose in His bosom eternally.

5. Your issue, my child, is primarily an issue regarding the elder. I have told you many times that the devil greatly fears elders, and that faith and love towards them is the greatest security for everyone who submits to them for the love of God. But whoever errs in his obedience to the elders immediately loses their protection, and his destruction begins. Since the devil knows this, he immediately begins the warfare with thoughts against the Elders, trying to exaggerate their weaknesses to such a degree as to convince the disciple that no benefit will come from them, that they are not in good standing, etc. And once the devil persuades him, he wins him. However, when he finds him with firm foundations, he leaves and opens another front. Rarely is a disciple spared from this type of warfare.

6. *(The Elder writes to a nun)*

My daughter, have love and reverence for the abbess. Who does not have weaknesses? We are all guilty on account of our passions. But this is one thing and your obligation to your spiritual mother is another. See her as the face of Christ! And the trust you have in her will be counted as trust in God.

I do not want you to pretend; I dearly love sincerity and honesty—this is also how I want my children to be. Always confess truly, listen to her counsels, and have faith in whatever the abbess says to you. If you do not accept with faith what she says, the result will be that you will criticize and become alienated and remote. This is unbecoming for you as a nun, under the protection of an abbess. It is not proper to criticize or become alienated towards any person, especially our spiritual mother. Struggle to love her and to see her as the face of Christ, and then, in accordance with your faith, you will reap the corresponding benefit. Do this and you will see the truth.

Now, during Great Lent, I want you to be especially forceful in your spiritual struggles. Be silent internally and externally. Remember death continuously and without flagging; the benefit from this meditation is enormous. Say the beloved little prayer. Compel yourself to be united more and more closely to your Eldress and never allow your thoughts to judge her, for this is characterized by the Fathers as a serious burn or poisoning. Be on guard lest you fall away from the Eldress, for then every good struggle of yours will be paralyzed.

Chapter Six

On Remembrance of
Death, Hell, and Judgment

The older I grow, the more I perceive the instability, the vanity of earthly things. Oh, why do we trouble ourselves in vain? Our life is short—dust, ashes, a dream—and in a little while, we shall taste corruption. Today you have your health, and tomorrow you lose it; today you are laughing, and tomorrow you are sullen. Now your eyes are shedding tears from an abundance of joy, and soon they will be shedding tears from pain and grief; today the economy is stable, and tomorrow misfortune strikes; today you receive good news, and in a little while bad news replaces it.

In vain we trouble ourselves; life is a shadow and a dream. Where are our parents, our siblings, our grandparents? The tomb has received them all; they have all decayed and have been eaten by worms. The tomb and decay await us also!

Ah, ah, death—bitter is your remembrance. Our Christ has given us the power to become sons of God[1] by arming us with so many divine weapons to fight our relentless enemy. But we—and I, above all—become prisoners of our enemy by neglecting the weapons Christ gave us, and as we approach death we tremble in agony and try by every means to prolong

---

[1] cf. Jn. 1:12

our life, because the soul is afraid to leave the body. Why is it afraid? Why does it not take courage as a child of God? Is it going perhaps to a foreign king? But the king is its Maker, its Savior, Who shed His Blood in order to redeem our soul from its enemy. Why then does it fear and lack courage?

Death is inherently cold—"My soul is exceedingly sorrowful, even to death,"[2] said our Jesus. Yes, death is cold by nature. But unfortunately, most of the fear comes from the conscience: the conscience does not assure the soul that it has lived properly; it has not put itself in order; it has not washed its wedding garment, and so it is ashamed to present itself to the King, thinking about what the verdict will be: yes or no? Will I be saved or not? And, if, the soul leaves without having confessed and without having repented completely, then woe—this is the evil day which the Prophet Jeremiah hints at.[3] Let us pray that our holy God will deliver us from this by giving us complete repentance, works worthy of repentance, works of mercy and love, and a spirit of repentance with true humility, so that the just Judge may be merciful towards us, so that when the fearful hour of death comes, the soul will take courage in the mercy of God and say, "I trust in God, that He will have mercy on my lowliness." Amen; so be it.

2. The years roll by and pass, and day by day each one of us draws closer and closer to the end of his life. Our precious time rolls by and disappears before our eyes, without our realizing, of course, what is escaping us unnoticed. For if the little child knew the worth of gold, he would not prefer to have a cheap candy instead. Doesn't this also hold true for people, and above all for me?

When our Lord comes at the appointed time to judge the world; when the Heavens are rolled up like a piece of paper, and the earth, which has been thoroughly defiled by those

---

[2] Mt. 26:38

[3] vid. Jer. 17:17

dwelling upon it, is renewed; when the sun, the moon, and the stars fall like autumn leaves; when the trumpet resounds throughout the entire world, and the scattered dry bones are reconstructed and flesh and life come upon them;[4] when the ranks of the angels gather in the vastness of Heaven in honor of the fearful Judge Who is to come; when small clouds rise up from the infinite multitude of resurrected people and lift upon themselves the holy and saved people to meet the Lord in the air—then those who have remained below and see all these things will weep most bitterly and beat their breasts in despair, reflecting that they wasted their precious time here in pleasures, in drunkenness, in acquiring wealth, in illicit deeds, in avarice, and in every sin, which now condemn them to this most pitiful and lamentable condition of theirs. Will they not pathetically seek to have a little time to run to the poor, to the sick, and to every destitute person, so that they also might hear the sweet voice of the Lord saying to them, "Come, you blessed of My Father, inherit the Kingdom prepared for you . . . for I was hungry and you gave Me food . . . I was naked and you clothed Me," etc.?[5]

At some time in their lives they heard these things. However, in Hades there is no repentance. For this reason, the utmost despair will seize them. They will seek death; they will have a burning desire for it to deliver them from their boundless sufferings, but unfortunately they will not find it, for everything will have already been transformed into immortality! (All this holds true for me. . . .)

3. Man comes into the light of this world crying, he passes his life in weeping and sorrows, and he leaves the world in tears and pain. O vanity of vanities! The dream vanishes, and man awakens into the reality of the true life. No one notices how this vain life flows by—the years pass, the months roll

---

[4] vid. Ez. 37:1-14

[5] Mt. 25:34-36

by, the hours disappear, the moments slip by imperceptibly, and then without any warning, the telegram comes: "Put your house in order, for you will die; you will live no longer!"[6]

Then the deception is uncovered, and a person dying realizes what an important role the world played for him. He feels regret and distress; he yearns for the time that is gone; he would give all his wealth to buy one day in order to repent and receive Communion. Unfortunately, though, not one favor is given to him. Previously, time was at his disposal for years; he, however, wasted it in business, in bars, in cinemas, and in every shameful desire.

Wise is the merchant who realized the deceit of this temporal life, became wise, and sent his merchandise to Heaven before the fair of life ended, in order to find it there in the treasuries of the heavenly city of God with accrued interest and dividends. Blessed is that wise man, for he will live the painless and blessed life unto the ages of ages, while the unwise, the drunkards, the greedy, the lovers of money, the lewd, the murderers, and the rest of my fellow sinners—of whom I am the first—will be thrown into the furnace of unquenchable fire!

Now that the sun is shining and the day casts its sweet light upon us, let us walk quickly along the road of our correction, before the night of the future afterlife overtakes us, at which time we shall no longer be able to walk. "Behold, now is the accepted time; behold, now is the day of salvation,"[7] cries the Apostle Paul in his immortal words.

4. Oh, how much the memory of death should flourish in the soul of the Christian! Since he believes in the real truth, it is impossible for him to ignore death.

After my Elder's heart condition had passed, he wept and recited a line from the funeral service: "Alas, what a struggle

---

[6] Is. 38:1

[7] 2 Cor. 6:2

the soul has as it parts from the body!" Indeed, this is the truth! How beautifully the psalmist expresses what peace a prepared soul has: "I prepared myself and was not troubled."[8]

At any moment, every soul can expect the telegram from Heaven to break off all relations with earthly things, to seal the time of this "fair," to render an exact account of his spiritual trading, and to seal his eternal fate either in the heights of Heaven or the depths of hell.

Ah, when I reflect upon this, what can I say! May the all-compassionate God be merciful to my wretched soul, which has nothing but its indifference and unreadiness. My mind stops when it contemplates this absolute truth about salvation.

Eternity—oh, what a great mystery! The world, the flesh, and the devil lead us astray and throw us into forgetfulness—and suddenly a voice is heard: "Behold, the Bridegroom comes!" When we are breathing our last, what preparation can we make then, when our conscience has already been cauterized and can no longer feel anything or cry out to us? Then the voice of truth is heard: "Only when the sun was setting did you remember God; what were you doing all day long when the sun was shining?"

"Watch and be ready,"[9] cries our Jesus! Blessed are those who have ears to hear, who hear and get ready, for they will be counted worthy of eternal happiness. Blessed are those servants whom the Lord will find ready when He comes, for they will rejoice eternally.

Let us patiently endure the sorrows of life, that we may attain the eternal things full of joy. "In vain does every mortal trouble himself; as soon as we conquer the world, we dwell in the tomb."[10] As long as there is light, let us walk towards our great destination, for the hour is coming when there will be darkness, and then we shall no longer be able to work for our soul.

---

[8] Ps. 118:60

[9] cf. Mt. 24:43,44

[10] from the funeral service

5. Raise your mind to the dread judgment seat of Christ—what defense shall we give on the day of judgment when our deeds are judged? How frightening is the hour in which the soul waits full of fear to hear the decision regarding where it will go to dwell eternally!

The word "eternity" is frightful! To understand in part what eternity means, I shall give you an example. Imagine that the whole earth is one big piece of granite, and every thousand years a bird comes to sharpen its beak on this rock. When the entire rock is worn away by the bird sharpening its beak, then we shall have some faint notion of what eternity means—not that we have actually understood eternity, immortality, or life without end! So this life of ours here on earth determines our eternity, like flipping a coin: paradise or hell! Therefore, how much caution must we have!

6. You were patient for so many years, and they passed like a dream. But even if we lived a thousand years, they would still pass like a dream. Oh, how vain is everything that belongs to this world here! Every life is followed by death. Death is man's transfer from this world to the other—the one that is immortal and eternal.

It is not important if someone loses this life here. One way or another, we shall all die someday anyway. The important thing is not to lose our immortal life, the life without end. Endless life in hell—oh, what a fearful thing! My God, save us all.

7. When God brings the new day, let us think that it is our last day and that when the sun sets we shall depart to the judgment seat of Christ. How should we spend our last day? In silence, prayer, obedience, tears, and repentance, begging God to be merciful!

Likewise at night, we should think that it is our last night, and our bed will be our tomb! Each one of us should think, "Ah, how will I pass through the toll-houses? I wonder, will I pass through them? Who knows which one will stop me? How will I look at the fearful face of the just Judge? How will I hear His frightful voice of reproof? What terror will seize me until I hear the eternal decision regarding where I shall be placed! And what if I am sent to hell—and justly so! Woe to my wretched soul! How will I be patient as I am punished with the demons in the darkness, in the filth, with no light, with no consolation at all—only the sight of demons and nothing else!"

We should ponder these and many other things every day and night, living them as if they were our last! For we do not know when the telegram will come from God's headquarters, from the capital, the Jerusalem above.

8. Be careful, my child; do not let time pass fruitlessly and without improvement in your soul, for death comes like a thief. Woe to us if it finds us in a state of sloth and laziness—then the mountains and hills will need to weep for us; then we shall be found empty of good works, and Hades will shepherd us eternally!

My child, why should we suffer such a lamentable shipwreck when we are able, with God's help, to avoid it and be rescued at the saving harbor of the Kingdom of God! I know that we have to wrestle with formidable enemies and that the labor is great. But with God—that is, with the power of God—everything gives way when man's will and strength cooperate with it.

9. When you are sitting in your cell, keep your mind meditating on death. Don't let your mind wander here and there, but collect your thoughts and reflect: see the mortality of your body; see how the body chills, changes, and the soul departs from it. What a struggle the soul has as it departs from the body! How much it weeps then; how much it sighs; how great is its regret! "It turns its eyes to the angels, but its entreaties are to no avail. It stretches out its hands to men but finds no helper."[11]

Meditate on the soul's ascent after it departs. When it ascends and encounters the hordes of evil demons, it trembles as they reveal sins it had committed but had completely forgotten, and wonders what will happen. It ascends from one toll-house to the next, and at every toll-house it gives a defense, until it passes them all. If it passes all of them and is not found guilty at any of the toll-houses, it then ascends to venerate Christ, according to the Fathers. If, however, it is found guilty and accountable for any passion, it is thrown into Hades!

There was one soul that had passed all except one, the last one, which is the toll-house of mercilessness. "Alas, alas!" said a certain saint who was having a vision of that soul. "He passed them all, and only at the last one was he shaken, and the demons flung him into Hades with a crash!"

There was another soul, a saved soul, being carried up by the angels of God into Heaven. Other angels, who had just taken another soul to Heaven, descended and embraced that soul, and he sensed an ineffable fragrance from the embrace of those angels who had approached the throne of God. And the angels said, "Glory to God, Who helped this soul to be saved!"

We should never lack this contemplation of death or other such meditations. All these contemplations create watchfulness in the soul and purify and cleanse the mind so that it may feel the contemplation better. This contemplation is a barrier for evil thoughts. When this spiritual contemplation is within us, we shut out evil thoughts; there is no room in us for them

---

[11] from the funeral service

because that contemplation has occupied the space of the mind. When we do not have godly contemplations, then indeed we are overcome by passionate contemplations.

If the soul does pass the aerial toll-houses, it should think, "Now all that is left is to venerate God. I wonder, how will I get there? In what way will I see Him? I wonder what He will say to me? Will He perhaps open a new book? Perhaps the demons with their incomplete knowledge did not have everything written or did not know everything I have done, and now I have to complete my defense before Christ! I wonder, what will Christ's decision be for my eternity? I wonder, will it be for eternal life or eternal damnation?"

If at this very moment we found ourselves before Christ, what fear and trembling we would have! If we could only understand, as much as possible through contemplation, what situation we shall find ourselves in then! "Alas, alas!" say the Fathers. "How much suffering will come upon us? What awaits us?" Yet we shun struggling; we are indifferent and drowsy, and we sleep the heavy slumber of ignorance!

The world is far from the truth. People work, sleep, travel overseas—without realizing what is about to happen beyond the grave! A thick darkness covers the truth, just as a thick cloud obstructs the sun's light. If a person contemplates and comes to grip with the fact that this life is like an ephemeral theater where people waste time by dancing and having fun, he would realize the tremendous insanity and foolishness of men and the great achievement of the demons.

There are two different ways of thinking: worldly people think of things before the grave, and we think of things after the grave! Worldly people think about present things; that is all that they see, and that is what they believe in. But the revelation of the Gospel of Christ casts abundant light into the souls that want to be saved. It opens to them a new horizon of awareness of the true God.

"The sufferings of this present time are not worthy to be compared with the glory which shall be revealed in us."[12] There will be unlimited, incomprehensible, inconceivable glory for those who will walk in the light of Christ!

We have no excuse before God because of His great benefactions: He has called us with a holy calling and shown us the road of light and truth! Great is the mercy of God! Let us not disregard it. Let us work at it. Let us reflect day and night upon our soul and how we should struggle. Meditating on God and practicing the virtues bring us close to God quickly.

We should never at any time stop remembering death. The Holy Fathers said that they were not overcome by negligence in their cells, because they had the remembrance of death night and day. Negligence found no room in them. The Fathers kept thinking, "If today or tomorrow is my last day, what should I do?" In this way, this remembrance kept their mind in the fear of God, and the fear of God gave light to their conscience regarding how to compel themselves.

In the beginning, of course, these thoughts do not make an impression on a person. His soul is, so to speak, dead—sluggish. But gradually, it begins to stir within him; it starts coming to life, and then it works normally.

10. Take care of your soul, my child. Read the Fathers; pray with the beloved little prayer, which will fortify the foundations of your soul.

Meditate on death, which is something that will most definitely come to us. Ah, death! The cup of death is extremely bitter for the soul when it powerfully separates the soul from the body. How much regret we shall feel then for everything we have done out of carelessness and laziness! Our conscience

----

[12] Rom. 8:18

will torment us as a foretaste of hell. So why should we let the pleasure of sin defeat us, for which we shall pay with much pain and no cure?

Man, with a dual nature, the elect and unique creation of God, is born on this planet, the earth, and gradually his body wears out and someday he dies, completely incapable of keeping himself alive. Because of conceit he blows up like a balloon, only to die because of just one illness. He has no power over himself. Without realizing it, he is governed by another's will and command, while he is led away involuntarily, completely helpless to resist.

What are you, O man, that you boast and brag, imagining outrageous things about yourself? Behold, an invisible microbe attacks you, and at once you feel ill, fall sick, and go to your grave. O conceited mortal, you see that death is coming and that you will yield to it and depart to an unknown land with no ability to object. Are you able to refuse, to resist, to escape what is going to happen to you at that fearsome hour? Not at all! Total helplessness. Then why do you boast, O man of clay, you helpless, wretched, useless one? What do you own that God has not given you? Can't He take it from you whenever He wants? Yes. Then bend your neck, humble yourself, and thus you will be saved.

11. Righteous Lot was afflicted night and day, living amidst profligate and licentious people. He was oppressed, seeing their shameful acts. Nevertheless, he didn't judge any of them, which is why he was counted worthy of the divine appearance of the angels and was considered worthy to be spared when God burned down the cities of the wicked and destroyed the licentious.

Aren't things here worse than Sodom and Gomorrah? Shouldn't we expect the fire and brimstone of God's wrath?

Therefore, let us pay heed to Lot's example so that we may not also be destroyed—not temporally, as of old, but eternally and endlessly!

Let us be vigilant, for we do not know in what hour the thief—death—is coming. Let us be watchful in order to guard our riches—not only the riches of our Orthodox faith, but also of the grace we were counted worthy of when we were baptized in the holy baptismal font.

What will come more certainly than death? It is the most certain thing that every person will encounter. We ought to keep the remembrance of death alive within us constantly, so that through this most saving remembrance, we may avoid the soul's death, which is nothing but complete separation from God in the afterlife.

Violently compel yourselves, says the Lord in the Gospel,[13] for you do not know when the Bridegroom of your soul will visit you, and woe to him whom He finds indolent and neglectful of his salvation. Pray also for me, for I do not practice what I preach. Woe to me the thrice-wretched! With what face will God look at me?

12. Take a look at death, my child, which reaps everyone. All human things melt and burn out like a candle. Only godly works—that is, whatever works were done for the love of God—will never burn out, but will shine for a person so that he may ascend the path to reach the throne of God.

Work the deeds of salvation, even if it takes great effort. Everything will be counted as a struggle, as asceticism, and as resistance to the devil, and your due reward will definitely be given to you. Compel yourself. Bear in mind your departure, your death, the toll-houses, and the fearsome judgment of God. Think about hell and the damned, my child. Count yourself as one of them also, and then all your sorrows will

---

13 cf. Mt. 11:12

seem like nothing to you, and a sweet consolation will come upon your entire soul.

13. My child, you should reflect upon the uncertainty of the time of your death and the demons and the terrifying toll-houses that our lowly souls will pass through! What a fearsome tribunal awaits them! Our souls will tremble out of fear and terror! Meditate on the painful torture together with the demons; alas, it is eternal with no end or termination!

Unfortunately, my child, the evil one takes all these salvific recollections from us so that we are not benefited, and he brings us all the evil recollections in order to defile our soul. Since we know his tricks, let us compel ourselves to say the most holy Jesus prayer and to contemplate spiritual meditations, which are so beneficial, so that our soul may be continually benefited and purified.

14. The remembrance of hell should always be in your mind, for it has much fruit within it. Who can remember eternal fire and remain without tears? Weep, my child, so that your heart and body may be cleansed of every passion, and that you may see days of holiness and be astonished by your wealth of purity.

15. How frightening is the question of where each person's soul will end up! Oh, how much do forgetfulness and indolence lead us astray—and me, first! If we think about it, it is terrifying to ponder whether we shall achieve our goal or not. Man's entire being is overcome by trembling when he carefully considers what will happen in the end! What judgment will be for me, who was conceived in iniquities?[14] Be merciful, be merciful upon me, my sweetest Jesus! Upon Thy compassions I cast my soul's despair.

16. May your prayers support the crumbling house of my wretched soul. There is nothing good in me. That is why I

---

[14] cf. Ps. 50:5

weep, calling to mind the things that will happen when I depart from this world and make the journey above without having the necessary provisions. Woe is me, for though I am now able to store them up, my negligence will bring about my eternal regret! But isn't this the truth! Oh, how precious this present time is—every moment is priceless. Yet this sound knowledge escapes us, and thus our precious time passes, and it is impossible to reclaim it.

17. Oh, at that time the internal judge—each person's conscience—will rise with a bold and powerful voice either to condemn or to acquit him. "If our conscience does not accuse us, we have boldness towards God." As long as we are on the road of life, how necessary it is to reconcile ourselves with our adversary[15]—our conscience—before it leads us to the judge, and then we shall not escape until we pay the last penny by giving an account for every idle word.[16]

Oh, what is going to happen in the end? How much toil and dread! Blessed are those who have the eyes of their soul open and prepare the provisions for the great journey, and woe to me whose eyes have been shut by the two great evils of mankind—forgetfulness and ignorance!

18. Oh, how watchful we must be in all things,[17] for the adversary walks about like a roaring lion, seeking to devour the universe![18] O God, my God! Arise! Why do you rest and sleep, my soul? Hour by hour we wait for the sound of the trumpet and to be brought to judgment! Woe is me! How horrifying that moment is, for our eternal life depends on it: either in God or in hell!

Let us sigh a little, and behold, God becomes merciful. He knows that we have nothing left that is healthy in His eyes; we are full of weaknesses, passions, and excuses. How will we meet God? I wonder, what will He tell us? How much exacti-

---

[15] cf. Mt. 5:25
[16] cf. Mt. 12:36
[17] cf. 2 Tim. 4:5
[18] cf. 1 Pet. 5:8

tude will He demand from us, who do not want to apply such exactitude to ourselves, because it conflicts with our desires?

19. Always remember death; meditating on it should become a rule of life for you. What a struggle the soul has when it separates from the body, when the books are opened and people's hidden deeds revealed! How much it sighs then, how much it weeps, but it has no help except from good deeds it has done! Therefore, struggle in good and beneficial works now that you have the breath of life, for an hour is coming when our members will stop working the deeds of salvation!

Weep bitterly if you want to find consolation in the distressing hour of death. Bear in mind the dreadful tribunal. Oh, what a fearsome hour awaits the poor soul, when it hears the decision for its eternal restoration! Even the saints feared this hour; how much more so should we! What can I, the wretched one, say? I moan bitterly when I remember it. You should also do so, and you will find great benefit.

20. The truth of God sounds forth like a mighty trumpet and says, "Vanity of vanities; all is vanity!"[19] "For what will it profit a man if he gains the whole world, and loses his own soul? Or what will a man give in exchange for his soul?"[20] "Remember your end and you shall not sin unto the ages."[21] "Riches do not remain, glory does not accompany one to the other world, for when death comes, all these things are obliterated."[22]

Behold the truth, which mightily crushes the lie! Within every trap and thought of the devil, a lie is camouflaged to deceive man. Therefore, let us pray that God will enlighten us with the light of truth, so that the darkness may be dispersed, and the bright day of triumph and the glorious truth may shine in all our thoughts, words, and deeds, so that as good stewards of grace we may be counted worthy of praise before the holy

---

[19] Eccl. 1:2

[20] Mk. 8:36-37

[21] Ecclesiasticus (Wisdom of Sirach) 7:36

[22] from the funeral service

angels. When will this be? When we shall no longer be in danger of falling into pride; for the devil has the power to fight us until our final breath. After this is the age of trophies, crowns, and the acquisition of God—the end of fear and tears. "And God will wipe away every tear from their eyes."[23]

Oh, what glory! Then no one will be able to take away the joy from the hearts of the saved. O my Jesus, glory to Thy dominion, glory to Thine inexpressible dispensation, O Master! Amen, amen, amen, sweetest Master. I kiss Thine immaculate feet that toiled and ran to find me, the lost sheep. Heal my wounds, O Master.

21. I pray that the grace of the Comforter will bring peace to your soul.

My child, I have already found complete peace, only by the grace of God. I feel myself as light as air. After sunset, I remain by myself in my little cell. I try to collect my nous and lead it within myself and into Christ. I usually weep for my many sins. I think about what awaits me, heavily laden as I am, at the impartial judgment when my mouth will be silenced, not having any excuse, for I know that I have done nothing truly good, nor will I ever in my whole life.

My beloved child in Christ, what will become of me? How will I endure the torments that await me? Woe to me, a prey of the eternal fire! I tremble, contemplating eternal damnation and the deprivation of the divine light! How will I, the wretched one, live without Christ and light?

22. When we remember death, we find an excellent guide that helps us discover the truth of things. Death says, "Why are you treasuring things up, why are you proud, why do you boast, O youth, O health, O science? When I come, I will render you your worth! When you are laid in the dark grave, you will know what the profit of earthly good things is!"

---

[23] Rev. 7:17

We are departing to the world that transcends the senses, my children. We do not stay in this world, which is full of bitterness, distress, sin, and miseries. There in the unfading life, God will wipe away every tear from the eyes of the saved, and there will be no pain, grief, or sighing, but an eternal day, a life without end or death! This is the life, my children, that we should long for wholeheartedly and fervently, so that by God's grace we may acquire it and be delivered from painful hell.

23. Everything in this vain world will pass. The world and life are a fair, and each person can buy eternal life with the "money" of his life. How wise is the person who spends his money—his life—buying whatever he will need for the hour of death and the tribunal of God! Let us buy precious things that are pleasing to the great King: confession, humility, godly love, purity of soul and body from carnal sins, and keeping ourselves far from criticizing others, idle talk, lying, etc. When we master all this, we shall be wealthy in God's blessed land.

24. "Vanity of vanities; all is vanity"[24] in this world, my child. This is what the wise Solomon cried out after he had tasted beyond satiety all the pleasures of the senses. He did not deprive his heart of any of the pleasures, and the end of all this was decay and destruction. On the contrary, he who works for God not only is not deprived of the necessities of life here, but also feels the true joy and peace of God already in this life.

Riches do not remain; glory does not accompany one to the other world; beauty changes; youth passes and old age comes; health fades; illness follows, and the grave disintegrates everything into nothing.

When we visit our final dwelling, our grave, we shall see with our own eyes all the vanity of man, as did Abba Sisoes

---

[24] Eccl. 1:2

when he saw the tomb of Alexander the Great and cried out, "Alas, alas, O death! The entire world was not big enough for you, Alexander. How then have you fit into two meters of earth now?"

There in the tomb the dreams of vain pleasures are sealed. Whatever preoccupied many people with love and sacrifices is trampled underfoot there. In the tomb, the souls that realized the world's deceit triumphantly ridicule it.

My child, be careful with this world, which is like a theater. For poor and ignoble people on stage in the theater wear the clothes of kings, tycoons, etc. and appear to be different from what they really are and fool the audience. But when the show is over and they take off their masks, then their true faces are revealed.

Abba  Sisoes

Chapter Seven

On Passions

Struggle, my child, for God's road is narrow and thorny—not inherently, but because of our passions. Since we want to eradicate from our heart the passions, which are like thorny roots, so that we may plant useful plants, naturally we shall toil greatly and our hands will bleed and our face will sweat. Sometimes even despair will overcome us, seeing roots and passions everywhere!

But with our hope in Christ, the Repairer of our souls, let us diligently work at clearing the earth of our heart. Patience, mourning, humility, obedience, cutting off one's will—all these virtues help cultivate it. We must apply all our strength, and then God, seeing our labor, comes and blesses it, and thus we make progress.

Take courage, for the toil is temporary and ephemeral, whereas the reward is great in Heaven. Struggle and be vigilant with your thoughts. Keep a firm hold on hope, for this shows that your house is founded on the rock—and the rock is our Christ.

2. Do not feed your passions by yielding to them, so that you do not suffer pain and affliction later! Labor now, as much as you can, because otherwise, if the passions are not tended to, in time they become second nature, and then try and deal with them! Whereas now, if you fight against them lawfully, as we advise you, you will be freed and will have happiness by the grace of God.

3. The thing that should preoccupy us above all is how to cleanse our heart from the passions and how to abate some passion or vice! The visitations of grace that God sends us from time to time for consolation do not play an important role, because they come and go. Ah, those passions! They are like roots with thorns. How much toil, how much pain, what tears, what prayers are necessary for a person to find slight relief—it is a real martyrdom!

4. I pray to the merciful God that He will show you the path of salvation and guide you as a hart to the springs of the living water of refreshment. Man is full of passions, shortcomings, etc., and in order to be freed of them, he must engage in a bloody battle. Once he wins, with God's help, he will receive here in this life the promise of the future marriage with the Lamb, Who was ruthlessly slaughtered by cruel hands accursed by God.

On Carnal Warfare

You wrote to me, my child, about your carnal warfare. Be patient—with the grace of God everything will pass. Nothing will be left of it, as long as you struggle. Whatever fights against you will be short-lived if you oppose it valiantly.

Carnal warfare will accompany you throughout your youth. But according to your struggle it will subside and become tolerable. The passion of pride, however, will continue for a long time, beyond your youth. But you will find some rest from this passion for a while according to the struggle and spiritual knowledge with which you resist.

These two passions are the strongest of all. Upon these two passions the entire edifice of sin stands; each one is a component of the other. Both are formidable lions. But our Jesus with a single cheerful glance is able to render them carrion for the vultures.

2. The terrible passion of fornication is difficult to fight against, especially when it is strengthened by former *predispositions.** But God knows how to deliver those who take refuge in Him with humility, for He knows how easily our nature slips.

3. My child, you wrote about your carnal warfare. Know that it stems from pride—so that you may humble yourself and learn that if grace leaves us, we fall and become a piteous spectacle.

So humble yourself; blame yourself; ask our Panagia to grant you a spirit of humility so that you may come to know and feel that you are nothing, a zero. For our Jesus says, "Without me you can do nothing."[1] From the temptation that came upon you, learn how man falls—and how low he can

---

[1] Jn. 15:5

fall. There are even worse falls for those who have more pride. Do not be distressed; it is a temptation and it will pass. God permits such things to happen for our benefit so that we may become wise through temptations. Be patient and brave! Take courage; it will pass. It is a storm, and in this way will the sea throw out all the rubbish that the preceding peace accumulated!

Do not grieve more than necessary, for this is from the devil, and this grief will lead you to negligence and laxity. Persist in your struggle and do not be afraid. Disregard Satan and show that you do not attach any importance to him. Then, since he is proud, he will leave, but as long as you pay attention to his attacks, he will not.

4. When you have carnal warfare, be very careful with filthy fantasies, which produce dirty thoughts. Stop and expel fantasies as soon as they come. Immediately say the prayer with pain of soul and at once you will be delivered from the warfare.

5. Do not lose heart, my child. It is a battle and it will pass. All the saints were fought against. They had such great warfare that in despair they took poisonous snakes and put them on their bodies so that they would be bitten and die. But since we are weak, God does not allow us to be fought beyond our strength, but instead He will help us. However, since we have pride, He permits this warfare so that we may humble ourselves. Do not grieve more than necessary, but with great humility throw yourself before God and blame yourself. Immediately drive away every evil thought as soon as it comes, and I hope that the grace of God will relieve you.

Do not fear; you will suffer no harm. Drive away cowardice; have courage. Everything will pass, as you will see, while this warfare will leave behind much benefit for you, and God will give you much grace. Just do not lose heart, because this is how we lose the contest.

6. *(From the Holy Mountain, June 30, 1958)*

My beloved brother in Christ, I received your letter and saw the mental warfare you are going through with the evil spirit of sin, of fornication.

My brother, listen to a pauper in knowledge with a soul bereft of any good. When one struggles against sin with humility and the fear of God, with fervent spiritual work and with the guidance of an experienced spiritual father, God will never let him be lost. Only when he neglects his spiritual duties, and especially when he becomes proud, thinking that he is something, then it is possible for him to slip. But even then, if he seeks forgiveness with humility, he gets up again and is healed again. For the Lord's mercy is near to those of a contrite heart.

However, many trials occur for one to gain experience and spiritual wisdom, for without temptations it is impossible to obtain experience. Experience is not a skill derived from learning, but it is to have practical knowledge of the benefit and harm of temptations. If God does not let a person fall into temptations a little, it is impossible for him to become conscientious. When someone does something with good intentions, yet later it turns out that what he did was not right, God— since He observes the heart and tries the purpose for every deed—will bring things back to normal and will enlighten him to realize what he should have done. Infallibility belongs to God alone. No matter how perfect the saints were, they still had some blemishes. Therefore, they would go through temptations to obtain greater humility and caution, and to grow patient with their weak nature. A touch of anger, laughter, or idle talk does not take away a saint's holiness.

Only one must keep in mind not to despair. Even if one slips and sins ten thousand times a day, it is not justifiable in God's eyes for him to despair, but rather he should be hopeful and prepare for a fight, until God's mercy comes and delivers him.

There was once a monk who happened to slip and sin by himself continually, yet he would always arise at once and do his prayer rule. The demon that kept throwing him into sin lost his patience seeing the courage and hopefulness of this brother. So he visibly appeared to him, and said to him with vexation:

"Don't you fear God, you defiled wretch? You have just sinned, so with what face can you now stand before God? Aren't you afraid that God will burn you?"

But since this brother had a valiant soul, he said to the demon:

"This cell is a forge: you hit and get hit. As God is my witness, Who came to save the world, I will not stop fighting you, falling and getting up, beating and being beaten, until my final breath—and let's see who will win: you or Christ!"

When the demon heard this unexpected reply, he said:

"I won't fight you any more, because if I do, I'll make you win crowns."

Thenceforth, this brother was delivered from the warfare, and he sat in his cell weeping for his sins.

When God enlightens a person and he repents for his sins and walks with humility and caution, God does not let him be lost. Of course, his predispositions for his previous sins will become thorns and hindrances to him, but when he sees the waves rising menacingly, he should not despair, thinking that he will fall and be lost. On the contrary, he should hope in God with faith and struggle with humility under the spiritual guidance and training of his spiritual father, without fearing the violent storm that rose.

7. The devil, of course, will not remain inactive; he also has his own weapons. Which ones? For instance, he whispers to us: "You can't do anything. I will throw you down again. Don't you see the magnitude of this passion, the bulk of that weakness? Bear in mind that I'm not defeated so easily and that I'm not about to retreat. Besides, what have you achieved until now? Nothing! Nor will I ever let you do anything in the future. All your efforts are going to waste. I am invincible. Don't you see my might?" And at once he displays filthy fantasies with intensely powerful carnal pleasure. He seems armed like a scorpion. And then he makes the struggler think that it is impossible for him to escape and that he should put up his hands and surrender!

These and countless other things does the insidious instigator craftily display. So, onward! Let us expose the lie of his traps, and let us reveal the rustiness of his weapons. The warrior of the mighty God, trusting in Christ's invincible power and actually feeling it, begins the serious battle courageously, raising the banner of the awesome Cross and armed with the name of Jesus, which is dreadful to the demons. He calls upon it constantly and vigorously, and thus keeps the *imagination** from giving in to the insidious and silly assaults of the devil, while always reflecting on death, judgment, hell, the delight of paradise and eternal glory beside Jesus, the feats of the saints, and so on—and all this is like ammunition supplying power to prayer! Then despair, negligence, egotism, and depravity are put to flight, the struggler is filled with zeal, and Satan's exaggerations collapse and burst like a thin balloon.

On Anger

Be meek and do not get angry, for anger is a fruit of egotism and self-will, while on the contrary, meekness is a fruit of a humble heart and of cutting off one's own will. When one gets angry, his mind loses its discretion, and as a result, it loses its equanimity and is carried away into saying improper words.

Even though the Holy Fathers liken all the passions to intoxication, primarily they liken anger to it, because when a person is intoxicated, he loses his dignity and makes a fool of himself in front of everyone—which is also what happens when an irascible person loses his temper.

The Lord tells us: "Learn from me for I am gentle and lowly in heart and you will find rest for your souls."[1] In order to find peace for our conscience, we must stifle and eradicate the beast of anger, whose lair is egotism.

When someone happens to criticize you, whether justly or out of tactlessness, take hold of yourself, repress the inward turmoil, close your mouth, and start saying the prayer internally, and at once you will see the beast choke! But every victory takes a struggle. If you want to subdue and eradicate your passions, learn to love humility and self-reproach. Only in this way are the passions diminished and obliterated.

When you are overcome by anger, you should realize that you are feeding it, only to find it stronger next time. But if, when it rises, you stifle it in the way we mentioned above, then you should realize that you are starving it, and so the next time it rises, it will be weaker, and the next time even weaker, and little by little your anger will be healed.

---

[1] Mt. 11:29

On the Warfare with the Demons

Hy child, always be careful, both when you are happy and when you are sad. When you are happy you should not lose control through vivacity and laughter, nor when you are sad should you be so gloomy that it shows. The reason why is that Satan shoots thoughts at us like arrows, but he cannot tell if our heart is receptive to them. But since he is an expert, once he shoots an arrow—that is, once he assaults us with an evil thought—he observes our face and all the movements of our body, and based on them, hc gauges how well the arrow struck our heart. If he sees that the soul is hit, then he shoots more arrows there to kill it. But if he deduces from the exterior signs that the soul is not wounded, he changes his attack, and so on.

Therefore, when you are happy, you should conceal it within yourself, so that he does not discover it through your carelessness and rob you of it with some temptation. Likewise, when you are sad, do not let it show lest he augment your grief after discerning the reason for your sadness. If you maintain a balanced state when you are happy and when you are sad, the devil does not know exactly what is happening inside you, and thus does not know how to fight you.

2. We are passing through the midst of many traps, so it is not permissible to proceed neglectfully if we want to avoid the snares. Let us keep our eyes wide open, imitating the many-eyed Cherubim, so that we may deride the clumsy tricks of Satan and ascend with the wings of divine thoughts through the spiritual ether. Thus we may offer the health of our souls as a fragrant incense to God, Who dwells in the Heavens. Just as the health of children brings joy to their parents, likewise our good Father—God—rejoices to see our souls healthy.

3. I am always praying to the Lord that He will give you sound judgment. Think before you speak. You are still inexperienced in the wiles of the devil, whose goal is never to let you have peace. Sometimes from the right and sometimes from the left, sometimes with your own affairs and sometimes with other people's he keeps you busy so that your soul is never calm and you are unable to see its depths, where there is still much rubbish. Do not occupy yourselves with anything other than yourselves. Become stupid to become smart; become ignorant for the Lord to reveal His wisdom to you.

4. Do not think that it escapes the devil's notice or that he doesn't care that you have formed a synodia, in other words, a bastion to fight him from. No; he has observed it carefully and has cunningly prepared himself with the guile of a fox and the power of a wolf, as much as he could. He has entered your sheepfold and is ravaging your souls. Do not leave him inside any longer; arise and be united with love, which paralyzes his strength. Reflect that you have left everything for Christ; you have sacrificed your youth; you have despised all worldly joys to obtain Christ. Pity your souls. Reflect that the devil is vigilantly seeking to devour someone. The abysmal dragon cannot stand to see you trampling upon him and not obeying him! He is jealous, and so as a cunning fox he causes discord and arguments so that he may succeed in destroying the brotherhood and then hurl you into various pits of sin.

5. Without the Lord's assistance, we are unable to do anything good. Therefore, we need much humility to find repose for our souls.

The evil one will never cease shooting at us with his flaming arrows and trying to overcome and dominate us. But we also have many deadly weapons. In particular, the prayer "Lord Jesus Christ, have mercy on me" literally burns him. This is why he tries to fight us in an indirect manner. But our Christ enlightens us with His holy commandments to fight him.

The devil is using that person to fight you and make you transgress God's holy commandments, and in this way to harm not only you, but primarily to grieve and fight God through your transgressions. Whereas, on the contrary, if we struggle to keep the word of God persistently, we not only save our souls, but also we become the means by which God is glorified. "Those who glorify me shall I glorify."[1]

Therefore, my child, struggle with love, patience, and humility to disable the traps of the devil with God's help. Perhaps through you, He will enlighten this person to repent. "Overcome evil with good."[2]

6. Do not think that it was you who thought such things about your Elder. No, my child, it was from the devil. Your soul is pure. The devil is dirty and he brings them to your mind. He tries to convince us that we thought them on our own in order to grieve us. The proof that this grief is diabolical is the ensuing negligence we have for our spiritual duties. For if it were from God, we would be eager in everything.

You have not grieved your Elder, as you imagine, for he knows from experience that it is from the demons and not from you. It seemed to you like that so that you would grieve and not have the courage to reveal to him your thoughts. No; no matter how many times such thoughts come, go and freely tell them to him. For the tempter brings such thoughts to make us feel ashamed and not reveal and confess them so that he may devour us whole. Be careful not to conceal your thoughts, or you will fall into a trap.

---

[1] 1 Kings 2:30
[2] Rom. 12:21

7. We must pass our days with great caution. The devil is very crafty and is always on the lookout to ensnare us at a time of spiritual drowsiness and render us accountable to God and our conscience. May God abolish him so that he cannot harm us! But since He is just, He does not remove the free will of man. And this is why we—and first of all, I—voluntarily follow the suggestions of the devil, and we sin.

8. Even in the eleventh hour, our all-good God accepts us as long as we realize He awaits our return. But the sly enemy of our soul does not remain inactive; nothing escapes his notice. For this scoundrel knows the inestimable value of time and endeavors through vain cares and allurements and comforts of the world to establish steadfast ignorance and forgetfulness, so as to bring complete despair at a man's last hour, and win the immortal souls for which Christ died on the Cross!

9. Do not grieve because of your warfare. Do not fear, but take courage. The demons do not have the authority to harm you. It is from the hand of God; through it the eyes of your soul will be opened, and it will set you on the right path. It takes extremely bitter medicines to heal difficult passions.

Entreat God: "Lead us not into temptation."[3] This warfare, as St. Isaac the Syrian says, is due to pride, conceit, and hardness of heart. The remedy is humility, the recognition of one's incorrect judgment, and obedience and trust in one's spiritual father.

Humble yourself, my child; only this medicine will save you. God has sent these temptations to you out of love to frighten you, so that you pull yourself together, come to your senses, humble yourself, and ask for forgiveness.

The demons get angry when you pray, because these evil ones see that you are beginning to break their nets, and they

---

3 Mt. 6:13

are afraid that you might escape from them. They want to make you despair or lose heart. Therefore, arm yourself with trust and hope in God and with the conviction that they are not allowed to do anything without the higher command of God.

Know that if you are patient in this warfare and humble yourself before God and your brethren, God will give you much grace and enlightenment; the eyes of your soul will be opened, and you will see in what great darkness you were.

The courage you have is due to the grace of God, which helps you in these temptations. For without courage and hope and faith, there is grave danger in such temptations. Do not be afraid of anything; have all your hope in God. Cry out the prayer without stopping and you will see how much help you will receive.

Fear God—not the demons. Fear God and His judgments, for when He decides to punish us with some kind of penance for our pride, who is able to stop Him? Therefore, when the evil is still small, let us take care to remedy it. For once it has grown worse, you will not be able to be delivered even if others help you.

So love God more, since He has sent you the medicine for your illness—that is, patience, humility, and courage—and see to it that you take it.

10. Do not be afraid of invisible enemies since you have put on Christ. But you should tremble when you do not see grace protecting you because of your sins. Even then, "every evil has a tinge of good." See to it that you serve God with fear and trembling, for the crafty devil, who trips up those who struggle, waits for a period of negligence, and then he furiously leaps out—may God abolish him—and tries, if possible, to drag us down into hell alive.

11. The devil is the source of every lie and deception and cunning and evil. This is why all thoughts aimed against Christians are in essence a lie and deception.

He promises to the young every kind of prosperity through fanciful thoughts and beguiles them through illusory dreams with riches, pleasure, delights, eternal life, etc. (for this is the devil's plan: to keep man from remembering death, since this ruins his plans), until they trust him as their best and most intimate friend. Then, once he entwines them in his webs as a spider its prey, with great ease he sucks up all their spiritual substance and renders them dead in relation to God.

12. Unbelief and blasphemy proceed from the envy of the devil. There is only one remedy: to disregard such thoughts as if they were only the barking of a dog. One is not held accountable for them. Other people who did not know this fasted and kept vigil and wept to be delivered. But blasphemous thoughts leave a person only if he disregards them.

Abba Agathon was also fought by blasphemous thoughts. He entreated God to deliver him and heard a voice telling him: "Agathon, Agathon! Take care of your sins, and let the devil bark as much as he wants. You are not accountable for those thoughts." If you do not disregard them, you will never be delivered.

On the Spiritual Struggle

The faster you acquire a virtue, the easier it is lost. The more slowly and laboriously you acquire it, the more steadfastly it remains—just like that squash plant that grew tall and said to the cypress tree: "See how much I've grown in just a few days! You've been here for so many years and haven't grown much at all!" "Yes," said the cypress tree, "but you still haven't seen storms, heat waves, and cold spells!"

And after a little while, the squash plant dried up, while the cypress tree remained where it was!

This is also how a spiritual man is. Both during a storm and in times of peace he remains the same. Why? Because the long period of time has created stability. When he first renounced the world, his spiritual condition was unstable, but with time, the grace of God gradually worked out his salvation and freedom from the passions. Thus, a person needs to force himself today, and the grace of God will start acting by itself tomorrow. Then you will not need to force yourselves to have good thoughts; the grace that remains within you is what brings them to your mind without your effort. Then you will see great mysteries! You will have a feeling, so to speak, of the remembrance of death, or of another beneficial recollection. When you wake up and are still opening your eyes, instead of feeling sleepy, you will have progressed; you will have already passed through the entire mystery of theoria and will say, "But how does this thing happen, since I am still getting up? How does this thing happen?" All the same, the grace of God acts by itself—it is a result of a long-standing habit.

The same thing happens with sin: whether awake or asleep, a sinful man constantly thinks about evil. When sin is helped by a bad habit and by the devil, it becomes a constant evil. Likewise with good—a good habit assisted by the grace of God becomes second nature to him.

2. To suspect that someone supposedly thinks ill of you or that they are saying things about you is called a lie of the mind by the Holy Fathers. A lie of the mouth is when, for example, instead of saying that I have five dollars, I say that I have ten. A lie of conduct is when, for example, instead of saying that I was late getting up for church due to my negligence, I say that I was tired because I worked a lot yesterday!

3. Fasting is an exceptional virtue; it represses bodily impulses and gives strength to the soul to fight against the poisoning of the heart through the senses, and provides it with a remedy against any past poisoning. Fasting causes the mind to be cleansed constantly. It withers up every evil thought and brings healthy, godly thoughts—holy thoughts that enlighten the mind and kindle it with more zeal and spiritual fervor.

4. No matter how much the frightening tyrant of our souls oppresses us out of envy and malice, the time will come for God to judge his malice and give eternal repose to us who are heavy laden.

Patience, my child. Let us also wear the thorny crown of life's afflictions, as did our archetype, Jesus. Let the thorns stick deeply into our head, and let it bleed painfully, so that the pain and the blood may beautify and glorify the garment of our soul, so that we will not be put to shame when we appear before Christ and see other souls full of glory and purity. Patience; the winter of afflictions will pass, and the beautiful spring will bring the fragrance of the grace of God.

5. Struggle with all the might of your soul for the love of our Christ. The devil strives day and night to make us his vessels and render us unworthy of our holy God. But let us strive to become vessels of our crucified Christ so that we may humiliate the devil and glorify the Love Who shed His All-holy Blood for us!

Struggle mightily. Do not fear, for we have before us our big brothers—the angels—who fight together with us. They are incomparably stronger than the demons. Therefore, take courage. Strengthen yourselves with true self-knowledge, for the truth protects a struggler like an almighty weapon.

6. Always pray with the beloved Jesus prayer. Retire into yourself through silence and reading. Care for your little soul, my daughter. Live more spiritually in your home. God is watching your situation, and the hour of grace will miraculously strike when the headquarters above decides.

Weep humbly, praying: "What profit is it to a man if he gains the whole world and loses his own soul?"[4] Satan employs all his means to prevent souls from ascending. Blessed is he who escapes from him and ridicules him.

Philosophize on the vanity of transitory things and on the authenticity of the constancy of the life in Heaven, where the Church Triumphant dwells, awaiting and praying for the Church Militant, which that fights the harsh fight today—for we will need the correct dogmas of our Holy Fathers and a burning faith in Christ. It is a time when the devil will deceive, if possible, even the elect.[5]

---

[4] Mt. 16:26
[5] cf. Mt. 24:24

Noah

The Flood

Chapter Eight

On Cowardice and Negligence

cowardly soldier lacks glory, boldness, prestige. Not a single one of his requests reaches the ears of the king. Whereas at the mere mention of a valiant soldier's name, his requests are immediately fulfilled!

O lofty boldness that adorns the valiant spiritual striver! Who does not desire it? And yet negligence, especially in prayer, scatters it to the four winds and leaves a person bare.

How much more should we be glorified when we are valiant, for we wear the angelic schema and have promised under oath to the King of kings to struggle till death—not to be negligent and to desert. So let us completely vanquish the enemy of God and of our soul through our struggle and forcefulness.

2. Regarding the fear that overcomes you at night, etc., know that it is from the tempter. You will defeat him with faith in God. In other words, you should reflect that God is everywhere present. "In God we live and move,"[1] and nothing happens without God allowing it. Even if we find ourselves with the devil or amongst wild beasts, God is present! Neither the devil nor the wild beasts are able to harm us if they do not have the authority from God to do so.

Why then should we lack this salvific truth of God—faith in His providence—and be afraid when there is nothing to

---

[1] cf. Acts 17:28

fear? How can I be harmed, since God has authority over the devil and an evil person and everything that can harm me? And how will a person's guardian angel—who, by God's providence, never leaves him—permit him to be harmed, if he does not receive a command from the Lord to let him?

Therefore, my child, take courage. And when this fear comes upon you, say: "Whom shall I fear? Who is able to harm me, since God governs everything? 'Even if I should walk in the midst of the shadow of death, I shall fear no evil, for Thou art with me.'"[2] At the same time, say the Jesus prayer, and fear nothing. Believe firmly in the truth of faith.

3. *(To a novice nun)*

My beloved child, may our Panagia strengthen you in your spiritual struggle until the end.

I see your soul's discouragement; you are like the "tyros" in a war, that is, like the newly recruited soldiers who are taken to the battlefront. As soon as they see bullets flying, bombs dropping, etc., they lose their courage and want to flee. But the experienced generals make sure to mingle them with old, seasoned soldiers, and they encourage them until they grow accustomed to war.

I commend your desire and your wish to attain perfection and dispassion. All your efforts should aim at this goal. However, you must not forget with whom you have to wrestle. You have to wrestle against rulers, against principalities, against very wicked, dark powers,[3] against legions very experienced in battle; furthermore, you have to wrestle against the flesh and the world of passions, which are like painful wounds, and it takes skill, time, patience, and diligence to heal them.

As for your discouragement, know that this is an attack—cannon shots of the enemy. It is one of the wounds of the passions. Therefore, it takes patience, perseverance, courage. Do

---

[2] Ps. 22:4
[3] cf. Eph. 6:12

not let this darken the heaven of your hopes. Trust that God knows all the inclinations of each person and that He has never overlooked good intentions and efforts without rewarding them sooner or later.

We see that the Holy Fathers in their early years endured droughts, terrible discouragement, and other deadly temptations. But they held on tightly to patience and forcefulness, and then grace visited them, in proportion to what they had previously endured.

You say that the eldress's mentality frightens you, as does your inexperience and the environment in general, as if it were inconducive to perfection because of temptations, etc. All these things are swept aside through humility and self-reproach. In other words, cast the blame on yourself. Say: "I am the cause of my discouragement, either because of my pride, or because I am still shortsighted and unable to orient myself properly, so it is only natural that I lose my hope." Likewise, the cloud can also be brushed aside through faith in your spiritual guide—as long as you abide by the rules of the fight.

We know from our patristic and hesychastic tradition that in the old days, young monks, after obtaining the blessing of some great Elder, would build cells and live by themselves, and only from time to time would they visit their Elder, tell him their thoughts, receive guidance, and depart again. And even though they did not have their Elder constantly hovering over their heads, they attained great heights of virtue only through his counsels. Know, my child, that above all these things is Christ—not only above our head, but even within us—and He rewards every good intention and effort.

Often humility—not genuine humility, of course, but humility poisoned by the devil—advises us with "humble" thoughts such as: "I am weak, so I need this and that in order to make progress, and since I am not given them, how can I be saved?" and so on. When we believe such thoughts, our spiritual nerves begin to be cut, resulting in spiritual torpor, etc. Whereas we should have been fortified by the counsels of an experienced spiritual father, so that we would not suffer this torpor. For we know that the devil transforms himself into an angel of light[4] and that every virtue can end up being extremely harmful in the absence of experienced discernment. This is why the Fathers said, "Above all is discernment."

My dear child in the Lord, cast away your discouragement and say: "I will compel myself until death. I will pursue perfection and attain dispassion. And if I do not attain it either because of my weaknesses or because my death intervenes, or for any other reason, I trust that, according to the teachings of our Fathers, God will rank me with the perfect."

"But I am seeking to enjoy the blessedness and the peace of God!" you might tell me. Yes; say to the enemy: "God is within me. If I compel myself with prayer, humility, and tears, He will show me His holy face! Not only here in the monastery, but even if I were in Sodom, like Lot, God is able to grant me this holy desire of my soul." So just attend to yourself and to your sins, and I trust that you will find more than you expect.

4. Consider those nightmares and turmoil to be a storm roused by the devil's jealousy. The devil wants to intimidate you in the beginning of your spiritual journey, so that you say, "If in the beginning of my journey I encounter such temptations that are beyond my strength, who could possibly endure until the end?" In this way, Satan works his evil craft with experience and skill, making thus a long list of damned souls. But we know his traps through experience. In the beginning the journey is difficult, but afterwards come repose, joy, and

---

[4] cf. 2 Cor. 11:14

high hopes of salvation. "Beholding the sea of life rising with the surging waves of temptations, I flee to Thy calm haven and cry to Thee: Raise my life from corruption, O Most Merciful One."[5] Tempests and fair weather, war and peace, health and illness, gain and loss—these characterize the journey of every soul. The end of this journey is death.

So, blessed soul, do not lose heart along the road of your salvation. Together we shall walk the road, helping each other. The grace of God, which heals weaknesses and makes up for deficiencies, will be with us, girding our flaccid thoughts and anointing us with patience, until the command comes from the Ruler of All that we leave our body here and that our soul ascend to the Heavens.

5. You wrote to me in your first letter that David states: "He shall never permit the righteous to be shaken."[6] Here he means that the righteous will not suffer the kind of storm that would have a deplorable end. However, out of His love, God does send them trials that have good results, for it is through the good kind of storms that righteous souls are not only saved but also perfected. If there were no storms, no one would be saved.

You wrote in your second letter that it is written in the Scriptures: "The fearful should not go out into battle."[7] Yes, but this holds for physical warfare, because the fearful can dishearten the brave. In the spiritual warfare, however, it is not so; rather, the fearful are encouraged by the brave and the experienced. Spiritual fathers can do harm only when they lack experience and teach erroneously. That is, when they give the wrong medicines for the illness of the person confessing. A fearful person in the spiritual warfare suffers harm in that he does not progress spiritually. But when he cries out for the mercy of God, he is delivered. He does not have the bravery for great battles, but at least he does something to be saved,

---

[5] Eirmos from the *Ochtoechos*, plagal second tone

[6] Ps. 54:22

[7] vid. Deut. 20:8

and he will receive a reward according to the amount of his work.

Having been justified, the saints were tried in this manner, either because they lacked something, or in order to be glorified more—for they had great patience, and since God did not want the rest of their patience to remain idle, He let them be tried. But their trials always had a good result.

6. I pray, my child, that you struggle. Do not forget the goal: salvation. The devil is roaring, seeking whom he may devour.[8] Time is not in our hands; our life is dangling by a single thread. Compel yourself; rise to your stature; prove that you are a servant of Christ and not of the devil. Don't you know that negligence will bring a thousand and one thoughts to take you captive? Pray with pain and tears. Take courage; Christ will not abandon you. Compel yourself a little, and the devil will leave. Grace is ready to help you; it awaits your resolve and forcefulness.

Negligence, my child, engenders unbelief and listlessness, which in turn brings a swarm of evil and harmful thoughts that leads its victim to filthiness. Arise, take the weapon, the dear little prayer, and cry out the glory of our God. Vanquish your adversary, the devil, who seeks to devour you. Compel yourself! I am praying and weeping especially for you, so that our Panagia may strengthen you in your struggle.

7. May the God of peace, my child, grant you His love and His divine peace, which surpasses all understanding.[9] May the love of God be the aspiration of your life.

You should fear negligence as your greatest enemy. Negligence brings all evils. It is through negligence of our duties that all spiritual goods corrode, resulting in an overall drought of soul and the consequences that follow. It is fought by continuous prayer, with the mouth or the nous, by the remem-

---

[8] cf. 1 Pet. 5:8
[9] cf. Phil. 4:7

brance of hell, paradise, the unknown time of our death, etc. So compel yourself in your duties—and especially with silence and the prayer.

8. Beloved of my heart, I give you my heart's greatest wish, that God may keep you from the evil one. Amen.

"Fight the good fight"[10] of your soul; be aware of where you fall and correct yourself. Strike your negligence with all your might—all evil originates from it.

Every time you fall, Satan comes that much closer to you to turn you into his plaything and make a spectacle of you. Awaken from your insensibility; meditate and reflect on the things above; we shall go on a journey with no return. Be careful, for some will go to the good things above, to the most beautiful Jerusalem, and have an endless Pascha with the angels, while others will go down to hell, having the demons as eternal companions!

Look above; pass through this sky with your mind and behold what is hidden beyond it! Our fatherland is there; that is where our labors go and are stored up. Therefore, do not neglect your duties—reading, prayer rule, vigil, watchfulness, and the prayer. Keep crying and shouting out, "Jesus, Master! I, the wretch, am perishing!"[11]

9. God does not want those whom He will save, who seek His mercy, to be ignoramuses, unmanly, cowardly, or spiritually untested. It is a matter of a divine inheritance stored up for experienced Christians. So He places temptations before us so that our obedience to His commandments may be demonstrated. His illumination is within us; knowledge of His will is taught by the Scriptures; furthermore, our conscience guides us like a compass. All of the above enlighten us in the face of temptations. But when evil prevails over our will, we do not obey His commandments.

---

[10] 1 Tim. 6:12
[11] cf. Lk. 8:24

We were created with free will, and free will cannot be controlled by others. As such, if we feared God, we would not fall into temptation. If we did not love ourselves more than God, we would not tend towards sin. But His goodness did not leave our falls without a rectifying remedy, whereby we return once again and a victory occurs in spite of our fall.

All who compel themselves to be saved, the Scriptures call righteous, justified by faith. God will not let them fall, for they are struggling properly. He will not let them be tempted beyond their strength when they are making every effort to be patient. But when we are cowardly and lukewarm, when we have a slothful will, this constitutes an occasion for a temptation beyond our strength.

Your grumbling is sinful; it is a result of self-love and unmanliness. Have patience in everything; thank God; blame your lukewarmness, and not God, Who was crucified for you and, consequently, must love you. Since He loves you, how can He let you fall into temptation? Seek forgiveness from Him, and secure yourself with patience.

10. Beware of indolence in saying the prayer, as well as in guarding your thoughts, not to mention slackness in the struggle of your vigil. Do not be negligent, my children, because negligence is a terrible evil, the mother of all the vile pleasures, the forerunner of hell, and a cause for a terrible captivity. Do not sleep the slumber of negligence, for the devil is awake and holds a lit torch in his hand, and endeavors to set us on fire. Wake up! A judgment and tribunal are one and the same without mercy awaits us!

Do not be disheartened; do not lose courage. Sometimes the holy nurse—the grace of God—leaves us, and we fall into ridiculous and indecent thoughts, and sometimes even words, so that we might be humbled and not think highly of ourselves, but rather become aware of our weakness, that we are unable to do any good without the grace of God.

11. Do not fear; struggle; arm yourself with courage and bravery. We have Jesus as our general, Who leads our army to a glorious victory! By no means lose heart; the evil one incites us to lose heart so that he may disarm us and take us prisoner. Have your hopes in Him Who said, "I will never leave you nor forsake you."[12] He will not let us be tempted beyond our strength.

12. My child, the tempter has visited you to test your intentions, based on your predispositions. Fight the good fight of a martyr; do not fear the dreadful enemy of our souls. Christ is observing your struggle, my good child. He allows the tempter to trouble you in order to show him the miracle He worked in you by detaching you from the world with His sweet grace.

Fight against your soul's enemy, my child, and do not let him get anything from you that he used to steal from you in the world "for free." Resist firmly, so that the angels may rejoice and leap for joy because the bodiless devil has been conquered by you with the aid of the invisible grace of God.

The labor of every struggle passes, but the victory remains. If you do not taste hell "by the bucket" during a temptation, you are not going to see the grace of God.

Meditate on death. We are departing to another world— how beautiful and blessed it is! I wonder, shall we dwell in that world of such beauty? Let us reflect upon this most blissful place constantly, so that we will be able to despise this false and deceptive world.

Pray continually, my child. Reflect upon your sins and shed scalding tears, which will greatly comfort you. You will mourn properly when you keep silent and do not laugh.

---

[12] Heb. 13:5

13. My blessed child, rejoice with the love of our good God, Who, like a most affectionate father, cares for us so well—even with his wise chastisement—for the salvation of our souls.

My child, many times we are daunted by some temptation—as you were—without realizing that nothing bad can happen to us without the Heavenly Father allowing it to happen through His divine providence in order to increase our spiritual knowledge. God will not put oxen (people spiritually uninitiated) in the other world, but people wise and faithful, knowledgeable through experience of the demons, and victorious over the various sins.

Have courage in the fight, my child! Through many tribulations and temptations we shall pass the sea of this life here to reach the calm harbor of that blessed life which will have no end, tribulations, or dangers. Keep a firm hold on the helm of chastity, so that we may pass the obstacles of dreadful hell.

God wants those who struggle to imitate Him by enduring the greatest sufferings for the sake of His love, because in this manner they show their true love for Him. It is during temptations that the love of each person really shows—how much he loves God!

Our Jesus, my children, wants us to have complete love for Him. In other words, two loves do not fit in one and the same heart. We cannot serve both God and mammon.[13] Rather, we ought to give Him an unadulterated, pure heart, so that He in turn may give us His undefiled, divine heart.

---

[13] cf. Mt. 6:24

On Forcefulness, Courage, and Self-Denial

I pray that you become fighters in a glorious battle whose victorious outcome the angelic powers will applaud, for we have the same Master, the same abode in the Heavens; in the very same abundant light shall we live the eternal, blissful life—a life without end or evening, a truly divine day! The Apostle of the Gentiles cried out in a stentorian voice: "Who shall separate us from the love of Christ? Shall tribulation, or distress, or persecution, or nakedness?"[1] I am convinced that no one is able to separate us from the love of Christ when our longing burns like a furnace sevenfold. Yes, this is how I pray that you will become, so that He may be glorified—He Who for our sake became the object of insults, reproaches, slappings, and death—even death on a cross!

Do not despair when you fall into temptations and afflictions. Do not think that God has abandoned us because of our sins. No, but He is chastising us in order to teach us wisdom. He does not want us to be ignoramuses, but wise in divine wisdom.

If we are not fought against, how will it show that we are soldiers of Christ? A soldier might get wounded in battle, but this does not mean that he has been defeated. Even if we are defeated, once again we shall rise and fight.

Of course, in the beginning of our calling, when we have chosen a life of chaste dedication to our Jesus, we are unable to meet His requirements because, as we know, there is another law within us which wars against the law of God and the lifestyle we have chosen, and it fights to separate us from the love of our Jesus. However, this fight does not mean that we are not worthy of our calling, but rather the fight to abolish

---

[1] Rom. 8:35

the law of sin within us will render us more fervent in our love for Christ. For if it were possible to acquire the love of Christ without a struggle, our own will would have no merit, since we would gain it without a struggle.

So this is why we shall be rewarded when, despite all the opposition caused by the love of the world, we obtain the life-giving love of God, and when, despite the attraction of sin, we stand as firm towers of virtue!

Clouds will rise up against our goal, threatening destruction and havoc; they will try to frighten and demoralize us with their thunder. But take courage and fear not; through many tribulations and trials shall we reach the gates of the Kingdom of Heaven![2]

The martyrs struggled with faith and complete self-denial, and thus they obtained promises[3] and crowns of eternal glory! Thus we, too, through faith in our Christ and complete self-denial, shall be able to prevail by His grace.

Our inner courage must reach the point of saying with resolution: "Even if I am put to death, I will not take a single step away from my faith in Christ, Who has called me. I will give up my life for Christ, but not one inch of concession will I concede to sin." If our inner courage boasts in this manner, we may hope that victory, by the grace of God, will be ours.

Say the prayer fervently; struggle mightily; abstain; pray; wear simple, humble clothes; read spiritual books; get up at night and pray in order to be warmed and become as sturdy as a rock. This is also how I, the wretch, used to struggle when I was still in the world; I secretly got up at night and did metanoias; I prayed and our Panagia miraculously intervened for me, the lowly one.

2. I see your struggle; I am counting the crowns; I envy your medallions; I plunge my mind into the age to come to

---

[2] cf. Acts 14:22

[3] cf. Heb. 11:33

hear the triumphant melodies that the angelic beings will compose; I am amazed and bemoan myself because I have not struggled as you struggle!

My children, just think about what the martyrs went through for our Christ! And the more martyrs were killed, the more did Christians flourish; our Church has been watered with the blood of martyrs. We are martyrs in this corrupt society of ours, for with our chaste—by God's grace—lifestyle, we censure the immorality of mankind and its estrangement from the worship of God.

Abide, my children, in this chaste lifestyle; abide close to our Jesus, and may you resemble Him by enduring slander and false accusations. This is what our Lord endured from the scribes and the Pharisees and the chief priests; unjustly did He suffer on the Cross. Therefore, those who want to be His followers will undergo similar trials.

Kneel at the holy feet of our Jesus and shed tears of love, follow Him with loyal dedication till death, and if the waves rise up to Heaven and descend to the abyss, so be it. Our Christ, the true God, with a dreadful, divine nod will calm all the waves, as long as we have faith. Believe truly and steadfastly in Him Who said, "I am with you always, even to the end of the age."[4] Jesus is with us; do not lose heart. He will fight for us, through the intercessions of the invincible Theotokos, and grant us the victory.

3. If indolence is harmful for those who are advanced, how much worse it is for those who are young. Therefore, my children, compel yourselves, for the less diligently we struggle to be saved, the more the enemy exerts himself to harm us.

Do not be drowsy if you want to be delivered from the snares of the enemy, for whoever is asleep can be mortally

---

[4] Mt. 28:20

wounded, whereas whoever is vigilant—no matter how much he is struck—fights and wounds his enemy as well.

Do not lose the prayer, my children, through daydreaming and neglectfulness. Do not forget the maxim "The way you begin follows you to the end." So fear the result and carefully attend to the beginning, for a day will come when you will realize the serious words I am stressing today.

Make a good beginning now, for "a good beginning is half the battle." Keep crying out the world-saving name of Jesus Christ so that not only your ears hear it, but so that it also echoes in the ravines. Struggle, for it is you who will be saved; you are the ones who will reap the sweet fruit of eternal life. I am doing my duty, for I want to act conscientiously before Christ in my effort and diligence for your salvation— as for your sins, that is something personal.

Compel yourself in your vigil, for from it springs forth eternal life. He who keeps vigil will enjoy great grace for the pains he takes to oppose his human nature. No work of the monastic life is greater than keeping vigil. He who is negligent in keeping vigil will reap vices instead of grace. And how shall he present himself before Christ with a patched-up garment? His shame will be indescribable when his brothers appear with garments all white and new. "A word to the wise suffices."

4. Sacrifice yourselves in order to find eternal life in paradise! Do not let forgetfulness overcome you and wipe away from you all spiritual dew, leaving you dry and dead in relation to God. Become valiant soldiers of Christ. Do not renounce Him by your deeds, but glorify His name. Become a whole burnt offering for God's sake, so that He may smell a fragrant aroma.

I beseech God for you; I weep for you, because I do not know how to do anything else other than to love and suffer for my children in Christ. I ask only this favor of you: love one another and be humble towards each other.

5. Struggle, my child, so that your soul may bear fruit, for the position that each person will receive beside the Lord Jesus corresponds to how much he has labored. Fear not; we shall pass through fire and water[5]—that is, through fire when the temptations seem like fire in the way they act, for example, carnal thoughts, thoughts of hatred, envy, etc., and through water when thoughts of despair and hopelessness come upon us and drown our soul as if in water. After passing through fire and water, God will raise us to the spiritual refreshment of deliverance from base thoughts and to the dispassion bestowed by grace.

6. My child, be silent, humble, obedient till death; be ready to sacrifice yourself by cutting off your will, even if it seems like a real martyrdom—this is what self-denial means. When you keep all this advice, fear nothing—no evil—neither from the demons, nor from men, for whoever keeps the divine commandments is kept by God from every evil.

Do not be abrupt when you answer; no matter how they criticize you, say, "Bless."

7. The devil deceives us, and we forget that we ought to compel ourselves, for the days are passing, and we are gradually approaching death to our inconsolable regret. Compel yourselves, my children; time is passing. Attend to yourselves; the devil does not sleep but vigilantly fights, seeking whom he may devour. My children, be careful not to lose your immortal and priceless souls, which are worth more than thousands of worlds.

8. During the fight, at the time of the struggle, the demons shoot arrows powerfully and wound us. They try to convince

---

[5] cf. Ps. 65:12

the soul that it is impossible for the passions to subside, so that the struggler will slacken, lose his fortitude, and give up.

But the struggler must realize the deceit of the demons and be patient and brave, saying, "Life or death—it is better to die for God rather than live with negligence and remorse." If he resists with this kind of knowledge and bravery, the dragon of the abyss, who devours the whole world with his cunning, departs until an opportune time—not that he is afraid, but he departs so that he will not cause the struggler to win crowns, for he sees the zeal of God surrounding him.

9. Why, my child, do you leave your "vineyard unfenced"? Why do you neglect to protect the fruit that you obtained after such a hard struggle? Why did you leave the watchdog—your soul's zeal—so hungry that it did not have the strength to bark and chase away the thieves and the wild animals? Have you forgotten that it is to those who compel themselves that the Kingdom of God is given? Didn't you consider that the eternal fire awaits those who neglect to cultivate their soul? "Arise; why do you sleep? The end draws near, and you are about to be troubled."[6] Wake up and cry out: "Lord Jesus Christ, have mercy on me, the sinner, and arouse me to do Thy work so that Thou mayest pardon my debt as the God Who loveth man."

The Judge of the contest is invisibly present, observing each soul's struggle and calculating how many trophies He will give. Let us eagerly desire the crowns and fight a good fight, and we shall obtain trophies corresponding to our zeal.

Do you remember, my child, the efforts you made in school to become an excellent student? Do likewise in spiritual learning, in the true philosophy, in the acquisition of piety, in the increase of faith, in the purity of ethics. Success in worldly learning can be an impediment for the soul, whereas spiritual success raises one to heavenly heights.

---

[6] Kontakion from the Great Canon of St. Andrew

Struggle, my child, for the sake of our Christ. Other people insult Him through their disgraceful conduct. But you should glorify Him with your intellect's shining purity from filthy thoughts. Drive away every thought that will defile your intellect and heart, which were sanctified during the divine washing by the Holy Spirit, Who came to dwell in us at baptism. Fear God—this is the true wisdom. "The fear of the Lord is the beginning of wisdom."[7] Do not fear the threats of thoughts from the demons, but lean a mighty arm on God, Who delivers you from faintheartedness and tempests.[8] Take courage and walk like a brave man towards the heavenly Jerusalem, and its light will meet you in exultation.

10. I received your letter, my child. Stand firm, tighten your belt, and put your best foot forward in the good fight, for the struggle is not to acquire material things, but to attain the heavenly inheritance of God! As the Apostle Paul tells us, "Eye has not seen, nor ear heard, nor have entered into the heart of man the things which God has prepared for those who love Him."[9] Furthermore, the sufferings of this present time are not worthy to be compared with these heavenly things.[10]

But if we do not fight well and lawfully, my child, then, unfortunately, evils await us instead of blessings—torment, misery, eternal damnation, and dwelling together with the demons forever! Fight bravely and do not fear the strength of the passions you see within you. For grace does not depend on the magnitude of the passions, but on our own forcefulness, and based on this, it provides the way out of our plight.

Attend to the good beginning you have made. That is, don't be negligent and lose the little compulsion you do have, for how much time was necessary just to attain it! So don't turn back; walk steadily ahead. Look up above—behold how

---

[7] Prov. 1:7

[8] cf. Ps. 54:8

[9] 1 Cor. 2:9

[10] cf. Rom. 8:18

Heaven shines. It awaits you; it has prepared an eternal abode for you! Christ is waiting to crown you; He is observing your struggle. Exert yourself as much as you can—only this will save you.

Don't despair when you see the strength of the passions and of the demons—nothing is impossible for God. Therefore, take courage and don't lose heart. The Lord will fight for us, and we shall be still.

Death comes without giving notice. Here in Portaria, a woman died while she was eating an apple. A nun at another monastery suddenly died within five minutes. They did an autopsy, but they couldn't find the cause of her death.

Be careful, my child. Whenever God gives the command, each person departs to Him. I wonder, when will He give the command for us to present ourselves before Him? Let us be ready so that we shall not be troubled in case He calls us suddenly.

Watch out, my child! Don't stray from the good beginning you have made. Instead, add struggle upon struggle so that you may reach the throne of God as one saved.

11. Struggle upon the spiritual battlements, for our struggle is for the acquisition of Heaven. What is more beautiful than a spiritual struggle! Just think what songs of victory the angels in Heaven will make for those who overcome sin, and what praise they will offer up to God, for there is a joyous celebration amongst the angels for the return of only one sinner![11] So then, why are we negligent? Our toil is nothing in comparison to the good things stored up in the Heavenly Kingdom!

Who is wise and will understand these things?[12] Who is the one who will raise the banner of revolution and roar like a lion against the enemy and seize the victory?

---

[11] cf. Lk. 15:7
[12] cf. Ps. 106:43

So, my children, onwards! Be brave; take courage—the Lord is with us. Hold on tightly to humility, lay hold of prayer, fortify yourself with reading. Run with courage, cry out the prayer "Upon Thee have I hoped, put me not to shame; upon Thee have I laid my hopes."[13] Encourage your governing mind. I am with you, strengthening you with my poor prayer.

12. My children, with a complete sacrifice of our self-will and desires we must declare war against the devil, the world, and our evil tendencies and weaknesses. The "old man"[14] of passions must leave our heart, and the man in God's likeness must be born, that is, with dispassion and purity of both heart and body.

Struggle with courage and with trust in God. The devil will attack you with worldly desires now and then. Nevertheless, you must keep the stance of a vigilant soldier so that you do not become spiritually drowsy and get killed by the devil. Be careful, for the adversary is roaring ferociously, seeking whom he may devour with vile passions.

13. Constant forcefulness is necessary for us not to remain outside the bridal chamber of Christ, as did the foolish virgins. Rather, our spiritual forcefulness should continuously light our lamps, so that we can see Christ entering His bridal chamber and enter together with Him into the eternal wedding of the Lamb!

Courage, my child; keep your chin up when you face the enemy, for we are soldiers of the great King, Who triumphed at the battlefront on Golgotha. If we are ever defeated, let us rise once again, and after we have bandaged our wounds, let us take up our weapons again with bravery and a firm heart. Since we have this kind of victorious Commander-in-Chief, we, too, shall be victorious with the power of our Christ, as long as a spirit of humble-mindedness dwells in our souls.

---

[13] cf. Ps. 24:2
[14] Rom. 6:6

14. Do not lose your courage, my child, no matter how much the tempestuous sea of various passions might rage at times. You should reflect that all these things—and even many more things—are incapable of preventing us from receiving the grace and love of God. If our longing for Christ grows, my child, all the obstacles will become very small and easy to pass. But when we have no love nor any longing for our Christ, they become difficult to bear, and they water our days with burning tears. Yes, my child, let us keep calling upon Jesus until His flame ignites within us, and then all the weeds will become ashes.

Always remember that we have to take up our cross every day, which means afflictions, labor, temptations, and every diabolical influence. Which saint has ever walked the dark paths of this world without afflictions and perils? And if we have been called to walk the same path, why do we find it strange to face afflictions? Since we have chosen to fight the devil, why are we surprised to encounter difficulties? Let us have the lamp of our eagerness lit, and let us await with patience and vigilance the coming of the Lord Jesus.

15. We should not postpone correcting ourselves, lest death find us. Then we shall weep and lament inconsolably—and I, first of all—without a single ray of hope that the tribulations will change.

Compel yourselves. Behold, Great Lent has come. However, it is not the fasting of the body as much as the fasting of the tongue, of the mind, of the heart, and of the senses that should preoccupy us especially now during Great Lent. Let us purify ourselves with this kind of fasting internally, where spiritual snakes are lurking that poison the life of our soul and deaden our spiritual strength, leaving it unable to correct and transfigure our soul.

Now, during Lent, compel yourselves even more. Become stubborn in your resolve; this stubbornness is holy and not egotistical. You will see how much you will profit spiritually. Merely for the promise that the passions will be suppressed and that we will avoid certain sins corresponding to our efforts, we have good reason to become stubborn with the devil, who continually throws us into the same old sins.

16. Struggle, my child; isn't the present life a time for struggling? Isn't the life of every earthly man but a dream? Raise the noetic eyes of your soul and behold heavenly hosts of angels and archangels. Lift up the eyes of your mind higher and behold the blissful place of Lucifer, who was once a rising star, now empty.

Oh, what a great destination! What a supremely holy calling! There, by the throne of God, souls will see the divine beauty of Christ and will be led up from knowledge to knowledge and from theoria to theoria with a superabundance of riches of divine grace!

But in order to obtain these heavenly blessings, we must display bravery and mettle, and must engage in battles without turning our backs in defeat, keeping before us Jesus, Who said to us: "Be of good cheer; I have overcome the world,"[15] and "The ruler of this world will be cast out."[16]

So, trusting in the invincible power of the crucified Christ, let us dedicate ourselves with simplicity to the struggle of the monastic life, and let us keep smothering the immaculate feet of our Savior with kisses, shedding tears of gratitude and joy.

Who, then, shall separate us from the love of Christ? Shall tribulation, or distress, or persecution, or nakedness, etc.?[17] "I count all things as rubbish, that I may gain Christ,"[18] cried out the mouth of Paul. Aren't we obliged to imitate Paul and attain the same grace and love towards Christ that he had? Yes,

---

[15] Jn. 16:33

[16] Jn. 12:31

[17] cf. Rom. 8:35

[18] Phil. 3:8

but do we struggle as he did? Have we—have I—also gone through everything that he went through for his beloved Christ? No. This is why I am bare—or rather dressed in rags and covered with shame, and I am deluded, thinking that I am wearing a glorious diadem. Woe to me, woe to me the wretch! Who shall illuminate my darkness, so that I may see my wretchedness?

17. Force yourselves in your spiritual duties, for forcefulness in spiritual things is like a solid wall that does not let the river run into the garden and destroy what the gardener has labored to grow. But if we are negligent, the river comes in and destroys everything!

The Lord speaks to us about this in the Holy Gospel: "While men slept, his enemy came and sowed tares among the wheat."[19] The more we compel ourselves, the more we shall gain. The more one works, the more he is paid. The life of a monk is a daily cross, a holy Golgotha, where Jesus is calling all of us who love Him to be crucified with Him, and then the soul will resurrect.

18. Do not remain sluggish; just compel yourselves, so that you will not be condemned as hearers and not doers of the law. For you seek divine words, and seeking presupposes a commitment to apply the advice; so compel yourselves.

Struggle, my children. Together with our Christ we shall endure everything. The world will hate us, primarily because it hates our Jesus—our love and adoration!

Love Christ; breathe Christ; make Jesus dwell within your soul. Fear no one, for we belong to God; the King of kings has us as His royal servants; no evil will touch us, for we serve Christ—to Him are all things subjugated!

19. My children, be brave in the fight. Our Christ is invisibly present, waiting to see your victory, in order to give you

---

[19] Mt. 13:25

the unfading crown of eternal glory! Whoever loves God sacrifices everything, solely to please God. Spare nothing, for before the love of God, everything is rubbish. The demons are troubled when they see us preparing for battle; the angels, though, rush to drive away every obstacle preventing victory. So let us ally ourselves with the angels of God, so that we may bear witness that "Jesus Christ is the same yesterday, today, and forever."[20]

20. *(To an Abbess)*

Struggle, for the duty of shepherds is to sacrifice themselves for the sheep they have undertaken to shepherd. Thrice-blessed are the shepherds who will guide their rational sheep well, for great eternal riches await them in Heaven.

Endure everything, my child, for the devil will strike in many ways to break down the wall of our patience; he will thus make a double profit: our own defeat as well as that of the sisters.

21. I pray that the grace of God will overshadow you and give you sufficient strength to confront our wicked ego, the dreadful root of all the evil activities of polymorphous evil.

Do not be afraid of the devil's pressure, my child. The power of our God is so mighty that it helps unreservedly those who want to fight using it. The devil's power is not trivial, but God miraculously protects us wretches.

Have courage in the struggle, my child; study the law of God; say the sanctifying and salvific Jesus prayer, and hurl yourself into the fire of the battle. God will reward this struggle of yours with alleviation—as has already happened countless times—with high hopes for an eternal, bright future.

Do not lose heart when facing any diabolical passion, no matter how gigantic it may look, for wherever God intervenes, the devil's opposition is overcome.

---

[20] Heb. 13:8

22. My blessed child, do not be afraid in the struggle. Nourish your soul with courage and hope. Disregard the adversities that come from the demons. See to it that every fight is crowned with success. In God's eyes nothing is in vain—even the slightest forcefulness is good. Do not lose your nerve at all; fight valiantly; coerce yourself, press yourself, for it is by pressing grapes that sweet wine is made, which gladdens the heart. Courage, my child; we shall prevail with God's help.

23. Bolster your courage for a new struggle, and thus you will repel every thought of cowardice and discouragement. We must continually revive our strength and regroup our front of resistance, as the devil also does.

Do not let an incidental fall—or even continual falls—drive you to despair. Our objective is not to turn our backs to the enemy in despair, so that he cannot boast before God and so that we do not sadden Him. Courage and bravery are appropriate for strugglers when they are struggling not for ephemeral crowns that fade, but for everlasting ones that are incorruptible!

So blessed are all who will have their lamps lit with oil in them. With joy and exultation they will enter along with Christ into the eternal wedding, full of spiritual delight.

24. The Christian struggle is glorious, for the prize is not something ephemeral, but it is eternal glory up in Heaven! Blessed is he who is wise in God, for no account will be demanded from him, and he will not find himself in a difficult position when God calls him to give an account for his time on earth.

We waste time with no regret. When we leave this world, we shall realize the damage we have suffered by letting time escape from us. The days are passing with no reckoning. Realizing this saves us, even if it is only during the final days of our life.

the SOWER

Christ ascending the Cross

Chapter Nine

On Condemnation

Slander is a great evil. Just as the little rudder steers the whole ship wherever it wants, likewise the tongue leads a person either to good or to evil. The Holy Fathers greatly censure judging other people's sins, faults, or evil habits.

When we judge our brother, we condemn ourselves to a great sin. But when we cover our brother, God will also protect us from great sins. When we expose our brother, we drive the grace of God away from us and He permits us to fall into the same sins so that we learn that we are all weak and that the grace of God supports us. Whoever guards his tongue guards his soul from great sins and grievous falls.

The chief cause of criticism and slander is pride and egotism, because one considers oneself better than the others. For this reason it is very beneficial for a person to think of himself as below everyone, so that he considers his brother better than him in order that, with the help of God, he may be delivered from this evil.

2. If something pushes you to criticism in any matter regarding a brother or the monastery, try to pray about the matter instead, without passing it under the judgment of your reason. If you turn within yourself through prayer, humility, and mourning, you will find a spiritual treasure—just keep pride and criticism far from you.

3. Be attentive, my child, that you not judge any soul. For God permits the one who judges his neighbor to fall, so that he learns to have sympathy for his weak brother. The mercy of God supports all of us, but if we become proud, God will remove His grace and we shall become worse than the others.

It is one thing to condemn someone and another to be fought by thoughts of condemnation. To condemn is a terrible passion, but to be fought by such thoughts and to fight back— this is an occasion for crowns.

4. Each person must bear the weaknesses of others. Who is perfect? Who can boast that he has kept his heart undefiled? Hence, we are all sick, and whoever condemns his brother does not perceive that he himself is sick, because a sick person does not condemn another sick person.

Love, endure, overlook, do not get angry, do not flare up, forgive one another, so that you resemble our Christ and are counted worthy to be near Him in His Kingdom. My children, avoid condemnation—it is a very great sin. God is greatly saddened when we condemn and loathe people. Let us concern ourselves only with our own faults—for these we should feel pain. Let us condemn ourselves and then we shall find mercy and grace from God.

5. Love one another, and do not be embittered out of egotism. Humility is a sure guide; it does not let the one who possesses it hit the reefs of carelessness and be shipwrecked, but as a luminous guide it leads him faultlessly on sure ground.

Egotism is the most evil of evils; it causes all our lapses through unsubmissive thoughts. Fear this and strive to get rid of it, for the more it remains within us, the more it will wound us with the proportionate pain.

I beg that you not criticize one another, for this is down-right egotism. Excuse your brother's fault; this is evidence of humility and love. The brother who acts thus will find much grace from God, but he who judges and scandalizes his neighbor should know that not only will he not find grace, but even if he has something he will lose it, so that he may learn the lesson of humility through suffering.

Be particularly afraid of inner criticism, that is, thoughts of criticism, because it does not come to light through the spoken word, in which case it is likely to be corrected by someone who hears it. Be careful, I say, about criticism from within, which imperceptibly makes us fatally guilty and deprives us of the life of divine grace and offers as a most bitter drink the death of the soul. I pray that love and freedom from criticism will reign in every expression among you, so that the Holy Spirit may rest in your souls.

6. Experience has shown that it is wrong to accuse and condemn someone without letting him defend himself. As also the sacred Gospel says: "Does our law judge a man before it hears him and knows what he is doing?"[1]

If we are not attentive, many sins of condemning others heap up within us, and then repentance is needed. How often a person repents because he spoke! Let us bear in mind the words of Abba Arsenios: "I have often repented for speaking, but I have never repented for keeping silent."

If we are often deceived by the sense of touch, how much more so we are by people's words. Therefore, much attention is needed, for the devil prowls around roaring to devour us.[2] A Christian ought to be like the many-eyed Cherubim, for evil has multiplied greatly, especially the sin of condemnation, which is as common as "bread and cheese." May God cleanse us and sanctify us for His glory.

---

[1] Jn. 7:51

[2] cf. 1 Pet. 5:8

"Do not let the sun go down on the wrath of your brother."[3] That is, let no one be angry and enraged against his brother past the setting of the sun.

Have you heard about that brother who was negligent and lazy, who did not go to the all-night vigils and did not do his duties, whom the brethren knew to be a negligent monk? When he fell ill and the hour of his death drew near, the brethren gathered to hear something beneficial, or to comfort him, or in case he wanted to say something to them, but they saw him joyful, cheerful. One brother was scandalized and said, "What is this we see in you, brother? We see that you are joyful even though you are approaching death. But we have the thought that you were not a violent[†] monk, so how do you have such courage and a cheerful face? How do you justify yourself?" "Yes, brethren," he said, "indeed I was a negligent person and I did not fulfill my duties. But I achieved one good thing, by the grace of God: not to condemn any brother and not to scandalize anyone; and never did I let my heart have something against any brother of the monastery when the sun set. And inasmuch as I did not judge any brother, I believe that God will not judge me either, for He said, 'Judge not, that you be not judged,'[4] and since I did not judge, I will not be judged." The brethren marveled and said, "Brother, you found the way of salvation very easily." And the brother died with much joy.

Do you see how the Fathers struggled and how they found the way of salvation?

---

3 cf. Eph. 4:26; 4 Mt. 7:1

† A "violent" or "forceful" monk or person is one who strives vigorously to "do violence to his nature constantly" (*Ladder* 1:4), for "the Kingdom of Heaven suffers violence, and the violent take it by force" (Mt. 11:12).

On Silence, Idle Talk, and Boldness

Compel yourselves in silence, the mother of all godly virtues. Keep silent in order to say the prayer. For when one speaks, how is it possible to avoid idle talk, which gives rise to every evil word, which weighs the soul down with blame?

At your work, flee conversation; only speak in moderation when necessary. Let the hands work for the needs of the body, and let the nous say the sweetest name of Christ, so that the need of the soul, which we must not forget even for a moment, will also be provided for.

2. Do not grieve for me, my child, but struggle ardently. Struggle in silence, prayer, and mourning, and you will find the elements of eternal life. Compel yourself: close your mouth both in joy and in mourning. This is a mark of experience, so that both states are kept safely. For the mouth does not know how to guard riches.

Silence is the greatest and most fruitful virtue; for this reason the God-bearing Fathers called it sinlessness. Silence and stillness, one and the same thing.

The first divine fruit of silence is mourning—godly sorrow, joyful sadness. Afterwards come luminous thoughts, which bring the holy flow of life-streaming tears, through which the second baptism† occurs and by which the soul is purified, shines, and becomes like the angels.

Where shall I place, child of Jesus, the spiritual visions springing forth from silence? How the eyes of the intellect are opened and see Jesus with sweetness greater than that of honey! What a novel wonder is worked from lawful silence and an attentive intellect! You know these things, so struggle. I have revealed a little to you; compel yourself and you will

---

† The Holy Fathers speak of four "baptisms": (1) the Mystery of Baptism; (2) the baptism of tears of repentance; (3) the baptism of tonsure into the monastic schema; and (4) the baptism of blood, i.e., martyrdom.

find yet greater. I keep you in my prayers just as I promised you. I wonder, are you ready?

3. Do not speak unnecessary words, my child, for they chill your soul's divine zeal. Love silence, which gives birth to all virtues and fences in the soul so that the devil's evil does not approach it. "Better to fall from a height than with the tongue." The tongue does the greatest harm to man.

4. Salvation is not gained when we speak idly or when we pass our days without keeping accounts. Be careful with your tongue and your thoughts, for guarding them fills the soul with the light of God. But he whose mouth is unbridled deposits various impurities in his soul.

5. Flee from idle words and laughter if you want your prayer to have boldness through tears and grace! Constantly say the prayer intensely, with zeal, with longing; only thus does one become strong in soul. Avoid idle words at all costs, for they weaken the soul and then it does not have the strength to struggle. This is no time for daydreaming, but a season for spiritual profit. Who can guarantee that after going to sleep, we shall wake up? Therefore, let us compel ourselves.

6. When one keeps silent, he is given time and freedom for prayer and concentration; but when he passes his hours carelessly, he does not have time to pray. Furthermore, through his careless speech he accumulates various sins. For this reason the Holy Fathers placed the virtue of silence at the summit of the virtues, for without it no virtue is able to remain in the soul of man.

7. Always be prudent in your words; that is, first think and then speak; do not let your tongue run ahead before you think what you have to say. Do not become bold in talking much, my child; many are the evils from this evil boldness. Flee from it as from fire or a viper!

8. Guard yourself from boldness in talking and untimely words; they dry up the soul of man. Silence, meekness, and the prayer, on the other hand, fill the soul with heavenly dew, with a mourning full of sweetness. Despise idle talk as the mother of coldness and dryness,[†] for idle talk drives the tears away from our eyes; that is, it takes them away from us and our soul withers.

9. My child, have patience, humility, and love, and guard your tongue, for when it defeats a person, it becomes an irrepressible evil for him, sweeping away also other people in its course and casting them down into the abysses of sin. Yes, my child, you must guard your mouth so that your heart may be kept pure. And when it stays pure, God comes and dwells in it, and then it becomes a temple of God. The holy angels rejoice to be in such a heart! Likewise, drive away filthy thoughts with anger and the prayer; the prayer is a fire that burns and expels the demons.

10. Be careful with your mouth, but primarily with your mind; do not let evil thoughts start talking with you. Do not let your mouth say words that could perhaps wound your brother. Let your mouth put forth words which are fragrant, words of consolation, courage, and hope. It is a person's mouth that reveals his interior, his inner man.

11. Struggle, my child, as much as you can to become forceful—force yourself in everything, especially in silence and in mournful tears. When silence is practiced with knowledge and maintained with tears, the foundation stone of monasticism is set, on which the secure house will be built wherein the soul will find spiritual warmth and comfort.

It is a bad omen for the soul's future if silence is not kept, since one who is not silent scatters whatever he gathers; for a monk who is free with his mouth will be disorderly in every-

---

[†] The Elder is using the words "coldness" and "dryness" in their metaphorical sense, of course, in reference to the soul's lack of fervor and spiritual "moisture" that is necessary for the seeds of virtue to grow.

thing. When we are silent, we have the time for interior prayer, which brings full assurance, and the time for luminous thoughts, which fill the intellect and heart with light. Therefore, my child, compel yourself in everything, for the good beginning is praised, but the negligent beginning is censured, for its end is most lamentable.

12. We have so much material offered by the devil, the world, and our carelessness to talk about idly, so many events and stories that are taking place and will take place, that we have plenty to occupy ourselves with; while "the one thing needful," to approach God through prayer, we have laid aside. Our need for this spiritual turning to God is so urgent that nothing else should preoccupy us other than how to be close to God by means of prayer and holy thoughts, which also greatly help us achieve this goal.

Saint
Isaac
the
Syrian

"Above all things,
love silence."

Chapter Ten

On Pride, Self-Reproach, and Humility

Be attentive to your thoughts. Your attention should mainly be turned to gathering humble thoughts. For humility saves man, and it is the chief aim of all spiritual pursuits. To see whether you have made spiritual progress in monasticism, search yourselves, and if you discover humility within yourselves, then you have made spiritual progress in proportion to the amount of humility you have. If instead of humility we see pride and egotism and their consequences, then we need to grieve and weep and mourn for our miserable condition, that the Lord may have compassion on us.

Let us flee far away from egotism; it emits an unbearable stench, and miserable is the person who possesses this as his wealth. Such a person will never find peace, not only because of the annoyance of the passions lurking in him, but also because he is far away from true humility. Rest for the soul is only granted to man through humility and meekness. This is what the Lord says to us: "Learn from Me, for I am meek and lowly in heart, and you will find rest for your souls."[1] For this reason, my dearly beloved children, let us love with all our soul the humility of our Christ together with His meekness, and then indeed we shall find, just as He said, manifold repose for our souls.

---

[1] Mt. 11:29

It is not easy to acquire humility; much labor and time are needed. To put egotism to death requires that we sacrifice ourselves. Let us trample our ego underfoot and embrace perfect self-denial. Let us fall in love with obedience, and then with bloody struggles, by the help of God, the death of the ego will be achieved.

Onward therefore, my children, let us run like athletes in the stadium of the glorious race, where the victor will be crowned with the unfading crown of eternal glory before the lofty throne of our most sweet God. I beg you, do not lose courage in the battle, for the Lord with a hidden hand will strengthen us so that we will vanquish the demon of egotism, and He will clothe us in the divinely woven robe of holy humility.

I write you these things and pray that these few words will fall like seeds into the good soil of your souls and bear a hundredfold the fruit of life eternal! Amen; so be it.

2. If we have struggled to acquire humility, we have inherited a luxurious garment. If we have love, we have prepared this garment most elegantly. If we have obtained unquestioning obedience, we have beautified it with colors and luster. And if we have labored at unceasing prayer, we have sprinkled it with the fragrance of the choicest myrrh. After we perfect it in this manner, we shall wear it and appear at the judgment seat of Christ with boldness and heavenly joy. Then the Lord of glory will smell a scent of spiritual fragrance and joyously open the infinite treasures of graces to us. Then indeed we shall be rich!

3. You, my child, should look only at yourself. You lack humility; your pride and obstinacy are causing those thoughts which you wrote about. If you humble yourself, if you blame yourself in all temptations and believe that you suffer them because of your passions and that the Elder and the brothers are not at fault, then immediately you will sense relief from those thoughts, and your wounds will heal. If you expect to be healed by any other means—namely, that the Elder or the brothers change—you labor in vain. Evil requires eradication from the root, and its root is pride, egotism, obstinacy, the will, anger, etc. All these are healed with one medicine: by casting the burden of the error and temptation on yourself. Always say: "It is my fault; I am the cause; because of my passions I suffer; the cause of my evils is no one else but me, the thrice-wretched one."

Yes, my child, this is the highest truth, the true reality. Walk in accordance with what I advise; walk along these guidelines, and you will truly find the health and cure of your soul.

4. Since we have pride—whether apparent or hidden without our realizing it—God, desiring to purify us from this stinking condition, raises a storm in order to cast out all the "dregs" which have accumulated mainly in a time of spiritual negligence.

All kinds of rubbish and refuse are thrown into the sea, especially in the harbor, and if there were no storms, the sea would become a source of pestilence. But the fact that the sea is pure and wholesome is due to the occasional storms.

Spiritually, the same thing happens with our soul, with the sea of our soul. Refuse accumulates little by little from our various passions and careless deeds, and the devil throws in his own trash, too. We do not see how much refuse has accumulated. God knows, however, and since He wants to purify us, He stirs up storms in proportion to the accumulation of refuse, and thus He purifies the sea of our soul. Sometimes, after we pass through a temptation with patience, we see that our soul is calmed, joyful, and light as air. On our part, we must be careful not to accumulate refuse, so that storms of corresponding magnitude do not become necessary.

Storms are stirred up also in saints, but those are of another nature, they have another purpose: sometimes a trial helps them become more holy, or it is for their greater glory, or it is so that they may glorify God more, or it has to do with the storms raised against Orthodoxy, etc.

See to it, my child, that you have much humility, obedience to the advice of your Elder, and love for all, and that you never trust your thoughts, but follow faithfully the suggestions of your Elder.

5. Never become overconfident in yourselves; never accept the thought that you are good and virtuous. Reproach yourselves; accuse yourselves inwardly in order to slay your ego, which is the wall that blocks the Sun of Righteousness, Christ, so that His rays do not reach us to illumine our nous with the knowledge of God and of self.

Love humility in everything, for our Jesus showed the example for us. When? When He girded Himself with a towel and washed the feet of His disciples and said, "Do you know what I have done to you?"[2] That is, just as I humbled Myself by washing your feet, you too should humble yourselves to one another.

6. Learn the monastic way of humility: whenever you are ordered to do something by the Elder, say, "May it be blessed," and whenever he censures you, say, "Bless." Through humility, contact with the divine occurs sooner, for our Christ says, "Learn from Me, for I am meek and lowly in heart, and you will find rest for your souls."[3] Rest for the soul is the truest sign of a healthy soul.

Humble yourselves, degrade yourselves, abase yourselves, that the peace of God may come into your souls. Do not jus-

---

[2] Jn. 13:12
[3] Mt. 11:29

tify yourselves when the Elder reproves you for one of your faults, but say, "Bless."

7. Let us love the humble disposition, my child, and if the Lord pities our nakedness and sends us some ability to pray and clothes our soul with some divine garment, we must be cautious lest we soil it out of carelessness: that is, through pride, criticism, negligence, disobedience, etc. But let us make a greater effort to whiten it through good works, especially through humble-mindedness and self-reproach. God is pleased more with these than with great works done with vainglory.

Always have perfect obedience. Obedience is the offspring of humility. Whereas back talk, quarrels, and disobedience are the offspring of pride, which a monk must hate as the causes of his soul's defilement.

8. Always seek in your prayers first and foremost that God grant you humble-mindedness. Persist in this request of yours, for without true humble-mindedness nothing good or worth a reward is achieved.

Just as the Apostle Paul says: "What do you have that you did not receive? Now if you did indeed receive it, why do you boast as if you had not received it?"[4] "Everyone that is proud in heart is an abomination to the Lord."[5] Therefore, my child, struggle against this miserable passion by being humble-minded and contemplating what great humility the Lord of glory showed in becoming man and humbling Himself to the point of abuse, slander, and the Cross. But also all the holy people of God showed exceptional humility, by which they became holy and attested to us that there is no road leading to salvation other than this.

Espouse whatever gives you humility, even if it hurts and makes you feel as if you were dying. The outcome of the pain

---

[4] 1 Cor. 4:7

[5] Prov. 16:5

will be a blessing from God and progress towards the most excellent of virtues, humility. I pray that our God, Jesus, will grant you this indelibly within your soul.

9. The whole essence of the matter, my child, is this: you are being attacked by a spirit of pride along with her sisters, vainglory and arrogance, along with their helpers, filthy and blasphemous thoughts.

Know, my child, that the spirit of pride is difficult to overcome; the spirit of vainglory is many-headed and thorny. No matter how you change your thoughts or your way of life, you will find it in front of you like a thorn. And if this is how things are, what can we do? We should employ every means, whether mental or material, that leads us towards humility. Above all we have to coerce our mind to think humbly, and leave it to divine providence to arrange the deliverance from or reduction of this passion. On our part, we should persevere with a fighting spirit, and God, in proportion to our struggle, will intervene as a succor and helper.

About the dreadful passion of vainglory, St. John of the Ladder says: "Vainglory till the tomb," that is, until we die we will be attacked by vainglory, with the difference that it will be weakened by the war against it and by long experience of its falsehood.

Weep before God so that He grants you a spirit of humility, for only through this will you advance towards higher things, towards the love of God. Spiritual progress is nothing but the acquisition of humble-mindedness. Jesus, even though He is God, humbled Himself so much, and we who are lowly by nature exalt ourselves and fluff out the feathers of vainglory like a peacock. However, when He throws us into some temptation and we peacocks see the ugliness of our feet, that is, the rotten condition of our soul, then we recognize what we, the race of Adam, are by nature, and that our pride is not humbled except by slaps and falls.

Tears and mourning bring much humility, therefore ask patiently from the Giver of good things. Pray: "Do not overlook me the prodigal one, O Thou Who wast born of a virgin; do not overlook my tears, O joy of the angels, but receive me in repentance and save me."

I pray that Jesus, the humble of heart, may give you His heart, so that you may experience His humility.

10. Humility is a wonderful virtue, which makes fragrant the one who has it. He who has humility also has obedience, love, patience, and every virtue. When we get angry, or become enraged, or criticize, or do not obey, it is evident that we have a corresponding amount of pride and egotism. The more we progress in humility, the more the evil offspring of egotism will retreat.

My children, let us humble ourselves for the Lord Who humbled Himself for us. The Lord showed so much humility, even to the point of crucifixion. So shouldn't we, who are lowly by nature, bow our head to our brother? Do we expect always to get our own way?

If we want Jesus to dwell within our heart, let us love and humble ourselves like Christ. Let us not grieve Him any more with egotistic manifestations. Let us not crucify Him again with expressions and conduct lacking brotherly love. No more bitterness in the holy heart of our most sweet Christ.

11. The angels were in Heaven in glory and hymns; men were happy in their mansions; but God the Creator was within a cave and in a manger of animals, as the last pauper! What humility of our Jesus! Acquire this humility, my children. Humility is the most grace-filled virtue, a garment interwoven with gold. Blessed is the one clothed in it; he will acquire an ineffable spiritual beauty. On the contrary, the most filthy passion is egotistical pride.

12. I entreat our Panagia very much that she grant me humility in all things, for it is a fundamental virtue, and without it the grace of the All-Holy Spirit does not validate any of our work!

When the Archbishop of Alexandria, Theophilos, visited the fathers of Mount Nitria, he asked the Elder of the mountain, "What have you found, Father, more than us in this way of asceticism?" And the venerable one replied, "To reproach myself at all times." "Truly," replied Theophilos, "there is no shorter road to God than this!"

Didn't Lucifer and Adam fall away from God through pride and rebellion? Wasn't Adam saved by the humility of the Theotokos—"Behold the handmaid of the Lord; let it be to me according to your word"[6]—and of the Son of God, Who was born of Her without change, Who taught and practiced extreme humility? He also said, "Learn from Me, for I am meek and lowly in heart, and you will find rest for your souls."[7]

Whenever a person looks upon himself with humble thoughts and self-reproach, he will see in his soul a sweet repose, peace, consolation, relief, and hope! While on the contrary, what shows him his pride of soul is restlessness, agitation, wrath, boasting, haughty tendencies, and so on.

Ah, how effortless the road of humility is! Even without laboring ascetically or enduring illness, a person with humility and self-reproach, along with thanksgiving to God, is able to reach spiritual heights and feel the gift of sonship! While on the contrary, toiling ascetically without realizing one's own infirmity and weakness and wretchedness is a struggle without prizes, sweat without wages, a road without hope.

---

[6] Lk. 1:38
[7] Mt. 11:29

What a misfortune to struggle without profit! To cultivate without reaping! Why does this happen? Because the struggle was not lawful. "If someone competes as an athlete, he is not crowned unless he competes according to the rules."[8] Even in physical competitions an athlete is not crowned if he does not struggle lawfully.

13. Our holy God lets temptations come upon those who love Him in order to teach them the art of war. The grace of God withdraws and then clouds of temptations rise and one reaches the point of saying, "See! God has abandoned me!" Then he has myriads of thoughts, strangulation of soul, and darkness and lapses everywhere!

Holy Wisdom, our holy God, causes all these, and we learn that only God is able to save us and that without God all our own works are rubbish and chaff, which all scatter with the slightest wind of temptation, and it becomes apparent that we are rusty things, feeble and unable to face any temptation whatsoever without the aid of our holy God's grace.

Through such things the grace of divine providence teaches us the lesson of self-knowledge—that is, of true, cognizant, solid, bedrock humility—for without it, it is impossible to build a spiritual house. He abandons us to the point of despair, so that we are compelled to cry out to Him mournfully and lamentably, so that our mouth and heart may be sanctified.

Temptations, therefore, bring about all these things. Indeed, let us pray that God will protect us from temptations, but when they come, we must pass through them with patience and wisdom to profit from them. Therefore, have patience in all things and thus save yourself.

14. My child, as a rule you should have continual self-reproach. In every controversy, do a prostration first; thus you receive the crown first, and you cause your brother to repent.

---

[8] 2 Tim. 2:5

At all times reflect on the Lord Who humbled Himself, so that your soul is ready to endure every kind of humiliation for His love.

That which plays the most important role in the spiritual struggle is for a person to learn to humble himself, reproach himself, and justify his neighbor. Whoever has learned this philosophy is surely gathering already the most sweet fruit of freedom from passions. Otherwise, he will drag his passions along with him to his great and constant grief.

My child, reproach yourself constantly. Do not consider yourself to be right; whenever you hear something bad being said about you, say, "My brothers are right; that is how I am. I deserve even more slander because of my sins."

Always consider yourself lower than everyone and refrain from giving orders as one having authority. In short, humility in everything.

15. Always reckon yourself as very sinful and polluted, so that Jesus Christ may have sympathy for you and send you mercy and forgiveness of your many sins. Have obedience to all the brethren; become last of all, the lowest, if you want your passions and weaknesses to depart from you. Never justify yourself, neither in word nor in thought, but always condemn yourself as the one being at fault and deserving many blows. Have faith in the Elder, show obedience and love to his words, and confess frankly each of your thoughts, for frank confession is characteristic of a humble soul.

16. Reproach yourself continually, for self-reproach is an offspring and fruit of a humble heart, and in a humble heart the Divine manifests itself, as it knows best. "Blessed are the pure in heart, for they shall see God." Examine each of your falls carefully and you will perceive that, to a greater or lesser degree, the seed of pride was the chief cause of the fall.

17. Keep in mind the existence of your ego: it causes every evil. Humble yourself; strangle your ego, which comes like a venomous serpent to poison your soul. Do not allow any proud thoughts to remain within you; only thus will you foil every activity of Satan.

The holy Triodion[†] begins with the beautiful example of the Publican and the Pharisee to instruct us that through a humble mind anyone can acquire justification, that is, the forgiveness of his sins from God. Likewise this parable also reveals the great evil—pride—which acts as a mighty obstacle to the forgiveness of sins, in spite of practicing all the other virtues and especially almsgiving.

From this and from many other Scriptural truths, we are taught that without humility and true repentance a person cannot be saved, even if he prospers in the other virtues.

18. Do not be obstinate, but humble; do not think that you are something, for this is pride, and God loathes the proud. My child, always assume that you are the most sinful person in the world and that, if the grace of God abandons you, you will do all the evil things in the world! Always accuse yourself.

Whenever you go to receive Communion, accuse yourself as unworthy to receive Christ the Master within you who are so sinful. You must weep when you receive Holy Communion for Christ to have compassion on you for your sins.

"Learn from Me, for I am meek and lowly in heart, and you will find rest for your souls."[9] Do you see, my child? Meekness is the fruit of humility, and both bestow God's blessed rest.

Grass does not sprout in trampled ground; likewise, passions and wickedness do not sprout in a humble soul. As long as we lack humility, God will not stop humbling us through trials, until we learn this serious and lifesaving lesson.

[†] The Triodion is the period of fasting and repentance preceding Pascha.

[9] Mt. 11:29

19. Onward, my children! Gird yourselves with the spiritual towel of Christ's humility[10] and submit to everything, so as to receive the Lord of all in your heart. Our Christ does not rest in a soul lacking the fragrance of humility, but rather departs because of its malodorous pride.

I entreat you with all my heart, detest talking back, quarreling, disobedience, self-will, boldness, and every other passionate state, for all these drive away God's love and bring bitterness into the soul instead.

Be sincere in everything you show and express: do not tell lies; speak the truth. Do not look at the spiritual illnesses of your brethren struggling together with you, for you will be greatly harmed. But rather, sympathetically overlook their illnesses for the sake of the Lord, so that He may also deem your own illnesses worthy of sympathy.

Never think anything great about yourselves, lest you be not abandoned by the grace of God, which is guarding you, and a great trial befall you.

20. There is no greater evil than egotism. It gives birth to all temptations and troubles, and woe to whomever it entangles—it will deform him! Only the good disciple will make his soul angelic with spiritual beauty. Do not let time pass unfruitfully, for the yarn is being wound, and suddenly we shall hear, "Put your house in order, for you will die; you will live no longer!"[11]

Strike egotism with all your might; learn humility. Work with contrition, with mourning, with the fragrance of humility. Only deeds which have humility will be rewarded. The deeds poisoned by egotism and self-will will be taken by the four winds and scattered like rubbish, and we shall be left empty-handed.

Let us come to our senses. Let us rejoice with the unadulterated love of Christ, for passionate souls will not enter into

---

[10] vid. Jn. 13:12

[11] Is. 38:1

the heavenly Jerusalem. Only pure souls will enter there with joy and delight.

21. Yes, my dearly beloved children, truly we lack this most holy virtue, humility. Egotism, this evil wickedness, has caused all the sufferings of man. Indeed, humility is holiness!

Why do we clash over a trifle? Because we do not have humility. He who has humility wards off troubles. Without true humility, troubles remain intact and increase, such that all hope of correction is lost. A humble person does not remember any past wrongs which his neighbor did to him, but with all his heart forgives and forgets everything for the love of God. Beg our humble Jesus in your prayers to give you a spirit of humble-mindedness and meekness.

22. Humble yourself and reproach yourself. Do not justify yourself, even if you are absolutely right, for self-justification is not conducive to the healing of our spiritual illness.

My daughter, try to please the Eldress, and the Spirit of God will overshadow you. Become a humble bride of Christ. The egotist is abominable to the most beautiful Bridegroom Christ. The Bridegroom is humble and meek; will the bride be a proud, ill-tempered soul?

If you want to be fragrant, embrace a humble, simple, obedient, and meek spirit. Despise egotism as a stench and stupidity. You do very well to reproach yourself in everything. This path is most true to the Fathers. Yes, my child, implant this manner of life deeply within your dear little soul and you will benefit enormously.

23. What is more beautiful than spiritual forcefulness? Indeed, it gives a hidden but perfect joy along with a holy, promising future.

Therefore, my child, struggle in holy self-reproach. Continually reproach yourself; cast the blame upon yourself and cry out: "My Jesus, here too I am at fault; neither the devil nor any person, but my evil self is at fault, because I don't pay attention to where I walk. Cast light upon the path of my life, send the dew of humility into my heart, so that I may feel Thee, my meek and humble Jesus. Do not disregard my tears, O joy of the angels, but accept them as a fragrant scent and grant me the petitions of my heart, so that I may find relief, and chant as an ecstatic youth the triumphal hymn of Thy glory."

Concentrate on yourself and see everything with a simple eye and as something that need not concern you. Work according to your strength and with a pure conscience. Pray for yourself and for all your brethren. May your love cover everything and may you fly over snares like a soaring eagle.

24. Be careful, my daughter, with your way of life. Be more meek, more tolerant; be humble, yielding. All these are characteristic of self-knowledge.

Blame yourself, saying, "If you think that the sisters scorn you and do not pay attention to you, and so forth, they do well to you. You are getting what you deserve for your deeds. For if you were worthy of attention, they would regard you; but because you are unworthy, an egotist, a grumbler, God allows this for you to be humbled. So how long will you fail to understand that you are such, and worse!"

By this and other means, smite yourself as with a club in order to smash the head of the dreadful beast which is called egotism! It is responsible for everything. Therefore, let us direct all our efforts against it. And if with God's help we humble it, immediately the vile passions of the bipartite[†] man will wither.

Reflect that God has given us everything: body, soul, mind, heart, earth, air, nourishment, breath, freedom in Christ, faith

---

[†] According to the Holy Fathers of the Church, man is bipartite, consisting of soul and body. In 1878, a local synod in Greece condemned a theologian named Apostolos Makrakis (1831-1905) for promulgating the heretical teaching that man is tripartite in composition (i.e., body, soul, and spirit).

in Him, His heavenly Kingdom, deliverance from hell, the holy mysteries, the holy guardian of our soul, and, above all, His invincible power, which He gives us in our battles; moreover, He has even given Himself to us.

How and for what can I boast, since God has given me everything and I have nothing of my own? Even if I think something good, the source of good is God; even my mind which thought it is God's. I have done something spiritual, and whether the heart or the body did it, both are God's. What is mine is the will, yet even the will is aided by Him. So all things derive from the true source, God.

What do we have, my child, that is not from God? From this point on we enter the domain of self-knowledge, of humility. What is the universe, in comparison with God's infinitude? Then what part of anything is man because of his nothingness, who boasts and is proud of his nothingness?

So this is the unshakeable truth: "His truth will encompass you like a shield."[12] With these truths you are very capable of opposing Satan powerfully.

25. Fight the good fight, my child. Do not fear; break away from every fetter of despair. God chose the weak and useless in order to shame those who think themselves healthy and useful. The power of God is more clearly manifest in weak creatures, and at the same time this choice of God pushes us towards involuntary humility, and impels us to send up like fragrant incense unlimited thanksgiving and gratitude to Him!

My child, God has shown much love to you. Therefore remain in God's bosom with humility, that you may be exalted with divine enjoyment.

Be careful of the spirit of arrogance. Do not think that you have something that others do not have, for the Holy Spirit

---

[12] Ps. 90:5

distributes Himself to each one of us as He wills. To one He appears as love, to another as wisdom, to another as knowledge, to another as great fear of God—one and the same Spirit. That is, all partake of the Holy Spirit, not according to one's works, but according to one's humility!

Nothing else in the absence of good deeds is capable of making us sons of God, other than the realization of our own weakness and the majesty of God. Without humility, our work lacks the seal of approval. When it partakes of humility, immediately it becomes valid.

God seeks useless beings: "Go out into the streets and into the roads and find as many as are poor, maimed, sick, lame, and compel them all to come in so that my house may be filled, for those who were called, who considered themselves blameless, shall not taste my Supper."[13] How joyful it is that we, too, are included among the useless beings because of our weaknesses and that He has called us into His house to make us His courtiers and friends, so that we may hear in our heart's chamber the divine voices of the heavenly bodiless powers!

You see, my child, that the evil one is lying when he tells you that you are physically useless and are not fit to be a monk. It is important that the soul be healthy—humble, that is—with self-knowledge. God does not desire an offering of health in order to give grace, for He is not a human with needs, but God without needs. It is He Who allows sicknesses, too. And once He has healed the soul through them, He has achieved His purpose. Health of body is not necessary to Him; love and humility are necessary to Him and beneficial to us.

26. Thoughts of both pride and vainglory are formidable and difficult to fight against. But before the humility of Jesus, they literally lose their strength. "The truth shall set you free from every sin and passion."[14]

---

[13] cf. Lk. 14:21-24

[14] cf. Jn. 8:32

The Holy Fathers write: "When you see Pilate and Herod reconcile, know that they are preparing to kill Jesus. And when you see vainglory and pride attacking you, know that they are plotting to destroy your soul!"

Fear and trembling should seize you when you discern such thoughts; for in proportion to the magnitude of your pride, the providence of God prepares to chasten you with trials so that you may learn to think humbly.

Force yourself to be humble, and when you see thoughts of pride, lay hold of a whip and start lashing yourself.[†] The bodily pain will drive away the pain of your soul, and God, Who sees how much you are struggling, will provide you with the corresponding strength, for according to our intention and struggle, Jesus sends His almighty power.

Just think how many people have preached, written, and dogmatized; they filled the world with books, as did Origen, who wrote many books and saved many people and strengthened a multitude of others to become martyrs; yet in the end he was labeled as the founder of a heresy and fell away from God.

Alas! How much evil does pride create in man! God reckons no man's works as his own, since man is merely a faucet, a tap—not the spring! And how can the faucet consider the water flowing through it as its own work, since it knows that the spring causes the water to flow? Even so, forgetfulness is a most evil teacher of the soul, for had it remembered the truth, it would not have gone mad.

What made Lucifer fall? Was it not haughty thinking? Let this be a lesson for us, for one acquires experience and caution not only from one's own misfortunes, but also from one's neighbor's.

How did great ascetics, who had renounced everything, fall and reach the point of demonic possession and then return

---

[†] The Elder is not referring to masochism, but suggests counteracting sinful inclinations with physical pain. Similar techniques were used by Sts. Benedict, Epiphanios, Nephon, and many other saints.

to the world so that monasticism was blamed? They fell because they thought that they were better and more virtuous than the others, and that they were supposedly accomplishing something.

27. Since we already know very well that the hunter of our souls has set and laid traps everywhere, let us not be drowsy. Whether at a store or in town, in the comfort of one's family or even in the church of God, we must watch out for the traps that happen to be set under the pretense of piety. Who is able to be delivered from these camouflaged traps and ridicule their masterly craftsman?

Behold—let us use the broad experience of our holy monastic Fathers to destroy them. They teach that it is essentially only the exalting virtue of humility that is almighty—a sword of the Spirit that destroys evil at its root and completely disables the traps of the tempter. So let us toil to acquire this most salvific virtue of humility, which destroys the devil!

28. Once a demon met St. Makarios the Great and said to him, "Makarios, what do you do more than we do by sitting in the desert? I reside in the desert, too; you fast, but I never eat; you pursue poverty, but I own nothing. Ah, Makarios, you have one thing that vanquishes me that I am unable to resist."

"What do I have?" asked Makarios.

"HUMILITY! It burns me!"

And as soon as he said this, he disappeared.

Let us make a little effort to acquire this saving virtue. The effort consists of constantly beseeching our God, Who is able to grant us everything. Let us be assured that we shall receive this virtue when with pain and patience and persistence we knock at the door of mercy, which opens easily when we use the key of the wronged widow in the Holy Gospel.[15] Let us shake off the burden of indolence, and let us imitate the clear-sightedness of the deer by quickly hastening to our God at every temptation and by seeking His assistance. In this way we can defeat Goliath the barbarian and glorify the majesty of the kingdom to which we belong—the majesty of the Kingdom of God.

29. When the evil spirit of pride fights against us, we shall never stop falling. But falls make us aware of our wretchedness and help us attain humility. Then Christ comes, Who is humble of heart and meek in soul. Then joy, peace, and sweetness will reign in our soul, and blessedness will warm our heart.

30. Compel yourselves, my children, in the spiritual struggle. Do not forget the vast experience of the devil and our own weakness. Just as a leaf in autumn falls at the slightest wind, likewise we fall at the slightest temptation or trial when the grace of God does not assist us. And when does the grace of God assist us? Only when humility guides our every thought and deed.

31. May true and genuine humble-mindedness increase in your soul, through which the fruit of the soul is preserved. Satan tries to make those who struggle forget their goal. He succeeds in doing so if he can make them grow proud so that they think it was by their own progress and forcefulness that they acquired this or that virtue. In this way, the labor remains without a reward—a struggle without hope, work without pay.

32. The voice you heard saying to you: "Christ has purged you of your sins and deadened your passions," is from the devil. It is the first stepping stone that leads man to delusion and destruction. If one listens and pays attention to him and his heart is sweetened and he accepts these words of the devil as

---

[15] vid. Lk. 18:2-5

true, immediately the devil comes more tangibly to him, and gradually he is overcome. Then it takes much toil to be freed.

This is why, my child, you did well not to pay attention to that voice, and to criticize yourself instead. Next time you hear something, say: "I will tell it to my Elder and will do whatever he tells me." The devil greatly fears confession to one's Elder, because he knows that all his traps will be ruined!

You should realize, my child, that thoughts of conceit (of pride, in other words) have sprouted within you, and this is why this happened to you. Be careful. Have much humility. Every day entreat God to grant you a spirit of humility. Just as nothing grows on a trodden path, likewise no delusion grows in a trodden humble spirit.

Excerpt from a Homily, "On Humility"

We need to be very careful; let us attend to ourselves and fear God. Fear is light, it is a lamp; the beginning of wisdom is the fear of God and the end of wisdom is the fear of God.[1]

Fear precedes even the love of Christ. When the love of Christ is acquired, fear is still mingled with love, for love can lead one to take liberties and thus depart from proper love. Fear is the brake that restrains a person.

Whenever we see within us malice, envy, criticism, grumbling, and whatever else is of the devil, we should realize that we do not have a pure heart. If we had a pure heart we would not be offended even if people insulted and derided us. The fact that we are offended, bothered, embittered, shows that our heart is not pure.

We lack humble-mindedness; humble-mindedness makes a person tolerant, forbearing, patient. When we do not have patience, when we do not have forbearance, when we are not tolerant, when we do not endure patiently, this is characteristic of a lack of the most fundamental virtues—humble-mindedness and love—which take us closer to the goal, which is purity. When genuine spiritual love and humble-mindedness do not exist, then we have not reached our goal.

A person does not need erudition and great knowledge to achieve purity. When I reflect that I have sacrificed everything in order to reach this goal, I cannot make excuses to justify myself. If we make excuses, we are defeating the purpose. It is not so much a question of whether or not the other person is at fault, as it is whether or not I really love my brother, or whether or not I feel that my heart is heavy. It is my fault; I need to change my soul and love him, even though

---

[1] cf. Prov. 1:7

within myself I feel bitterness towards him because he reproved me once or because he does not think well of me.

If I have a dark and somewhat bitter image of him within myself, this burdens only me. That brother may indeed be thus inclined towards me, but thinking like this does not help me reach my goal. No matter how that brother is disposed towards me, if I want to reach my goal and be united to God, I must see him differently. For this reason the Fathers never justified people, especially monks, if they had something against someone.

One father was going to bring another brother to trial, or rather, prosecute him. So he went to Abba Sisoes and said to him:

"Father, I am going to bring charges against my brother because he has done such and such an evil to me." "Forgive him, pardon him."

"No," he answered, "if I pardon him he will do it to me again. This man must be punished."

"Eh, fine, my child. Let us say a prayer and then go."

So they knelt, and Abba Sisoes began praying: "Our Father, . . . and do not forgive us our debts, as we do not forgive our debtors. . . ."

"That's not right, father," he said, "you made a mistake."

"Since you want to take your brother to the judge, this is how we will pray."

Then the brother realized his mistake, repented, and did not go to denounce his brother.

So there is one great truth: just as our heart is disposed towards our brother, in the same way the heart of God will be disposed towards us. Do you want God to forgive your errors? Do you want Him to love you with all His heart? Then you too should love and forgive with all your heart.

Do you want God to forget your errors and not remember them? "I want it, I desire it," cries the soul. Then no matter how your neighbor has wronged you, neither think about it nor remember it. This is the enormous truth. So whoever departs from this goal will make many and great mistakes in his life. If we apply this patristic wisdom, the devil will have no power over us.

Let all of us be attentive and compel ourselves, so that we do not lose our goal and repent bitterly tomorrow. We must keep these things in mind and work as if it were our last day.

Our aim is one: to come to see ourselves, to see our own guilt, and to reprove ourselves in everything, to criticize ourselves, to consider ourselves responsible and guilty, and to pay no attention to whether our neighbor is guilty or not.

The Fathers say, "If we desire to bring peace to ourselves by trying to reconcile others, we shall never have peace." That is, if we want to derive peace from others becoming peaceful, we shall not be at peace. So a person must find peace within himself, internally. "Make peace within yourself," says Abba Isaac, "and then Heaven and earth will make peace with you."

Let us ingrain this indelibly within our heart, for this is the spiritual wealth that the holy Gospel and the patristic texts give us to save our wretched souls!

dionysiou monastery
mt. athos

Chapter Eleven

On Love and Forgiveness
towards the Brethren

My children, fight the good fight;[1] let brotherly love continue;[2] may love be the center of all actions within the synodia—may egotism be far from your thoughts and words.

"Whoever wants to be first must be the slave of all,"[3] says the Lord. And if we do not become like little children in terms of innocence and simplicity, we shall by no means enter the Kingdom of Heaven.[4]

When love governs a synodia, Christ invisibly blesses everything; joy, peace, and self-sacrifice for the brethren are afire in the heart of every brother—but also prayer intensifies then. The more love abounds, the more love in Christ and self-sacrifice enriches their souls, and then Christ is glorified and worshipped, and we become humble instruments for the glorification of the holy name of God.

Genuine love does not envy the good gifts of one's brother; it does not rejoice when it hears humiliating words or criticism of a brother; it does not restrain itself from constantly commending a brother's progress. Love does not envy; love does not parade itself, does not behave rudely,

---

[1] 1 Tim. 6:12
[2] cf. Heb. 13:1
[3] Mk. 10:44
[4] cf. Mt. 18:3

does not seek its own, but its brother's interests; it is not provoked; it thinks no evil; it bears all things, endures all things.[5] Whoever has genuine love never falls by sinning against his brother.

So my children, pray that Love itself—our God—will grant you the gift of love in Christ. When this love comes to reign in our hearts, words, and deeds, then we should hope for prospects of forming a synodia in Christ with a Christian spirit, with spiritual radiance and an unshakeable foundation—a synodia closely united with one mind and one soul in many bodies.

2. My beloved children, I pray that the God of love will strengthen you in mutual love and give you the love that does not act wickedly, that does not create scandals, but rather averts them with the wisdom it engenders.

I pray that the Lord will give you pure love—love which guards the mouth of him who possesses it and does not let him fall into the pit of criticism, malicious gossip, lying, hypocrisy, and the countless other evils which the lack of this true, godly love begets through the tongue.

"He who has love abides in God, and God in him."[6] The evidence that we are of God and that we love Him is when we have true and unadulterated love for one another. "Whoever hates his brother is a murderer"[7] and is in spiritual darkness and does not know where he is going.[8]

We have received a very important commandment from our Lord Jesus: to love one another. Likewise, the devil has given a commandment to those who obey him, that they hate one another. Therefore, we are disciples and subjects of him whose commandment we keep.

My children, let us fear coldness and enmity towards our brethren, as well as the various thoughts that accompany

---

[5] cf. 1 Cor. 13:4-7

[6] cf. 1 Jn. 4:16

[7] 1 Jn. 3:15

[8] cf. Jn. 12:35

these attitudes, which little by little lead the soul to demonic hatred. For in this manner we subject ourselves to the devil—the enemy of our salvation—as to a master, and then innumerable evils will accumulate in our poor souls!

Love is the base, the foundation, and the roof of the soul that possesses it. When such a soul has the God of love dwelling within it, it rejoices splendidly at every moment.

In a monastery, mutual love among its members is extremely necessary for its establishment and preservation, because love is the golden link that unites the brethren in every way in a closely knit body, which will withstand the temptations that the lord of enmity and hatred—the devil—will always create. Love is that invincible power that holds the members together in one body, with the abbot as the head. And every time it is necessary, this power will fight against the other completely opposite power of evil, which will endeavor to break off members from their unity.

When we are lax and slack in love, the opposing power of the devil will have victories for its side corresponding to the laxity that our previously fervent and powerful love has suffered. What are the victories of the opposing power? Troubles within the brotherhood, such as back talk, disobedience, quarrels, pride, bragging, envy, hatred, and finally, deserting the monastery!

Let us reflect, my children: do the angels in Heaven perhaps talk back, disobey, do their own will, bear malice, hate, or desert the place where they serve before the throne of God? Of course not. This is what Lucifer did, who was once a rising star, and was cast down and became Satan!

Therefore, since we have worn the angelic schema, aren't we also obliged to live in an angelic manner? How can you be considered to be living an angelic life when I see amongst you back talk, complaining, self-will, enmity, and, worst of all, disobedience? By doing such things, wouldn't you be doing the opposite of what you have been counseled to do by my lowliness? Won't you receive a greater condemnation by doing the opposite, according to the scriptural saying that "he who knows and does not do shall be beaten with many blows"?[9] That is, he will be strictly chastised with many terrible blows and punishments.

Let us fear disobedience to counsels, my children, because every transgression and disobedience inevitably receives a punishment.[10] On the contrary, let us struggle to apply them. Be obedient to what you have been advised to do, so that you may receive the unfading crown of love and obedience when the trophies and crowns are given by the Judge of the contest, Jesus Christ.

I pray that the Christians' Champion Lady of the world will count you worthy, through her prayers and those of all the saints, to receive this unfading crown of eternal glory!

3. My child, see to it that you drive away the evil thoughts which the devil urges you to *consent** to—especially thoughts of hatred towards the brethren you should pay no attention to, because he aims to steal from you the greatest virtue: love. And if he achieves this, he has completely won your soul. Once we have lost love—God, that is, for God is love and he who abides in love abides in God and God in him[11]—then what is there left to save us?

My child, do not listen at all to these thoughts of hatred towards the brethren, but drive them away immediately, and start saying the prayer, or tell Satan, "The more you bring me thoughts of hatred, devil, the more I will love my brethren. For I have an order from my Christ not only to love them, but even to sacrifice myself for them, just as Christ sacrificed

---

[9] cf. Lk. 12:47

[10] cf. Heb. 2:2

[11] 1 Jn. 4:16

Himself for me, the wretch." And at once embrace the things about them that annoy you, and say, "Just look how much I love them, O envious Satan! I will die for them!" By doing this, God sees your good intentions and the method you are using to conquer the devil, and He will come at once to your aid to deliver you.

4. I pray that the all-good God will send down upon you the All-Holy Spirit, as He did to His divinely sent Holy Apostles, so that you may be enlightened to walk the arduous path of salvation. "Behold now, what is so good or joyous as for brethren to dwell together in unity with love?"[12] There is nothing more beautiful than for a synodia to be replete with godly love. Then, everything is radiant; everything is full of beauty, while God above delights, and the holy angelic spirits rejoice above where love is boundless. "Love one another, as I have loved you. By this all will know that you are My disciples, if you have love for one another."[13]

O love, whoever possesses you has a truly blessed heart, for within love, what could one possibly want and not find! Humility, joy, patience, goodness, compassion, forbearance, enlightenment, and so on, are all there. But in order to obtain this supremely wondrous love, we must constantly call upon the God of love to give it to us. When the name of God is remembered through the prayer "Lord Jesus Christ, have mercy on me," it contains within it eternal life, and eternal life is the God of love! Therefore, he who prays this prayer obtains true, godly love.

So, onwards; behold the way and means of victoriously conquering love. Take courage and bravely proceed into the battle. Say the prayer constantly: orally and noetically. It is more beneficial to say it orally during the day, because at that time the nous is scattered by one's work.

---

[12] cf. Ps. 132:1
[13] Jn. 13:34,35

5. The beautiful road of love is effortless, and there is neither blemish nor stain in love, but rather the conscience testifies that the soul has boldness towards God. But when there is no love, the soul has no boldness in prayer, and as one defeated and cowardly, it cannot lift its head because it feels remorse for not having loved as God has loved it; it is a transgressor of the commandment of God.

If we do not love our brother whom we have seen, how can we love God Whom we have not seen?[14] He who has true love has God; whoever does not have love does not have God in himself. The Holy Fathers say, "If you have seen your brother, you have seen God; your salvation depends on your brother."

The holy monastic fathers of old walked the path of salvation effortlessly, because they sacrificed everything so that they would not fall away from love. Love was their goal in life. Our path, though, is completely strewn with thorns which sprouted because we lack love. And this is why when we walk, we constantly bleed. The foundations of the house shake when we do not lay the foundation of love well.

6. Compel yourself, my child, for the sake of your soul. Compel yourself to comfort the brethren, and the Lord will comfort you—He will give you His grace. Have patience, have patience. Let everyone treat you like dirt, and He will give you His grace.

Great is he who has more humility. God gives grace to the person who has fear of God and obeys everyone like a small child and constantly seeks God's holy will. Such a person never seeks that his own will be done, but the will of God and of the others. He always says, "As you wish, as you know best." He does not give his own opinion because he considers himself lower than everyone. When they tell him to do something, he eagerly says, "May it be blessed."

---

[14] cf. 1 Jn. 4:20

So, my child, this is what you should do, too. This makes the demons tremble, flee far away, and not approach anymore. They are very afraid when they see humility, obedience, and love towards all.

7. My child, just do your duty. If the others do not obey, leave it to God and be at peace. It is due to the devil's jealousy, my child. Will the devil go out perhaps to the mountains to create temptations? He goes wherever people are struggling for their salvation. And since we, too, are seeking our salvation, he jumbles us up without our realizing it.

Carry the burden of the brethren. God rewards everyone justly. The time will come when you will see how much He will give you for the pains you went through to look after so many souls. Labor in this world; keep helping, and you will never be deprived of God's help. Now you are sowing; the time will come for you to reap. Pray that God will make you strong in patience, discernment, enlightenment, etc. I am constantly praying for you, but I have no boldness before God, and thus my prayer bears no fruit.

Just think what the Fathers went through to save others. It is no small matter; you are helping the others, which is why the devil will take it out on you and afflict you. So start showing patience and bravery, and say: "I am ready to die in the battle helping my brethren to be saved, but God will not let me perish, since I am doing it for the sake of His love."

Yes, do so, and you will see how much strength and joy you will receive in the struggle. For sometimes impatience, despair, and pessimism deprive a person of God's grace, and then he wrongly attributes it to the burdens he is bearing. But courage, self-sacrifice, bravery, and faith in God bring the grace of God. I pray that God will invigorate your spiritual nerves to fight with renewed strength.

8. Abide in the bond of mutual love, for love is the beginning and the end—the foundation. It is on love towards God and your brothers that "all the law and the prophets hang."[15] Without love we are a clanging cymbal—a big zero. According to the Apostle Paul, even if we give our body to be burned for Christ and distribute our belongings to the poor and mortify our life with harsh asceticism for Christ, yet lack love, we have accomplished nothing.[16] Therefore, with all our strength we must see to it that we keep a strong hold on mutual love, so that our trivial works may be approved by Him Who examines the secret thoughts of our hearts.

9. You write, my child, about someone who kept grieving you, and you cursed him, etc. No, my child, do not curse anyone, no matter how much he has harmed you. Our Christ tells us to love our enemies, so how can we speak evil? Seek forgiveness from God, and henceforth love him as your brother, regardless of whether or not you agree with him. Didn't Christ on the Cross forgive his crucifiers? Then how can we do otherwise? Yes, my child, we must love everyone, regardless of whether they love us or not—that is their business.

10. My child, always justify your brother and reproach yourself. Never justify your deeds. Learn to say, "Bless"—in other words, "Forgive me"—and humility will dwell within you. Have patience and overlook your brother's faults, remembering God's forbearance towards your own faults. Love as Jesus loves you and as you want others to love you. Hold on to silence, constant prayer, and self-reproach, and then you will see how much mourning and tears and joy you will feel. But if you fail to hold on to them, in other words, if you neglect to apply them, then coldness and dryness will replace the above graces.

Love the brethren. Your love will show when, despite all your brother's weaknesses, you count them as nothing and

---

[15] cf. Mt. 22:40
[16] cf. 1 Cor. 13:13

love him. Love will keep you from all sins. Think of nothing but your own sinfulness. Reproach yourself constantly—this is the best path.

11. I pray your soul is in good health, for when it is healthy, it has patience in afflictions, it has self-denial with the body and in its thoughts, and it fears neither illnesses nor selfish thoughts. When the soul is healthy, it has love within itself; it does not scandalize others; it endures a brother's harsh words; it does not expose his faults in public; it always has something good to say about his brother; it gives way in quarrels and escapes having bitter thoughts and distress. When the soul is healthy, it does not get angry, complain, talk back, murmur, disobey; it does not follow its own whims, and it does so many other things indicative of spiritual health. This health is what I seek from you; this is what I advise; for this do I pray.

12. *(To a struggling Christian)*

First Letter

Put up with that person who grieves you and creates temptations. Put up with him joyfully. Pray for him every day. Always try to do good to him, to commend him, to speak to him with love, and God will work His miracle and he will reform. Then our Christ will be glorified, and the devil, who sets up all the stumbling-blocks, will be foiled. Force yourself especially to stop criticizing and lying. Your penance is to do one *prayer rope** every day for this person who hates you, so that God may enlighten him to repent, and do ten more metanoias daily for one month.

If this person does something against you, overlook it, be patient. Let yourself be wronged, but do not wrong; let yourself be slapped, but do not slap; let yourself be criticized, but do not criticize. When you do all this, then the Son of God, along with the Father and the Holy Spirit, will dwell in your soul. Fight the good fight;[17] overlook the deeds of this person, just as our Christ has overlooked your sins.

Second Letter

I rejoiced to find out that you are compelling yourself to defeat in this way that person who harasses you so much. Yes, my child, love always conquers. Pursue love, humility, purity. Keep doing a prayer rope for this person. Christ shall enlighten him. The devil is behind it all. When Christ drives the devil away, your brother will become like a little lamb.

13. Give preference to your brother in everything. Let deference towards others characterize you. In the name of God, do not quarrel, do not criticize. These are not actions of a monk, but of a worldly person far from God. You are dedicated to God; whatever He wants is what you should do—this is what should govern your conduct towards others.

When you see that you are quarreling, etc., you should realize that you are doing the devil's will and that God is greatly distressed. The angels who see you say with sorrow, "What's wrong with him that makes him fight? Doesn't he take into consideration God's commandment to love?" Whereas, when they see you sacrificing yourself for the love of Christ, they rejoice and glorify God, Who gives His grace so that man may conquer the devil.

14. I entreat you, my child, compel yourself to show brotherly love. A monk without love is spiritually dead. Do not judge anyone; do not say things that are unnecessary, useless, harmful, and unbecoming for monks.

Why did you leave the world, my child? Wasn't it to become holy? Wasn't it to have genuine godly love? When you complain and judge your seniors, can you possibly be fulfilling the goal for which you have withdrawn from the world?

---

[17] 1 Tim. 6:12

How long will the devil laugh, and when will you start repenting and correcting yourself? Time is passing and the end draws near. We must compel ourselves now; now everything can be rectified—later we will bang our heads against the wall to no avail.

15. It is now the eve of holy Theophany. Oh, what condescension! Naked, He entered the waters of the Jordan! Who did? He Who is the Logos of the beginningless Father, Who said of old, "Let there be. . .," and lo, everything came into being in front of Him! Naked, so that He would bestow sonship upon us, who were spiritually bare.

When the Jordan saw the Invisible One visible, the Fleshless One incarnate, it was frightened and turned back its flow! St. John the Baptist trembled and said, "How can a servant baptize his Master, how can a lamp illuminate the light?" Which light? That blessed, triple-sun light, "which gives light to every man coming into the world."[18] The beginningless Father bore witness to His co-beginningless Son, while the Comforter descended in the form of a dove and remained on the immaculate head of Jesus, confirming the certainty of the word.

Every Christian soul rejoices and leaps for joy before the grandeur of the mystery of Theophany! Oh, what a God and Father we have! Ah, this heart of God which loves man so much has been ignored, forgotten. He cries out through the prophet: "Can a woman forget her child and have no compassion upon the offspring of her womb? Though she may forget her children, I will not forget you."[19] "For if when we were enemies we were reconciled to God through the death of His Son, how much more, having been reconciled, shall we be saved by His life!"[20]

Oh, how much comfort these words of the Apostle Paul give to a newly repenting soul! A soul that shows compassion

---

[18] Jn. 1:9

[19] Is. 49:15

[20] Rom. 5:10

and sympathizes with its neighbor in words and deeds has great boldness before God!

Once, when St. Andrew the Fool-for-Christ was feigning foolishness in the middle of Constantinople, the spiritual eyes of a God-fearing woman were opened, and in a vision she saw blessed Andrew shining brighter than the sun. People were striking him, spitting at him, loathing him, while the demons were rejoicing because they would condemn them at their death, since they were beating and tormenting in every way this saint of God! But St. Andrew said to the demons, "No—I have entreated God that this not be counted as a sin for those who strike and torment me"!

Then Barbara—that was her name—saw Heaven open, and a huge dove descended with a flower in its mouth and sat upon the head of blessed Andrew and said, "Accept this flower, which the Father of lights has sent to you because you are merciful towards those who strike you, just as He is merciful." Around the dove were countless little birds of every kind, chanting heavenly songs to the delight of his blessed soul, which suffered so much for Christ!

Shortly thereafter, the vision ended. When the blessed one approached Barbara, by the Holy Spirit he knew of her vision and said to her, "Keep this a secret, Barbara, until I leave this life, until I go to the place of the wondrous tabernacle."[21]

A merciful soul resembles God and has great boldness towards Him! May God give us a compassionate, merciful heart, so that when we depart, we may find God's heart open and full of mercy, compassion, and love! Amen. So be it!

16. Great is our honor—though we are unworthy—to have been called by God to serve as His tools in the work of saving souls, but let us bear in mind that if others (apostles, etc.) had not sacrificed their lives for our sake, we would not be children

---

[21] cf. Ps. 41:4

of God and heirs of heavenly blessings. Therefore, let us do whatever we can; the work will be completed by Him Who has the power to perfect it.

Think about how the first Christians struggled during the times of the catacombs; with what self-sacrifice, with what love they sacrificed things dear to them when Christian duty called. And in the end, their sacrifices brought them eternal glory.

Oh, we are unworthy, and unfortunately we lose everything because of our lack of faith—and I am the first amongst those of little faith. But we hope that the Lord's mercy will strengthen us, so that we, too, may humbly bear a small cross for our solace.

17. Blessed is he who endures the harsh words of his brother in silence and circumspection lest there be hatred or criticism or rancor in his heart. He resembles Christ, Whom, when He was casting out demons from people, the Jews criticized by saying, "He casts out demons by the ruler of the demons,"[22] and "He has a demon. Why do you listen to him?"[23]

Do you see, my child, that they said such things even to Christ? Therefore, do not be upset. If you are patient, if you humble yourself and say, "Indeed, I have many demons— since every passion is a demon—and I am just as my brother says, and even worse"; if you try to love and obey him, the day will come when you will be freed from the passions, and then Christ will reign in your heart and give you the priceless peace of God.

18. Do not ruin salvific love for trifles; do not harbor suspicions against each other and create bad conditions within yourselves that corrupt your souls. Fear the judgment of God; woe to him from whom the offense comes.[24]

---

[22] Mt. 9:34

[23] cf. Jn. 10:20

[24] cf. Mt. 18:7

Do not justify yourselves; take the burden of any matter upon yourselves, and then you will experience much benefit in your soul. But if you justify your actions and judge your neighbor and your brother, you will always feel sorrow and distress as a punishment for your transgression.

A monk without self-reproach isn't worth a penny, nor will he ever make any progress. Consider whatever the elder tells you to be the will of God and that the Lord speaks through his mouth. Only when you think like this will you practice obedience the way our Christ wants you to.

19. The Lord will condemn to eternal fire those who create temptations. Sincerely love one another—not falsely and superficially, but with spiritual depth. Our Christ showed us so much love that His holy example should become a holy reason for us also to love one another similarly.

If we do not show love through our deeds—not only in words—in vain do we labor in our struggle, for we are beating the air[25] and are straying from the goal of our salvation. Let us not be deceived, thinking that we shall be saved while neglecting the basic virtue of love. If we are not characterized by the unadulterated love of Christ, in vain do we run, in which case all hope of salvation is lost.

20. Regarding your question, my brother in the Lord, if we should correct our fellow human being when he is ungrateful, unfair, etc., or if we should not in order to be rewarded for being patient, I shall answer: If you think that he will benefit through admonitions and advice, we should do so, choosing to benefit our brother rather than ourselves, thus performing the greatest virtue, love. If you think that no benefit will result from your admonitions, choose your own benefit by putting up with his ingratitude and injustice.

---

[25] cf. 1 Cor. 9:26

Chapter Twelve

On Trials and Temptations

God allows temptations so that they might rouse us to remember Him. When we call upon Him, He acts as though He does not hear us so that we multiply our supplications and cry out His holy name, in fear of the various passions. Then, through the pain of the entreaties, our heart is sanctified, and through experience we learn the weakness of our lame nature. And thus we realize in practice that without God's help we are not able to do anything.

This deep experience is acquired with the blood of the heart and remains indelible; it becomes a foundation for the remainder of one's life. The grace of God leaves and comes again, but experience never leaves, because it has been branded within the heart. And no matter how much Satan praises the heart, it points to what is indelibly written within its depths, that without God it is impossible to do anything.

If there were no temptations, then pride and other passions would have turned us into other lucifers. But our good Father, God, allows afflictions to come upon us so that we may be guarded by humility, which will lighten the burden of our sins.

When we are still in our youth, we must be tempted, for youth is easily derailed. In time the war will cease and the desired peace will come. Just have courage and patience. Do not despair, no matter how much the passions may fight you. God loves one who is fought against and fights back. Be brave, and pray also for me, the indolent, the unclean, the unworthy, the abomination!

2. If a trial benefited the Apostle Paul—as he said: "A thorn in the flesh was given to me, an angel of Satan to torment me, lest I be exalted above measure"[1]—how much more will trials benefit us when we bear them patiently?

The Apostle Paul was a chosen vessel, the mouth of Christ, dead to the world, one in whom the whole Holy Trinity dwelt. And even though the trial hindered his apostolic preaching, and even though he entreated God so much to take away the trial, God, looking after the benefit of his soul, did not fulfill his prayer—although he besought Him three times—but he received the answer, "My grace is sufficient for you: for My strength is made perfect in weakness."[2] My grace, He said to him, is sufficient for your consolation; you will have this trial in order to benefit by acquiring more humility.

Therefore, my children, bear with joy whatever trial God sends you, whether it be grief or ferocity of the passions, for God sends them to us for our benefit, in order that patience in all these things may be considered as asceticism, which we are otherwise unable to do. So thank God; glorify Him with your mouth and heart, because the consolation of grace will come after the trial when we bear it with patience and thanksgiving.

Is there anyone who has entered paradise by a different path, a path without temptations, whom we can imitate? No. All the saints passed through fire and water, through various temptations and afflictions, and they glorified God with their patience and received crowns of eternal glory!

---

[1] 2 Cor. 12:7
[2] 2 Cor. 12:9

Do not lose courage in the struggle; our Christ is invisibly standing by, observing the struggle of each one of us. Therefore, struggle patiently; call out the name of our Jesus, so that it may be implanted within your hearts and so that you may become rich in the grace of God. Struggle to acquire a pure intellect, so that you may feel the grace of the Holy Resurrection.

3. Two kinds of grace are acquired when struggling according to God: one is the comfort of the Holy Spirit, Who fills the soul with joy, peace, delight, etc.; the other is called experience of temptations. This grace of experience is indelibly imprinted upon the soul, that is, it does not leave a person, because it is united with the heart which experienced the temptations. Whereas the first, the grace of the Holy Spirit, sometimes comes and sometimes goes.

In a time of temptations, the second grace, experience, is more beneficial because it enlightens the soul how to pass through them. Since experience comes from temptations, it knows how to free the soul from danger whenever it comes.

So temptations, when we bear them with patience, bestow upon us the wisdom of temptations, and thus we become true philosophers. If we do not humble ourselves, instruction through temptations is not going to cease. Egotism creates temptations, but temptations in turn subdue the ego.

Therefore be humble, my child, if you want the demons who oppress you to be humbled. Throw yourself beneath all and say, "I am the worst person in the world and everything is my fault."

4. Struggle, my children, struggle. No matter how much the enemy fights against you, take courage and we shall overcome him. We have our Christ, the Commander-in-Chief Who said, "I have overcome the world."[3] We, too, will over-

---

[3] Jn. 16:33

come it; just do not lose hope. God will not overlook the supplication of anyone who has hope and calls upon Him, if he prays humbly.

Humble yourselves. Do not think highly of yourselves, and you will attain lofty things. The more gold is tried in the fire, the purer it becomes. And the more a Christian is tried by temptations, the more his soul is purified. The more deeply we plow the earth and the more often we prune and look after the vine, the sweeter and more abundant will the fruit be. The more deeply and frequently afflictions and temptations plow the heart of a Christian, the more pure and fruitful he will become.

Therefore, have courage, hope, and patience to receive the crown of glory! Temptations and afflictions will save us, whereas whoever flees from afflictions should not expect joyful things to come.

5. Do not grieve for what has happened. May His will be done always, and let us say, "May it be blessed."

I pray that you acquire monastic forcefulness. All people suffer. We are blessed, because for the sake of Christ we show patience in temptations. For the monk who endures them patiently, temptations will cause an eternal glory that far outweighs them all.[4]

We owe thousands of thanks to the sweetest Heavenly Father, Who providentially allows painful events to occur in our lives, so that we will not find ourselves in the other world incapable of showing that we endured something for the sake of His love.

Courage, my children; do not fall to your knees on your way uphill. We shall ascend little by little because we are weak. All will pass and be forgotten on the never-ending day of the glorious common resurrection.

---

[4] cf. 2 Cor. 4:17

6. You wrote me about your temptations, my child, but it is clear that whoever wants to walk the road of God—the road of *purification,** sanctification, and dispassion—must first consider the necessary commitment he will shoulder. That is, he must be prepared to encounter temptations regardless of their origin, and to be powerfully forged in the virtue of humility.

We are full of egotism, my good child, and since we are ill with this great illness of irrational egotism, naturally it follows that we undergo a painful treatment—that is, temptations—for several years, until we learn humility in practice. The Lord of glory wore humility; it is a God-adorning virtue. However, my good child, it is acquired with the blood of the heart. "May it be blessed." "Forgive me." "I do not know." "Whatever you want." These are the words of a humble monk—a clear sign of progress.

Concerning the matter of the brother who afflicts you, you must be patient. Be tolerant, overlook his faults, be philosophical about it, and reproach yourself for being more ill spiritually in other ways and not having been tested yet, and therefore, it is improper for you to speak.

7. The grief which you wrote about, my child, is clearly from the devil, because one who has confessed his sins must believe that they were entirely forgiven, and all grief must be banished without delay; so he must rejoice that God pitied him and enlightened him to wash his dirty garment by means of a frank confession, and should have good hope for the salvation of his soul. This untimely grief has destroyed many. Therefore, do not grieve at all; "Rejoice, and again I shall say rejoice."[5]

8. Every time a person falls, my child, he must arise, and he will be saved. When someone falls and voluntarily does

---

[5] cf. Phil. 4:4

not get up, this is from the demons. Despair is a demonic weapon which has broken down many; hope, however, has saved many from the filthy pit of mire.

9. Satan leads us astray—and me, first of all—because we do not show patience and thus we lose the profit of each temptation.

There was a monk who entreated God to deliver him from the passions. So God took the passions away from him and gave him dispassion. Then he went to an experienced abba and said to him:

"Geronda, I have found rest from the passions and am at peace" (he was still young).

"Listen, my child," said the great Elder to him, "go and entreat God to bring the passions back to you, for man profits not in dispassion but in warfare, because dispassion is not labor but rest. In temptations a person is perfected and becomes spiritual, whereas without temptations, he remains unwise, uneducated, and useless."

Therefore be patient, no matter what fights you. In these end times that we are living in, let us not expect anything other than temptations, and they will save us!

10. The darkness which you have, my child, comes both from nature and from the tempter. Both are healed by the arrival of God's grace. For this reason, entreat God to give you sobriety and the ability to remember good things and forget bad things. When you persist, little by little the grace of God will help you.

11. My blessed child, I pray that the Lord of glory will give you the finest spiritual gift for your soul, so that your heart leaps from the divine joy and peace.

As for temptations, they are inevitable, and we must realize that they are not about to subside, so we must always be ready to show patience. In any case, the wages of the one who patiently bears the infirmities of the weak will be great, for he will have suffered much and it is very just that he be rewarded proportionately.

I pray that you will become as strong as granite, on which all the billows of temptation will break, and that you will remain unshakeable in faith towards God.

12. Be patient, my child, be patient. It is for us to acquire humility that we are allowed to be tempted. These are medicines which cure our sick souls. Rejoice that God is caring for your wounds. Bless Him that He considers you His child and disciplines you in order to teach you wisdom from His Law. "Blessed is the one whom You will discipline and teach," and "What son is there whom a father does not discipline? But if you are without discipline, then you are illegitimate and not sons."[6] But our temptations testify that we are children of God, and this is cause for much joy and honor. So take courage, my child. "Wait patiently for the Lord and do good."[7]

13. My child, we must understand that we shall pass through this present life with many and various temptations. We shall often water every step of our life with bitter tears and sighs. It is in this way that the all-wise God wanted man to live. But even He Himself did not escape this law, since the whole life of our Christ was a life of afflictions and trials. Who among men can demand to escape fulfilling this common law? No one! Therefore let us be brave, fighting valiantly in each oppressive adversity of this life, until the divine command calls us to abandon the present things and depart to the eternal dwellings.

14. Sometimes a person seeks the will of God or to be delivered from some passion, and God allows some predicament to befall us which will bring the desired result. But at

---

[6] cf. Heb. 12:7-8
[7] cf. Ps. 26:14

first sight the thing seems arduous, and he thinks that it is a temptation due to his carelessness. Yet when the benefit ensuing from the predicament or the temptation is revealed, it is seen clearly that hidden within it was God's will or the deliverance from the passion for which he had begged God.

Thus we learn that in each temptation we need patience and forbearance in order to ascertain what is hidden within it once it passes. Many times a temptation happens which, at first glance, does not seem to conceal anything salvific within it. Yet afterwards, we see that within it is eternal life!

15. Just as night succeeds day, winter eventually succeeds summer, spring succeeds winter, and so on, similarly one spiritual state succeeds another.

Today, for example, I am in a good state in terms of purity of thoughts, and my soul glides like a dolphin in a tranquil sea. Everything is peaceful, and you think that it will continue like this forever. But the road which the wisdom of God has mapped out does not change its course. And behold, in a corner of the sky little clouds, simple unhealthy ideas, arise in the horizon and gather in the sky, in the mind. Soon afterwards, the wind begins; thunder follows; the sea becomes rough, and before long a tempest of thoughts is formed. Thus a state of bitter thoughts, etc., succeeds the purity, and various disturbances follow the calm.

If those who fear God lacked the various trials and temptations, some of us would have ended up in satanic pride, others in debauchery worse than Sodom, others in the darkness of unbelief and impiety, and so forth. So then, it is to afflictions that we owe this little piety of ours, as well as our hope of salvation.

One who is physically ill abhors the bitter medicines and painful operations. However, he endures patiently, knowing that the physician effects his health through these things. And when he gets well, he renders many thanks to the physician for the good which he did, and no longer remembers the pain, because it has passed.

We should also understand spiritual matters in the same way. All the various afflictions make the one afflicted abhor them, but they result in the cure of the soul's spiritual members. And if those afflictions had not been sent by God, the great Physician, that sickly member of the soul would have constantly grown worse, and then the soul would have been poisoned and suffered spiritual death, which is separation from God. Therefore, we ought to thank God in every situation so that we do not fall away from piety.

The Apostle James teaches us beautifully concerning this matter: "My brethren, count it all joy when you fall into various trials, knowing that the testing of your faith produces patience."[8]

Temptations attest to the inner state of each person. When many kinds of storms appear, it is then that the nautical experience of the captain shows. And godly afflictions reveal who the Christian is.

"Take away temptations and no one would be saved." This does not mean, however, that we should lead ourselves into temptation on purpose, but as we struggle according to God and look out for ourselves, we shall encounter temptations coming from His fatherly endearment, from the demons' envy, from our carelessness and inexperience, from the cunning of men, etc. But the goal is one: to struggle with patience and perseverance, reflecting that nothing happens without the will of God. Therefore, we need patience and gratitude.

---

[8] Jam. 1:2-3

St. Nilos the Ascetic

Chapter Thirteen

On Faith, Hope, and Patience

L et not your heart be troubled, nor let it be afraid."[1] My children, trust that God will not allow us to be tempted beyond our strength; along with the temptation will come the help of God.

Our Christ tells us that if they hated Me they will also hate you;[2] if they persecuted and blasphemed and cursed Me, they will also persecute and blaspheme and curse you. And they will do these things to you because they do not know God and "they know not what they do."[3]

We, my children, know God, and because we love Him and are His, the world hates us, since it does not agree with Him. Therefore have courage, my children; we are followers of the One Who was crucified by them; so we too will be crucified by trials and temptations. Just as He was resurrected, we too will be resurrected and glorified together with Him unto the ages of ages.

The devil has raised a storm, but it will die down because God is all-powerful, and nothing can happen without His divine will. God is with us. Christ reigns within us, within as many of us as were baptized into Christ, and we are not afraid. Perhaps we shall enter into temptations, but our Deliverer is near, for He said, "I have overcome the world."[4] There-

---

[1] Jn. 14:27
[2] cf. Jn. 15:18
[3] Lk. 23:43
[4] Jn. 16:33

fore, we will also be victorious, even if the sea surges threateningly for the moment. Do not be afraid of anyone; fear only God Who is able to cast us into the fire of hell, if we are not careful.

So, "Blessed are those who are persecuted for righteousness' sake, for theirs is the Kingdom of Heaven."[5] Do not forget what the Christians of the past suffered in order to keep their faith in our Christ: they hid within the catacombs; they were persecuted and afflicted. We also are blessed, who are persecuted because of our desire to worship God and to guard our chastity.

We shall go through much. But in the end, the crucified Jesus will be victorious, for the Cross is our glorious banner. So do not fear; God is with us.

2. Trust in God, Who has created them and keeps them under His care. For if a leaf does not fall from a tree without His divine will, how much more shall the affairs of a man, His son by grace, a Christian, be under His care? But the devil, who knows your weakness, troubles you with it in order to harass you.

When we have laid our foundation on trust in God, the foundation is on the rock, and even if the winds blow and thunderstorms come, they will not overcome us. But when we have laid our foundation on trust in our own efforts, the foundation is on sand and we shall easily fall.

Do not grieve; everything will pass. This is how the path of those who are being saved is marked out: in torments and afflictions.

3. Why are you gloomy and devoured by grief? The spirit of grief requires self-consolation for you to overcome the thoughts of despair from the evil one. When you listen to any suggestion of the evil spirit of grief, you will never be able to

---

[5] Mt. 5:10

see the joy of hope. Everything written in the divine Scriptures was written for our admonition, so that with them we may fight back against the one who deceived us, the pernicious dragon.

When the greatly compassionate father saw the prodigal son coming, he hastened to embrace him, kissed him tenderly, and abhorred neither his filthiness nor his whole inward and outward wretched condition. Who can describe his paternal feelings when he embraced his beloved child, whom he had considered dead and lost but then saw alive and returning in repentance? His actions showed his feelings: immediately he raised him to his original position as son and heir.

To whom did the revered mouth of the Lord say these things? Was it not to us for our consolation, so that when the tempest of despair tosses us about, we may tie our boat to the saving anchor of hope in the love and compassion of our Heavenly Father?

The Lord founded His Church on earth as His bride, to intercede for His children. He left us the great mystery of the divine Eucharist so that we may be purified, sanctified, and united with God. If the blood of bulls and goats purified sinners in the Old Testament, how much more will the Blood of Christ purify us from all sin! "For if the blood of bulls and goats and the ashes of a heifer, sprinkling the unclean, sanctifies them for the purifying of the flesh, how much more shall the Blood of Christ, Who through the eternal Spirit offered Himself without spot to God, cleanse your conscience from dead works?"[6]

The devil, who out of hatred and envy does not like to see a person spiritually happy, stirs up everything in order to cause bitterness and poison. This is his joy and gain. But as for us, let us keep striving to produce self-consolation through spiritual means, opposing his various machinations.

---

[6] Heb. 9:13-14

Who has ever hoped in God and was put to shame? And who has despaired and was ever saved? The devil fears a person who hopes, because he knows from experience what a greatly compassionate God we have. If the child who hopes in his own father will never go wrong, how much more will he who hopes in the Father of fathers, Whose love cannot be compared with any other love and is as far from any other love as the Heaven is from the abyss! If someone sins fatally ten thousand times but exerts himself in repentance with all his strength, as long as he hopes, he will never be put to shame.

For whom did our Christ suffer? Was it not for our souls that are wounded by the dragon? "And whoever looked upon the bronze serpent was saved."[7]

You too, humble soul, should hope in the sweetest compassion of our Heavenly Father, Who never loathed or rejected anyone. He receives everyone; the boundless space of His compassion is never filled. He has mercy on the first and likewise does not exclude the last, but receives all equally out of His great goodness.

The more sinful the penitent, the greater the honor given to the compassion of God. "Glory to Thy compassion, glory to Thy dispensation, O only Lover of mankind."

4. Why do you worry and grieve more than necessary for the various incidents? We are not outside of divine providence, so as to be directed by mere chance. Therefore, whatever happens to us happens with God's knowledge, and so nothing will happen to us beyond our strength!

Let those who do not believe in divine providence drown in worry; they are certainly justified. But we, who believe that God is present everywhere and that there is no creature outside His providence, are not justified when we worry more

---

[7] Num. 21:9

than necessary, for through this action we show a lack of faith and illumination.

"Blessed is the man who hopes in God, for as a lion he will trust in Him."[8] If God is the One Who permits it, Thy will be done, Lord. "Who has known the mind of the Lord? Or who has become His counselor?"[9] Who is able to search out the will of the Lord! "If you do not become as little children, you will by no means enter the Kingdom of Heaven,"[10] that is, through faith and innocence.

5. A dreadful storm was raised on the sea of Tiberias. A threatening wind was trying to sink the tiny little boat of Jesus and His disciples. The disciples were terrified. No one was resting, except the Lord of life and death. "Arise, Master," they cried out in despair, "we are perishing!"[11] Then He Who holds all in His hand arose and rebuked the sea and the wind, and there was a great calm. Let us also believe in the power of our Jesus, and the tempter will surrender his weapons and there will be a great calm.

For whose love do you bear afflictions? For whose sake did you jeopardize your very lives for the sisters? Out of love, whose command are you carrying out? You will answer, "For the love of our Christ, in Whom we hope that all things, through His power, will have a good ending."

Good, very good—for He is the One Who numbers all the hairs of our head. How could we think that anything will happen without His willing it? And if we are protected by divine providence, what are we to fear? Should we not rather fear Him Who is able to put us into the fire of hell on account of our sins?

Instead of having courage and pride in our Christ unto His glory, Who counted you worthy to struggle in this way, you, on the contrary, are filled with grief and thoughts and mur-

---

[8] cf. Prov. 28:1

[9] Rom. 11:34

[10] Mt. 18:3

[11] cf. Mt. 8:25

muring. I repeat: you ought to be proud that God deemed you, the base and unworthy, worthy to become instruments of His divine providence for the salvation of select souls, for whom our Christ died. Do not grieve, for God's sake! Do not seek to lose your reward, which will be great in Heaven.

Preaching the divine word is the smallest virtue, but sacrificing ourselves for Him is PERFECT LOVE—that is, to lay down our lives out of love for our neighbor. Certainly this virtue is laborious and dangerous, but are any high offices attained without labor and toil? Let us not forget the meaning of the divine Crucifixion, that we also ought to become small saviors, when the time calls for it, by the divine will.

Let us see God as our Father; let us rest in the warmth of His secure embrace, for He knows how to arrange everything for our benefit. As humans we—and first of all, I—lose courage in the beginning, so that our human weakness shows; but then the good Cyrenian, divine grace, comes and bears our cross and thus we ascend Golgotha more easily.

Wasn't our Christ afraid in Gethsemane? What were the great drops of holy sweat for? These and other things characterized the human weakness; but afterwards, as God, quiet and meek as an innocent lamb, He sacrificed His life for the sake of ungrateful man.

6. Let us bear everything patiently, that we may gain the God of all. When we patiently bear sufferings, immediately the future blessings are confirmed. When we are deprived of the joy of this world, then without a doubt, we store up the joy of God in our immortal soul. It is impossible not to enjoy with an everlasting recompense the good which we are deprived of here!

Let us give a little here on earth so as to receive it with interest from the impregnable treasury of the gifts of God. Let us sow the seeds of virtue so that we may crown our heads with most fragrant flowers in a crown of eternal glory.

7. We should not find it strange if the passions and sicknesses war against us, but rather we should entreat God to give us patience, that great balm for the wounds of the soul as well as of the body. Patience is the one and only diamond which beautifies the Christian and makes straight the rough road of our salvation. Patience is the fortitude of the soul, the support, the deep root that holds the tree when the winds beat against it and the streams strike it.

When you fall, rise, and when you sin, repent. Just never let the poison of despair penetrate into your heart, seeing the great sea of God's compassion. No matter how many sins one commits, they go away and vanish in the sea of God's goodness.

8. Wholeheartedly thank God, Who loves you—as I can see—very much. For if He did not love you, you would not be as you are. You think that you are lost, etc., but I see that spiritually you are very well off. Just do not despair; do not lose hope. He who has hope will by no means be put to shame.

Even if someone is covered by an abyss of sins, if he repents and does not lose hope, the devil fears him, because the paternal heart of the Heavenly Father yields when His prodigal son says, "I have sinned." He runs first, embraces him, kisses him, and kills the fatted calf in celebration, for His son was dead and is alive again.[12] The despair of the sinner is completely unjustified. Is a handful of sand ever able to cover the ocean?

9. Blessed is a man who has a living hope in God; he shows faith, trust, glory, and honor to Him. God is then obliged to keep him in His providence, and the saying of the

---

[12] cf. Lk. 15:19-24

holy Gospel applies: "As you have believed, so let it be done for you."[13]

But unfortunately, temptations come to us, creating great spiritual confusion, and the bright sun of sweet hope is covered by deep darkness. Then we lose our orientation and end up thinking and doing something unbecoming to our calling as Christians. But the goodness of God, Who knows that the mind of man is inclined to evil from his youth,[14] and that men are not able to remain in the height of Christian perfection, gave us glorious and endless repentance.

10. Have patience, my children; do not lose your courage in the struggle, and do not let your knees weaken under the pressure of temptations, for our good God will not allow us to be tempted beyond our strength.

Why do you give room to Satan to war against you with greater intensity? Have faith in God, and whatever He permits will be to our advantage. Do we perhaps know better than He?

Cast your care upon the Lord, and He will take care of you. Do not put forth your will, for faith is the offspring of grace and divine visitation. Has not each one of us experienced personally miracles of God's divine providence? Didn't divine grace visit N.? If you had not sacrificed yourselves, would N. be in the army of Christ now? Didn't Christ sacrifice Himself for us? Certainly! And had He not given Himself to death on the Cross, we would not be what we are by divine grace.

This shows that things that are very good, those that are on a higher spiritual level, are bought with blood. But their reward is so great that it cannot be measured, and their glory is equal to the angels'!

I feel for you, and this is why I also suffer. In times of temptation, man forgets everything and is brought to a state that he did not want in times of peace.

---

[13] Mt. 8:13

[14] cf. Gen. 8:21

11. In general, your thoughts are human. Start trusting in the almighty God, and the four winds will take everything away; "Not a hair of our head will perish."[15] "Christ is the same yesterday, today, and forever."[16]

Bear in mind the temptations of the saints and be calm. Do not grieve, for the demon of the passion fabricates misleading and provocative images in order to induce a bad and dangerous predisposition. Whereas by reflecting on the uncertainty of the time of our death, we become peaceful.

Pray, my children, and do not fear. The Theotokos, our champion, will again give us the victory. Reflect on the precious soul of your sister and its incalculable worth—for Christ died also for her.

12. Be patient in everything; remember that Christ was reviled, slapped, whipped, and finally crucified on the Cross. Since He endured these things for us, we too must endure similar things for His love, but also for the salvation of us who have so many sins.

Regard every evil word they say to you as a golden crown. When one is reviled or spoken to harshly, he feels pain, but this pain becomes a healing balm for his passions, for the wounds of his soul. No virtue purifies the passions of pride and unchastity as much as bearing insults and contempt with patience and silence.

13. I received your sorrowful letter and read it attentively. My soul was filled with pain for you, and I wept and prayed in tears and mourning after reading your letter. Nevertheless, be patient, my child, because God made you like that because He loves you very much. Maybe if you were well, you would not have been attentive to yourself. Whereas now, in your sickness, God gives you so much humility and self-reproach and patience, and He is very pleased.

---

[15] Lk. 21:18

[16] Heb. 13:8

You should always thank Him, for as our Father—which God is—He knows what is advantageous for each soul, and accordingly, as He knows best, gives us various means of salvation, regardless of whether or not we understand it due to our narrow-mindedness and human imperfection.

Endure patiently, my child; God, Who gave you this sickness, knows that hidden within it is much benefit. Every evil has a tinge of good; therefore, endure patiently and it will be counted to you as a martyrdom.

Reflect that all who have entered paradise, the Kingdom of God, passed their lives like martyrs, some in sickness, others in labor, others in pain and persecution. Each one of us bears a cross in accordance with his strength, in order that we all may resemble Christ, Who in His life on earth also bore the Cross for our sake. So if we suffer together with our Christ, only then will we also be glorified together with Him.

14. Never lose hope of salvation. Constantly cry out to God and weep. God never overlooks a soul that wants to be saved and repents, no matter how much it may be wounded in the fight.

God knows how weak our nature is. Where will the clay find the strength to support the pressure of the water, if God does not bake it with the grace of the Holy Spirit? He knows, as the all-seeing eye, that as soon as He leaves us, we fall down and are lost. For this reason, He does not allow us to be tempted as much as the devil wants. Were he to leave us, the devil would cast us all together into hell. But the good God prevents him and allows him to tempt us only as much as each soul is able to bear.

No matter how much we are wounded in the fight, let us not lose courage, but let us take care of our wounds and continue the fight. When God sees our labor and our small desire for salvation, He will give us the victory.

It is a great evil for a combatant to lose courage in the fight, for immediately the adversary pounces ferociously to vanquish him. Therefore, my child, encourage your soul and be hopeful. Say to yourself: "I would rather die in the battle for the glory of God than grieve my God by abandoning my fight against the devil."

15. My child, if only we would have patience and not get tired of seeking divine mercy until our last breath! Why was the Canaanite woman called blessed? She was called blessed for the faith and perseverance which she showed while crying out behind Jesus, "Have mercy on me, son of David! My daughter is severely possessed by a demon."[17] Jesus dismissed her, overlooked her. She, however, showed no sign of keeping quiet, but kept crying out until our Christ grew weary of her— or rather until He had tested her—and granted her request. "O woman, great is your faith! Let it be to you as you desire."[18]

16. Endure all things, my child, as a slave sold for the sake of Christ. People scold, berate, scorn, and do many other things to a slave, yet he endures everything as a man without freedom. You too, my child, should think of yourself like this so that you can endure everything for the sake of glorious slavery to Jesus, and so that our Christ may give you eternal freedom in the heavenly Jerusalem.

17. My child, support the brothers. I know their weight; it does not escape my notice what you bear. But for whom do you endure these things? For Christ and Him alone. So is He not worthy of this? Oh, what good work, what virtue is able to measure up to the love of God and the forbearance which He shows to us? But is it we who are patient, or is it really Christ Who strengthens us invisibly? It is Christ Who helps

---

[17] Mt. 15:22
[18] Mt. 15:28

us; otherwise, who would be able to support such a weight of souls, when we are not even able to support ourselves? The only thing which we must do is to pray that God will give us patience, and we shall try, as is our duty, to bear the weaknesses of those for whom we have assumed responsibility.

Each of us has a burden in proportion to his power; but God perceives our weaknesses and helps us. Do not murmur; do not fall to your knees, my child. It is time to run the race; run in order to take hold of the prize of the heavenly calling. Do not lose courage; Christ is invisibly present. It is for His love that you undertook the struggle.

18. I pray for you that the Lord will give you patience, enlightenment, discernment, and health, so that you are able to navigate the ship of the synodia with wisdom and meekness. Scandals will never cease, inasmuch as the devil exists, who continually attacks us with his evil. Bear without murmuring the weaknesses of your brethren and humble your inner self. But as regards governing the synodia, you must keep your position as Elder.

Have patience, my child. The harvest is in accordance to the labor. Let us labor for God. We should not worry and despair while awaiting our recompense from God.

19. We must do all things with faith and hope, for "whatever is not from faith is sin."[19] No matter how rough the sea of passions becomes, and even if the waves have the power to sink us, we must place our hope in the Lord. Then the waves will break like soap bubbles on the rock of our hope and love towards Jesus.

Do not lose your spiritual courage when temptations surround you, but rouse your zeal with good thoughts, that is, with various sayings of the Lord which give us the enlightenment to deal with every temptation. Let us continuously com-

---

[19] Rom. 14:23

pel ourselves in order to put oil in the lamps of our souls, so that when the Lord comes, He may find us vigilant, filled with the oil of good works. And then, we shall enter into the divine bridal chamber of eternal joy and delight.

The struggle is not small; it does not last for only one day, but until our last breath. Therefore, let us arm ourselves with the sweetest name of our Jesus, so that the devil finds no room in our heart. But to acquire the memory of our Jesus, much diligence, forcefulness, faith, hope, perseverance, patience, and time are needed.

20. Place your hope in our Christ and do not fear the threats of the demons, but establish yourself beside Him and say, "By my God shall I leap over a wall";[20] that is, I shall pass over the barriers of demonic temptations with the power of my God.

Try to make a good start, for then you will have an excellent end. How you begin is how you will continue to walk. Do not disregard your small imperfections and say, "This is nothing." No. Small things will become large and will give birth to other evils as well. He who does not pay attention to small vices will fall into great ones.

21. Do not grieve for anything other than your lack of patience in some matter. This is because when you are impatient, you lose eternal rewards and a great deal of boldness in prayer! Pray that the Lord adds to you a wealth of patience and forbearance, and through these riches you will also make others rich. Do not lose your spiritual courage, I entreat you, but draw this up from mighty faith in God, Who does not allow us to be tempted beyond our strength.

22. My child, be patient with your children. What can we do? Of course they are rambunctious, but they cannot be otherwise. In any case, we must be patient. Do not let things pile

---

[20] Ps. 18:29

up in your soul; do not demand details. For by constantly worrying, you will harm your health, and that will be worse. Just overlook their shortcomings and increase your prayer, for prayer works miracles. And then miraculously, without exertion, they will become calm and quiet children. Many children were very rambunctious when they were small; afterwards, however, they became wonderful in everything. The rambunctious children are usually smart, too, and someday they may achieve much.

My child, do not lose your courage, and as long as I live in this vain world, with God's help, I hope to help you in all of your difficulties. I realize that I am continually burdened with responsibilities, and consequently my free time is reduced. Nevertheless, I shall try to help you with whatever strength I have left over.

23. The road that leads man to the life of dispassion has been strewn with thorns and thistles, and those who desire to walk along it will often bleed and feel pain; many times they will even despair. But they strengthen their hearts in patience till the end, because their hope is in Him Who says to them, "I will never leave you nor forsake you."[21] Likewise, they bear in mind the words of the Apostle Paul: "What tribulation is able to separate us from the love of Christ?"[22]

When someone wants to cross a sea and reach the opposite shore where deliverance awaits him, he ponders it carefully, weighs his strength, and when he is certain that he is capable, he throws himself into the sea and swims. As he progresses, he begins to tire; the waves seem rougher than they did in the beginning; timidity begins to enter his heart. This timidity weakens the powers of his body and soul even more. If he shakes off the timidity and takes courage by pondering that there is but one solution—to strain every nerve of his to get

---

[21] Deut. 31:6
[22] cf. Rom. 8:35

across, for timidity will result in his drowning—by acting courageously, he will cross to the other shore and be saved.

Furthermore, if there are two swimmers and one of them loses courage and starts sinking, the other one encourages him, boosts his low morale, points out to him the danger that cowardice leads to, and helps him also with his hands, and in this way he is saved. "A brother helped by a brother is like a fortified city."[23]

24. It is unbecoming for a monk to despair, as it is also for a soldier. For where will he find the strength to lift his rifle, make laborious night marches and attacks, and obtain victories! Likewise a monk, the spiritual soldier of Christ Who fights against his spiritual enemy, will be able to accomplish his spiritual purpose only by having an invigorating hope and by sacrificing himself.

25. Do not worry at all; everything will pass and the storm will die down. Do not despair; have hope in God and in our Panagia. God will never ever abandon pained souls seeking salvation. The devil has become rabid because his plans were ruined—and what big plans! Glory to Thee, O God, for everything. Carry the cross, my children, and crucify yourselves with our Christ, and soon the bright Resurrection will come. The more afflicted you are now, the more you will feel the joy of freedom. This is how the life of the Christian is mapped out: in afflictions and troubles. All who desire to live according to God will suffer.

Take courage and do not fear; have firm faith in our Christ. He is omnipotent. No matter how wild Satan becomes, before our Christ, before His power, all his machinations are destroyed. Just say the prayer and be at peace. Trust in divine providence. All your afflictions will turn out to be for your own good. During great trials, my Elder experienced theoria!

---

[23] Prov. 13:19

Chapter Fourteen

On Thoughts, Fantasies, and Distraction

Fasting is not just abstention from food, but primarily strict abstinence of the senses. When the senses are fed by external things, they transmit a corresponding amount of poison to the nous and the heart, which kills the poor soul's life in God. Our Watchful Fathers have so much to tell us about the holy fasting of the senses. Their entire teaching is mainly directed at the purification of the nous from sinful fantasies and thoughts, and the purification of the heart from feelings that defile it. Furthermore, they teach that we must eradicate every evil in its beginning to keep the soul clean. As soon as any evil thought whatsoever approaches even slightly, it is absolutely necessary that we drive it away and say the Jesus prayer right away. And when in this manner we confront the thoughts coming from the senses and the devil, very soon we will feel the joy and the profit derived from the fasting of the senses. If Eve had restrained her sense of vision, she would not have poisoned the offspring of her womb, that is, all the people who were born from her. In short, abstinence with the senses saves man from hell.

2. I pray, my child, that you resist egotistic and proud thoughts, for from them and from similar passions all the other evil passions originate, and by them a poor soul is pushed over the cliff of destruction.

Pay no attention to passionate thoughts; disregard them completely, since the ugliness of evil is written all over their face. Disregarding the thoughts suggested by the devil brings salvation. Humility is the best stratagem, for not engaging in a battle of *rebuttal** with them and fleeing for refuge in Christ through prayer is humility.

Passionate thoughts may also be expelled by means of rebuttal, but the fight is difficult and the soldier of Christ must be very experienced to get by without damage, because Satan is also an expert in the Scriptures and he cites arguments to trip up the soldier. Therefore, whatever he suggests to you through your thoughts—whether it is pride, vainglory, criticism, etc.—let it go in one ear and out the other. Since they are passionate thoughts, it is unnecessary to hold a conversation with them. Lock them out! Tell them, "I do not tolerate associating and speaking with heretical thoughts," and remain firm in your prayer.

3. Pay no attention to whatever the enemy says to you. As soon as he is about to whisper something in your ear, immediately say, "Lord Jesus Christ, have mercy on me," or "Save me," rapidly and without stopping, and soon you will see that the thought—or rather the pressure to accept the thought—has weakened, and you will not remember what exactly he was trying to say.

This method is simpler and more effective than rebuttal—that is, to contradict the thoughts suggested—because after the demon has left and finished everything he had to say, there is nothing left behind as a remnant or shadow. Whereas with rebuttal, when he is defeated and departs, he leaves behind remnants and shadows of whatever he suggested to the soul, that is, faint memories of what one fought against. The first method—i.e., to take refuge immediately in the prayer—

is relaxing, and the soul is quickly calmed. On the other hand, the second method—rebuttal—is laborious, and if the soul does not succeed with rebuttal, one is likely to be wounded in proportion to the demon's skill of persuasion.

4. Flee from sinful thoughts; cut off fantasies, the idol of provocativeness, because Satan—that "know-it-all"—wants to separate you from God your Creator. For when he makes a person guilty by means of sinful consent, the grace of the Holy Spirit leaves, just as a bee flies away from smoke, and then the soul is left without grace and joy, and full of despondency and sorrow. But when we oppose evil fantasies as soon as they first appear in the mind by destroying or repulsing them and immediately seize the sword of the spirit—the holy little prayer of our Jesus—with eagerness and zeal, at once we shall see the knavish evil thought abandoning its post and conceding the victory to the governing mind, which the grace and mercy of God strengthened.

The cunning devil cannot tolerate seeing the holy guardian angel of our soul stand near us. This abysmal dragon strives to distance him in order to catch us bereft of a bodyguard and swoop down on us like a fearful tempest and devour us. And since he knows that only unchaste thoughts distance this angel, we see him rouse a multitude of filthy thoughts and fantasies of vain idols in order to defile the mind, heart, and body. But when the soldier of God realizes his malice, he seizes the weapon of Christ immediately and disperses his machinations.

5. My child, be careful with your imagination. All sins originate from the imagination; it is the root of sin. So be careful. As soon as a fantasy of a person or deed comes, of something you saw or heard, immediately drive it away from your mind with anger and the prayer. Say it rapidly and intensely, and at once entreat our Panagia mentally with pain to help you, and I trust in God that you will obtain the victory.

You were proud, and this is why the devil started fighting you. Humble yourself now; abase yourself; insult yourself mentally, and God, seeing your humility, will help you. Just as you avoid fire so that you do not get burned, and a snake so that you do not get bitten, likewise—and even more so— you should avoid the devil's fantasies! Be careful, I repeat, with filthy fantasies, because this is how great spiritual men have fallen and perished.

6. Be careful that your mind does not wander here and there, but affix it tightly to the name of Christ. Entreat Him as if He were in front of you by invoking His name with pain of soul, and then you will see how much benefit you will derive.

Drive evil thoughts away quickly—kick them out! Shout, "Get out of here, you tramps, out of the temple of God, out of my soul!" Do not leave them inside yourself, because you run the risk of being wounded, and then you will weep and sigh. Be patient, my child. Flee from thoughts as from a fire, for they ravage, chill, and deaden the soul! But if we drive them away with anger, vigilance, and the prayer, they give rise to great benefit.

So struggle; do not be afraid. Call upon our ready Physician. Not many entreaties are needed; He does not ask for money; He is not disgusted by wounds; He accepts tears like a good Samaritan; He nurses and attends to a person wounded by the noetic thieves. Therefore, let us hasten to Him.

7. As for obscene thoughts, they spring from the imaginative part of the soul. That is, within the mind appear people, things, and deeds that the five senses of the body have gathered and transported into the storehouse of the imagination. And in time, the devil will present to the imagination people or things or songs, etc., that the senses have stored up, and in order to create thoughts he incites the passion so that he may sack the city of God—the heart, that is—and defile it.

Therefore, the whole trick is to drive away fantasies, people, and so on, as soon as they are depicted in our mind. And if we accomplish this, by the grace of God, the evil temptation is eradicated in its beginning and we win with little effort. But if the thoughts persist, we should resist by invoking the name of Christ and confronting those thoughts with anger.

Furthermore, when we see people who scandalize us, we should try not to let the images of them be deposited within us, but we should drive them away at once, lest these images be taken into the imaginative part of our soul, and thus enable the devil to fight us by showing them to us again later.

8. Regarding your blasphemous thoughts, my child, which the devil is putting in your mind, do not fear. It is due to the jealousy of the evil sower. The devil tries to choke the Christian's soul with the idea that he himself is blaspheming, and in this way to poison his heart! Such thoughts should go in one ear and out the other. That is how much you should disregard them, because these thoughts are not yours.

I am telling you, my child, do not fear. I shall take the responsibility for them. When these thoughts come, say to Satan: "Bring whatever you want. From now on I couldn't care less about anything you say, since all these things are contrivances of your malice!"

Even though blasphemous thoughts are clearly from the devil, nevertheless we are also partly responsible for them. How? We are responsible because of the hidden pride of our mind that thinks that we are important; this is revealed by the blasphemous thoughts. They can also originate from our anger, wrath, hatred, etc. Therefore, along with disregarding them, we should take care to reproach ourselves inwardly and fight off every proud thought. Furthermore, we should be at peace with everyone, even if someone harms us.

9. Do not talk a lot. Stay away from back talk, quarreling, loquacity, and everything that issues from a careless tongue. Drive away evil thoughts and filthy fantasies from your mind as soon as they appear. For when they linger inside the mind and heart, they create a grave condition. Whereas when we are careful at the first appearance of the filthy fantasy and the filthy thought that follows, we remain in peace and enjoy the moral gratification of purity.

Therefore, my children, let us pay attention to ourselves every time various bad thoughts enter, because the same approach applies for every bad thought. Whatever kind it may be, when it finds the nous careless, it enters and creates—corresponding to the passion—the aforementioned unhealthy condition.

Therefore, since a monk is fought primarily by thoughts, the thing that saves him is watchfulness! Watchfulness (nepsis) is derived from the verb "nēfo," that is, to be careful, vigilant, alert, and on our guard. When we are careful, vigilant, alert, and on our guard, the house of our soul will be well kept and we shall save our souls for which we struggle our whole life.

10. When a person is young, it is impossible not to be fought by filthy thoughts and fantasies. One must drive them away immediately and say the Jesus prayer, and they will leave. But once again they will return; once more he needs to drive them away through the prayer and watchfulness, that is, through the attention and vigilance of the nous.

One must be careful not to let the temptation form an image, because first a fantasy comes, then a thought, and then a

filthy pleasure. So when through watchfulness we do not allow an evil fantasy to form and at the same time we say the
prayer, we are delivered from the disturbance. In addition, we
are crowned by God for our good intention and desire to
please Him.

11. You should always keep in mind, my child, that whatever your thoughts tell you is from the devil with the aim of
making you despair, while he sits back and chortles. Therefore, you should also scoff at him and pay no attention to his
silly words. You will never suffer harm when you disregard
him. Take care to pay no attention to whatever he says, and
you are saved. You will suffer no harm whatsoever if you ad-
here to this advice. Anyone who has believed his thoughts has
suffered harm. This is why disregarding them and saying the
prayer does wonders.

Do not sorrow, my child, do not despair, do not lose your
courage. No matter what the devil whispers in your mind, it
is a lie, deceit. Do not believe him at all! He rejoices when he
sees people believing him and becoming embittered. On the
other hand, he is tremendously grieved when they do not believe him and remain in peace!

As for me, when my Elder told me that these thoughts need
to be disregarded, I believed him completely right away and
immediately put his advice into practice—which is how I was
cured.

For the cure to be complete, you must disregard these
thoughts. Believe me, this is the best medicine. See to it that
you do not neglect it. All your effort should be how not to
think of those thoughts that the devil puts in your mind. Pay
no attention to them, and do not grieve at all.

Show no mercy towards filthy fantasies; strike at them
with anger, with divine fear, with the double-edged sword of

the prayer: "Lord Jesus Christ, have mercy on me." Shout it intensely, cry out; Jesus is invisibly present to help. "The Lord is near to all that call upon Him."[1]

12. Youth does not forget its natural laws. For this reason it hurls rough waves of filthy thoughts against the citadels of the temple of God to render them dirty dens of bestial thoughts. Flee from filthy fantasies. Destroy them and kill the Babylonian thoughts[2] with the sword of the spirit, the prayer, in order to be blessed on the day when the secret deeds of men will be revealed.

13. Do not be dismayed, my child, by the thoughts of fornication; just learn how to drive them away. If you learn this you will reduce them by half, and your head will be crowned with victories.

As soon as the person who causes filthy thoughts appears in your imagination, immediately, without the slightest delay, drive the image away—just as you shut your eyes when you do not want to see something—get angry with the devil, and say the prayer rapidly with pain and tears, and you will see immediately that the evil thought withdraws. But if the fantasy intensifies, cut the person depicted to pieces and make him ugly so that the repugnance will drive away the pleasure created.

Be very careful not to grow bold and not to pay attention to any evil thought, because this small carelessness will give rise to an enormous battle. Be careful lest the sweetness of the filthy fantasy allure you, and your soul converse with the person imagined, because afterwards, you will extricate yourself only with difficulty, and after this experience, you will see how necessary it is to have vigilance with thoughts.

14. When we struggle against demonic thoughts, the struggle will be considered as a martyrdom. This is because one

---

[1] Ps. 144:18
[2] cf. Ps. 136:11-12

suffers a great deal when evil thoughts attack, and God, seeing the toil and pain of his soul, considers it to be a martyrdom.

Thoughts of unbelief are caused by pride and egotism. Therefore, my child, drive away egotistical thoughts and think very humbly about yourself. Do not criticize others; look at only your own faults. Be careful with your words and do not embitter anyone.

Disregard thoughts of unbelief totally since they are demonic and plan to rob you of your fighting spirit. If you don't, they will hand you over to the carnal demon and thereafter to spiritual death. As soon as you begin the struggle, thoughts of pride will come to you—that you are a fighter, and so on—and the thoughts of unbelief will fall aside. Thus you will see how the demons deceive us.

Pay no attention at all to thoughts; disregard them completely. Take hold of the prayer and the remembrance of death, and you will see how the devil changes his guise.

15. We should constantly occupy our mind with beneficial spiritual thoughts, so that the cunning devil will not find the opportunity to bring us a thousand and one filthy and sinful thoughts that defile our soul and render us guilty and unclean before God. So let us attend, my child, to every thought of ours as well as our every word and deed so that we will not grieve our sweetest Jesus Who suffered a cruel and painful death for us, the guilty ones.

My child, attend to your thoughts. Have a fighting spirit and always be ready to confront thoughts. Do not yield, for we pay dearly and gravely for every concession.

16. I received your letter, in which you write about blasphemous thoughts in general. Thoughts of this kind originate from pride. You are deluded in saying that the temptations have ostracized pride from your soul. A tree is known by its fruit, and a cause by its effect.

An elder has written that the amount of pride dwelling within us corresponds to the number of temptations we shall have. If we had true humble-mindedness, the peace of God would gloriously ripple in the seat of our heart, and everything would be quiet and peaceful. But since the peace of the city is being disturbed, it seems that there are revolts and espionage, and this is why there is trouble amongst the citizens, the thoughts. The remedy is as follows: not reading heretical books; total disregard of blasphemous thoughts, regarding them as foreign and alien, as barking dogs, as products of the devil; humble prayer; reconciliation, if perchance as a human you are upset with someone; vigilance, if negligence has set in. These are the remedies that cure this illness—but it is cured above all by completely despising blasphemous thoughts as "hogwash" of the devil.

When Abba Pambo was being fought by a spirit of blasphemy, he prayed saying: "Lord, how shall I be saved from these thoughts?" And an angel answered him: "Pambo, Pambo, stop worrying about foreign things—that is, blasphemous thoughts—and attend to your sins."

As far as the truth of Orthodoxy is concerned, there is no room for the slightest doubt. The Holy Spirit presided over the Ecumenical Councils. Whatever the saints of God said, they said with the Spirit of God, and as proof of this, we have the sanctity of their holy relics.

17. Do not be discouraged at all, my child. Every passion that springs up and disconcerts us is a salutary medicine. Drive away the image of every person or matter that disturbs you and leads you into temptation. Get rid of any person's image in your imagination, and let your mouth say the prayer nonstop, and immediately you will see the benefit of this method. Strive not to let desire and the image of that person win your heart and mind.

Usually in the beginning of one's monastic life, the devil brings to mind dear friends in order to break our soul's strength and crush our soul's struggle, and thus bring about a defeat with uncertain consequences. Therefore, we must not take things lightly, but must bravely resist temptation from the beginning by driving away images of people from our imagination, by saying the prayer, and by abstaining somewhat from food. Then with sincere and perpetual confession and with God's grace as our ally, we trust that the enemy will retreat.

18. I received your letter, my child, and saw the trick the devil played on you. Do not be distressed in such instances, but deal with this "expert" very simply: when he brings thoughts of unbelief, blasphemous thoughts, etc., have nothing to do with him, but pick up your prayer rope and start saying the prayer intensely—continuously, like a motor—and you will see in a little while that the distress and thoughts have left you. In such instances, do not dispute with him! Just say the prayer without any other thought or fantasy, and you will see everything fall apart like a spider's web. Let no anxiety ruin your peacefulness.

19. To progress in the spiritual life, it is necessary to drive away the various evil thoughts as well as their evil fantasies that provoke us and defile our soul. We must not remain tepid in driving away evil thoughts and fantasies, because every sin originates from the imagination and thoughts. So if we uproot evil thoughts and fantasies by diligently driving them away, we should realize that we are undertaking a systematic struggle towards purity from passions, and thereafter one is freed from spiritual and mental disturbances. But when, on the contrary, we neglect to undertake this struggle to purify our nous from evil thoughts and fantasies, inevitably the vile passions will conquer us and henceforth the demons and sins will control us.

20. Be extremely careful with your imagination. Do not accept any image, because it will become an idol that you will worship. A wandering mind is a shameless bird and paints the most grotesque images: it enters into the depths of our neighbor's conscience and depicts his secret and hidden things. Immediately destroy the image with the prayer as soon as it begins to form. The more you delay, the more you will toil and suffer later.

21. Each one of us needs to attend to himself, to his work, and primarily to his heart—to see if he has remembrance of God, death, hell, heaven, and every other beneficial divine recollection. The fact that we do not have spiritual consolation is due to our daydreaming and lack of introspection along with remembrance of God. Your thoughts should revolve upon yourselves; give spiritual work to your mind, and do not let it wander about here and there. Force yourselves a little to be silent; do not speak unnecessarily; pray constantly; criticize yourselves internally—do not justify yourselves. In conclusion, without compelling and constraining ourselves, nothing spiritual can be accomplished.

Face to Face
(vid. Ex. 33:11)

Chapter Fifteen

On Prayer and Watchfulness

Time is short, and it is unknown when it will expire. Therefore, let us struggle and be careful and expel every evil thought with anger and fervent prayer. And if we shed tears we shall benefit greatly, for tears cleanse the soul and make it whiter than snow. Let us stand ready for battle courageously, for we wrestle against the powers of darkness, which never make allies and never lessen their attacks. Therefore, let us also rouse ourselves and not be drowsy, for our eternal life is at stake. If we lose the victory, we have lost our soul, have utterly lost eternal rest and joy in God, and have condemned ourselves to the second death, which is eternal separation from God—may this not come to pass.

While practicing watchfulness, let us be vigilant with thoughts. We fall into sin because of our thoughts. So let us fight powerfully against our thoughts and not allow thoughts to become strong within us due to our negligence, but as soon as they arrive let us drive away the fantasy and with anger seize the sword of the Spirit, which is the word of God—that is, "Lord Jesus Christ, have mercy on me." So as we call on the sweet Jesus, He immediately rushes to help us and the demons flee at once. We must not, however, say the prayer negligently, but with a fervent spirit cry out from the depths, "Master, save me, I am perishing!"[1] The struggle to ward off thoughts in the beginning is small. If, however, we allow the thoughts to become stronger, then the struggle becomes difficult, and often we are defeated and wounded as well. But when we arise and cry out, the good captain Jesus comes again and steers our boat to the calm and peaceful harbor.

It is in our thoughts that we either suffer damage and are defiled, or progress and become better. For this reason let us place our nous—that is, our attention—in our heart as a brave guard, armed with courage, the prayer, silence, and self-reproach. If we struggle in this manner, the outcome will be sweet peace, joy, purity, spiritual philosophy, and the prayer, which as a most fragrant incense will cense the temple of God, the inner man. "Do you not know," says the Apostle Paul, "that you are the temple of God and that the Spirit of God dwells in you?"[2] I write these things in order to rouse your souls to spiritual vigilance, so that you may find the inner peace of God and rejoice. Amen; so be it.

2. Let us fast according to our strength; but in the fasting of the senses, of the nous, and of the heart, let us wrestle against our soul's enemy with all our strength. My child, guard your senses and especially your eyes. The eyes are like the tentacles of the octopus which grasp whatever moves in front of them. They catch the prey of sin more easily. With the eyes spiritual towers fell and were lost. When David was careless with his eyes, he committed murder and adultery, even though he was a great prophet of God Who had grace and the gift of foresight.

My child, since you are in the midst of occasions for various sins, be careful with your senses. Above all be careful with your nous, the navigator, "the most shameless bird," according

---

[1] Lk. 8:24
[2] 1 Cor. 3:16

to Abba Isaac the Syrian. The nous pries into the secrets of the actions of one's neighbor; it can be a filthy artist when it depicts shameful things. Therefore, at all costs take care to keep your nous pure by immediately driving away every thought and sinful fantasy, having as strong aids the Jesus prayer and the kind of anger for which it was said: "Be angry and do not sin."[3]

3. Be ceaselessly vigilant with the guarding of your nous, for the life and death of the immortal soul depend on our diligence or our lack thereof. Everything starts from the imaginative part of the nous. There is no sin or virtue which does not have the imaginative faculty of the nous as its beginning and starting point. Therefore, the holy goal of salvation is attained by diligently attending to this noetic starting point.

Spiritual watchfulness primarily means to keep our nous pure of passionate imaginations and to oppose every attack of the enemy with rebuttal and the holy name of Jesus. Without watchfulness, the purification of the soul and body is not obtained, in which case God is not perceived by the senses of the nous and heart.

If the Lord does not visit a man's soul, he remains in the darkness of sin indefinitely. We, however, as monks dedicated to attaining inner purification in Christ from the passions, ought to be instructed very well in this most important lesson of watchfulness, through which we shall draw near to God through the senses of the heart.

The devil fights intensely against this most salvific practice of watchfulness, and he employs every means in order to hinder it, creating occasions for sin and attacking us with all kinds of thoughts. But we, too, must at all costs do everything to resist him in order to attain the reward of inner purification and be crowned by the Judge of the contest, Christ our God.

---

[3] Eph. 4:26

Do not falter before the satanic attacks of our common enemy, but struggle with courage and hope in our Lord, Who does not allow us to be tempted beyond our strength.

Therefore, take courage, my children, and go forward with sweet hope in our Christ and the powerful protection of our Panagia; and I firmly believe we will obtain eternal life with all those who have struggled well and have been crowned in the Church Triumphant in Heaven. Amen; so be it.

4. There was a holy man who cast out demons—the demons feared him. One of his disciples asked him, "Geronda, why are the demons afraid of you?"

"My child, I will tell you," said the Elder. "I had a mental war with carnal thoughts, but I never allowed myself to yield to them. I had always arranged the battle so that the war front was at the stage of *assault,* * and I never allowed the devil to advance further than the stage of assault. And since I had a continuous warfare, God gave me this blessing, this grace that, in spite of my unworthiness, the demons fear me and are cast out."

Just think—he cut off temptations outside the door, as soon as they knocked; he did not open at all. Why didn't he open? What did he have within himself that hindered them? He had holy recollections which occupied his mind. Temptations knocked from the outside, trying to enter, but there was no place for them; they were given no room to put their own thoughts inside—he had stopped them with the remembrance of God. Through this continual victory this holy man received the grace to be feared by the demons and to cast them out of people. It is a great boast for someone to succeed, by the grace of God, in keeping the devil at the stage of assault.

There is no mortal, no spiritual man, no struggler who is not subject to the assaults of the enemy, that is, every human being should expect to be tempted. If people leave their doors and windows open—as people in the world usually do, who do not have knowledge of God—then the enemy advances and conquers them. Spiritual people struggle not to open to the enemy a door, a window, or even a hole.

It is often difficult to commit a sin in deed—not a sin that is done in the heart, but a sin done by the mouth or in deeds. Many things must coincide in order for this kind of sin to take place. To sin with the mind, however, is very, very easy. One is able at any hour, place and time to commit a sin in the mind without anybody knowing it. Outward deeds are often prevented from occurring, not only because many factors must coincide, but also because of shame. On the contrary, an inward sin, a sin done by the mind, can persuade a person to commit crimes inwardly, without being noticed.

This inward sin is not visible; people do not see it—but God does. And if we do not fear people and do not feel shame, because they do not see the sin, we should fear God, because this moral crime done with the mind takes place in His presence. Many people are deceived; deep down it is due to egotism—it is egotism that does most of the damage. This treason first occurs inwardly, and then it is expressed through the members of the body.

So we need intense and constant attentiveness, as we have said—intense vigilance. There should be a guard and sentry within us, which observes the thoughts coming and going and checks their identities, so that spies do not enter and cause a civil war within the soul. The eye of the soul needs to be very clear and strong in order to see the enemy from afar and take suitable measures.

What a great variety of thoughts assail us all the time! Every passion attacks with its own thoughts. If the soul sees clearly, it cuts off the thoughts from afar. Even from their "smell" it realizes which passion is about to rise up and immediately prepares itself, posts sentries, sets up trenches, and gets ready to face the attack of that passion.

People become captives. Passion is like a snake that has poison within it. There are said to be big snakes with poisonous breath that poisons any living thing in the area so that they can devour it. The same holds true for the snake of sin: it spreads poison—pleasure—from afar, and the nous is paralyzed; its powers are paralyzed. The person is captured by the passion and involuntarily is carried toward evil.

When people are in this state of captivity, they protest and say, "But I am unable to resist; at that time I am unable to do anything." The answer is: they must take the proper measures, so that the mind and heart will not reach the point of being captured and disarmed. By experience, as soon as the spiritual serpent spreads its poison, while it is still far off and before it reaches us and poisons our mind and soul, we must take measures to escape the danger. For once we are poisoned, we are no longer able to act at all.

When a person yields to fantasies and is overcome by sinful thoughts, it is from there, from the imagination, that all evil comes! And when he has suffered many spiritual shipwrecks mentally and has been wounded repeatedly by hedonistic fantasies, then as soon as Satan comes back again with similar fantasies and shows them to the mind, immediately the person is captured. This is why one must not yield to them, so that the passions and fantasies do not become firm and strong.

5. Keep the eyes of your soul wide open; guard your senses, both those of the body (primarily the eyes) as well as those of the soul (especially by keeping the mind from wan-

dering). This is necessary because it is through these senses that all the poisonous germs of spiritual diseases creep in. And thus, in time, the careless Christian contracts many diseases and loses the invaluable health of his immortal soul.

Adultery of the soul occurs very easily when we allow filthy thoughts with their corresponding fantasies within us to overcome us. My child, be careful with your eyes if you want to conquer the demon of lust. Likewise, it is no less dangerous to look at indecent images, newspapers, magazines, etc.

6. My child, fight the good fight of eternal life. Make a good beginning to obtain an excellent end. Keep your nous entirely engrossed in the recollection of Jesus, and He will become everything for you—joy, peace, mourning, and a multitude of life-flowing tears, which will make your soul whiter than snow and lighter than a cloud.

My child, when you keep silent and say the prayer with attention—that is, when the nous pays attention to the prayer being said, without wandering off into something else other than the prayer—then your nous will begin to draw near to the sweetness of Jesus. Constantly humbling yourself will greatly help you achieve this goal. Humility is reproaching yourself always in any temptation or any matter whatsoever, and always justifying your brother.

7. The greatest temple, in which God delights to dwell, is that which He skillfully crafted with His own hands—our entire being, our soul, as long as it is pure. Purity of heart consists in the nous being free from evil thoughts, from which evil and passionate feelings originate which cause the body to be passionately excited. For it is then that both soul and body are defiled, and to a certain degree their purity and spotlessness are lost.

The first evil and passionate thought—but primarily the corresponding passionate fantasy—is the starting point of all forms of sin. No sin occurs in deed if an evil thought does not precede it by means of the imagination.

Therefore, in order to attain the greatest good—purity in the full sense of the word—we need to purify our nous from sinful imaginations and thoughts. Only in this way is purity acquired with a firm foundation.

If we want to stop doing evil deeds without paying attention to our inward thoughts, we labor in vain. When we have taken care to purify our soul, the God of glory will dwell in it, and it will become His holy and luxurious temple, giving forth the fragrance of the incense of unceasing prayer to Him.

8. What is the use of laboring and toiling with the body night and day, if inwardly we do not take care to pull out the roots from which all evil sprouts? We have an absolute need for watchfulness and unceasing prayer in order to cast off the evil which lurks within us and replace it with spiritual good.

Make sure that your daytime work does not rob you of oral prayer; cry out the supremely glorious and sweet name of our Jesus, and it will not be long before He comes to help and console you. What is there that the blessed prayer cannot set aright and renew! Constrain yourselves in the prayer; why should your mind wander around here and there and not turn towards our Jesus, when for Him we left everything and for Him we endure everything?

9. I know by experience that piety through silence, prayer, meditation, cleansing tears, true repentance, and contemplation of divine things renews the physical aspect as well as the spiritual aspect of him who struggles. Asceticism helps, of course, when the body is strong, but when it is weak, thanksgiving and self-reproach make up for asceticism.

Overall piety and vigilance are everything; they are the true marks of a soul living in Christ. When these are absent and one practices asceticism one-sidedly, either he benefits little or he is totally lost because he becomes puffed up by the praises of others as well as by his own thoughts. Without watchfulness—that all-embracing light of the soul, inestimable in value—he loses his labors. This is what happened with many ascetics in the desert, and they literally lost their souls, as we read in the writings of the Desert Fathers.

Asceticism is depicted by the Fathers as the leaves of the tree, while vigilance is the fruit.[4] By their fruits you shall know them[5]—it is fruits that we have been commanded to bear. May God enlighten us how to walk, for true guides have vanished and everyone walks his own way. May God be a true guide for all of us.

10. My children, whatever grievous thing the devil, the enemy of our souls, reminds you of, make an effort to drive it away immediately without delay, for every delay brings about unfavorable consequences.

The devil is completely vanquished with prayer and vigilance. The essence of watchfulness consists of being sleeplessly vigilant with the nous, pitting it against the passionate thoughts and fantasies of the vile demons. On this depends life or death, degradation or improvement. In other words, a soul that prays noetically and loathes and scorns the various evil thoughts is purified and sanctified with time.

11. In the war of the flesh, only turning our back saves us—that is, we must flee from fantasies and thoughts as soon as they appear. Do not linger at all in order to examine or to converse with fantasies! The imagination is a great and terrible snare; things avoided by the eyes and the touch are approached with the greatest of ease by the imagination.

---

[4] Abba Agathon, vid. *The Philokalia,* Vol. IV, p. 199.

[5] Mt. 7:16

Strive to keep your mind from imagining any worldly thing outside of your monastery. Only one thought should replace them all—the remembrance of our adored Jesus. If something in your cell reminds you of someone, you must necessarily get rid of it, to avert by all means any occasion for war. Make an effort to erase your past. When it rouses itself and tries to choke you, call on Jesus and He will be ready to help you.

12. My child, guard your nous from evil thoughts; as soon as they come, chase them off immediately with the Jesus prayer. For just as bees leave when there is smoke, so also does the Holy Spirit leave at the foul odor of the smoke of shameful thoughts. And just as bees go to flowers which have nectar that makes honey, so also does the Holy Spirit go to the nous and heart where the nectar of virtues and good thoughts is produced.

Without imagining anything, the nous should pay attention to the words of the prayer, which are pronounced either by the nous or by the mouth. The objective and focal point of all methods is to pray without imagining anything, while paying attention to the words which either the nous or the mouth is saying.

On Prayer of the Nous and Heart

Pray, I beg you, according to the instruction of the Apostle Paul: "Pray without ceasing."[1] The Watchful Fathers say, "If you are a theologian, you will pray truly, and if you pray truly, you are a theologian."[2] Indeed, the Watchful Fathers of the desert teach that through various kinds of asceticism, *praxis,** contemplation, and the moral and spiritual philosophy of watchfulness and prayer, the nous of man is purified, illumined, and perfected, and subsequently it acquires the gift of theology—not academic theology which the theologians in universities possess, but theology proceeding and gushing forth from the divine spring from which the rivers of true, divine theology eternally flow forth.

The holy Watchful Fathers say that a nous that has ceased to contemplate God becomes either carnal or savage. But conversely, through prayer and especially through noetic prayer, the nous becomes godlike and is illuminated by divine radiance.

A person's salvation depends on prayer, for this is what unites him with God and brings him near God. When he is near God, it is natural for him not to deviate from the moral road because he pays attention to every step he takes. Nevertheless, in spite of all this attentiveness, the devil never stops stalking us constantly, in order to find us at a moment of weakness and thus drag us onto his road, which always leads sharply downhill. For this reason, my beloved children, it is a must, an indispensable requirement that we always be armed with the continuous prayer of our sweetest Jesus.

We must not forget that the demons assail and attack prayer in order to render it ineffective by means of evil dis-

---

[1] 1 Thes. 5:17
[2] *The Philokalia,* Vol. I, p. 62.

tractions. Thoughts of every kind encircle the poor man's nous at the time of prayer in order to plunder the fruit of prayer and leave only its bones—that is, the labor and effort—for him who prays.

This is why one who desires to pray well should drive away every sort of care and any thought whatsoever in advance, before beginning to say the prayer. The nous as an overseer should supervise very attentively the words spoken by the mouth, so that prayer becomes a fruitful spring of divine help and grace.

According to the Fathers, Satan will always position himself as a thorn and stumbling block for holy prayer. This is because he is greatly troubled and burned by it. Therefore, my children, compel yourselves in prayer, and also remember me, your wretched Elder, so that the Lord may have mercy on me.

2. The main goal of the monastic life is to unite monks very strongly with God, Who is the ultimate. When a person is united with God and God dwells within his heart, he lacks nothing. There is no void within his soul. Furthermore, he does not even lack any material thing necessary for living in this present life. This is but one more proof of how much God loves those who obey Him.

Prayer is the means by which we are united very closely with God. By "prayer," we do not mean just praying now and then in front of icons, but along with this—which we must do—a monk uses seven words of prayer, which he says when he works, when he eats, when he sits, and when he occupies himself with anything whatsoever, without stopping! We say these words with the mouth, with the nous, or with the heart: "LORD JESUS CHRIST, HAVE MERCY ON ME."

Saying them constantly does not tire us. In the beginning one must persist a little; but later, he becomes accustomed to it and says the prayer with great ease and does not want to stop. When he says it, he feels so much spiritual exultation that even at the most difficult moments, if there are any, he is not disturbed or troubled. Rather, with patience he takes refuge in Christ, Whom he entreats to have mercy on him, and Christ consoles him and gives him joy. What is more beautiful than to entreat Christ at every moment and to say His holy name with these lips of clay? Is there a greater honor?

These words contain our whole faith. In saying "Lord," we believe that we are servants of God and that He is our lord. This honors Christ, that we make Him our lord, but it also honors us, who are servants of such a lord, Who is God.

When we say "Jesus," which is the human name of God, all the earthly life of Christ, from His birth to His Ascension, comes to mind.

In saying "Christ," which means anointed by God, king of Heaven and earth, we confess and believe that Christ is our God, Who created everything and is in Heaven and will come again to judge the world.

In saying "have mercy on me," we entreat God to send us His help and His mercy, for we acknowledge that without divine help we are not able to do anything. This, in brief, is the explanation of these holy words. Whoever says them experiences many things.

With my whole heart I pray that our sweet Jesus will give you this prayer within your soul, that you may taste the spiritual ambrosia of prayer and are replenished overall.

3. To guard love, the pinnacle of virtues, diligence in prayer is an immediate spiritual necessity. Struggle in prayer if you want our Christ to dwell in you, and He, the most experienced general, will struggle together with you. He will fight for us and grant us the victory.

We become like roaring lions when we get a good grip on the prayer—not when we pray carelessly or lukewarmly, but with strength of soul! Invigorate yourselves with the thought that the prayer is everything. Without the prayer, expect a general decline, going from one fall to another. If we hold on to the prayer with all our strength during temptations, we will certainly overcome the devil and we shall ascribe the victory to the all-holy name of Christ.

4. My child, with the weapon of prayer in your hands, fight for the divine battlements. Whoever struggles is crowned, not with olive branches, but with the unfading crown of eternal glory in the heavenly Jerusalem!

This struggle is worth it because the glory it brings remains unfading and eternal, whereas the glory of athletes who struggle for transient things is ephemeral and vain! Therefore, we must struggle by making sacrifices and bearing privations, so that the holy name of God may be also glorified by us worthless ones.

5. My children, I beg you, for the love of God, do not stop saying the prayer of our Christ, not even for a moment. Your lips should continuously murmur the name of Jesus Who destroys the devil and all his plots. Cry out incessantly to our Christ, and at once He will hasten wholeheartedly to help us.

Just as iron cannot be grabbed or even approached when it is red-hot, the same thing happens with the soul of him who says the prayer with the fervor of Christ. The demons do not approach it—and how could they? For if they draw near it, they will be burned by the divine fire which the divine name contains.

Whoever prays is enlightened, and whoever does not pray is darkened. Prayer is the provider of divine light. This is why everyone who prays well becomes all radiant, and the Spirit of God dwells in him. If despondency, indifference, listlessness, etc., approach us, let us pray with fear, pain, and great noetic vigilance, and we will immediately experience the miracle of consolation and joy by the grace of God. It is not possible for a person who prays to hold a grudge against someone or to refuse to forgive him for any fault whatsoever. Everything is reduced to ashes when it comes near the fire of the Jesus prayer.

So, my children, struggle in the salvific and sanctifying prayer of our Christ, so that you may become radiant and holy. Pray also for me, the indolent sinner, so that God may be merciful on the multitude of my sins, as well as on my countless liabilities.

6. My children, always remember Jesus so that in all your weaknesses you may find the appropriate medicine. Are you in pain? By calling on Jesus you will find relief and enlightenment. Are you in affliction? Call on Jesus and behold, consolation will dawn in the realm of your heart. Are you overcome by discouragement? Do not neglect to set your hopes on Jesus, and your soul will be filled with courage and strength. Are you bothered by carnal thoughts that allure you to sensual pleasure? Take the consuming fire of the name of Jesus and set fire to the tares. Are you oppressed by some worldly affair? Say: "Enlighten me, my Jesus, how to deal with the matter which lies before me. Work it out in accordance with Thy holy will." And behold, you will be at peace and will walk with hope.

In all and through all, set the name of Jesus as a foundation, support, adornment, and protection, and do not be afraid of the enemies. But when you go through anything without Jesus, then you should be afraid. Without medication do not expect to be healed—putrefaction will be the result. Make an effort in the prayer, my child, and then you will experience enormous benefit and refreshment and repose of soul.

7. Cry out the name of God; He is ready to help everyone who asks. Do not forget the prayer; man's entire being is sanctified by the prayer. It is the only thing which those who do not struggle to the point of shedding blood are unable to do.

What is more beautiful than prayer! Whoever prays is enlightened and comes to know the will of God. And how does he know it? When he prays well, of course. And when does he pray well? When he sends his prayers to God with all the right ingredients. And what are the ingredients that make prayer savory? Humility, tears, self-reproach, simplicity, and especially obedience with love. Prayer sheds light, and this light shows the right path which God wills.

The prayer should be said without flagging; by praying thus you will remain invulnerable on all sides. When you find yourselves in a state of passionate thoughts, resume the prayer eagerly and assiduously, and immediately you will find relief. Hold on to the Jesus prayer steadfastly.

8. Say the prayer with pain and mourning of soul, and then you will feel different. Pay attention only to yourself! Then you will see yourself and you will feel pain, and that pain will bring you the mercy of God. Do not pay attention to heartbeats when you say the prayer. Just keep your mind from wandering away from the prayer—this is the center and the aim of prayer.

Pray continuously with the Jesus prayer; it will set everything right. Whoever prays is enlightened, whereas whoever neglects prayer—like me—is darkened. Prayer is heavenly light, and whoever has the prayer within him or on his lips has the light of prayer welling up within his heart, and this enlightens him what to think and how to guard himself against the snares of the devil.

9. Compel yourselves in the Jesus prayer; this will become everything for you—food and drink and clothing and light and consolation and spiritual life. This prayer becomes everything for him who possesses it. Without it, the emptiness of the soul cannot be satisfied. Do you want to love Christ? Long for the prayer and embrace humility, and then you will realize that the Kingdom of God is within us.

Do not let evil thoughts rule over you; drive them out immediately with the prayer. Oh, this prayer—what miracles it performs! Cry out the prayer, and your guardian angel will send you spiritual fragrance! The angels greatly rejoice when a person prays with the prayer of our sweetest Jesus. May Jesus be the delight of your soul.

10. Cry out the prayer without ceasing. May God grant you a blessed beginning! May it not abandon you, or rather, may you not abandon the prayer—the life of the soul, the breath of the heart, the sweet-scented springtime which creates a spiritual spring in the struggling soul.

My children, prayer and humility are the all-powerful weapons which we must keep continuously in our hands with sleepless attentiveness, because these, with God's help, will give us the victory against the demons.

11. Patience, my children; do not lose your courage. Say the prayer intensely; do not scatter your mind among earthly things, even if you have cares—consider them as passing. Just keep prayer and the remembrance of death continually before your eyes: "I beheld the Lord always before me, that I might not be shaken."[3] If you pray intensely and without ceasing, you will not fall. You should realize, though, that if you neglect prayer, you will suffer a general fall.

---

[3] Ps. 15:8

12. Persist in the prayer; do not think that great things are achieved so easily. You will labor; you will sweat—and God will see your labor and humility, and then He will easily bestow upon you the gift of prayer.

The more you say the prayer, the more you will bring joy to me—primarily to God—and the more you will alleviate your souls. You must help each other in this sense: when you say the prayer out loud, and someone else is not saying it and his mind is wandering elsewhere, as soon as he hears the others saying it, he wakes up from his daydreaming. Then his conscience reproves him because he is not saying the prayer, too, but is just sitting there, letting his mind wander. So he also begins to say the prayer, and thus the sayings are fulfilled: "A brother helped by a brother is like a strong city,"[4] and, "bear one another's burdens."[5]

13. Pray as often as possible. Try to feel compunction and to weep, and you will see how much you will be relieved from thoughts and grief.

Prayer is a conversation of man with God. He who prays with a broken and humbled spirit is filled with divine gifts and blessings—that is, with joy, peace, comfort, illumination, and consolation—and he, too, becomes blessed. Prayer is the double-edged sword that slays despair, saves from danger, assuages grief, and so on. Prayer is a preventive medicine for all diseases of soul and body.

Likewise, entreat the Mother of Light, the spotless Theotokos, to help you, for she is the greatest means of consolation after God. When a person calls upon Her holy name, he immediately senses Her help. She is a mother; when she was on earth, as a human being and fellow-sufferer she suffered the same things we do, and for this reason, she has great sympathy for pained souls and swiftly comes to help them.

---

[4] Prov. 18:19

[5] Gal. 6:2

14. Let our throat become hoarse from crying out the sweetest name of Jesus all day long, and it will become "sweeter than honey and honeycomb"[6] to the noetic larynx—the heart. With no other name will we be able to overcome the passions within us, except with the name of Jesus. With no other name will we be able to expel the darkness from our heart and to have the radiance of luminous knowledge shine forth in our nous, except with the name of Jesus. With this name we shall arm ourselves, and in every war and battle we shall call on Him as our general for help. And at the first call, He comes; then our soul is filled with courage and we fearlessly advance towards the unseen war, with Jesus as our champion.

Let us struggle in our thoughts, always hoping on God. Let us always stand armed with the prayer and vigilance. Let us always be on the watch for thieves—thoughts from the left—without leaving those from the right unexamined, lest we accept evil thoughts which feign innocence.

15. Work at noetic prayer with much diligence, patience, persistence, and humility. You should know that this method of prayer is not achieved by chance; it takes quite a struggle, as well as much time. We must not forget that the devil hates noetic prayer more than we can imagine, and consequently we shall face fierce opposition from him in various ways. Therefore, have forcefulness, courage, patience, persistence, humility, and a loving disposition towards our Jesus.

Do not be discouraged at the first difficulties of the struggle; good things are achieved with labor and pain. But when you see fruit—and oh, what fruit!—then you yourselves will say, "It was worth the effort for such a spiritual harvest."

16. Pray, pray—just pray continuously now. The miracles of ardent prayer are beyond description and explanation. One

---

6 Ps. 18:10

marvels how the sea subsides and how the fierce winds stop! Many times temptations arise like a fearful storm and relentless winds that threaten us with total destruction. But by crying out the prayer: "Master, save us, we are perishing,"[7] you will see that all becomes calm miraculously, and we are saved. Amen.

17. My child, I received both of your letters. You seek to acquire divine love and unceasing prayer—supremely rich gifts; gifts which require afflictions, trials, time, etc. Therefore, my child, your trials are normal, and you should not wonder why you have them. So struggle to obtain divine love by constantly saying the Jesus prayer. At every fall, do not despair, but rally yourself for a counterattack!

18. We live in this vain world, but it must not attract and engross our heart so as to deaden its spiritual stamina and separate it from its Maker and God. Therefore, we ought to pray constantly, my child, in order to communicate ceaselessly with our Christ and draw spiritual strength from Him, so that we may face every demonic attack victoriously. Pray with the Jesus prayer, and He, the wonder-working Lord, first of all will forgive us the multitude of our sins, and second, by His grace will help us defeat the flesh, the world, and the devil— our three great enemies. Moreover, prayer is the provider of joy and peace in God.

Consider how much we need joy of soul and especially divine joy. Therefore, let us see to it that at all costs we take advantage of all our spare time and utilize it for prayer.

19. Pray, my child, because everything depends on prayer—especially the salvation of our souls. When we pray with pain and humility, God hears our prayer and responds according to what is beneficial to us. Often it happens that after we pray for something, the will of God is expressed in a

---

[7] Lk. 8:24

way that is completely different from what we had prayed for. This often grieves us, because our own will was not done. We do not understand the depth of the divine judgments and that, despite all the disparity between the expression of the divine will and our own will, the omniscient God is working things out for our benefit in many different ways. Therefore, my child, let us muster all the strength of our soul to persevere and implement that great virtue which is called Patience.

20. Glory to His holy name, because we came to know Him and worship Him as much as we are able, and we shun the confusion and vanity of this age. "Glory to God Who loved us and washed us from our sins in His own Blood."[8]

Know, my child, that when the heart is free from the things of this world and occupies itself with the study of the divine Scriptures, vain thoughts flee, and the nous is confined to thinking divine thoughts. It is not interested in this present life, but by the great pleasure of continuous meditation it is lifted up to God. Through the continuous invocation of the name of God by means of the unceasing prayer "Lord Jesus Christ, have mercy on me," man receives a sense of the other life, of the age to come, and of the hope which is stored up for the righteous. He foretastes the magnificence of that life and says with astonishment, "Oh, the depth of the riches of the wisdom and knowledge of the unsearchable God!"[9]—for He has prepared another world that is so wondrous in order to bring into it all the prudent people to keep them there in life everlasting.

21. My children, work diligently at the spiritual fragrance—I am speaking of prayer—this holy conversation with Jesus, which abundantly provides His blessings. Yes, children of the Spirit, love prayer with your whole heart so that all of you become a fragrance of grace, and that you

---

[8] Rev. 1:5
[9] cf. Rom. 11:33

smell sweet to those near you and make them say, "Truly, monasticism makes monks give off an angelic fragrance through spiritual grace." So, let the filthy passions be far from you, for they cause a foul smell and make a bad impression.

22. Let us compel ourselves, children, in the prayer of our sweetest Jesus, so that He may grant us His mercy, so that we may be united with His grace in order to carry out His divine commandments and acquire His love. And when we acquire it, it makes us gods by grace and by participation—and then the path of our Christ will not be harsh and steep for us, but sweet and pleasant. And then we shall carry out His commandments with great ease.

Homilies on Prayer

On Watchfulness and Noetic Prayer

The Watchful Fathers labored greatly in order to find the grace of God through prayer. This is why we, their children, owe them eternal thanks, for they showed us a road which leads the soul to union with God. One wonders and says, "But how is it possible for people, and especially for monks and priests, to live spiritually and satisfy their spiritual needs without prayer, which our Watchful Fathers gave us out of their experience?"

St. Gregory Palamas—the great luminary of hesychia, vigilance, and especially unceasing prayer—wrote the greatest and most systematic lessons on prayer and received the title: "the head and chief of the Watchful Fathers."

When he lived ascetically outside the Great Lavra on Mt. Athos, together with his synodia, he had a vision in which he saw that he had before him a vessel like a pitcher, which contained a liquid material. It was so full that the liquid was overflowing and was going to waste. That beautiful white beverage which was within the vessel looked like milk. A man of sacred appearance said to him, "Gregory, why do you let so much spiritual material overflow and go to waste, instead of giving it to those who need it?" The saint, of course, understood that it was the grace of God. It was that spiritual material and drink which he had within himself as the grace of God, as wisdom, as experience, as watchfulness, as the gift of speaking. "Why do you neglect these gifts," he said, "and confine them here in this place instead of imparting them to the weak, the hungry, the starving, the thirsty people?" Indeed, years later, with God's help and guidance, of course, he found himself among many people and he dispersed spiritual benefit and quenched the thirst of souls in need.

Even when he was in the world, he prayed by himself; he practiced hesychasm alone in his cell, and only on Saturday and Sunday did he attend the Liturgy. All the other days of the week, he confined himself to his cell and did not go out at all. He neither ate nor drank. Only on Saturday did he break his silence and go to the Divine Liturgy. After receiving Communion, he would go to the refectory and speak with the fathers and the brethren. Then once again he kept silence from Sunday afternoon until Saturday.

These great Fathers taught us that when a person's soul is attacked by thoughts that are filthy, proud, egotistical, blasphemous, sinful, etc., the soul must struggle to expel the thoughts with anger and wrath, as well as with the prayer and rebuttal. It is not enough to employ only anger and wrath against evil fantasies and thoughts. It is absolutely necessary for the person who is being fought against to pray with the unceasing prayer, with the invocation of the divine name, "Lord Jesus Christ, have mercy on me."

According to the Fathers, the name of Christ has restorative power within it. That is, this prayer of Christ has power to restore the soul which has fallen low and has become weak, which has become negligent and has sinned.

There are days and times in the life of a spiritual person when he feels an emptiness within himself, a weakness of soul. Something is missing; something within him has left, and he does not quite know how to come to himself, how to bring back the initial strength and grace which his soul had. He does not know how to bring back the fullness which he lost. In this case, the Holy Fathers teach us: Resume the prayer; begin prayer again, either with the mouth, with the mind, or with the heart, and this lost fullness will return. You will find it again, provided that you force yourself to pray.

It is of great value when a person does not stop the prayer. "But when one is working," someone will object, "the mind is scattered here and there." Nevertheless, it is possible to say the prayer very well with the mouth at such a time, discreetly and quietly, and thus to restore the feeling of grace to his soul.

Our Fathers have left us a great inheritance of limitless value, which cannot be measured, weighed, or calculated. This inheritance is called watchfulness. Watchfulness means attention to thoughts, fantasies, and the movements of the senses; it is a spiritual strength that opposes evil; it is clear perception, that is, the nous sees temptations from afar and flees, taking the appropriate safety measures; it is when the nous oversees the heart and the thoughts coming in and going out of it.

Before the Holy Fathers, those teachers of watchfulness, systematized noetic prayer, monks occupied themselves primarily with virtues belonging to praxis. Asceticism done with the body is called praxis, whether it is fasting, abstinence, prostrations, vigil, the church services, obedience, humility, etc. They called this praxis "somewhat beneficial," while they called watchfulness "greatly beneficial."

From the 14th century onward, prayer began to be systematized and organized by the Fathers. They left writings about prayer. They made known the work of watchfulness as something necessary for the perfection of man.

Before the teaching concerning the work of vigilance had been systematized, before it was known and freely circulated, the Fathers and spiritual people toiled greatly in praxis. They kept many fasts, many vigils, endured hardships, etc. But when the work of vigilance came to light as a systematic method, then the amount of asceticism was reduced—not because it is unnecessary, but because the Fathers dedicated themselves more to spiritual work than to praxis. Through the work of watchfulness they were freed from thoughts, and the passions were reduced. The work of watchfulness gave them purity of heart. This is why they did not have such an absolute need for bodily asceticism to attain purity of soul.

For this reason, we monks must not lay aside this prayer, for it is guaranteed to bring benefit 1000%. For when the work of watchfulness purifies the nous and heart and gives prudent care to the exterior senses of the body as well as to the interior senses of the soul, then a monk does not need much asceticism to attain the same goal.

Asceticism through praxis is a helpful means towards watchfulness. For this reason, the Fathers—in part and according to their strength—also exercised themselves in asceticism through praxis, in order, of course, to help the work of watchfulness. But for the most part, they pursued the work of watchfulness, because prayer and watchfulness teach the most thorough lessons about spiritual matters and theoria.

The work of watchfulness leads the watchful person to theoria, from theoria to wisdom, from wisdom to love, and it is from love that divine eros proceeds. Purity was a natural result of this work of watchfulness. Purity of both soul and body came on its own. While in physical asceticism the Fathers exerted themselves to death and suffered greatly, the work of watchfulness took away most of the labor and toil.

The work of watchfulness led the Watchful Fathers to freedom from care, for they saw that caring unduly for many things and various matters is a serious obstacle to the pursuit of watchfulness, because it gives birth to thoughts. Thoughts draw the attention of the nous away from prayer and theoria.

For this reason, the Fathers call the care for things which are unnecessary and superfluous, spiritual tuberculosis.

*Cenobites** live under obedience. A natural consequence of obedience is freedom from cares for the one who obeys. For as long as I practice obedience and as long as someone else bears the concerns, I can have peace and tranquillity, carrying out only my diakonema.

When I carry out a diakonema, and I consider that beyond this I do not need to worry about anything else, I can combine my work with prayer very well. If I see that my nous is unable to attend to the handicraft with prayer because it is distracted by many things unrelated to the duties it has at its diakonema, then out of necessity I will begin the oral invocation of the name of Christ, saying in a whisper, "Lord Jesus Christ, have mercy on me. . . ."

When the mouth prays and the hands work, the work has twice the grace: the grace of obedience and the grace of prayer. Obedience gives us a reward for our work, while prayer sanctifies it; any work escorted by prayer has a special grace.

In the monastery of Tabenesi in Egypt there was so much stillness that they called it a necropolis, a city of the dead. By this they meant that the fathers were so silent that it was as if they were not living people, who have need of speech and bustle. Furthermore, since they had this stillness, they certainly had the time to say the prayer or to be occupied with the theoria of God. It is clear that someone who loves stillness has understood the benefit of stillness and prayer.

We do not know the benefit of being vigilant with our thoughts. We do not know the value of silence. We have not found out how much benefit comes from remaining in stillness in our cell.

A monk who lacks prayer feels empty, unless he has not tasted the benefit of prayer and does not realize his emptiness. If a poor man never had anything, he is not troubled. But if a monk who has been taught the prayer becomes neglectful and loses it, he knows his loss and is troubled. Therefore, monks must pray not only to carry out their duty as monks, but at the same time to be monks in deed; not just monks in name and outward appearance, but also inwardly. According to the Watchful Fathers, one is not called a monk if he does not have this hidden work within him. Therefore, we too must compel ourselves to pray for our soul to be full of benefit. Only then can we consider ourselves to be monks. Just as someone could wonder how a body could live without a soul, likewise a person experienced in prayer would be at a loss and say, "But how can people live without this spiritual nourishment!"

The Watchful Fathers tell us that those who pray in this manner acquire great gifts. Through fasting, prayer, abstinence, and vigil we are given grace, the varied grace of the Holy Spirit. The grace of the Holy Spirit has many forms and many sensations. The Holy Spirit, through advanced prayer and the work of watchfulness, bestows the grace of tears, the grace of joy, the grace of foresight, the grace of teaching, the grace of the apostolic charisma, the power of forbearance, of patience, of divine consolation, of great hope, the grace of divine eros, of theoria, of rapture.

We, of course, are continuously being taught, and the more we are taught, the more our obligation to God and the Fathers increases.

Our passions of soul and body are remedied in proportion to the progress we have made in prayer and the benefit we have received from it. The healing of one's passions and weaknesses marks how much a person has advanced in prayer.

Consequently, we must compel ourselves. We must constantly urge ourselves not to forget the prayer, not to neglect it. When we notice that the prayer has "sprung a leak," has weakened and begins to waver and stumble, it is necessary as quickly as possible to strive to correct it, to work with diligence, to restore strength to our prayer. How will this be accomplished? The soul must collect itself immediately, must concentrate, "tighten the belt," as we say, and vigorously begin to pray. It must drive away thoughts, expel worries, free the mind from distraction and say, "I will occupy myself with the prayer now." And when we occupy ourselves with it in this way for a while, we shall soon feel the power which proceeds from diligence in prayer.

Prayer is the catapult against the demons, against the passions, against sin, and in general against everything that opposes us on the road of salvation. If you call prayer a harbor you are not mistaken; for in the harbor a small boat which was rocked by the storm finds its peace, salvation, and safety. If you call prayer a pick, if you call it an ax, if you call it a compass, if you call it a light, if you call it a thousand other such names, you will not err.

Therefore, we monks must not neglect it at all. There are laypeople in the world, mainly women, who occupy themselves with and struggle extensively in prayer, even though they have cares, they have children, they have work, they have so many obligations—yet they find time to pray and to meditate upon the name of God. What do we have to say for ourselves, since God has given us so much liberty and freedom from cares? What do we have to say for ourselves, when we neglect prayer and say it so weakly that its weakness allows the disease of sin and of the passions to crush us and make us ill?

Do thoughts war against us? Prayer is a great weapon. The attraction of sin pulls the mind towards evil. But when the mind takes hold of the ax of prayer and lifts it and begins to chop, it uproots even the hardest of thoughts. As long as one gets a good grip of the ax and wields it skillfully, it really brings about wonderful results.

Because the devil knows this, he hinders us from saying the prayer so that he can capture us more easily. He brings negligence upon us; he brings us cares; he brings us a thousand and one obstacles with the sole aim of hindering prayer. As experience has shown many times, the demons shudder at the name of Christ. They themselves admit, through people's mouths, that they are burned when a person prays.

There was a monk who had fallen into so much negligence that he not only abandoned his rule but was also ready to return to the world. He went to his homeland, the island of Cephalonia, where people possessed by demons stream to be healed at the shrine of St. Gerasimos.

Since he was near the shrine he also went to venerate the saint, but a possessed woman met him on the way and said to him, "Do you know what you're holding in your hand? Ah, if you only knew what you're holding in your hand, you wretch! If you only knew how much that prayer rope of yours burns me! And you just carry it like that out of habit, as a formality!"

The monk stood thunderstruck. It was from God that the demon spoke like that. The monk came to himself. God enlightened him, and he said to himself, "See what a fool I am! I hold in my hand the most powerful weapon and I can't even strike one demon. And not only am I unable to strike him, but he drags me captive wherever he wants. I have sinned, my God!"

And at that very moment, he set out in repentance for his monastery. Once he got there, he made a good beginning again. He made so much progress in the prayer and in the monastic life in general that he became a model for the benefit of many others. I, the lowly one, also had the chance to meet with this Elder. All you ever heard him say was, "Lord Jesus Christ, have mercy on me!"—unceasingly. If you said something to him, he would answer with a few words and then his tongue immediately returned to the prayer. That is how accustomed to it he was. That is how much it had changed him. And imagine that the value of the prayer and of the prayer rope had been revealed to him by the devil—involuntarily, of course— according to the judgments and the unfathomable plans of the Most High!

Let me tell you another similar story: When we were at New Skete, when my Elder, Joseph, was still alive, a young man who was possessed came to us. The Elder, out of compassion, welcomed these unfortunate people. They stayed as long as they liked and then left of their own accord. These people are not able to stay for long in one place. All those who lack consolation from God within themselves seek it by moving from place to place, and from one group of people to another.

This young man had the demon of a prostitute. When it seized him, his voice changed into the voice of a common woman, and he said things which "it is shameful even to speak of," as the Apostle says.[1] He was a barrel maker by trade. He stayed in our synodia for some time, and during the work hours he came to help however he could. On the third day he said to me, "Father, won't you teach me to carve *prosphoron** seals, too? Those barrels I make are hard work, and I've got this thing inside me that constantly disgraces me."

---

[1] Eph. 5:12

"I will teach you, my brother; may it be blessed! Look, this is how you do it. The tools are here, the wood is there, and the samples are in front of you. You will work at this bench. The only thing is that, as you see, all the fathers here in this synodia don't talk; they are always saying the prayer."

I said this to avoid, as much as possible, idle talk and distraction from prayer. But also something else crossed my mind at that moment: I wondered if demoniacs can say "the prayer." So we began to work, saying the prayer. Only a few moments passed and the demon flared up within him. His speech changed and he started shouting, using foul language, threatening, and swearing: "Shut up, you scum!" it said from within him. "Shut up! Stop that muttering! Why do you keep saying the same words over and over again? Quit saying those words. You make me dizzy. I'm fine inside you—why do you want to disturb me?"

It went on like this for a while. It tormented him. Then it stopped.

"See what it does to me?" the poor fellow said. "This is what I go through all the time."

"Patience, my brother, patience!" I said to him. "Don't pay any attention to it. These are not your own words, so don't get upset. You just concentrate on the prayer."

We stopped working and went to the Elder. On the way, he said to me, "Father, should I say a prayer also for the one inside me, for God to have mercy on him as well?" What a thing for that poor fellow to say! At once the demon seized him, lifted him up, and slammed him down. The whole place shook. His voice changed and it started up again:

"Shut up, you scum!!! Shut up, I told you. What are you saying? What do you mean, "mercy"? Not mercy! I don't want mercy! No! What have I done to ask for mercy? God is unjust! For one little sin, for one proud thought, He banished me from my glory. It's not our fault; it's His fault! He should repent, not us! Get mercy far away from me!"

It tormented him terribly and left him a wreck. I shuddered at what the demon said. In a few minutes I had learned more about demons through experience than I could have grasped from reading thousands of books. We went on to my Elder. My Elder always received him and talked to him with great love, and that young man was always calm when he was with him. He prayed a great deal for such people, for he knew what a martyrdom they went through from the demons. And he said to us:

"If we, who have the demons outside of us, are so tormented by thoughts and passions, what a martyrdom must these unfortunate people endure, who have the demons inside them day and night!" And shaking his head sadly, he concluded, "Perhaps they are going through their hell here. But woe to those who will not repent so that God may chasten them compassionately in one way or another in this present life!" And he quoted the words of a saint, who said, "If you see a person who sins openly and does not repent, and nothing grievous happens to him in the present life up to the hour of his death, then know that the examination of this person will be without mercy in the hour of judgment." As the Elder said these things, we regarded that troubled brother with more and more sympathy.

During the services, he did not come inside the church with the fathers, but wandered around outside on the rocks with his prayer rope and kept shouting out the prayer continuously: "Lord Jesus Christ, have mercy on me! Lord Jesus Christ, have mercy on me! Lord Jesus Christ, have mercy on me!" The whole place echoed with it.

He had experienced how much the prayer burns the demon. And as he roamed around the rocks, incessantly saying the prayer, suddenly his voice would change and the demon would start: "Shut up, I told you, shut up! You're choking me! Why do you stay out here wandering around the rocks and muttering? Go inside with the others and stop this muttering. Why do you keep repeating the same thing day and night and not give me a moment's rest? You've made me dizzy, you've scorched me; you're burning me—don't you understand?" And when the time of temptation was over, he would go back to the prayer with the prayer rope: "Lord Jesus Christ, have mercy on me. . . ." He had understood very well something that the demon thought he could not understand. It was with pain of soul and yet with hope that we saw him suffer, struggle, and endure. Anyway, he stayed with us for a while and then left, considerably improved. We never saw him again, though. God knows what became of him.

Do you see the power of the prayer and the demons' refusal to repent? They are consumed with fire and they cry out, "Not mercy!" And they never stop blaming God. Oh, what satanic pride! I wonder, how does an egotist, a person who is utterly unrepentant, differ from a demon? Someone who does not deign to confess Christ as God and man and to seek His mercy and compassion as long as he lives? Do you now see the deeper significance of the prayer and that it reveals how near or far people are from Christ?

We let our thoughts loose, and they take control of us. We let our thoughts loose, and they imprison us, while we could use the resplendent weapon of prayer—that weapon which is called fire and flame. This prayer is a whip that scourges every demonic thought.

But we—first of all, I—are unworthy to occupy ourselves

with it. Not that we are unable or that we do not have the calling for prayer, but we are lazy and negligent. The devil leads us astray, and we obey him and do not occupy ourselves with prayer as we should. If we did occupy ourselves with it, we would not have let so many passions and weaknesses conquer us.

We see that even laypeople who occupied themselves with prayer were sanctified. The father of St. Gregory Palamas was within the palace, in the Imperial Council of Andronikos, the Byzantine Emperor. Despite the fact that he had so many concerns, worries, and business matters, he was involved with prayer and experienced the benefit and progress which come from it. This goes to show that wherever a person may find himself, wherever he may be, whatever life he may lead, he can attain the grace of God when he occupies himself with this wonder-working prayer.

We see also St. Maximos Kafsokalyvis, who wandered around the wilderness of the Holy Mountain in quiet places to be able to increase prayer. The fathers asked him, "Father, why do you go into the wilderness, and why do you flee men and not come near them?" He answered, "I wander out in desolate places in order to increase prayer." Experience has shown that without the proper stillness, prayer does not achieve the greater and additional gifts which issue from it.

Both in the world and in the stillness of the mountains, much is accomplished by prayer. We who are in a *cenobium** must hold on to the prayer and implement the virtues of praxis: being obedient, cutting off our will, loving each other, being tolerant towards one another, confessing our thoughts frankly, remaining spiritually obedient to our Elders, saying the prayer continually at our diakonema. And when we have carried out all these things, the grace of God will come in proportion to our intention and our faith, in proportion to the faith and obedience which we have towards our Elders, in proportion to our ascetical struggle.

We here, under one roof, under the guidance of one shepherd, are also able to attain a sufficient measure of grace, for God does not show favoritism. He rewards those who work at His commandments with a pure heart, with a pure conscience, and He comforts them and gives them the hope of salvation.

In conclusion, there is nothing left for us to do except to compel ourselves; to compel ourselves constantly. We should occupy ourselves with prayer above all, saying continuously: "Lord Jesus Christ, have mercy on me." As we wake up in the morning we should say the prayer; then, we should do our work with the name of Christ on our lips. By saying the prayer like this, we cut down on idle talk, superfluous words, criticism, anger, and grumbling, and each one of us keeps stillness within himself.

Woe to us when we are taught and do not practice, when we do not compel ourselves, when we are furnished with the means to compel ourselves and yet do nothing. What is left for us to do except to condemn ourselves continuously as unworthy, wretched, and lazy? At least through self-reproach and humility, we may regain forcefulness in prayer. For humility and self-reproach bring the grace of God. And grace in turn brings eagerness and facilitates prayer.

As I also said in the beginning of this homily, we owe continual gratitude to our Watchful Fathers. Let us revere them, love them, and glorify them. Let us seek their prayers and intercessions, and let us entreat them to send us also a small gift, a little blessing of prayer.

The Art of Prayer

For a monk, prayer must be like an inseparable companion. During the time which we have set aside to pray somewhat more collectedly and attentively, we must force ourselves, in a sense, to try and fix our nous in the place of the heart—without imagining it, of course.

We should breathe slowly and with our *inner voice** say the prayer: "Lord Jesus Christ, have mercy on me." We should set our nous as a guard, as an overseer, to follow the inner voice which is saying the prayer. Furthermore, our nous should make sure that the imagination does not accept any image. Together with this, we shall rouse a loving disposition in our soul, so that our prayer will be strengthened and made whole with good results. This result may be ease in saying the prayer, spiritual warmth, joy, tears, etc.

Of course, before we start saying the prayer, it is helpful to look back for two or three minutes at our sins, our passions, and to reflect on our sinfulness, our passionate condition, the lowly state of our soul, and that we cannot do anything without God. Likewise, one can call to mind the judgment of God or a state of damnation in the other world. With the feeling which will be created within the soul in this manner, we shall be moved to regulate the prayer with our breathing.

In this way the soul is prepared so that after a few minutes, when we begin praying, the prayer will have a certain spiritual impetus and hue. By doing so, the nous is more collected, more attentive. This contemplation, this meditation, encloses the nous and confines it. Thereupon we give the prayer to the nous, and thus it begins to pray well.

When a person acquires the habit of praying in this way, after a period of time (the length of time is different for each person, depending on his eagerness) he progresses in prayer—of course, by the grace of God, for I believe that the entire matter of prayer clearly depends on the grace of God. One becomes a co-worker with grace through his methods of praying, but it is an accomplishment of grace for him to remember the name of God. The proof of this is that a person is able to think any other kind of thought that he wants; but to keep the name of God in mind requires a very great effort.

Something similar happens with plants, to offer an illustration. Wild plants and thorns sprout on their own, without anyone making an effort, whereas cultivated plants must be looked after with much labor. Furthermore, if God does not help, if He does not send sunlight with its wonder-working rays, nothing is able to sprout and grow and flower. This is how it is spiritually, too: man strives to attain union with God through various methods of prayer, but if God does not send His blessing, if He does not assist, all these methods and the great effort man makes in prayer remain spiritually fruitless.

For this reason, before beginning prayer, we need contemplation—spiritual contemplation, that is—with humble thoughts, thoughts of self-reproach, the remembrance of death, and so on, in order to elicit help from God when we pray.

Even when a person is praying, if he accepts vainglorious thoughts, prayer ceases—that is, the grace of God is immediately obstructed; it does not act. Then he becomes indignant with these thoughts and thinks: "As soon as the prayer began to act and I started feeling the grace of God, thoughts intruded and grace withdrew."

Furthermore, many times various evil thoughts approach and at once the prayer is cut and one asks oneself, "But I did not accept these evil thoughts; why am I now deprived of prayer and its grace?" Even so, this happens certainly by the providence of God to instruct a person. It is as if God were saying to him: "Do not think that it is only when you accept proud thoughts that you are deprived of the grace of prayer; but also whenever I will, even without proud thoughts, I take away from you the impression and conviction that through your own preparation and effort you can succeed in finding active prayer."

This is something I have come to know so fully from experience that nothing can take this thought, this conviction away from me, that prayer is the work of grace. Of course, we mean active prayer, prayer when one perceives the presence of grace—because any other kind of prayer, without the perception of grace, is also called prayer.

So it is to one's advantage to be deprived of prayer from time to time in order to learn this lesson of humility well. After years, after losing prayer many times because of thoughts, a natural inner conviction develops, that it is only with the help of God that prayer is achieved. Abba Isaac the Syrian says, "It is not when you prepare yourself with every means and way of prayer that you will obtain the grace of God, but it is when God wants to that He will give it to you. When you have not prepared, it happens that He gives it to you; and when you have prepared, it may happen that He does not give you prayer."

This is a very great truth. Many times when I, the lowly one, had taken all measures to find prayer at night, for the most part I would not find it. I would get up on time, in my stillness, according to my schedule; I would do everything attentively; I would not make a sound. I struggled for hours, yet I would not find prayer. Then, after this lengthy struggle to pray attentively, I would do something else, some other spiritual work, and would find so much grace from God. I thought to myself, "So much labor, such a great effort, so much attention resulted in nothing, and now suddenly so much grace?" God gave me to understand that I should not abandon my efforts, but that I should not trust in my own efforts to find prayer.

It is within the power, within the authority of God to make the prayer be felt even without effort. At any rate, he who prays must, on his part, take all measures necessary to find prayer, without believing that these measures will definitely bring prayer. Rather, he should believe that if God wills, he will be given prayer—otherwise he will accomplish nothing.

The farmer sows: he cultivates the field well, makes sure that the plow goes deep, rakes up the earth, brings what is underneath to the top, and then he sows. Afterwards, he waits for rain and fair weather. If fair weather coincides with rain and the proper atmospheric conditions, the seeds will sprout, grow, and yield their fruit. Otherwise, nothing will happen— or if they do sprout, they will yield so little that the farmer will not even recover the seeds he sowed. However, the farmer hopes in God and says, "If God wills, I shall obtain fruit." And in times of drought, the poor farmer prays and has the fields blessed with holy water, because he believes that if God wills to send rain, sun, etc., his labor will bear fruit. Otherwise, in spite of all the measures he has taken, he will not obtain fruit.

The same thing happens in the spiritual realm: no matter how well a person may prepare, he will bear fruit only if God wills. For this reason, humility must precede all spiritual pursuits.

One reaches the point of being convinced that absolutely nothing can happen without God's help. He believes this and says, "I sign with my own blood that I am nothing and that I am unable to do any good." And while he has not yet finished signing that he is nothing, immediately he sees vainglorious thoughts! And he reflects, "Just now I was signing with my blood that I am nothing—how could a vainglorious thought attack me?"

So it is clear that God must even give us humility. Despite all the work we do to realize our nothingness, it is still God Who must give us the sense of this nothingness. So then, what is one to do, since this is how things are? Should he do nothing good and make no effort, waiting for God to give him humility and grace? No. He must do whatever is required of him concerning this or that virtue, and then wait humbly with the awareness that, if God wills, this virtue will receive flesh and bones, and then he will be able to bear fruit. Otherwise, only the labor remains.

Getting back to the subject of prayer, I repeat that we must prepare ourselves for it. We must enclose ourselves within our cells at the appointed time. We must make an effort to reflect on something related to prayer: for example, our sins, or the fact that time is passing and we are not doing anything, or that death and the tribunal await us, and so on.

After this sort of improvised and brief meditation, immediately a mood for prayer comes. We put our nous into our heart and breathe in a restrained manner, saying the dear little prayer, "Lord Jesus Christ, have mercy on me." And if sometimes we feel that it is laborious or that we are sleepy, we must persist. We don't seem to get anything out of it, of course, but imperceptibly something good is created within us. The next time we sit down to pray, we shall feel somewhat better, and the next time, better yet. Thus, little by little, we shall begin to get something out of prayer, and, with time, we shall find more and more. Of course, in this effort the devil shall most certainly attack us. He will distract us and bring us various fantasies. Our effort must be to exclude all these things and attend to prayer.

The work is not easy. It seems simple: you bow your head, collect your thoughts, and follow the prayer. In essence, however, it is difficult, because the evil one does not want to hear this prayer. Noetic prayer is an implacable enemy of Satan! Consequently, it is not so easy for the devil to tolerate it burning and scalding him, to permit it to establish Christ in man's heart and expel him from the region surrounding the heart. As we have said, the purpose of prayer is to bring Christ within the heart of man—something unacceptable to the opposition, to Satan.

This simple, single-phrased prayer is so powerful that it is not possible for man's mind to contain it. For this reason Satan combats it, fights hard against it, and brings us distraction, restlessness, distress, and suffocation, with the sole aim that the person not pray.

"Continuing steadfastly in prayer."[2] Prayer takes patience, persistence, forbearance. Let us not say that we are unable to do anything, because then we shall not succeed in acquiring this prayer, which is so vast that it contains heavenly things within it! Let me explain:

When prayer becomes active, the nous becomes so clear, so illumined, so dynamic, it receives such strong wings, that it ascends very high and meets God with all His graces. Then the nous becomes so receptive to spiritual contemplations that one says, "Which contemplation shall I choose?" On the other hand, when the nous is not enlightened by prayer, it is extremely sluggish; it cannot be moved fruitfully to even a single contemplation.

---

[2] Rom. 12:12

When one makes an effort and does not find prayer, the evil one comes and says, "See, you made such an effort and didn't find anything, so give up this prayer." But experience tells us in its own language that patience and persistence are needed, for the heart does not easily open to prayer. Many blows and much effort in prayer are needed.

What happens with a seed? It sprouts; little by little it rises upwards; it breaks the surface of the soil and emerges into the light of this world. Then it puts out a shoot, grows, blossoms, and bears fruit. The same thing happens with prayer as well. Little by little it will break the hardness of the heart; it will emerge at its surface, and when it emerges into the light of the spiritual world, it will begin to sprout, grow, blossom, and bear fruit.

When God counts a person worthy, after years of working at this spiritual prayer, then—although previously he himself had felt that he was weak in humility and lost prayer easily— he sees humility established as a spiritually natural state. Then prayer is also established and retained.

A little child, when he first begins to walk, is not strong. His knees are not strong, and he easily falls and hurts himself. As he gets older, of course, his ankles become stronger. Then it is easy for him to walk without falling. The same thing happens with prayer, too.

So we must do all these godly labors, because they predispose God to send His grace. That which is harmful in the spiritual struggle is despair and hopelessness. There is no need for despair. Despair, in any spiritual sector whatsoever, is from the devil. It is never from God but always from the devil. And whenever it approaches us, we should say, "This is from the devil."

The devil does attack every prayer, but he is particularly aggressive towards this one. One can say all other prayers easily with the inner voice. When one begins this prayer, however, all the demons gather. Satan's opposition and the war he wages against it reveal how good, spiritual, and fruitful this prayer is. We have not understood what we shall gain, how much we shall benefit from this prayer. That is why we do not have the appetite and patience for prayer.

So let us struggle; let us labor in prayer until God sends His grace—and then, when grace comes, it will instruct us in everything.

On the Practical Method of Noetic Prayer

When we were in the wilderness, our vigil began at sunset and lasted until the morning hours. My Elder of blessed memory, Joseph, in teaching us the duties of the monastic life, greatly emphasized the practical method of noetic prayer. Just as he continually forced himself in prayer, he insisted that we also force ourselves as much as we could, in order to establish deeply within our nous and heart the name of the Lord, which is the cornerstone of the whole spiritual building.

After sleep, my Elder would tell us, man's nous is fresh and clear. It is in a perfect condition for us to give it, as its first spiritual food, the name of our Lord and God and Savior Jesus Christ. But since the devil knows this, he hurries as quick as lightning to sow the tares of his evil thoughts when we wake up, so that the memory like a mill will begin to grind them and the noise made by its turning will sound like his kind of "prayer."

In millers' jargon, the part of the mill where they put the wheat, the barley, the corn, or whatever else is to be ground, is called the hopper [in Greek it is called the "desire"]. It is open and wide on the top, but becomes so narrow on the bottom that it permits only a few grains to fall rhythmically between the millstones. Whatever enters the "desire" will pass between the millstones and be ground. But whatever enters the heart—which has all the human desires within it—does not have to ascend and pass between the millstones of the nous. "Out of the heart," said the Lord, "proceed evil thoughts,"[3] and ascend and pass one by one and are ground. The more unclean and earthly the heart is, the more dirty and base the thoughts are.

---

[3] Mt. 15:19

Therefore, in order to keep all the muddiness of thoughts from ascending into the nous and to cleanse the heart, as its Creator desires, we bring our nous down into the heaven of our heart through noetic prayer, and thus we transform the place of the passions, where Satan is indirectly worshipped, into a holy temple of God, a dwelling place of the Holy Trinity.

This figure we have sketched is simple to describe with words, but to apply it requires all man's powers with the full cooperation of divine grace. And since God always offers Himself, and even entreats, "Son, give Me your heart,"[4] it is necessary that we also offer ourselves entirely and obediently to the ascetical rules of our Watchful Fathers.

So be careful with your first thoughts after sleep. Dreams, fantasies—whether good or bad—whatever sleep bequeathed to us, we must obliterate immediately. And right away we must immediately take the name of Christ as the breath of our soul. Meanwhile, after we throw a little water on our face to wake up, and after we have a cup of coffee or something else to invigorate us—as long as our vigil begins long before midnight—we say the Trisagion, recite the Creed and "It is truly meet" to the most holy Theotokos, and then we sit in our place of prayer with the weapon against the devil—the prayer rope—in hand.

"Did you sit down on your stool?" my Elder would ask. "Wait a minute! Don't start praying in the prescribed way before you concentrate your thoughts and meditate a little on death and on what follows it."

Consider that this is the last night of your life. As for all the other days and nights, you are sure that they have passed and have brought you to this point of your life. But as for this night ahead of you, you are not sure whether it will hand you over to the day that will come, or to death, which is coming. How

---

[4] Prov. 23:26

many people will die tonight! And how do you know that you
will not be among them?

So reflect that you are about to leave shortly, and either the
angels or the demons will come to claim your soul, according
to what you have done. At the hour of death the demons are
bitter prosecutors and bring all the works of our life to our
memory and push us towards despair. The angels, on the contrary, show the things we have done for God. And from this
preliminary court, the course of the soul is determined. Then
come the aerial toll-houses, the dread tribunal of the Judge,
and the verdict. And if the outcome of all these proceedings
will be damnation, then what will you do, wretched soul?
What wouldn't you give at that hour to be delivered! Come to
yourself like the prodigal son, and repent and seek the mercy
of the most merciful God. Whatever you would want to do
then, do now. Have you sinned? Repent. Behold, now is the
acceptable time.[5]

If one meditates upon these thoughts for even a short time,
without images or fantasies, he is moved to contrition; his
heart is softened like wax and his mind stops wandering. The
memory of death has this natural advantage: to overcome all
the illusions of life and create godly mourning in the heart.
Within this contrite atmosphere you can begin your single-
phrased, unceasing noetic prayer.

While your thoughts are collected and your spirit is broken
and humbled, bow your head slightly and turn your attention
towards the place of your heart. It is also broken and humbled
and waits for the nous to descend in order for them (the nous
and the heart) to offer a supplication to the most compassionate God with the hope that He will not disregard it.

The bodily process of respiration begins with breathing in
through the nostrils. Attach there, too, the respiration of your

---

[5] 2 Cor. 6:2

soul through prayer. As you inhale, say the prayer once, following it to the heart, and as you exhale, repeat it once again. Establish your nous where the breath stops, in the place of the heart, and without distraction follow, through inhaling and exhaling, the prayer being inhaled and exhaled: "Lord Jesus Christ, have mercy on me!"

Assume the disposition of someone in love, and without fantasies or images, say the name of the Lord Jesus with the inner voice. Send away every thought, even the most beautiful, the most pure and the most salvific. They are from the evil one, from the right, to stop your prayer. Disregard all evil thoughts, however obscene, profane, and blasphemous they may be. They are not yours; do not be concerned about them; you are not responsible. God sees where they come from. Just do not be enticed by them; do not fear; do not be carried away; do not consent to them.

If you are distracted for a little while, as soon as you perceive that you have strayed from the place and the manner of your prayer, immediately return. And if you are carried away again, return once more. If you keep returning every time you are distracted, God will see your labor and your eagerness, and by His grace, little by little, He will make your nous steady.

The nous is accustomed to run around and only remains where we feel pain. Therefore, pause momentarily after you inhale; do not exhale immediately. This will cause a slight, harmless pain in the heart, which is the place where we want to establish our nous. This small pain greatly assists by attracting the intellect like a magnet and holding it there to serve the nous somewhat like a servant.

Indeed, little by little as time passes, the sweet name of the Lord, the name which is above every name, when called upon with pain and contrition, works the change of the right hand of the Most High[6] on our soul in the place where sin had previously encamped. The *circular** movement of prayer in the place of the heart enlarges its boundaries so much that it becomes another heaven, a heaven of the heart, able to contain the Uncontainable.

There will be a war, a mighty struggle for the throne of the heart. In the beginning, the devil will act through the passions and their fumes—that is, various thoughts opposed to prayer. And the more he loses ground through fasting, vigil, prayer, and other ascetical efforts, the more he will roar and the more forcefully—by the permission of God—he will try to manifest his evil and cunning through various influences, temptations, and afflictions. But the affectionate providence of the Heavenly Father will always trace out the limits of his jurisdiction, in proportion to our strength to resist his attacks.

Before a temptation, Christ, the Judge of the contest, always provides hidden grace to the combatant so that the rage of the enemy is crushed by it, and the combatant prevails and emerges victorious. We have to please the Lord by bearing afflictions in order to make up for all the grief we caused Him when we were lured by sin. At that time the devil rejoiced and God was grieved; now it is God's turn to rejoice and the devil's turn to be grieved and be torn apart.

---

[6] cf. Ps. 76:10

The Path to Unceasing Prayer

The heart of man is the center of movements above nature, in accordance with nature, and contrary to nature. Everything begins from the heart. If the heart of man is purified, he sees God.

But how can we see God? Does God perhaps have human form? Does He have the shape of a human? No, of course not! God is invisible; God is Spirit. He is able, however, to reign in man's heart when it becomes a vessel fit to receive Him. For the heart of man to become a vessel fit to receive God, it must be cleansed of unclean thoughts. But in order for the heart to be cleansed, some kind of cleaner must enter into it. This cleaner is prayer.

Wherever the king goes, his enemies are driven out. And when Christ—or rather, His holy name—enters into the heart, the phalanxes of demons are put to flight. When Christ is enthroned well within, then everything becomes submissive. It is like when a good king conquers a country and is enthroned in the capital; then he subjugates all the rebels with his army. That is, he pursues the enemies and pacifies the country from internal troubles, and then there is peace. Meanwhile, the king sits on his throne and sees that everything has been subdued. Then he rejoices and delights in seeing that the labor and fight have ended and that they have brought obedience, peace, and all the desired results.

Thus it is also with the kingdom of our heart. It has enemies within it; it has rebels; it has thoughts; it has passions and weaknesses; it has storms and disturbances—all these are within man's heart. For the kingdom of the heart to be pacified and subjugated, Christ, the King, must come with His regiments to take control of it and drive out the enemy, the devil. He must subjugate every agitation from the passions and weaknesses, and reign as an omnipotent emperor. The resulting condition is called by the Fathers "stillness of the heart"—when prayer reigns unceasingly, bringing about purity and stillness of heart.

There are many ways to pray. In the beginning, we must first pray orally in order to attain our final goal. This method is necessary because the nous of man is in perpetual motion. And since it moves not in accordance with nature as it should, but rather is misused because of our indifference, it roams the entire world and rests in different pleasures. Sometimes it goes to carnal thoughts and enjoys their pleasure; sometimes it goes to other passions, and at other times it loafs around indifferently here and there. Wherever it may go, wherever it may stay, it finds some sort of pleasure.

Therefore, a person who aims to gain "prayer without ceasing"[7] must collect his scattered nous—that vagabond that roams around all the alleys—so that it may be tidied up and become neat and clean. In order to collect it, however, we have to offer it something sweet; for as we have said, it finds pleasure and delight in roaming here and there. Again, we have to attract it with something that has pleasure. For this reason, in the beginning we need to say the prayer with the mouth.

The beginner who is taught the prayer must begin to say with his mouth, "Lord Jesus Christ, have mercy on me," and must make an effort to pull his nous away from worldly things. The sound that comes out—the sound of his voice—will attract his nous to pay attention to the prayer, and thus, little by little it will get used to being collected instead of scattered. Of course, the effort, the attention, the intention with which we pursue unceasing prayer, as well as keeping the goal in mind, all help us to concentrate our nous.

---

[7] cf. 1 Thes. 5:17

In time, as we say the prayer in this manner, it also begins to create within us a certain pleasure, a certain joy and peace, something spiritual which we did not have before. Little by little this attracts the nous. As oral prayer progresses and attracts the nous inward, it also begins to give the nous the freedom to say the prayer on its own, without the mouth saying it—that is, it begins to bear some fruit. Later, when the prayer is said sometimes with the mouth, sometimes with the nous, it begins to take over the soul. Then, as the nous occupies itself with the prayer, it begins to enter the heart, to the effect that one feels his heart saying the prayer as he just stands there. However, in order to reach this point, the correct method of saying the prayer will greatly help.

When we abandon the regular and natural rhythm of inhaling and exhaling, and breathe in and out slowly, less oxygen goes to the heart. This creates a certain pain, a kind of constriction in the heart. This pain naturally results in attracting the nous and making it pay attention to the heart. This attraction of the nous to the heart brings about their union. It is just as when one has a toothache: the nous may roam about, but it returns to the tooth because of the pain.

So as the prayer is said rhythmically with controlled breathing, the nous will go down where the pain is, and thus distraction is eliminated. Once distraction has been eliminated in this way, the nous will find stillness—it will not find a reason to be scattered, since the pain collects it.

Controlled breathing (along with attentiveness) is necessary to keep the nous from escaping. In this way we shall be able to cut off distraction, which bleeds the essence out of prayer. In other words, distraction takes away the benefit of saying the prayer.

By eliminating distraction, we give the nous the ease to pay attention to the heart. So we begin by breathing very slowly and joining to our breath the prayer "Lord Jesus Christ, have mercy on me." We may say the prayer either once, twice, or three times as we inhale. Then as we exhale, again we join the prayer to it. We might say the prayer three times when we exhale and two times when we inhale—however we are able. In any case, it is in this sense that we say the prayer rhythmically with our breathing.

Now then, if we are able to say the prayer noetically with controlled breathing, fine. If, however, we have difficulty because the tempter creates problems, we should breathe through the mouth and our tongue may move slightly, which is very beneficial in the beginning.

As we inhale through the mouth or the nose, we should be saying the prayer while the nous is in the heart. The nous should pay attention to the heart without imagining it. The nous should simply position itself in the place of the heart, and we should not imagine the heart, because if we imagine it, delusion will gradually enter, and we will be praying with the imagination.

Prayer has no danger of delusion when it is done without distraction, without form, with a simple nous, without any shape or figure at all. The nous must be pure of every divine and human imagination. We must not imagine Christ or the Panagia or anything else. Only the nous should be noetically present in the heart, in the chest—nothing else. It should only take care to be in there. But at the same time, along with the breathing, the nous should say the prayer without imagining anything else. The heart should work the prayer like a motor, and the nous should follow the words of the prayer as a simple observer. This is the unerring path of prayer.

When we practice this method, in the beginning we will find some difficulty, but afterwards we will find breadth, height, depth. First, a certain joy mixed with pain will come. Then gradually come joy, peace, tranquillity; and once the nous is sweetened, it will not be able to tear itself away from prayer in the heart. Such a state will arise that we will not want to tear ourselves away from it. We will sit or stand in a corner, bend our heads down, and we will not want to tear ourselves away from it for hours on end. We might sit there for one, two, three, four, five, six hours rooted to the spot, without wanting to get up and without the nous going anywhere else. We will observe that as soon as it wants to go somewhere else, bending our head down brings it right back. In other words, a kind of captivity in prayer occurs.

This method of prayer is very effective. First, it will bring undistracted prayer; it will bring joy and peace. Simultaneously, it will bring clarity of the nous and tears of joy. The nous will become receptive to theorias. Afterwards, it will create absolute stillness of the heart. One will not want to listen to anything at all. He will think he is in the Sahara desert. At the same time the prayer will be said more rapidly. He might want to say it rapidly, or he might want to say it slowly. We should say it however it pleases the soul, however the soul wants it at that time.

So we will say, "Lord. . .Jesus. . .Christ. . .have mercy. . . on me. . .Lord. . .Jesus. . .," while the nous will be following the prayer as a machinist follows the machine that is working. And then once we cannot inhale anymore, we will exhale slowly, "Lord. . .Jesus. . .Christ. . .have mercy. . .on me. . . Lord. . .Jesus. . .," until we reach the end. Then we inhale again slowly—not hastily, but gently, calmly, quietly, without haste, "Lord Jesus Christ, have mercy on me."

And you will see later, while you are working, that as soon as you take a breath you will say, "Lord Jesus Christ, have mercy on me." Then as you exhale, you will say the prayer again.

The heart and the nous on their own will be so pleased with this method that no matter where you are, the nous will say the prayer at every breath. Of course, you might not say the prayer three times at each breath—in any case, you will say it at least once. Then later, you will acquire a rhythm like the rhythm of a machine masterfully tuned, and then you will see the results that this prayer has. It will attract you more and more. You will say, "Fifteen minutes must have passed," whereas in fact, two hours will have passed. That is how much a person will not want to take his nous away from his heart and from listening to the prayer.

Who needs chanting, or anything else for that matter? This is why the Fathers in the desert did not need such things. Of course, these are sanctioned by the Church, but the people who have found this method of noetic prayer, which is much higher than the conventional prayers, abandoned the conventionalities and laid hold of the essence. Since we have lost the essence—perhaps because we don't have teachers to tell us how to pray, or because we don't have the motivation and the desire—we have laid hold of the conventional prayers. Thus, today's monks do their Vespers, their services, and beyond that, nothing. They also work and say that they do their duty in doing so—but they haven't done their duty!

St. John the Almsgiver formed a monastery and said, "Fathers, you do your spiritual duties, and I shall take care of your food, so that you won't have material cares and thus deprive yourselves of prayer. I shall provide you with the necessities, and you pray."

The abbot answered, "Your All-Holiness, Master, we do fulfill our duties. We read the First Hour, the Third, the Sixth, the Ninth, Vespers, Compline, and serve Liturgy."

"Ah!" he replied. "It is obvious that you are negligent! Then what do you do the rest of the time?"

What was the saint trying to say with this? He was saying that they did not fulfill their duty because they did not pray without ceasing.

When we get up for our vigil, after we say the "Heavenly King," the Trisagion, the Fiftieth Psalm, and the Creed, we should bend our head a little on top of our chest, and we should try to tear our nous away from everything and put it inside our chest, within our heart. As we bend our head, we should compel our nous to go in there. Once it enters, we should begin by saying with the breathing, "Lord Jesus Christ, have mercy on me." And you will see. Of course in the beginning, there may be some small difficulty, but a little perseverance and patience will bring the desired result. Then once one's heart has been ignited and sweetened and he gets the knack of it, nothing can stop him, even if he sits there all night. And then you will see that time passes and you will say, "But I just started to pray." And you will find immense benefit from this method of prayer.

For what purpose did we come here? Didn't we come to find God? Didn't we come to find His grace? Didn't we come to find peace? Didn't we come to be delivered from the passions? Well then, with this prayer all these things are accomplished. The prayer will produce a warmth, a flame within the soul. After the prayer generates this warmth, the warmth will bring more prayer, and so forth. Then once this happens, you will see that little by little, weaknesses are burned up, thoughts are burned up, the passions are burned up, and we end up with purity of heart. And then the Father, the Son, and the Holy Spirit will come and make an abode, a dwelling in the heart.

The Holy Fathers say that the nous is easily defiled and easily purified, whereas the heart is purified with difficulty and defiled with difficulty.[8] The nous is easily defiled when it is distracted by something evil. The heart, however, does not immediately participate in the defilement. When the heart has created a good spiritual condition but later loses it somehow and the nous begins to be defiled by various things, the heart does not change easily—for previously it had been changed by grace, and so evil progresses slowly and with difficulty.

Therefore, prayer is needed to transform the heart from being fleshy, passionate, and egocentric, into dispassionate, so that it feels no passions. When the center is purified, the rays and the circumference will become pure. Prayer will drive out despair, hopelessness, negligence, and laziness, because it will produce a new resolve, a fresh desire for new struggles.

So when we sense this transformation within us, then we will understand precisely what the fruit and the goal of prayer are. Then we will understand that the Kingdom of Heaven is within our heart: "The Kingdom of God is within you."[9]

It is there, within the heart, that we will find the precious pearl, by digging with the prayer, breathing in and out, and striving to keep our nous attentive in our heart. What is that pearl? It is the grace of the Holy Spirit, which we received when we were baptized. But whether out of ignorance or because we progressed in the passions, this grace has been buried.

Another helpful method is to inhale and follow the air as it descends from the nose to the larynx, to the lungs, and then to the heart. There is where we should stay, once we take several

---

[8] Vid. *The Ascetical Homilies of Saint Isaac the Syrian,* Holy Transfiguration Monastery, Boston, 2011, p. 133.

[9] Lk. 17:21

breaths. This is where we should hold the nous: in the heart. In the meantime, we should breathe slowly, gently, calmly—not hastily. In the beginning, the devil brings distress and the heart feels some difficulty, and other negative feelings. But gradually it will begin to break through this difficulty and the beauty of it will begin. And then there is no need for a teacher—the prayer itself will teach us.

You will see that, automatically, the nous and the heart on their own will desire to pray in this manner, because they perceive the benefit to be much more than what you imagine it to be now. For here everything is capitalized on. Here is gold—not coins or silver or anything else. This is solid gold. Who can discover gold somewhere and not go there to collect it with all his eagerness and greediness?

I marveled at my Elder. We had special stools for prayer; they were just like regular chairs but lower, and the armrests were higher for more comfort. He would sit there for hours on end, saying, "Lord Jesus Christ, have mercy on me." And when divine grace was active and the nous was clear, he would stop saying the prayer and begin theoria with his nous. But when he didn't find theoria and his nous was wandering, he put it in his heart again and obtained benefit from prayer. Thus he obtained benefit either from the prayer or from theoria, and in this way he would spend seven, eight, nine hours.

After praying and praying, you think that you have just started. What are three or four hours? And if the nous wants to escape, to "unwind," it is pulled back as if there were something in the heart pulling it back and attracting it. Little by little, a person who occupies himself with this prayer is perfected inwardly. His heart is purified more and more, and subsequently he acquires *prayer of the heart*.* Then he attains high levels of prayer. On its own, the nous follows the heart as it says the prayer. At this level, inhaling and exhaling the prayer is unnecessary. This is called prayer of the heart.

Our Holy Fathers, after occupying themselves with the prayer for many years, gradually acquired ardor and then eros for God. Then, once divine eros greatly increased, they went out of themselves and came to theoria and had ecstasies; God took them. Did He take them with their soul? With their body?[9] It is not important; in any case, they went out of themselves. A person does not know if he goes up there with his heart or with his body. He only knows that this high level of prayer brought him to theoria.

We see that when St. Gregory of Sinai went to St. Maximos Kafsokalyvis, whom they considered deluded, he asked him, "Geronda, tell me: have you acquired the prayer?"

He answered, "Forgive me, father, I am deluded. Do you have anything to eat?"

Then St. Gregory answered, "I wish I had your delusion," and repeated, "Tell me, have you acquired the prayer?"

"Well . . . that is precisely why I go into the wilderness, so that I can retain the prayer," said St. Maximos.

"Have you experienced the fruits of the Holy Spirit?" St. Gregory continued asking.

"Eh, those things are from God," answered St. Maximos.

"And where does your nous go when you have the prayer and the grace of God comes?"

"It ascends to divine things. It goes to the Last Judgment, to paradise, to hell, to the Second Coming; God takes it to heavenly light, to the state of Heaven."

All these things spring from noetic prayer. Without it, none of this happens. We see how much this method of prayer helps one to attain ceaseless prayer. He who practices prayer in this manner, even when he is at work doing his handicraft,

---

[10] cf. 2 Cor. 12:2

will say the prayer as he inhales and exhales, without even wanting to. The prayer will stick to his breathing. As soon as he inhales, he will start saying the prayer without wanting to—this method has such beautiful results.

We must begin with desire, with eagerness, with zeal. One has a little difficulty in the beginning, but the road will open, and then no one can stop him. Let the others say whatever they want afterwards—his soul has been sweetened, and no one can stop him. Then you will see that you find grace, alleviation from the passions, and especially alleviation from filthy thoughts. You will find great relief. They will be obliterated with time. They will be wiped out from the nous through prayer, and the heart will become completely well. The heart will become like the heart of a child who feels no passions. It will see everything naturally.

Since we had acquired the habit of saying the prayer with inhaling and exhaling, when we served and had to say the petitions, sometimes—in the beginning, of course—I nearly said, "Lord Jesus Christ . . ." instead of the words of the petitions! For it was a matter of breathing, and the prayer had stuck to it. A person grows so accustomed to it that nothing can make it leave afterwards. That is how much it overcomes a person—of course, in proportion to the energy he employs. In the beginning, he will be able to say it for a short period of time; the next day, more; the next day even more; and then he will say it constantly.

When we were on the Holy Mountain and our Elder was alive, we said the prayer for two, three, four, five hours with inhaling and exhaling. Of course, when sleep fought us, we got up and went outside to say the prayer out loud, for more "relaxation," so to speak. But when sleep was not an issue, we stayed inside all night.

St. Gregory Palamas says that when the prayer is said with every breath, in time a subtle fragrance comes out of the nostrils. Indeed, this is the case. Through prayer a fragrant air will be produced which is nothing but a fruit of prayer. When we were beginners and were saying the prayer like that, there was so much fragrance that everything smelled sweet—our beards, and even out of our chests came so much fragrance. The air we inhaled and exhaled was all fragrant, and I thought to myself, "What is this prayer?" It is the name of Christ! And what doesn't the name of Christ contain within it? By the name of Christ, the Holy Gifts are sanctified; by the name of Christ, Baptism is done, the Holy Spirit comes, the saints raised the dead. By the name of Christ, everything is done.

One of the Watchful Fathers said that when the soul departs from a person who has acquired the prayer, it is not possible for the demons to remain near him, since his soul departs with this prayer. The name of Christ is his weapon. His soul is armored with the prayer. How can the demons approach him? That is how great its benefit is.

This is why the angel who taught St. Pachomios said, "Many learned men abandoned their studies and their scholarly works, occupied themselves with this prayer, and attained sanctity." Likewise, the hermitess Photini[†] wrote that the services are like one's daily wages: if you worked, you are paid and can buy food; if you didn't work, you don't get anything. This is how the conventional prayers of the Church are. But unceasing, noetic prayer gives you not only your daily wages, but it produces great spiritual wealth, and you can put it in the bank and get rich.

With this prayer, a person sits and listens to his heart working. This work is very productive! Just as a machine works

---

[†] The hermitess Photini lived in complete seclusion near the Jordan River in the beginning of the twentieth century. Her life has been published in Greek by Archimandrite Joachim Spetsieris. Our monastery published the story of her life in English in 2000.

on its own once we get it started, the same thing happens when one progresses in the science of prayer. As in the old days, machines were manually operated and required a lot of labor, but once it is made automatic and electric, it is more productive and requires less labor. The same thing happens with prayer. In the beginning, it requires labor to regulate the prayer with one's breathing. But afterwards the work becomes automatic, and the nous monitors it as a machinist monitors a motor.

Prayer is aided by keeping silent, by not having boldness or pride. Pride is a very great obstacle to prayer. When praying, as soon as the nous has proud thoughts, criticize yourselves constantly so that pride does not raise its ugly head. It is beneficial even to hit yourselves with a cane and call yourselves names so that pride does not raise its head at all. A person should not be thinking anything at times of prayer but should only try to pray with fear. The more he adorns his prayer with love and humility and the fear of God, the more progress he will have. If you try this out in practice, you will see for yourselves.

Just as when we go into a candy store we find chocolates, pastries, and various sweets, so also in the spiritual candy store one finds many different sweets, and we will take whatever the baker gives us. We will do our duty to regulate our prayer and humble ourselves, and then whatever God sends is His business. We will do all the formalities, but it is God Who will give the substance to prayer. But the more humbly we pray, the more benefit we will have. Most importantly, though, the nous must be attentive to the words of the prayer, without thinking anything else at all. This is the heart of the whole matter. It is impossible for a person praying in this manner to be deluded.

So this is how we will pray from now on. This method will be our rule of prayer, because it will greatly assist us to see our passions, our faults. All this effort will help us collect our nous. However, light and moving around create commotion in the nous. But when a person remains in one place, whether standing, sitting, or kneeling, his nous has no commotion. This method has a lot of substance in it. If you work at it, you will see for yourselves, and you will find great things.

There was a certain pilgrim who had been initiated in noetic prayer. Because he had much meditation, self-denial, and freedom from cares—since he was not bound with a family, work, or any other things—he said the prayer continuously and felt very great love for Christ. That is, he really did have divine eros in his soul. He had a great desire to go to the all-holy tomb of Christ; he thought that there he would in some way have his fill of love for his dearly beloved Christ. So he went down to Jerusalem to the tomb of Christ and went inside to venerate it. Certainly he felt intense feelings of passionate spiritual eros. He reflected that here the One Whom he worshipped—Jesus Christ—had been buried and that here was His empty tomb, and so forth. As he venerated the holy tomb, right there upon the tomb, he gave up his soul! When the others saw this, they said, "Let's see what this man had hidden in his heart!" They did an autopsy, cut open his heart, and were amazed: there within his heart were written the words, "Jesus, my sweet love."[†]

Do you see how rich the prayer had made this man? How much it had enriched him with divine love? Just think where he found himself after his death! Certainly angels received his soul and took it before the throne of Christ crowned in splendor.

Only through noetic prayer does man reach dispassion. Neither by much reading nor with much chanting or by any other way is it possible to attain dispassion. He who prays in

---

[†] A similar miracle occurred with the heart of St. Ignatius the God-bearer.

this way will learn on his own to hate idle talk and boldness, and will try to find time alone in order not to lose the spiritual state he finds through prayer.

I pray that God will give you the feeling of this prayer. And when grace comes, then you will discover these things in practice and understand what I am telling you now.

Saint Anthony the Great

Patristic Counsels on Prayer

T he work of the Jesus prayer is not just for one or two days, but it lasts a long time and many years," observes the divine Chrysostom. "For much struggle and time is needed for the devil to be expelled and for Christ to take up His dwelling. . . . Devote yourselves to prayer, therefore, and wait on the Lord our God, until He has mercy on us. Seek nothing but mercy from the Lord of glory, with a humble and piteous heart. Cry out from morning to evening and, if possible, all night: 'Lord Jesus Christ, have mercy on me.' And compel your nous in this work until death."

All our Fathers give similar advice, each in his own way and with his own words, depending on his experience of war and victory over the enemy—who is literally unnerved and totally enfeebled by unceasing noetic prayer.

"Brethren, always breathe Christ," urges St. Anthony the Great, the Professor of the Desert.

"Always remember God, and your mind will become Heaven," declares St. Nilos the Wise.

The more one persists in prayer, the more the heart is purified, the more the nous is illumined, the better one's disposition becomes, and the more the Kingdom of God spreads its joy and its presence within man, who is in the image of God and for whom the God-Man Jesus covered all the ends of Heaven and earth with His virtue, His Passion, and His Resurrection.

A person who withers his sense of taste through asceticism, who restrains his senses from all the delights of the world, and who stands courageously until the end against the influences of the ruler of this world, will receive here in this life a foretaste of the good things of the Heavenly Kingdom: tranquility of thoughts, peace of heart, sweet flowing tears, rapture of the nous, knowledge of mysteries, superabundance of love, theoria of God, perfection "as far as possible for human nature." All this is attained through a systematic, continual, persistent, unyielding struggle for noetic prayer. But for this unceasing noetic meditation to be heard by God, a person who prays must also fulfill the monastic (and in general Christian) terms of the spiritual life, which in turn help prayer.

As for a disciple monk, unshakeable obedience is required towards the Elder, who is the visible model of the life of Christ the Savior. As for all Christians, it is required that they regulate their lives according to the advice of their spiritual fathers and that they obey the Canons of the One, Holy, Orthodox Church, so that each individual does not wander off on his own road of wishes and desires, just as the Holy Scriptures advise that we be attentive.

The very simple and comprehensive view of Abba Minoos is cited in *The Sayings of the Desert Fathers*: "Obedience in return for obedience: when someone obeys God, God obeys him." And Abba Isaiah elucidates this at greater length: "It is impossible for God not to hear a person, if that person does not disobey God; for He is not far from man, but it is our will that does not let Him hear our prayer."

If you pray and are not heard, make sure that you are not perchance being disobedient. If you pray at night and are not careful with your lifestyle during the day, it is as though you are building and destroying at the same time. If you are indifferent in little things, you will definitely succumb and fall in big things. Attend to yourself.

God will not send His grace permanently into a heart that does not put up a fence against its desires, or into a mind that shows no sign of restraining itself from its aimless wandering. In the beginning God gives His grace to help us, to rouse us, to sweeten the senses of our soul, to attract us. But if we do not labor along with it, grace will have no effect and will withdraw. Appetite comes from eating, and prayer from praying.

Are you at your diakonema, at your work? Remember what the Holy Fathers said to themselves as they worked: "Body, work so that you may be fed; soul, be watchful so that you may be saved." Is your mind wandering? Say the prayer in a whisper and do not talk idly, for you will also harm others, including yourself, through idle talk.

Abba Philemon said, "Many of the Holy Fathers could see the angels watching them, which is why they guarded themselves with silence and did not converse with anyone."

Instead of wasting your time, say the prayer. And the more that listlessness and indifference come upon you, the more you should fear the threat which the Lord addressed to the wicked and slothful servant.[1] If you let the days and nights pass with increasing negligence, soon you will end up extremely negligent. Will you perhaps boast of your negligence, when others will receive crowns for their labors?

Brother, labor a little in prayer and watchfulness, and you will see joy well up in your heart and light dawn in the firmament of your mind—not the kind of joy that disappears before you enjoy it, but the joy that is sweet, similar to the sweetness of the angels, and the light without evening of the other world, which Christ, the light of the world, Who comes through the prayer, will bestow upon you before you depart from this world. Didn't this happen to our Fathers, and can't this happen to us as well if our lack of faith and our negligence do not prevent it?

My Elder also used to say, "Labor a little in order to have God as your debtor, and in time He will send you much more than what you labored for or sought."

---

[1] cf. Mt. 25:26

But do not forget the words of St. Isaac the Syrian: "First the devil struggles to do away with the unceasing prayer of the heart, and then persuades the monk to disregard also the appointed times of prayer and his prayer rule, which is done with bows and prostrations."

So do not listen to the whispers of negligence, and if you want God to cover your faults, you also cover your brother's and bear with him during his temptations and pain.

Do not talk back and do not conceal thoughts from your spiritual father, for you will labor your whole life in vain, and your prayer will remain fruitless.

If you are not cleansed through frank confession, how will you approach to receive the immaculate and life-creating Mysteries of Christ? Haven't you heard that they bring life to those who partake worthily, and death to those who receive unworthily?

Do not say, "I am just like the others," for this is foolishness, and the Judge cannot be deceived.

Every thought which brings despair and excessive grief is from the devil, and you should reject it immediately, for it will cut the thread of prayer. Every thought which causes moderate grief within the soul, mixed with joy and tears, is from God. The grace of God never drives a person to despair, but only leads him to repentance.

Anthology on Noetic Prayer

1. Prayer is one of the foremost and strongest powers that causes him who prays to be born again, and it grants him bodily and spiritual well-being.

2. Prayer is the eyes and wings of the soul; it gives us the boldness and strength to behold God.

3. My brother, keep praying with your mouth until divine grace enlightens you to pray also with your heart. Then a celebration and festival will take place within you in a wondrous way, and you will no longer pray with your mouth, but with the attention which works in the heart.

4. If you truly desire to expel every anti-Christian thought and to purify your nous, you will achieve this only through prayer, for nothing is able to regulate our thoughts as well as prayer.

5. Be careful, because if you are lazy and inattentive in prayer, you shall not make any progress either in your pursuit of devotion towards the Lord, or in the acquisition of salvation and peace of thoughts.

6. The name of Jesus Christ, which we invoke in prayer, contains within it self-existing and self-acting restorative power. So do not worry about the imperfection and dryness of your prayer, but with perseverance await the fruit of the repeated invocation of the divine name.

7. When guided by prayer, the moral powers within us become stronger than all our temptations and conquer them.

8. Frequency in prayer creates a habit of prayer, which quickly becomes second nature and which frequently brings the nous and the heart to a higher spiritual state. It is the only way to reach the height of true and pure prayer. It constitutes the best means of effective preparation for prayer and the surest road for one to reach the destination of prayer and salvation.

9. Each one of us is able to acquire interior prayer—that is, to make it a means of communication with the Lord. It does not cost anything except the effort to plunge into silence and into the depths of our heart, and the care to call upon the name of our sweetest Jesus Christ as often as possible, which fills one with elation. Plunging into ourselves and examining the world of our soul give us the opportunity to know what a mystery man is, to feel the delight of self-knowledge, and to shed bitter tears of repentance for our falls and the weakness of our will.

10. May your entire soul cleave with love to the meaning of the prayer, so that your nous, your inner voice, and your will—these three components of your soul—become one, and the one become three; for in this way man, who is an image of the Holy Trinity, comes into contact with and is united to the prototype. As the great worker and teacher of noetic prayer, the divine Gregory Palamas of Thessalonica said, "When the oneness of the nous becomes threefold, yet remains single, then it is united with the divine Triadic Unity, and it closes the door to every form of delusion and is raised above the flesh, the world, and the prince of the world."[1]

11. Wherever the prayer is active, there is Christ with the Father and the Holy Spirit, the Holy Trinity, one in essence and indivisible. Wherever there is Christ, the Light of the world, there is the eternal light of the other world; there is peace and joy; there are the angels and the saints; there is the splendor of the Kingdom. Blessed are those who in this present life have clothed themselves with the Light of the world—Christ—for they have already put on the garment of incorruption.

---

[1] *The Philokalia,* Vol. IV, p. 343.

12. Since Christ is the light of the world, those who do not see Him, who do not believe in Him, are all most certainly blind. Conversely, all who strive to practice the commandments of Christ walk in the light; they confess Christ and venerate and worship Him as God. Whoever confesses Christ and regards Him as his Lord and God is strengthened by the power of the invocation of His name to do His will. But if he is not strengthened, it is evident that he confesses Christ only with his mouth, while in his heart he is far from Him.

13. Just as it is impossible for someone who walks at night not to stumble, likewise it is impossible for someone who has not yet seen the divine light not to sin.

14. The goal of noetic prayer is to unite God with man, to bring Christ into man's heart, banishing the devil from there and destroying all the work that he has accomplished there through sin. For, as the beloved disciple says, "For this purpose the Son of God was manifested, that He might destroy the works of the devil."[2] Only the devil knows the inexpressible power of these seven words of the Jesus prayer, and this is why he wars and fights against the prayer with furious rage. Countless times the demons have confessed through the mouths of possessed people that they are burned by the action of the prayer.

15. The more the prayer unites us with Christ, the more it separates us from the devil—and not only from the devil, but also from the spirit of the world, which engenders and sustains the passions.

16. The prayer's satan [i.e., adversary] is listlessness. Satan's satan is the desire for the prayer, the fervor of the heart. "Be fervent in spirit," says the Apostle, "serving the Lord."[3] This fervor draws and retains grace for the one who prays, and it becomes light and joy and indescribable consolation for

---

[2] 1 Jn. 3:8
[3] Rom. 12:11

him—but to the demons it is fire and bitterness and persecution. When this grace comes, it collects the nous from its wandering and sweetens it with the mindfulness of God, healing it of all evil and unclean thoughts.

17. Is the prayer on your lips? Then grace is there as well. But from the lips it must pass into the nous and descend into the heart—and this takes much time and labor. The tongue must toil in order to pay for all its idle talk and its falls, and it must acquire the habit of praying. For without labor and practice, a habit cannot be formed. Humility must also appear for grace to come. After that, the road is clear; the prayer cleaves to our breathing and the nous wakes up and follows it. With time the passions abate, thoughts subside, and the heart grows calm.

18. Do not get tired of bringing your nous back every time it wanders. God will see your eagerness and your toil, and will send His grace to collect it. When grace is present, all is done with joy, without toil.

19. With the prayer, we pass from one joy to another; without the prayer, we pass from one fall to another, from affliction to affliction, and heavy is our remorse. In short, with a little labor and pain in the prayer, we obtain much joy-making mourning, compunction, and tears, along with the sweetness of the presence of God and the immaculate fear of Him, which cleanses and purifies nous and heart.

20. The heart must be purified for the nous also to be enlightened by it with the pure thoughts reflected towards the nous from above.

21. It is not the unrepentant who enter the Kingdom of God, but sinners who are transformed through repentance and tears. Nothing helps man fight and conquer the passions as much as unceasing noetic prayer.

22. When you are attacked by listlessness, when the nous, the tongue, and the fingers on the prayer rope are flagging, I beg you not to give up. Make a little more effort, so that God will see your resolve and strengthen you. There is something more that God wants from you, and He allows this time of temptation so that you may give it. For He knows—and you know—that you can do more.

Therefore, compel yourself as much as you can at your appointed time of prayer; do your duty to have God as your debtor. And if you do not receive grace, you have prepared yourself for the next time or the time after that. In any case, sooner or later you shall receive grace; it is impossible for you not to. In fact, it is God's practice to give much more when He delays.

23. The field of the heart yields in accordance to how well it has been plowed by prayer, watered by tears, and weeded of thoughts.

24. From time to time it happens that, without your being at fault, grace withdraws. It is as if God were saying to you, "All your works are fine, but do not think that everything depends on you. I shall come and go as I see fit, to teach you to completely cut off your will and to be patient, so that you learn the lesson of humility well."

25. Those who are advanced in the prayer have the indubitable conviction that, in spite of all man's labor, prayer is the work of grace.

26. St. Symeon the New Theologian says clearly that no one is able to glorify God on his own, but it is the grace of Christ, which has taken abode in him, that glorifies and hymns God and prays within him.

27. It is a sign that the grace of God has visited the soul when one prays with fear and reverence, standing with much orderliness and giving great attention to what one is praying.

28. Attention must be inseparably bound to prayer in the same way the body is inseparably bound to the soul. In other words, the nous should guard the heart at times of prayer, always circling around within it, and from there, from the depths of the heart, it should send up prayers to God, continuously saying "Lord Jesus Christ, have mercy on me." Once it tastes and experiences there in the heart that the Lord is good, and it is sweetened, the nous no longer wants to leave the place of the heart, but says along with the Apostle Peter, "It is good for us to be here."[4] It wants to circle around, pushing out and expelling, so to speak, all ideas sown in there by the devil, not allowing any thought of this world to remain, and thus becoming poor in spirit—bereft of every worldly thought.

Such a task seems very arduous and oppressive to those who do not know about it. But those who have tasted its sweetness and enjoyed its pleasure in the depths of their hearts, cry out with the divine Paul, "Who shall separate us from the love of Christ?"[5]

29. Our Holy Fathers, heeding the Lord Who said that the evil thoughts which defile man proceed out of the heart[6] and that we must cleanse the inside of the cup for the outside to be clean also,[7] left every other spiritual work and devoted themselves completely to this work—namely, to the guarding of the heart—being certain that, together with this work, they would easily acquire every other virtue as well.

30. The God-bearing St. Symeon the New Theologian says, "Let us purify our hearts, so that we may find the omnipresent Lord within us. Let us purify our hearts with the fire of His grace, that we may see within ourselves the light and glory of His divinity."

---

[4] Mt. 17:4

[5] Rom. 8:35

[6] cf. Mt. 15:19-20

[7] cf. Mt. 23:26

31. Fortunate are those who have approached the divine light and entered into it, and have been united to the light and become all light; for they have completely stripped themselves of the defiled garment of their sins and will no longer weep bitter tears. Fortunate are those who have known already in this life the light of the Lord as the Lord Himself, for they will stand before Him with boldness in the life to come. Fortunate are those who have received Christ, Who came as light to them, who were formerly in darkness, for they have now become sons of the light and of the day without evening.

32. St. Gregory Palamas says that when the prayer is practiced in conjunction with breathing in and out, in time it causes a sweet breath of grace, a savor of spiritual fragrance, to come forth from the nostrils of the person praying—"a savor of life unto life,"[8] according to the great Paul. Truly, there is nothing like the breath of the prayer, of unceasing noetic prayer. The prayer sheds grace not only on the person praying, but it also overflows and is diffused, spreading through him to creation. As he breathes in, he is purified, vivified, and sanctified; as he breathes out, he purifies, vivifies, and sanctifies creation—it is not he, but divine grace that accomplishes this.

33. In these last days, when the breath of the Antichrist pollutes land and sea and every breath of life, God fans the activity of noetic prayer in the bosom and heart of the Church like a refreshing dew of grace, like the breeze heard by the Prophet Elias,[9] as an antidote for the health and salvation of soul and body in the days that are upon us and those to come.

34. I know thousands of souls in the world—throughout the whole world, I would say—who compel themselves in the prayer with wondrous results. The prayer fortifies them in their spiritual struggle; it enlightens them inwardly, and they

---

[8] 2 Cor. 2:16
[9] vid. 3 Kings 19:12

confess thoroughly and sincerely. Distressed by the thoughts and temptations which the demons rouse against those who say the prayer, they run with longing to the immaculate Mysteries. Then, they run back to the struggle with thoughts and passions, and then, back again to the Mysteries—they can no longer do without the prayer.

35. The prayer is breath. When a person breathes, he is alive, and he attends to his whole life. Whoever begins to say the prayer, also begins to correct his whole life, with his spiritual father as a guide. Just as the rising sun awakens, illuminates, and gives life to creation, so also when Christ, the Sun of Righteousness, rises by means of the prayer in man's nous and heart, He awakens him to do the works of light and of the day without evening.

36. Therefore, brethren, "breathe Christ continuously," as St. Anthony the Great, the chief of the ascetics, used to say. And the Apostle to the Gentiles advises, exhorts, and commands all Christians of every place and time to "pray without ceasing."[10] The divine Fathers explain that "without ceasing" means that there is no end or measure to it.

So in time of peace do not be negligent, but pray; correct yourself; prepare for war. Take courage. Do not fear temptations. Everyone experiences changes, but patience and perseverance are needed in the struggle. The righteous man, even if he falls a thousand times a day, rises again and it is considered a victory for him. This is what the prayer means: continuous repentance, incessant calling on divine mercy.

To Christ our God, Who gives prayer to him who prays,[11] be glory and thanksgiving unto the ages. Amen.

---

10 1 Thes. 5:17
11 1 Kings 2:9

Chapter Sixteen

On Contemplation

a nous that has ceased to contemplate God becomes either carnal or savage."[1] In other words, when the mind of man strays from the various ways of contemplating God—that is, praying, meditating on spiritual contemplations such as hell, paradise, one's sins, one's passions, the countless benefactions of the Lord which He bestows upon each of us in a wondrous manner, and so forth—then evil demons come and fill him with their own contemplations which lead him into the mire of carnal, passionate sins, or into the sins of wrath and anger!

When the mind does not contemplate salvific thoughts—except for thoughts necessary for the sustenance of life—it will be obsessed with sinful contemplations, and then it will be either carnal or savage! Let us then, my children, pay close attention to what we are thinking, so that we do not let our mind slip into passionate, sinful thoughts, because this is a very serious sin with grave consequences.

Be careful with your imagination. Do not let your mind accept fantasies of people and sinful images that carnally scandalize you or lead you to wrath and anger! Rather, see to it

---

[1] cf. St. Mark the Ascetic, *The Philokalia,* Vol. I, p. 132.

that with every good effort you keep your mind pure of such fantasies, so that being free and pure of such things, it will be able henceforth to pray constantly and have godly contemplations. Through them it will be made spiritual and make heavenly ascents towards the soul's sanctification.

2. Fear of God is necessary. "I beheld the Lord ever before me . . . so that I not be shaken."[2] One must remember that God is everywhere present and fills all things; we must remember that we breathe God, we eat God, we wear God, and that we have God within our heart and nous.

God knows our thoughts, our recollections, our words, our deeds, our intentions. Nothing escapes His all-seeing eye—not only present things, but even past and future events; not only those of men alive now, but of all men from Adam until the last man before the end of the world. Man is unable to do anything without God knowing, since everything is done before His eyes.

When a person meditates upon and contemplates all these things, he feels sharp pangs of conscience for his transgressions and weaknesses. A genuine fear of God overcomes him, and he tries to change his life and conform it to the divine commandments. By meditating upon these things, he feels the presence of God, which previously had escaped his notice due to his ignorance. A genuine fear guides him to clean the inside of the cup, as the Lord has said[3]—not saying one thing with the mouth and another in the heart. By meditating upon these things, his conscience awakens, and at the slightest thing, it cries out through the voice of censure. He then acquires keenness in his spiritual life: his spiritual eyes are opened, and he sees clearly what is lurking within him. He prays fervently to God: "From my secret sins cleanse me, and from those of others spare Thy servant."[4]

---

2 Ps. 15:8
3 vid. Mt. 23:26
4 Ps. 18:13

3. It is not so easy for the demons to harm a person who keeps the constant remembrance of God in his soul. They can tempt him, but it is difficult for them to harm him. This is because he does not permit them to trip him up, for he is armed with the weapon of the constant remembrance of God. Whoever has his soul's eyes open and sees God is not easily harmed by the enemies.

The very spiritual men of old did not need spiritual books. They did not have such a great need to read many patristic books, because they constantly meditated upon things about God. Whatever they saw immediately gave them an opportunity to meditate upon something, to discover something unknown. All of creation was a university for them. Wherever they turned their eyes, they saw something to meditate upon—sometimes the providence of God, other times His wisdom; sometimes His judgment, other times His teachings, and so on. With the eyes of their soul they saw invisible things. Meditating upon them filled their hearts with spiritual knowledge.

We people of today—since we do not have the eyes of our soul open—do not have the ability to remain in this spiritual meditation. Even when we do see something, we need religious books to know something about God.

The minds of these spiritual men were so strong that they could conceive thoughts and ideas with deep wisdom. Our minds are so weak that they can barely retain anything. The Fathers then were, for the most part, simple people; yet, they acquired full knowledge, because the Holy Spirit helped them understand the Scriptures.

The remembrance of God is an all-powerful weapon, a mighty suit of armor against Satan and the various sins. When the mind ceases to remember God and meditate upon divine things, man is overcome by negligence, indolence, forgetfulness, and then by evil desires!

If you see your mind rushing towards the world, know that your soul lacks divine consolation, which is why it turns to the world for consolation. When a person's soul is warm towards God, he is enlightened and feels compunction, and it is impossible for his mind to incline towards the world at the same time. The soul inclines towards the world when it is not united, in a sense, with God.

The mind is an area, a place. If God does not occupy it, then the enemy will occupy it. This place cannot remain empty, having neither God nor evil, sin, temptation, or the activity of Satan.

The mind is like a mill that is turning. Whatever is thrown into the funnel, which leads to the millstones below, will come out as flour of that type. If you throw wheat in, you will get wheat flour. If you throw thorns in, you will get thorn flour—a harmful substance.

The mill is always turning; the mind of man is always working—like a mill. Do you want to have good results? Put good material into the mill. Do you want to find compunction, tears, joy, peace, etc.? Put good thoughts into the mill of your mind—for example, thoughts about the soul, about the Judgment, the remembrance of death, and so on—and then you will get corresponding spiritual results! But if a person puts sinful thoughts into the mill of his mind, he will definitely have sin as a result. The material that will be given to the mind depends on the intentions of man. And these intentions will be either commended or censured.

We should always strive to have salvific thoughts and beneficial images in our mind, so that we do not leave room for Satan to throw in his garbage—sinful thoughts and fantasies!

4. Progress in prayer brings us to theoria, and we may even see indescribable things. It brings us to the Last Judgment, to paradise, to the sight of hell, before the throne of God, to heavenly light, and so forth. One might begin chanting and then stop at a point, and be overcome by the meaning of the words chanted. He might start reading something from The Song of Songs, and then stop somewhere, and the theoria may widen and end up wherever God leads it. One might be reading the Gospel about the Passion of Christ, and then stop at a point—for example, at His arrest, His suffering, His crucifixion, His resurrection, etc.—and contemplate it with feeling, compunction, and self-reproach. Sometimes we might be fathoming the Judgment, thinking for example, "If I die now, how shall I present myself to God? What will the decision be for me? Shall I be damned, perhaps? How shall I pass the tollhouses?" Other times we might be contemplating the Panagia, her glory, her virginity, etc., or contemplating the saints, and so on.

5. "When Thou openest Thy hand, all things will be filled with goodness; when Thou turnest away Thy face, they will be troubled."[5] Our all-good and munificent God created two worlds. First He made the spiritual world in the heavenly realm with the orders of the innumerable angels, the countless hosts of these ministering spirits, with many "mansions,"[6] and various dwellings. Then He made this tangible world with man as the crown of His divine wisdom, and He commanded him to reign and exercise dominion over everything therein. The goodness of the all-good God inundated the heavenly realm with holy angels, and due to the extreme bliss, they chanted and incessantly hymned with ceaseless doxologies, thanking in this way the eternal goodness and compassion of our holy God, Who blessed them with such

---

[5] Ps. 103:28-29

[6] cf. Jn. 14:2

honor and glory and delight! But alas! The first of the angels, called Lucifer, revolted and rebelled against God. He wanted, desired, wished for equality with God. "I shall ascend above the clouds," he said in his heart, "and be like the Most High."[7] As soon as he consented to this blasphemous and proud thought, the just God turned His sweet, beautiful, divine face away, and immediately with a most frightful crash, Lucifer fell down from his lofty position and rank, and was bound with unbreakable bonds in the gloom of Hades, dragging along with him the entire order which had followed his most evil will! These events took place in the heavenly realm.

Now, here I come, the ignorant and wretched one, to recount and briefly set forth the point and significance for man of the psalmic verse, "When Thou openest Thy hand, all things will be filled with goodness; when Thou turnest away Thy face, they will be troubled."[8]

So, once God created man with such wisdom, He bestowed upon him His image and likeness; He endowed him with reason and freedom; He made in the east the palace of exquisite paradise abounding in countless very fragrant flowers, plants, and trees varying in kind and fruit: "God made trees grow out of the earth," say the Scriptures, "trees that were pleasing to the eyes and good for food."[9] Furthermore, He enriched it with birds of various shapes and colors to fly and sing most sweetly.

In addition, He placed the wild animals and the cattle in the plains as companions for Adam, and made a river to pass through the middle of Paradise and water it with brooks and streams of profuse, crystal-clear water to vitalize and feed the roots of the trees. He also made fresh air and fragrant breezes to bathe the face of the small god, man.

In a word, the Scriptures tell us, "And God made . . . all the animals of the earth . . . and all the birds of the sky . . . and a

---

[7] Is. 14:14
[8] Ps. 103:28-29
[9] Gen. 2:9

river coming out of Eden to water Paradise."[10] This paradisiacal day bathed in sun was not followed by night. And behold, the goodness of our holy God dwelled and rested in the palace of the first-formed man. But who can truly describe the goodness and majesty of God, which His almighty right hand lavishly bestowed upon man? He honored him with His image and likeness; He made him immortal; He made him worthy of speaking with Him, so that by sweetly communicating with God and delighting in His infinite source of blessedness, he would be amazed at the riches of spiritual pleasure.

Throughout his body and soul, dispassion reigned; nothing disturbed him; he ruled over everything; simplicity and innocence enriched his entire state. Everything was subject to him, as to their small god and king. His soul was adorned with virginal purity, which reflected on his exquisitely beautiful body, an original creation of the omnipotent hand of God. God's supervision and goodness reigned over both this earthly king and his palace, as well as over all of creation. Everything had a divine hue, for man, too, kept the divine commandment.

But alas and woe to me! How and from where shall I, the wretch, begin to recount with lamentation the terrible storm that broke out when God turned His face away? With what words and with how much mourning shall I declaim the miserable plight and tragic fall of man from the delight of Paradise—he who was so honored yet so ungrateful? Who could ever honestly grasp in its entirety the tragedy of God turning away His face, of the exile of Adam, of the affliction of nature? Certainly, no one! And who can fathom the abyss of lamentation and inconsolable wailing of the miserable transgressor, sitting at the place of condemnation and gazing from afar at his lost palace? Adam was deceived by Lucifer; he

---

[10] Gen. 2:10

voluntarily consented to proud thoughts; he, too, entertained fantasies of being equal to God! Adam transgressed the commandment, and the punishment of God fell upon him as a fearful tempest and changed the paradisiacal blessedness into a life full of misery and tears. The poor king of earth became proud, and behold, he was driven out of the exceedingly beautiful and delightful Paradise, from his splendid palace. And fallen thenceforth, he was exiled to the bitter earth, full of thorns and thistles, to work laboriously and eat the bread of pain in sweat, with a despairing and deeply sighing soul.

"When Thou turnest away Thy face they will be troubled."[11] Everything is troubled, all things lose their harmony and grace, they get out of order, they forget the joy of Paradise and fall into corruption. This holds true for all of nature, but especially for man.

The ghastly face of accursed sin, which first appeared in Paradise, drove the sovereign out of his delight, once he himself approached it and was lured by it. Thus, from immortal, man became mortal, and from dispassionate, he became passionate! The elements, which were previously submissive and harmless, were altogether shaken at once and arose to destroy him, to mangle him; for they, too, were condemned along with him to the accursed earth. Earth groaned beneath the burden of transgressions that were committed on it, as it awaited with an intense desire and hope the revealing of the children of God so that it might be delivered from its bondage and glorified, as the divine Paul writes to the Romans.[12]

God turns away His face and everything changes. Right after the first fall a second one followed, when Cain killed Abel—that wicked fratricide—and thenceforth sin reigned. God turns away His face because of the impious deeds of men, and water floods the whole world, turning it into a hor-

---

[11] Ps. 103:29
[12] vid. Rom. 8:19-21

rifying tomb for the entire race of man, except for Noah and his family. God turns away His divine manifestation because of man's lechery, and fire burns up the land of Sodom and Gomorrah. God turns away His face and His forbearance, and the proud Pharaoh is engulfed along with all his army, and the water of the sea becomes his eternal tomb.

Time and again, moral evil and sin—as a transgression of the divine law—cause God to turn His face away from men, so that natural evil follows as an inevitable consequence, in the form of diseases, various afflictions, and ultimately—death.

But when the munificent God opens the hand of His goodness, the heart of man becomes a royal palace! The luxuriousness of the royal majesty occupies the most prominent position within him. The royal servants serve their king as he sits upon his inconceivably resplendent and extraordinarily beautiful throne of grace. The royal guards, both those of the high throne and those of the gates, guard the king with vigilant attention! Everything bears witness to the wealth and magnitude of the king's presence and favor. But who is this king, and who are the servants and his guards?

The king? Who else could he be but He Who through Holy Baptism made the heart of man His own house, the Kingdom of the Heavens! As He Himself declared in His Gospel: "The Kingdom of God is within you."[13] The royal servants? They are the divine thoughts that minister to the grace of God so that the royal palace is decorated and so that the glory and comeliness of God shine in it! And who are the royal guards? They are watchfulness, attention, and the thoughts of divine zeal, through which the palace and the king are guarded! Then, goodness and sweet repose in God prevail in the realm of the heart.

---

[13] Lk. 17:21

When, however, some of the royal guards neglect their duty, some give themselves over to gluttony and drinking, while others rush into licentiousness, and yet others betray the king to his enemies—then this good King, the grace of Holy Baptism, hides, leaves, and is no longer visible. Grace turns away its face from those servants and the palace, for the betrayal defiled it.

Then—oh, then—the last state of that man is worse than the first. Then he becomes like him who goes down into the pit of the tomb, whose lot is an unbearable stench. This is why the psalmist prayed fervently, "Turn not Thy face away from me, lest I become like them that go down into the pit."[14]

When youth is in the glory of its blossom, oh, how much beauty it has! It is so beautiful that some people do not differ from heavenly angels. But when the sharpened scythe of death strikes and reaps them, they have to be buried quickly, because there is an imminent danger of infection. They are hidden in frigid tombs, for soon a terrible stink will replace beautiful, fragrant youth!

Something similar takes place with the soul of man. When man is pure of sins and attentive to himself, the grace of God reigns in him, divine goodness adorns him, and everyone delights at the very sight of such a person. But unfortunately, when man sins and does not repent, God turns away His divine eyes, and at once moral darkness overcomes his soul. Then he begins to work evil deeds, and the unclean demons defile that miserable soul more and more each day, and lower it from sin to sin and from passion to passion, thus rendering the soul so fetid that even the holy angels cannot tolerate the stench or stay beside him to help. Therefore, divine grace withdraws, and the putrefaction of sin begins its destructive work. Then the soul resembles a corpse that is tossed in the

---

14 cf. Ps. 27:1

grave: if by chance it is opened shortly thereafter, the sight and stink of the worms, and its revolting condition in general, evoke horror.

My dear children, let us say along with the Archangel of God Who, wishing to prevent other heavenly angels from slipping perchance into Lucifer's dark road of disobedience and pride, said: "Let us stand well." Let us raise our soul every time it stoops, my beloved children. "Let us stand with fear," for the gloomy tomb of sin opens its mouth menacingly, if we are not careful at every moment.

But if we are careful, vigilant, and watchful, then by all means the open hand of the Ruler of All shall fill our heart with divine goodness, and He Himself shall visit the assiduously kept palace of our soul, so that it may taste in this life divine exultation and delight, followed, according to His promise, by the full rendering in His endless Kingdom of the good things prepared as a reward since the foundation of the world for those who love and fulfill His commandments. Amen; so be it.

THE
GIVER

OF
LIFE

Chapter Seventeen

On the Love and Humility of God, on Grace, and on the Fear of God

May the Lord our God give you peace and love, for God is love. Always remember the words of the Lord, Who said: "He who keeps My commandments, it is he who loves Me. And he who loves Me will be loved by My Father . . . and We shall come to him and make Our abode with him."[1]

Let us love God with all our soul, with all our heart, and with all our strength, and may our works keep in step. That is, our works should be a reflection of our love towards Him. And when our works are wrought lawfully, God will repay us with divine love in our souls. He who has found love partakes of Christ every day, and thus he becomes immortal. "If anyone eats of this bread, which I shall give, he will live forever,"[2] says the Holy Gospel.

He who partakes of the love of Christ bears much fruit. The souls that love Jesus breathe the spiritual air of the other world, the world of the spirit, which is the Kingdom of Heaven. Even in this life they taste the waters that flow from the throne of God's grace!

The drink at the heavenly table is divine love. The licentious drank this drink, and the wounds of their sins were

---

[1] Jn. 14:21, 23
[2] cf. Jn. 6:51

soothed; drunkards became fasters; rich men desired poverty in Christ; paupers were enriched with godly hopes; the weak became strong; the unlearned became wise!

Love is the Christian's triumph over the devil, hatred, and envy. In order to reach the divine harbor of God's love, we must first fear Him as God, Who chastens sin and transgression. It is not possible to cross the sea and reach the harbor without a boat. Likewise, it is impossible to reach the harbor of love without repentance. The fear of God, as commander and captain, makes us sit in the boat of repentance and takes us across the murky sea of life and guides us to the divine harbor of divine love. Just as we are unable to live without air, likewise it is impossible to live in the eternal life with God if we do not breathe the very sweet and fragrant air of God's love.

Let us shake off the burden of our sins with the power of repentance, and thenceforth light and free as eagles, let us fly high above where the eternal God has stored up the inexhaustible treasures of virtue and wisdom, so that we may drink the waters of eternal life and be deified, as the Scriptures say: "You are gods, and all of you are the sons of the Most High."[3]

Let us compel ourselves, my children, for the love of God is not gained through negligence and sluggishness but through eagerness, obedience, patience, forbearance, silence, prayer, and forcefulness in everything. So shall we be negligent for such an eternal gift? No! Then let us cry out in lamentation: "Christ, our Master, shut us not out of Thy Kingdom, but open unto us out of Thy compassionate mercy. Amen."

2. God is love and full of compassion. Let us not sadden Him in anything! He endured the Cross for us; His head was

---

[3] Ps. 81:6

pricked by the crown of thorns; His side was pierced by the spear; His feet were nailed; His back was scourged; His All-holy mouth was given gall and vinegar; His heart ached from the insolence and ingratitude; He was naked up on the Cross in front of such a demonic mob. This, my children, is Whom we should not sadden with our carelessness, which intensifies His suffering. The Jews were His enemies, whereas we have been baptized in His holy name—we are His disciples who are devoted to serving Him!

His disciples abandoned Him out of fear of the Jews, and how much He was grieved is beyond description! And now, how will all who deny Him, all who abandon Him, all who promise Him one thing and do another, find themselves before Him at the hour of judgment? What shall they say when our Christ begins to enumerate His sufferings one by one, while they will have only their denial and a multitude of evils to present?

Let us attend to our life, my children. Let us have love and patience in everything. Let us not criticize, let us drive away every evil thought, let us humble ourselves, let us bear in mind the difficult hour of death and judgment.

When you do all these things, know that you will live with Christ eternally! Like angels beside His throne, you will chant everlasting hymns full of joy! What bliss we shall have then! All things here will be forgotten! Only joy and Pascha with no end! Glory to God, Who gives us the victory.

3. I pray that the love of God will refresh your thirsty soul, as the hart quenches its thirst at the fountains of water. "Thus does my soul yearn for Thee, O God. When shall I come and appear before the face of my God?"[4]

Glory to Thee, O God, for Thy great mercy upon me! Without my doing anything good on earth, He consoles and

---

[4] Ps. 41:1, 2

comforts my soul. From time to time the blessed dew of God's love affects my callous soul. Ah, how much it soothes my wretched soul! How much it refreshes my soul and lightens the burdens of life and temptations! Oh, if only God would count me worthy through your prayers to rest eternally in the dew of God's love for which I long!

The salvation of man requires much toil. The tempter—the devil—has activated all his experience and knowledge to annihilate man. Do not depart from us, O God, my God, but be for us as the brass serpent was for Moses,[5] so that by looking at You, we may be healed from the bites of the spiritual serpents.

"When you lift up the Son of Man, then you will know that I am He."[6] My Christ, my light, my crucified love, Who was lifted up on the Cross for our sins, the Serpent that saves souls wounded by the evil serpents, heal us who have been wounded by the stings of sin.

May God bless us and in His good will open His sea of compassion to us, so that we may all be found united together in the eternal and blessed life, where there is neither pain nor sorrow nor sighing, but life unending. "God will wipe away every tear from their eyes."[7]

Oh, what joy that cannot be taken away! What a confident awareness that henceforth the torments of this toilsome life have ended! "What god is as great as our God?"[8] He is a Father overflowing with compassion, Who does not take sins into account, as long as His repenting son says: "I have sinned against Heaven and in your sight."[9] Then at once the Father embraces and kisses him and obliterates from His heart every trace of displeasure that the child's profligacy may have occasioned! I lose my senses when I contemplate His abyss of paternal compassion towards sinners!

---

[5] vid. Num. 21:6-9
[6] Jn. 8:28
[7] Rev. 7:17
[8] Ps. 76:13
[9] Lk. 15:21

4. With what love the blessed souls will be fed in the Kingdom of Heaven! It is He—my Christ, my Jesus, my dearest, the living Logos—Who gave us our existence, as well as the means to exist, eternal redemption, and repose in the bosom of the Heavenly Father. "He spoke and they came into being; He commanded and they were created!"[10]

He chastens us a little in order to keep us humble, for He knows how easily our weak human nature changes, how easily it turns towards evil. He treats us with paternal solicitude and chastens us lovingly, so that we may obtain firm wisdom.

This is the knowledge of the perfect saints: (it is not as some people explain it, but it has its own special power) to put it simply, one must confess that even when one is at the heavenly height of virtue, it is possible—if God abandons him—for him to fall into the abyss of corruption and debauchery! It is not a matter of just saying this with empty words, but one must really feel this way. But one cannot say this with conviction if one does not first pass through the Babylonian furnace of temptations, and if one's human nature does not slip by God's permission, so that he realizes his weak constitution. He then sees with whom he has to wrestle, what the wickedness and malice of his adversary (the devil) is, and how difficult it is to rise after a fall! In brief, this is what "know thyself" means.

When one obtains this knowledge, the Holy Trinity dwells in his heart. Then bliss gushes forth endlessly, and he reaches the point of seeing revelations! This is what Abba Isaac writes—that great boast of hesychasts.

One holy monk stood up to say his evening prayers and stretched out his arms. When the grace of God came upon him—he had his back to the setting sun—it overcame him so

---

[10] Ps. 32:9

much that he didn't come to himself until the sun rose the next morning and warmed his face. Then he realized that it was the next day, and he glorified God Who counts men made of earth worthy to see such mysteries.

Oh! Those days of grace have passed, and now there is a bitter cold even in the warm countries, that is, in the dwellings of monks and hermits. Good examples and virtue have vanished!

How vividly the monastic saints must have felt grace in prayer! God visits us somewhat faintly in prayer, and we feel a little bit of grace. But they who were engrossed in theoria all night long—how intensely they must have felt the Kingdom of Heaven! "The Kingdom of Heaven is within us."[11]

Oh, how much I would have liked to live in those days when sanctity and good examples were abundant—now there is only aridity and misery. Let us once again thank God immensely that in such a moral darkness He has given us a little light, so that even by stumbling forward we are able to reach the gates of the heavenly Jerusalem and not be shut out in the eternal darkness. May this not happen to any Christian, my dear Christ, but may all of us together be counted worthy to reach there with joy and a joyful step, celebrating the eternal Pascha![12] Amen.

5. A person whose mouth always thanks God will by no means lack the blessings of God, but a person whose mouth grumbles and wounds his great Benefactor shall certainly be chastened by God.

He gave us our being; He gives us life; He preserves us in various ways with His divine providence. Through the death of His Son, He reconciled us who were previously His enemies and made us sons and heirs of His Kingdom! He purifies us and sanctifies us through His holy Mysteries! He gives us

---

[11] cf. Lk. 17:21

[12] Paschal Canon, Ode Five

the heavenly, most holy food and drink, that is, His All-holy Body and precious Blood! He has also given us a guardian for our whole life! He will receive our soul and guide it to the eternal inheritance! But what am I saying? Time would fail me to recount everything; I would be laboring in vain, trying to count the sand in the sea—the infinite benefactions of our good God!

Then, even after so many countless good things, we grumble! Oh, my God, overlook our ingratitude and open our mind so that we grasp what Your paternal heart has bestowed upon us, and so that we render a little thanks in order that we may find forgiveness and mercy.

6. Regarding the holy angel that you wrote to me about, it is true that when he receives a decree from the Lord, he neither adds nor subtracts anything, but he remains beside a person, enlightens him, looks after him, delivers him from dangers, and defends him from the devil, as we see in the life of St. Andrew the Fool for Christ, in which an angel was fighting against the devil in order to defend a guilty monk, and so on. Read it and you will see.

Man is given a guardian angel as an older brother who, being closer to God and having more boldness, prays for his younger brother. And man entreats his guardian angel as his older brother to protect him and pray for him, since he has more boldness towards God.

How many times he whispers in our soul's ear, "Don't do this," or "Do it," or "Be careful here." There are many such instances with those who have the eyes of their soul open.

Do not forget the parable of the gardener and the fruitless fig tree in the Holy Gospel. "Let it alone this year also, until I dig around it and fertilize it. And if it bears fruit, fine. But if not, after that you can cut it down."[13] The gardener symbol-

---

[13] Lk. 13:8-9

izes the holy angel who looks after a person, until he bears
fruit and is saved.

In *The Sayings of the Desert Fathers*, many things are written about the angels' solicitude for man—they were seen
weeping while the people they protected were sinning. Just
think how much they prayed for them! Their "tears" show
their love and compassion for man.

7. My blessed children in the Lord, may the love of our
Lord keep you in spiritual and bodily health.

Truly how lamentable it is for a child to be living in his father's house, to enjoy all the comforts of life, and not to acknowledge his own father—or even if he does give him a
little respect and attention, not to feel his profuse love and affection—but on the contrary, when the remembrance of his
father does come, he considers it something not worth thinking about or occupying his mind with!

What verdict could be given for such an ungrateful and ar-
rogant child? Surely, everyone would label him as an unworthy heir of his father's love and fortune. Unfortunately,
though, in this example and in the person of this unworthy
child, we see today's man who is ungodly in his relationship
with God, his Father, and, sad to say, we also see today's
Christians, except for a select few.

We live in this world, which God has designated as our
temporary abode. He gave us the freedom to enjoy the good
things of the earth, without leaving Himself unattested to in
everything that we see and think, so that through our reason
we would render glory and honor to Him, with whole-hearted
love for Him as our supreme offering.

Let us briefly go over the world-saving and momentous
events, beginning with the disobedience of Adam and Eve, so
that we may perceive more clearly the wealth of God's love.

Because of their pride and disobedience, Adam and Eve were banished from the garden of delight and inhabited the land of thorns and thistles. But the infinite love of the Heavenly Father, Who had been forgotten by the human race, sent His only-begotten and beloved Son into the world, to remove man's enmity towards Him. We see His supreme love leading Him to sacrifice His sweetest Son through a tragic death on the Cross, since this is what the grave fall of guilty mankind required!

The Apostle Paul presents this sacrifice with the following words: "He (the Father) who did not spare His own Son, but delivered Him up for us all."[14] He also says: "He became obedient to the point of death, even death on a cross."[15]

But after three days He rose by His own authority, as befits God, becoming the firstfruits of those who have fallen asleep, to confirm that most truly the entire race shall be raised by a common resurrection. Before His Ascension, He commanded the Holy Apostles to baptize in the name of the Father and of the Son and of the Holy Spirit all who believe in His name, simultaneously giving them the power to become children of God through faith.

He even handed down to us the Holy Mysteries, so that through them we may be united with Him and always live with Him in true happiness, which only union with God can provide. He also gave us a vigilant guardian for our soul and body, our holy guardian angel, whom He sends to us at Holy Baptism to be our guide and protector. It is through the Mystery of Holy Baptism that a Christian becomes a child of God by grace, an heir of God and a joint heir with Christ.[16]

But I shall not proceed to recount the events that show the infinite riches of the ineffable love of the Heavenly Father towards us; for the more man's mind is enlightened to grasp the

---

[14] Rom. 8:32

[15] Phil. 2:8

[16] cf. Rom. 8:17

love of the Creator for His creation, the more evident our ingratitude and failure to recognize such an affectionate and true Father becomes.

We live in this vain world and are truly ignorant—or rather, we have not yet understood why we are alive, what goal this life of ours has, and what purpose man has on earth! Unfortunately, we have become almost like the irrational beasts; we live without considering that the time of our life here is the most precious thing for our future restoration. We use up and waste this time with no regret, and when we come to our senses we shall be unable to bring this time back. Therefore, how truly wise is the man who has realized the great value of time in this transient life and takes advantage of it accordingly, enriching his life with good works, so that when the grievous hour of death comes, his conscience will be confident and say in his defense before the spiritual prosecutors, the demons: "I have done what I should. So why are you still raging?"

In the Holy Gospel, Jesus spoke about the purpose of man: "I came forth from the Father and have come into the world. Again, I leave the world and go to the Father."[17] Here our Savior is speaking humanly, for as God, consubstantial with the Father, He was never separated from Him. The fact that man is destined to leave the world at the time determined by God and to go to God where he came from, can be inferred from the Holy Scriptures in Genesis: "And God formed man from the dust of the earth and breathed upon his face the breath of life, and man became a living soul."[18] The divine breath came out of the tri-hypostatic God—not that the breath itself became a soul in man, but the soul of man was created by a divine insufflation, which is why it has to return to its God.

---

[17] Jn. 16:28
[18] Gen. 2:7

Here is something remarkable: the breath of God went out and created the soul of man. He made it holy, pure, innocent, good, etc. So when the frightful hour of death comes for the soul, I wonder, will it still have its original sanctity and purity? Unfortunately not, for we have all sinned as descendants of Adam. God, however, Who knows our weakness and that the mind of man is inclined to evil from his youth,[19] certainly does not demand the impeccable purity of its initial state, but what does He seek? He seeks true, sincere repentance, abstention from sin, a heart broken and humbled; He seeks mourning and tears in order to give us a consoling ambrosia, "which the unrepentant world knows not."[20]

So when a person sincerely repents, God welcomes him with open arms, simultaneously giving him the divine features with which he will be able to ascend unimpeded into the boundless Kingdom of God, so that he may live thenceforth with the Heavenly Father. Behold, the purpose of man!

The mind stands in amazement when it grasps this grand and lofty divine purpose! And yet how great is man's insensibility and how thick a darkness covers the eyes of his soul, so that he does not think why he exists here on earth and what God wants from him. Unfortunately, his mind's vision has been impaired by the illness of sin, and especially by self-love.

How long, my God, shall we remain sluggish and callous towards this great purpose of ours? Send us a little illumination. Why, has the sun ever stopped sending its abundant light? How much more so will You, the infinite Sun of love, never stop shining! Woe to us, my Lord, for we voluntarily do every evil deed. But since You have endless oceans of love, pour upon us love and affection, compassion and forbearance again and again—perhaps some more souls will be saved be-

---

[19] cf. Gen. 8:21

[20] cf. Jn. 1:10

fore Your just judgment breaks out upon us! Yes, Lord, take pity on me, the miserable one, who does not practice what he preaches, and grant me repentance before I leave this world! Enlighten Your world, for which You poured out Your awesome and All-holy Blood, and give repentance to all.

8. Beloved children in the Lord, I pray that my poor letter will find you in love, obedience, prayer, and circumspection in everything.

Today we celebrate the assembly of all the Heavenly Powers; just think what a festival is taking place in Heaven! What hymns! What joy for the angels of God! The holy angels, the guardians of our souls, are celebrating today, and since they are our older brothers, we should share in their joy and grace.

They invisibly help us so much! From how many temptations and deaths they deliver us! How many prayers they say for us when they see the face of God! When they stand beside us, they offer each person's prayers! And when we die, it is they who will help us in the hour of death and in the ascent through the toll-houses, and for this reason we should bear a special love towards God's angels. However, it is more advantageous for us to resemble them in their virtues. The holy angels have perfect obedience to the commands of God; they execute His orders with no objections. They have perfect love towards God and men. The angels have undefiled chastity and invincible humility, while their innocence is beyond description.

Other virtues also adorn the angels. If we sincerely love them, if we want to live in the same place that they do, we must compel ourselves to resemble them.

The monastic way of life is called the angelic life by the Church Fathers. This is because monastics must live a life similar to the angels. However, when they do not live like that, but live a life contrary to it, they will be ranked with the evil angels.

Struggle, my children, my joy and consolation, so that you attain the angels' level of obedience, love, prayer, and chastity, and so that you may also live together with the angels in the life after death! Amen; so be it.

9. The more you perceive the mercy of God, my child, the more lovingly you will be united with Him. And the more you fathom the magnificence of God's majesty, the more you will immerse yourself in your nothingness, with a corresponding ascent to the state of spiritual knowledge.

The more humility you mix with your unceasing prayer, the more intensely you will feel Jesus, and your heart will feel like another burning bush.

Raise your mind up above, where our life and joy are, for according to the Apostle Paul, "our citizenship is in Heaven."[21] Long whole-heartedly for the things above, and this holy longing will make monasticism light and very sweet for you.

During rapture of the nous by the grace of God, wonder will follow upon wonder, and it will stand completely ecstatic before the abundant light of apprehending the knowledge of God.

10. When Christ lives within you, fear nothing. In order for Christ to live within you, much humility is needed. Mentally fall at His immaculate feet and weep, saying: "My Jesus, Thou alone art left for me in this humble life of mine as light and life. Show me Thy spiritual beauty, so that I may be filled with divine eros and run after Thy myrrh and cry out, 'My soul has cleaved to Thee, Thy right hand has helped me.'[22] Oh, my Jesus, when shall I come and appear before Thy

---

[21] Phil. 3:20
[22] Ps. 62:8

face?[23] When, O light of my soul, shall I see Thee and be filled and say, 'Oh, the depth of the riches of the wisdom and knowledge of God!'"[24]

Yes, my child, love humility above all, and then you will obtain Jesus, Who is lowly in heart, as an everlasting possession in your soul.

Inhale Jesus; exhale Jesus, and then you will know what Jesus is! Where is earthly love then! Is it possible for a fire-brand to fall upon a parched forest and for anything to survive? The same thing happens with the twigs of human thoughts when the love of Jesus falls upon them.

11. Take courage, my child; through many tribulations we shall ascend to the boundless, divine light of Mount Tabor, and there we shall hear the divine voice of our beloved Jesus. "How beloved are Thy dwellings, O Lord of hosts! My soul longs and faints for the courts of the Lord. My heart and my flesh have exulted in the living God."[25] Yes, O Giver of life, Christ our God. "I have come that they may have life, and that they may have it more abundantly."[26]

Yes, I pray that Christ, the eternal life, will live and reign within you, so that you cry out, "Abba, Father!"[27] Oh, what is more delightful than Jesus! Who has tasted Christ's love and then desired another sinful love? No one! For this love is so potent, that even if one goes through a life of afflictions for a hundred years and then feels divine love for only a short time, this love is able to dispel all the afflictions and leave him astounded before God's majesty.

12. Out of His infinite goodness, and wanting to impart His innumerable spiritual blessings to us, God invites and exhorts us to seek them from Him—and He wants to give them to us; He wants us to knock at the door of His mercy, and certainly He shall open it for us.

---

[23] cf. Ps. 41:2
[24] Rom. 11:33
[25] Ps. 83:1-2

[26] Jn. 10:10
[27] Gal. 4:6

God wants us to knock, but the devil—that primeval evil, God's enemy and ours—what does he do to make man not believe God's exhortations? He gives us thoughts of unbelief, and then thoughts of hopelessness and despair, so that we will not believe that God shall by all means fulfill His divine words. Then he tells us, "You are a sinner, you are a loser—God won't listen to you; He won't pay any attention to you, so cry out all you want." In this way, he weakens our faith and willpower.

13. Christ does not need us, for He has thousands of angels who serve Him impeccably. In addition, by a word He is able to create thousands more of these most holy beings. But His infinite love constrains Him to be concerned about us, without being disgusted by our stench and our festering wounds. So let us remember this love of God at every moment of our life, so that we shall do our worthless deeds solely for the love of God.

Just think—we were not crucified for our Christ, our Savior, whereas on behalf of us monstrosities, He endured death on a cross for the sake of obedience!

14. May the grace of Christ be with you, within your soul, my child, to enlighten you and increase your love for Him, so that you may be kept near Him and not be swept away by the current of worldliness and fall away from God and lose your immortal soul, which is worth more than the entire world.

The amount of grace that came to you is small; the saints, though, had much grace. In order to increase it, you must humble yourself. If you become proud it will leave, and then you will weep. So be very careful to bear in mind your sins and passions, so that vainglory will not sprout in you and drive away the Jesus prayer.

15. The goodness of God sometimes seems like a rod that disciplines man—for his own good, though. When He sees that the rod is too burdensome, He changes His approach, and it becomes a cane that relieves the burden and thus comforts man's soul, so that everything turns out for his benefit and spiritual progress.

When a person lacks spiritual knowledge, he thinks that the rod, the "chastisement of the Lord," will kill him, and that it will stay like that forever. But along with the temptation the good God brings the way out, that is, the end of the temptation.

Man has discernment and can determine, for example, how much an animal can carry, so he does not overload it. How much more discernment does God have not to overload us with a temptation beyond our strength! So it is not God, but our faintheartedness that leads us to impatience, which makes our burden seem so heavy.

Sometimes, however, God allows very strong temptations to come upon people who have much pride and conceit dwelling in them, in order to crush their haughty spirit. But in the end, He does not abandon them; His mercy will come back again. Oh, how good God is!

16. "Today the Virgin gives birth to the Transcendent One." What can I, the unworthy and filthy one, say about the grandeur of the innumerable dispensations of the Most High God! I am astonished and unable to look directly at it as I contemplate this mystery.

How did God condescend to be an infant in a cave of irrational beasts? How was He wrapped in swaddling clothes and carried in the holy arms of the Holy Virgin, He Who was born by the Father without a mother! "Great art Thou, O Lord, and wondrous are Thy deeds, and no word sufficeth to hymn Thy wonders!" "Oh, the depth of the riches of the wisdom and knowledge of God!"[28]

---

[28] Rom. 11:33

My soul shall rejoice in the Lord; I shall noetically smother with kisses that most sweet and blessed Infant, so that He may deliver me from my irrational passions.

17. Christ commanded that we forgive our enemies seventy times seven every day. How much more so does He forgive, He Who is the Abyss of forgiveness!

If you were able to count the drops of rain and the grains of sand, you would be able to measure a small part of the infinite compassion of the infinite God.

18. Let us fall down before the heavenly Queen, the immaculate Theotokos, the Maiden quick-to-hear, that she may help us, for "no one who runs to thee is turned away ashamed, but he asks for a favor and receives the gift from thee, to the profit of his request."[29] After God, only she is able to help us. Let us trust in her, and we shall not be put to shame.

19. I pray from my heart that you are well and rejoice in peace of soul, for the peace of God is nothing but a place of God, repose, bliss, and divine delight.

The peace of God, which surpasses all understanding,[30] is given to souls that struggle as a prize and royal gift; it is a property of the children of God. In order for it to dwell in the soul of a Christian, first, godly labor is necessary—labor of a spiritual nature. Then it takes discernment and a blameless, clear conscience shining brighter than the sun, which knows that one has done what he should.

Then this soul receives the precious gift of "the peace of God" and delights in it and converses like a bride with her most beautiful Bridegroom Jesus about their eternal marriage and the spiritual riches of Heaven. And while one thinks about these things, the peace increases, and one ends up in very sweet tears.

---

[29] from the Small Supplicatory Canon to the Theotokos

[30] Phil. 4:7

The peace of God is one's betrothal for the future wedding with the slaughtered Lamb. O peace of God, come even to me the troublemaker, who does not know Your beauty! Come and refresh my wretched, condemned soul!

20. I pray that the love of Jesus will inflame your heart with love, that you will run like a thirsty hart to the monastic fountains of spiritual water and drink your fill of heavenly nectar. May you become entirely spiritual, entirely devoted with divine eros to worshipping Him Who loved you to the point of death, even death on a cross.

Only in God will you find true happiness and joy, for the unchangeable and true God is their source. The enjoyment of earthly things is obtained with much labor and hard work, and afterwards it turns out to be harmful, meriting punishment. "Truly all human things are vain; riches do not remain; glory does not accompany one to the other world; when death comes, it obliterates all these things."[31]

Do you want to live a pleasant and peaceful life? Keep the commandments of God; keep the fear of God in your every thought, as well as in everything you say and do. The fear of the Lord is the beginning and the end of wisdom.[32]

Just as a lamp illuminates the path we are walking on, in the same way the fear of God illuminates us spiritually so that we can see how we must walk the path of our salvation. Also, as a lamp keeps us from tripping and falling, likewise the fear of God frees us from the obstacles of sin and guides us to our destination, which is the acquisition of God.

21. What defense shall we have when our Christ shows us His pierced hands or His speared side or His immaculate head pricked by the thorns or His dry lips embittered by the vinegar and gall, and says, "For you, my dearest soul, did I suffer all these things, out of the great love I have for you. Now

---

[31] from the funeral service
[32] cf. Prov. 1:7

show me your marks of love for Me, which will be like balsam on My wounds." Then, my children, what shall we show? Our ingratitude, our negligence, our ego, our disobedience, and the multitude of our other passions? And then, instead of balsam, we shall put poison in the wounds of His love! So then, onwards! Let us compel ourselves. From now on let us be careful to put balsam on His wounds and be called His true, beloved children.

22. "The Divine is beyond explanation and understanding." We do not know the nature of our nous; we do not see it, and yet the nous directs everything in man. So how can our finite nous see the infinite Nous, God, in order to believe in Him? God is beyond spirit, beyond everything that man can think of. "Oh, the depth of the wisdom and knowledge of God!"[33]

23. I, too, my child, have my sickly body as a thorn along my way. It does not allow me to progress, and thus I remain behind until God has mercy on my weakness.

Sin gives birth to all evil, but out of His goodness, God transforms the chastisement of sins into forgiveness, but also into a means of acquiring boldness towards Him.

Oh, how great is the love of God for man! Who is able to look directly at this ocean of love? One cries like a baby when his nous is enlightened and sees even in a small way how much God loves him. But how much he must labor beforehand to be given this enlightenment! For it is a gift from above, from the Father of lights; it comes as dew, as a delightful spring day to souls being scorched by the hardships of various trials.

24. Man has failed to recognize his own Father, the Most High God, Who brought him into being out of nothingness. Oh! How harmful this failure to recognize Him has been!

---

[33] cf. Rom. 11:33

This is the cause of all human suffering, the first transgression of Adam and Eve. And their sin of disobedience and lack of repentance brought upon their children—upon us—all the evil results, and we harvest the thorns and thistles of various tribulations.

"You shall surely die."[34] Death is corruption of our former incorruption, with all of its attributes: illness, affliction, misery, pain. However, the good God did not overlook His own creation, but gave grace through the death of His Son on the Cross—"by grace you have been saved."[35]

Just as the evil one used the crafty serpent as a tool, in a like manner did our Lord Jesus Christ put on human nature to deceive the devil.

O Lord Jesus Christ, the light of my darkened soul, the goal of my life, how great has our guilt become with the passing of time! One disobedience resulted in bringing God down to earth—and where did it lead Him? To be crucified at Golgotha! And the small taste of the forbidden fruit was paid by the awesome drama of the God-Man. Oh, how much God loves man! So let us be confident in our repentance, my fellow sinners. "Though your sins are like scarlet, I shall make them as white as snow; though they are red like crimson, I shall make them as white as wool."[36] So, my child, let us cleave with love to such a merciful God. Amen.

25. Yes, my child, Jesus alone will become everything to you. Put your trust in Him Who said, "I will never leave you nor forsake you."[37] Never lose your courage. Always stand tall with Jesus as your boast and with your nothingness as your pride.

When the devil raises you high, humble yourself and bring yourself down below the earth through self-reproach; when he brings you down to hell, to despair, fly to the Heaven of

---

[34] Gen. 2:17

[35] Eph. 2:5

[36] Is. 1:18

[37] Deut. 31:6

God's grace and love—this is the game you should play with him. Do not fear him; you have put on Christ; you are the inheritance of Christ; you have been enrolled with the saints. You still have much to go through to show the measure of your love towards Him to Whom you have devoted yourself.

Do not accept any thoughts of pride suggested by Satan, but constantly criticize yourself, for that evil rascal has defiled us with disgraceful passions, so how can we be proud? We need weeping and a river of tears to wash away our filth and sores.

Bear in mind the humility of the crucified Lord: "Learn from Me, for I am gentle and humble in heart, and you will find rest for your souls."[38] Only by achieving true humility shall we find tranquility and peace in the tempestuous state of our soul.

26. Man suffers because of his sins. However, the goodness of God counts the pain as spiritual work, and He gives wages and a reward. How can we not love such a God? How can we not devote our whole life to worshipping Him! But unfortunately, despite all this, we forget Him—and I do more than all—which is why we transgress His commandments. For if we remembered God, we would remember what God commands, and fear of Him would make us law-abiding and careful; we would remember the Judgment, the fire of hell, and we would shed tears of repentance. The farther we are from tears and mourning, the more attached we are to earthly and corruptible things. Concern for things above engenders the desire to inherit those everlasting good things, and this good concern breaks our sinful attachment to corruptible, transient things that seem good.

May God the Lord give us the good sense to take care of our soul before we depart for the other world.

---

[38] Mt. 11:29

27. I pray with all my heart that the love of Jesus Christ be poured abundantly into your hearts, and that by His grace you will be counted worthy to live in purity of soul and body all the days of your life.

"By this all will know that you are My disciples, if you have love for one another."[39] Thus spoke the life-bringing fountain, our Christ. He also said: "As the branch cannot bear fruit of itself, unless it abides in the vine, neither can you, unless you abide in Me. I am the vine, you are the branches. He who abides in Me, and I in him, bears much fruit."[40]

With such sublime imagery our sweetest Jesus teaches us that if we do not stay beside Him, it is impossible for us to bear the fruit of eternal life. And in order for us to be near Him, we have to approach Him by practicing His divine commandments. His commandments are not burdensome,[41] but indolence and our soul's lack of humility render the commandments an overwhelming burden; yet it is through these very commandments that Christ has secured for us the dominion of happiness and peace.

When love establishes its throne in the soul, it bestows the most beautiful spiritual springtime. Everything glistens with the breeze of love's refreshing fragrance, for it bears all things, believes all things, hopes all things, endures all things, thinks no evil,[42] does not act wickedly, sees everything simply; love covers everything. For this reason, it has earned the crowning achievement: "Love never fails."[43]

When a bride adores her bridegroom, night and day she thinks about him, imagines him, and lives only for him. Not a single moment goes by without him passing through her thoughts and dripping into her heart the sweetness of love and of hoping to meet. In this way she communicates with her beloved unceasingly.

---

[39] Jn. 13:35
[40] Jn. 15:4-5
[41] 1 Jn. 5:3

[42] 1 Cor. 13:7, 5
[43] 1 Cor. 13:8

So in the same way, we too should remain with our Lord Jesus Christ. It is not permissible for us to limit our love by offering it only to a particular individual, be it to parents and relatives, or even to another member of the synodia, which the Fathers label "particular friendship." All of the above are considered to be kinds of spiritual adultery, for the soul exchanges the eternal love of an immaculate, spotless Bridegroom for the love of earthly and corruptible men.

Humble yourselves, my children, if you do not want God to let you fall into temptations. For corresponding to the pride we have, temptations will follow us. Temptations will not cease until we humble ourselves with knowledge and consciousness of soul.

28. There were ten lepers in the holy Gospel, and the divine bath—the command of the living Logos of God—cleansed all ten of them. But only one returned to give thanks to his great Benefactor. And then Truth itself, Jesus, asked, "Were there not ten cleansed? But where are the nine? Were there not any found who returned to give glory to God except this foreigner?"[44]

Therefore, in every good turn of events, but also in attacks of misfortune, in good health, as well as in encounters with illness, in joy, but also in sorrow, we should always offer up the fragrant incense of our thankfulness before the throne of God as unprofitable servants who have received mercy through the precious Blood of Christ.

"Our dear Christ, our good God, give us the gift of thankfulness, so that we will not be condemned even more—the guilt for our other various sins is enough."

29. Fear nothing but God. Have the fear of God as a lamp, and it will illuminate your path and show you exactly how you should walk. For without the fear of God, we can neither form a clear conscience, nor confess frankly, or ever obtain

---

[44] Lk. 17:17-18

spiritual wisdom, for the beginning of wisdom and the end of wisdom is the fear of the Lord.[45]

30. The death of the Lord on the Cross brought us back to our former status as sons, in which the children of God cry out, "Abba, Father!"[46] The terrible sufferings of the Lord made us worthy to become children of God, heirs of God and joint heirs of Christ![47] I am so filled with elation when I reflect that I am a child of God and that the good Father has a place of ineffable repose and bliss prepared for me!

"O death, where is your sting? O Hades, where is your victory?"[48] What joy the Christian feels when he considers that when the time comes for these physical eyes to close, at once the eyes of the soul will open, and he will see a new world, new beings, new creations, things that are incomparably superior, incorruptible, eternal!

The Heavenly Kingdom is not eating and drinking,[49] but spiritual ambrosia of the holy love of God, eternal delight, unspeakable joy.

"I desire that they may be with Me where I am, that they may behold My glory."[50] Oh, the infinite depth of God's love! How much has He honored wretched man by exalting him up to God Himself and bestowing upon him eternal glory and blessedness!

So shall we deprive ourselves of such glory and blessedness for the sake of a short-lived, sinful pleasure? May God show compassion on all Christians and enlighten them to follow the path of salvation and repentance. Amen, my Panagia!

31. If one meditates on the crucified Lord and penetrates the mystery of God's love for man, he sees how much the Lord endured for each one of us personally. What shall we render unto the Lord for everything?[51] Man, however, was not found worthy of this great and immense love.

---

[45] cf. Prov. 1:7

[46] Gal. 4:6

[47] Rom. 8:17

[48] 1 Cor. 15:55

[49] cf. Rom. 14:17

[50] cf. Jn. 17:24

[51] cf. Ps. 115:3

As soon as we do something good, we see our ego jump up as if we had created Heaven and earth. Whereas God made everything out of nothing, and yet He humbled Himself so much!

The compassion of God has no bounds, and blessed is the man who through prudence has come to realize the love of God. For the sake of earthy, disobedient, insubordinate man, who had become a prey to the passions and demons, the Son of God Himself came down and was hanged on the Cross! Alongside this we see our own laziness, coldness, indifference, while God on the other hand shows us His providence and love in many different ways. Truly, man is a mystery.

Boundless and unlimited is God's patience! What doesn't He hear and see within each person! When we see some ingratitude in a person close to us; when we see him behave harshly, ungratefully, inhumanly, mercilessly; when we see that he does not say at least one "thanks," we hold it against him. How many things could God hold against us men who behave callously and abominably towards Him?

Every person in this world, every one of us, is more or less ungrateful. God feeds us, He clothes us, He protects us, He has given us a guardian angel, He feeds us with His holy Mysteries, with His Flesh and Blood, He has prepared a vast Kingdom for us, He puts up with us when we go astray, He welcomes us when we repent. But we are impious, we blaspheme Him, insult Him, disregard Him, and He is forbearing and tolerant; He awaits our return. But as if God were indebted to us, we never even think in passing about the fear of God, reverence for Him, or the piety we should have when we remember His presence. We forget that we should bow our heads in veneration of this great God—the most wondrous, inexpressible, unsearchable, boundless, and most sweet God.

If each one of us had thousands of mouths, we would still be unable to extol Him worthily and fittingly for His countless gifts for us! This is why the Apostle Paul, after repeated ecstasies and theorias and delights of God, was often overcome with amazement and cried out those immortal words: "Oh, the depth of the riches of the wisdom and knowledge of God! How unsearchable are His judgments and His ways beyond finding out!"[52]

"Who has known the mind of the Lord? Or who has become His counselor?"[53] Who can know how the infinite Nous works, not only in the heavenly realm, but also in the earth and the underworld?

Just think—effortlessly, without toil, He feeds every living thing: men, the animals, the fields, the reptiles, the fish, the microbes, the millions of living creatures. He cares for everything and looks after everything.

"How magnified are Thy works, O Lord! In wisdom hast Thou made them all; the earth is filled with Thy creation."[54] "He spake and they came to be; He commanded, and they were created!"[55] Let there be light, and there was light; let there be earth, and there was earth; let there be stars, sun, and moon,[56] and there were these stupendous creations, these colossal, huge bodies, hanging and moving in space, which illuminate and beautify the sky—all came to be at a single command of God!

"The Word became flesh and dwelt among us,"[57] the Word of the Father. "In the beginning was the Word, and the Word was with God, and the Word was God."[58] He came and took on flesh and became man, and the world came into being through Him—He made the world! He gave us the right to become children of God.[59] He came to His creatures, and they did not receive Him. Now just think—He made the world and

---

[52] Rom. 11:33
[53] Rom. 11:34
[54] Ps. 103:26
[55] Ps. 148:5
[56] cf. Gen. 1:3-18
[57] Jn. 1:14
[58] Jn. 1:1
[59] cf. Jn. 1:12

the people, and they were cold and callous and did not receive Him. He came as a stranger; He was given hospitality on the wood of the Cross instead of on a mattress; He was given hospitality in a grave; the earth was shaken, the veil was rent, the sun was darkened, the universe was terrified!

"What god is as great as our God?"[60] "Great art Thou, O Lord, and wondrous are Thy deeds, and no word will ever suffice to hymn Thee fittingly!"

The Word became flesh.[61] What grandeur this hides! God became man, He descended from the Heavens; the bodiless God, the infinite, incomprehensible Spirit came and dwelt within human nature in order to save it. He became a slave to deliver us from slavery; He became man, so that we may become gods by grace; "You are gods, and all of you are the sons of the Most High."[62] We have become a special people,[63] a holy nation,[64] a priesthood of God, through the advent of the divine Child! The divine Word—Who lives, reigns, and governs all of creation— the Only-begotten Word of God, the boundless sweetness of God's existence, the glory and hymn of the martyrs, the endurance of the holy monks, the sole Bridegroom of pure souls. And as many as received Him, to them He gave the right to become children of God—who were born, not of blood, nor of the will of the flesh, but of God.[65] Those who will be saved are not born of the will of the flesh and desire, but of God, and they will reign beside Him.

"We have received grace for grace. For the law was given through Moses, but grace and truth came through Jesus Christ."[66] He gave us the ten commandments; He gave us precepts in the new grace of the Gospel, and disregarding the gratitude we owed Him, He gave us even more grace! And from His fullness we have received grace for grace.[67] God was not deprived by giving us His glory, but He gave out of

---

[60] Ps. 76:13
[61] cf. Jn. 1:14
[62] Ps. 81:6
[63] cf. Tit. 2:14
[64] cf. 1 Pet. 2:9
[65] cf. Jn. 1:12-13
[66] Jn. 1:16-17
[67] cf. Jn. 1:16

His abundance. He was not diminished by giving and creating the whole world, but rather the complete, infinitely perfect God created man and the angels, so that there would be other beings to delight in Him, so that other spirits would become blessed, and so that other souls and beings would possess free will—not subjugated slaves, but free beings that obey and glorify Him freely.

"I do not want slavery," says God. "I do not want them like animals which are enslaved by man and led wherever he wants. I want free will." This is how great the magnificence of God is.

Oh, what the demons lost by falling away from such an infinite, most sweet, inexpressible God! What did the dominion of God lose by the insubordination of Lucifer? Nothing: God has no need of anything or anyone. It is we who have need of God—gratuitously He saves man.

God is perfect, incomprehensible, blessed unto the ages of ages; He came and saved us gratis. We owe him our entire existence—and even if we gave it to Him, we would have done nothing, we would have merely done our duty. He is our Creator; He is our Savior.

Chapter Eighteen

On the Divine Liturgy and Holy Communion

hat grandeur the Divine Liturgy has! When God looks upon His humble priest, how strongly he feels the majesty of the Liturgy! How much benefit the commemorated receive! How much God honors man by descending with the angelic orders during every Liturgy and nourishing man with His All-holy Body and Blood!

Everything has been given to us. What thing, bodily or spiritual, corruptible or incorruptible, do we lack? Nothing. If He gives His deified, holy Body and Blood to us every day, what is higher than this? Nothing, of course. In what mysteries God counts man worthy to serve, though he is made of earth! Oh, heavenly, inestimable love! One drop of divine love surpasses all the physical, worldly love under the sun.

2. In the Skete of St. Anne lived a certain *hieromonk** Savvas, the famous "Papa-Savvas," as he was called. Fr. Joachim Spetsieris had him as his spiritual father. The Empress of Russia, Catherine, also had him as her spiritual father. He served the Liturgy every day; he was a God-bearing, clairvoyant teacher of noetic prayer.

Once some people asked him, "What motivates you to commemorate so many names in the *proskomidi**?" He answered, "When I was younger, we called the bishop to conse-

crate the church above the Holy Monastery of St. Dionysios"
(It was there that he first practiced hesychasm, with his elder,
Papa-Hilarion, another famous spiritual father.) "After the
consecration, the bishop said to my Elder, 'May I give Papa-
Savvas some names to commemorate for forty days, since he
serves Liturgy every day?' My Elder told him, 'Give him as
many as you want.' So he gave me sixty-two names. When I
had completed thirty-nine Liturgies and was about to serve
the fortieth, I leaned against the chanter's stand and waited
for my Elder to come, so that I could say the entrance prayers
to serve Liturgy. I fell asleep and saw in my sleep that I was
wearing priestly vestments and was standing before the Holy
Table. On the Holy Table was the holy diskos[†] for the Liturgy,
and the holy chalice full of the holy Blood of Christ. Then I
saw Papa-Stephen come and take the Communion spoon and
the paper from the proskomidi, approach the Holy Table, and
put the paper on it beside the holy diskos. Then he dipped the
spoon into the holy Blood of Christ and a name was erased.
He dipped it again, and another one was erased, and so forth
until all were done and the paper was clean. "Then I awoke,
and in a little while my Elder came. Immediately I told him
what I saw. The Elder said to me, 'Didn't I tell you not to believe in dreams?' After the Liturgy he added, 'You are not
worthy for their sins to be forgiven; through the power of the
Blood of Christ their sins were forgiven.' So this is the reason
why I commemorate the names of everyone."

3. Immense is the benefit of the Divine Liturgy, of com-
memorations for the departed, etc.—of course, they are only
full of benefit for those who repented, who had some signs of
virtues, but did not have time to knead the bread of virtues
due to negligence, indolence, and procrastination. For those
people, the prayers of the Church and personal prayers, alms,

---

[†] The "diskos" is a small plate with a large base used in the Divine Liturgy
to carry the bread of the Eucharist. In Western Christianity it is called the
paten.

philanthropic deeds, etc., fill up their deficiencies, through the abundance of God's mercy!

St. Cyril of Jerusalem says that in every Liturgy, all who are commemorated, for whom intercession is being made, receive immense benefit.

The new Saint Photini the Nun of Asia Minor, in one of her many ecstasies of soul, saw a man who looked like a priest who said to her, "My daughter, give your names to the priest; give him also money for his toil to commemorate them, for the souls of those who have died receive great benefit! See to it that you do not forget to give the names to the priest!"

The greatest charity, the greatest good, which more than anything else relieves a soul that finds itself in the other world, is the sacrifice of the divine Lamb upon the holy altar in the holy Liturgy. The benefit is immense because the innocent Lamb of God is sacrificed in order to purify men from their sins and to free them from the various bonds of captivity to the passions.

4. "As Moses lifted up the serpent in the wilderness, even so must the Son of Man be lifted up."[1] And just as all who were bitten by the serpents and looked upon the suspended brass serpent were healed, likewise every Christian who believes in our Christ and hastens to His life-bearing wounds (by eating His Flesh and drinking His All-holy Blood), is cured from the bites of the spiritual serpent of sin. By this most holy nourishment, he is given life unto renewal in a new creation, that is, a new life in conformity with His life-giving commandments.

Oh, how essential it is for us in every way to approach this heavenly banquet, which this supernatural mystery of the Holy Table provides for us! The angels stand by invisibly. With utmost reverence the priests, who at this moment of the

---

[1] Jn. 3:14

mystery are more honored than the angels, sacrifice the blameless Lamb. The angels minister and the faithful approach to eat and drink the Body and Blood of Christ: "Partake of the Body of Christ; taste of the fountain of immortality" to live in Christ and not die in sin.

Therefore, "let a man examine himself, and so let him eat of the bread and drink of the cup," according to the divine Apostle, because "he who eats and drinks in an unworthy manner, eats and drinks judgment to himself. For if we would judge ourselves, we would not be judged. But when we are judged, we are chastened by the Lord."[2]

When someone wants to present himself to the king, he prepares himself for days—that is, with an overall preparation in cleanliness, speech, approach, manners, and so on—to attract the king's sympathy and thus obtain the desired request. Corresponding to the incomparable difference between the two kings, every Christian ought to prepare for Holy Communion in order to obtain mercy and forgiveness.

Cunning, flattery, affectation, and lies often adorn someone who approaches an earthly king so that he may obtain what he wants. Whereas holiness, a humble spirit, and simplicity of soul—which is more precious than perishable gold—must adorn the faithful Christian approaching the King of kings, Who looks upon the inner man.

Let us also prepare ourselves with purified intellects, and, aspiring to the mortification of our senses from the passions, let us enter together with the Holy Apostles into the Mystical Supper in purity, and let us partake of our sweet Jesus, so that He may abide with us unto the endless ages of ages. Amen; so be it!

5. With fear and reverence you should stand in church, for our Christ is invisibly present with the holy angels. He fills

---

2 cf. 1 Cor. 11:28-32

the attentive and reverent with grace and blessings, whereas He censures the inattentive as unworthy. Try to receive Communion as often as possible—you have my permission to do so freely—for Holy Communion is an excellent aid for those who struggle against sin.

6. You should approach the divine Mystery with much compunction, contrition, and awareness of your sins. Great is the mercy of God, Who condescends to enter within you without abhorring the multitude of your sins. Instead, out of boundless love and affection He comes to sanctify you and count you worthy to become a child of His and a co-heir of His Kingdom.

7. Unworthily I serve the Liturgy to my God. The office is holy and awesome. Every day I offer the Lamb of God as a sacrifice pleasing to God, the Blameless One to the blameless Father and God, in order that He be merciful to us for everything through which we grieve Him, the most good God, Who sacrificed His Son for us. Oh, my God, Your beloved Son for us! Who are we to deserve such a supreme sacrifice? "When we were enemies we were reconciled to God through the death of His Son."[3] The image of the prodigal son, who squandered the property of his father, shows us very clearly the reason why Christ died.

The sin of Adam and Eve was the beginning and root of all grievous events that occurred until today and will occur until the end of the ages. That one disobedience, like a seed in the womb of Eve, gave birth to and transmitted a physical and spiritual death to the human race that proceeded from her. And how could poor Eve have imagined that a small taste of the fruit would create so much destruction and punishment that the Holy Trinity would be compelled to send one Person of the life-originating Trinity into the world to suffer from the

---

[3] Rom. 5:10

work of His hands—from man—slaps, blows, scourging, spitting, and all kinds of cursing, and to be hanged on the Cross as a curse: "Cursed is everyone who hangs on a tree."[4]

The Passion on the Cross and the life-bearing Resurrection of our Jesus—our sweet deliverance and the light of our darkened souls—which expiate every sinful soul, are reenacted in every Divine Liturgy. And if in the old law, in the shadow of things to come, the blood of bulls and goats and the ashes of a heifer cleansed those who partook, how much more the All-holy Blood of Christ, which is partaken of in the holy altars of the holy Orthodox churches of God, will cleanse us from every sin and warm our souls with the divine eros of our sweetest Jesus![5]

Love is born of understanding. For if we do not comprehend and feel what God has given us and in particular to each one of us, and if we do not realize who we were because of our sins when God did this great deed of mercy—in short, if we do not come to know Him and ourselves—we will not bind our souls to the fear of Him, and we will not rejoice in the beauty of His eros.

The Apostle Paul said to the Christians in order to arouse in them greater love and thanksgiving to God: "What fruit did you have then (in idolatry) in the things of which you are now ashamed? . . . For the wages of sin is death."[6]

If God had not called us to follow His holy way of self-knowledge and to be aware of our previous sinful life, and if divine illumination were absent, we never would have seen the way of light and of truth. He has called us all—some from childhood, others in middle age, others in old age. Being good, He took all of us as a hen gathers her chicks under her wings, in order to make us participants in His divine Kingdom. He loathed nothing—neither sore nor wound nor sick-

---

[4] cf. Deut. 21:23, Gal. 3:13

[5] cf. Heb. 9:13-14

[6] Rom. 6:21, 23

ness nor the deformity of our souls' spiritual features. But as a father He received us, as a mother He suckled us, and as an unmercenary physician He healed and clothed us in the first garment of sonship, of grace, overlooking the great debt of the sins of each one of us. Therefore, we owe Him infinite love and adoration. May love abide in the heart, as a living fountain gushing forth torrents of water, streams of divine eros. Not as the Israel of old—only honoring with their lips, while their heart was far from Christ—but as living fire saying, "Come to the Father."

Just as the athlete is tested in the arena and in the field of action, likewise the Christian is tested in the arena of struggles as to whether he truly loves God. Patience in the struggle against the various sins and courage at their onset to apply the divine commandments characterize the fervent worshipper of Jesus.

Let us not grieve with transgressions, grumbling, disobedience, and various forms of sin, Him Who showed us boundless love and affection, but as grateful servants, let us strive to give rest to His compassionate heart, so that He may be comforted as the psalmist said: "He shall be comforted because of His servants."[7]

---

[7] Ps. 134:14

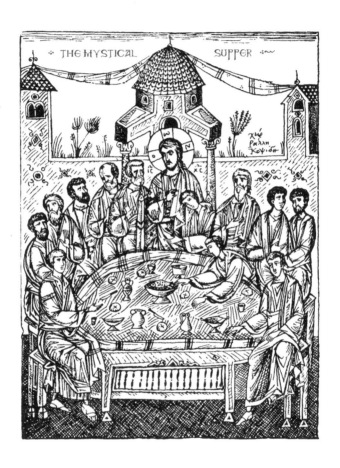

THE MYSTICAL SUPPER

Chapter Nineteen

On the Departed

We received the bitterly joyful news of your child's departure to the Lord. We mourned and wept along with you, but such behavior is not fitting for such a soul that we hope our Christ has accepted and delivered from the torments of this life in order to give him repose in the eternal abodes. This soul will adorn your noble family as the most bright and sacred decoration, and henceforth will be an everlasting torch interceding with the Lord for us. His virginity, the many years of illness and patience, the second baptism—that is, the Angelic Schema—assure us that our sweet Jesus has accepted him as a fragrant incense. I beg you, do not be sad, but rejoice, for you have deposited a great treasure in God's treasury, a large sum which will support you. Death is a momentary separation, because Christ came to earth and cast light upon this dark mystery of death. For "he who believes in Me, though he may die, shall live. I am the resurrection and the life."[1] I pray with all my heart that our holy God gives you patience, consolation, and holy thoughts for deeper spirituality.

2. Do you know how much help the departed seek! Since there is no repentance after death, and as humans they also departed with stains and blemishes, and since they see that the

---

[1] Jn. 11:25

help of the living greatly assists them to be perfected and find rest, they yearn, seek, and long for someone to commemorate them. They also long for one of their descendants to become a priest or a virtuous Christian who will care for them.

Let me tell you about a vision of a certain bishop which he himself told me while we were serving together years ago. He told us that there was a priest who had a drinking problem and often got drunk; this was going on for many years. Other than this, though, the priest was virtuous and pious. One day he drank wine as usual and got drunk, and then before he was fully sober, he went and served Liturgy. So God allowed an accident to happen: he spilled the holy Body and Blood of the Lord! The poor fellow froze with fear, while also thinking about the heavy penance his bishop would give him!

Finally, after he confessed, his bishop told him, "Go—I will notify you when to return, and then I'll give you the penance." So as the bishop was all alone reflecting and pondering, and as he picked up a pen to write his decision to depose him, he saw an endless multitude of people of every age, kind, and class unwind before him like a movie. The bishop was stunned by this vision but was also overcome with fear. Then all those people together said to him, "Your Eminence, do not punish the priest; do not depose him." Then, little by little, they disappeared.

Afterwards, the bishop called the priest to come. The poor priest was terrified, thinking about being deposed. The bishop said to him, "Tell me something, do you commemorate many names when you serve Liturgy?" The priest answered, "In the proskomidi, Your Eminence, I commemorate names for a long time—from kings and emperors down to the last pauper." The bishop then said to him, "Go, then, and whenever you serve Liturgy, commemorate as many people as you can, and take care not to get drunk anymore. You are pardoned." Thereafter, the priest—with the help of God—was delivered from drinking.

3. We received the telegram regarding the departure of our beloved sister, and, as is human, we grieved. We shed tears, which bear witness to our souls' unity through the unbreakable bond of love in Christ.

But we must also rejoice for the great "lottery" she won. First of all, because she kept her virginity—that great jewel on the garment of her pure soul. Second, because for years she endured the Lord's visitation through her illness and lifted her cross until the Golgotha of her perfection, thus proving to be a true disciple of Jesus. Third, because she was given the Angelic Schema, which she did not defile with new sins, and which the Holy Fathers have decreed to be a second baptism!

So, cleansed thenceforth by the baptism of repentance, she departed. Our sweet Jesus has called her to be by His side from now on so that she may see His theandric face to her utmost delight. There she will intercede perpetually not only for her parents and the rest of her relatives, but also for the whole world.

Once St. Anthony the Great was in ecstasy and saw himself being lifted by the angels to Heaven, as if he were departing to the Lord. But the adverse powers—the demons, the tollhouses—were obstructing him and accusing him of sins he had done. The holy angels were objecting, saying, "All the sins he committed before becoming a monk were forgiven by God the moment he wore the Schema. Only sins he did after receiving the Schema you have the right to use against him." Once the angels said this, the demons could not find anything culpable, and thus he ascended freely.

Glossary

Asceticism (ἄσκησις)

Asceticism is man's struggle to keep the commandments of Christ. It encompasses not only his bodily and spiritual effort, but also the method by which he passes through the three stages of the spiritual life—namely, *purification* of the *heart*, *illumination* of the *nous*, and *theosis*. Thus, it is an essential tool for one's sanctification. According to St. Gregory Palamas, it is primarily "the evangelic life which is based on repentance. It is man's preparation for his union with Christ." See also *praxis* and *theoria*.

Assault (προσβολή)

Assault is the first stage of a temptation. See *consent* for more details.

Athos (Ἄθως)

Mt. Athos, or the Holy Mountain, is a self-governed monastic community on a peninsula in Northern Greece. The term can also refer to the mountain at the tip of this peninsula.

Bless (εὐλογεῖτε, εὐλόγησον)

In addition to its regular meaning, "bless" is used by monastics also to mean (1) "Forgive me," (2) "Hello," or (3) "Good-bye."

Blessing (εὐλογία)

Besides its usual meanings, a "blessing" can also mean the permission given by one's spiritual father for a particular action.

Cenobite, Cenobium (κοινοβιάτης, κοινόβιον)

Cenobites are monastics who live in a cenobitic monastery or cenobium, that is, a monastery where all things are held in common.

Circular prayer (κυκλικὴ προσευχή)

St. Nikodemos the Hagiorite writes: "St. Dionysios the Areopagite refers to three forms [of prayer]: direct, spiral, and circular—which alone is without deception. It is called circular prayer because as the perimeter of a circle returns to its starting point, so also in this circular movement, the *nous* returns to itself and becomes one. This is why St. Dionysios, that superb theologian, said, 'The movement of the soul is circular because it leaves the externals, enters into itself, and unites its *noetic* powers in a circular movement which keeps the soul from deception' (*Divine Names*, ch. IV). St. Basil also noted, 'A nous that is not distracted toward externals or scattered through the senses to the world, returns to itself and through itself rises to the understanding of God' (Epistle 1). St. Gregory Palamas also mentions in his letter to Barlaam that deception can enter into direct and spiral prayers, but not into circular prayer. According to St. Dionysios the Areopagite, direct prayer is the activity of the nous based on external perceptions that raise it to a simple intellectual activity. Spiral prayer occurs when the nous is illumined by divine knowledge, not entirely noetically and changelessly, but rather intellectually and by transitions, combining direct and some circular prayer. Therefore, whoever wishes to pray without deception must occupy himself more with the circular prayer of the nous, which is accomplished by the return of the nous to the *heart* and by *noetic prayer* in the heart.

"This prayer is very arduous and toilsome, yet correspondingly fruitful because it is free of deception. This is the most important, the most sublime activity of the nous, for it unites the nous with God Who is above all things. In short, this circular movement of the nous purifies, illumines, and perfects the nous more than all the algebra, physics, metaphysics, and other sciences of secular philosophy. This noetic prayer makes man spiritual and a seer of God, whereas those other intellectual disciplines make him only a natural (ψυχικός) man. But as St. Paul says, 'The natural [unspiritual] man receiveth not the gifts of the Spirit, for they are folly to him' (1 Cor. 2:14)."

—St. Nikodemos the Hagiorite,
A Handbook of Spiritual Counsel, pp. 116-117 (Greek ed.)

Consent (συγκατάθεσις)
Consent is one of the stages of temptation. St. John of the Ladder describes the stages as follows: "Assault is a simple conception or an image encountered for the first time, which has entered the heart. Coupling is mentally conversing with what has been encountered, accompanied by passion or dispassion. And consent is the yielding of the soul to what has been presented to it, accompanied by delight. But captivity is a forcible and involuntary abduction of the heart, or a permanent association with what has been encountered which destroys the good condition of our soul. Struggle is power equal to the attacking force, which either wins or loses according to the soul's desire. Passion is primarily that which nestles with

persistence in the soul for a long time, forming a habit in the soul by its long-standing association with it, since the soul of its own accord clings to it. The first of these states is without sin, the second not always, but the third is sinful or sinless according to the state of the struggler. Struggle can earn crowns or punishments. Captivity is judged differently, according to whether it occurs at the time of prayer or at other times; whether it happens in things neither good nor bad, or in the context of evil thoughts. But passion is unequivocally condemned in every situation, and requires either corresponding repentance or future punishment. Therefore, he who regards the first assault dispassionately cuts off with one blow all the rest which follow."

—*The Ladder of Divine Ascent*, Step 15:73

Contemplation (θεωρία)

The Holy Fathers use the word "θεωρία" (theh-oh-ree'ah) in three different ways. Its first meaning is simply "seeing" or "beholding" physically. Its second meaning metaphorically refers to intellectual perception, that is, "consideration," "speculation," and "philosophical contemplation." In this case, we chose to translate θεωρία with the word "contemplation." Its third meaning refers to *noetic* contemplation, which is the highest state of prayer. When used in reference to this noetic contemplation, we merely transliterated the word as "theoria," instead of using the term "contemplation," to avoid confusion with the second meaning of the word, i.e., intellectual contemplation. See also *theoria*.

Diakonema (διακόνημα)

A diakonema is a monastic's assigned job at a monastery. Some translators use the word "obedience" for this term.

Discern, discernment (διακρίνω, διάκρισις)

Discernment is a spiritual gift pertaining to the *nous*. Through discernment, one discerns the inner states of the spiritual life, distinguishing between uncreated and created things: between the energies of God and the energies of the devil. Through discernment, one is also able to distinguish between the energies of God and the psychosomatic energies of man, thereby distinguishing emotional states from spiritual experiences.

Disciple (ὑποτακτικός)

Taken in the broad sense, the word "disciple" refers to every Christian who receives spiritual guidance from his spiritual father. In the monastic life, it applies to a monk who obeys an elder so that his soul may be healed from the *passions* and attain *theosis* by the grace of God.

Dispassion (ἀπάθεια)

Dispassion is achieved when all three aspects of the soul (i.e., the intelligent, appetitive, and incensive aspects) are directed towards God. It is the transfiguration of the *passionate* aspects of the soul (i.e., the aspects of the soul which are more vulnerable to *passion*, namely, the appetitive and incensive aspects), rather than its mortification. Thus dispassion in this context does not signify a stoic indifference, but rather, a transfiguration and sanctification of the powers of the soul and eventually of the body also.

Ecstasy (ἔκστασις)

One experiences ecstasy when, with the synergy of grace, one detaches his *nous* from reason and the surrounding environment and brings it back to the *heart*. Then, "through the heart the nous ascends to God," according to St. Gregory Palamas. During ecstasy, the nous is found in a different, spiritual realm. It is not a respite of the actions of the soul and nous, but a respite of physical actions, such as eating, sleeping, etc.

Eros (ἔρως)

Although "eros" can mean sensual love in other contexts— as the ancient Greeks used it—the elder uses it in the *patristic* sense, which denotes exclusively the burning or intense longing or love (completely void of any sensuality) that impels man towards union with God.

Fantasy (φαντασία)

In the *patristic* sense, a fantasy is a mental image formed in the *nous* either by oneself or by the demons. Fantasies are the chief instruments of the demons to lead man into sin. As St. Hesychios the Priest writes, "It is impossible for sin to enter the heart without first knocking at its door in the form of a fantasy provoked by the devil" (*Philokalia*, Vol. I, p. 173). Fantasies created in one's own nous, though, can be either beneficial or harmful. For example, it is helpful to *contemplate* death, heaven, hell, etc. with our nous at the outset of prayer, because in this way one's *heart* is predisposed to prayer. However, it is also possible with one's nous to meditate on worldly or sinful things. Nevertheless, all fantasies are an obstacle to pure prayer, which requires an undistracted *nous*.

Flesh (σάρξ)

In addition to its literal meaning, the word "flesh" denotes the carnal *passions* or a carnal way of thinking.

Geronda (Γέρων)

Usually translated as "Elder," a geronda (pronounced "yeh'-ron-da") is a *hieromonk*, priest, or monk who, ideally, has reached *dispassion* by the grace of God. Thus, because of his own experience, he is able to lead his spiritual children to dispassion as well. In a broader sense, it is used as a respectful title for any spiritual father and any elderly hieromonk, priest, or monk.

Heart (καρδία)

In *patristic* usage, the heart is both spiritual and physical. The spiritual heart is "deep" (Ps. 64:6), an "immeasurable abyss" (St. Makarios, *Philokalia*, Vol. III, pp. 321, 83), the "inner man" (St. Gregory Palamas, *To Xeni*, Gk. Philokalia, Vol. IV, p. 109), the "hidden person" (1 Pet. 3:4), the "battle-ground of the spiritual struggle" (Archimandrite Sophrony, *Saint Silouan*, p. 10), identified with *nous* (St. Maximos the Confessor, *Philokalia*, Vol. II, pp. 109, 73), that into whose depths the grace of God enters through baptism (St. Diadochos of Photiki, *Philokalia,* Vol. I, p. 279, 77), where God may be made manifest (St. Theoleptos, Metropolitan of Philadelphia, *Writings*, pp. 385f. Gk. Philokalia, Vol. IV, p. 6) and may dwell (Eph. 3:17) and writes His laws (Rom. 2:15 and St. Maximos, *Philokalia*, Vol. II, pp. 158, 81). It is located in the physical heart as in an organ (St. Gregory Palamas, *Triads*, 1, 2, 3, CWS p. 43), which is man's "natural, para-natural, and supernatural center" (*St. Nikodemos the Hagiorite—a Handbook of Spiritual Counsel,* CWS, p.154-157), and is the path for the nous to return to the spiritual heart (Archimandrite Sophrony, *Saint Silouan*, p. 47).

Hesychast (ἡσυχαστής)

A hesychast is someone who lives a life of *hesychia* in seclusion from the world and is wholly dedicated to God. His chief struggle is to bring his *nous* into his *heart*.

Hesychia (ἡσυχία)

The term ἡσυχία can mean either external stillness or internal, *noetic* stillness. In the former instance, the word is translated as "stillness," whereas in the latter instance, it is transliterated as "hesychia."

Hesychia is the ascetical practice of noetic stillness linked with *watchfulness* and deepened by the unceasing *Jesus prayer*. Hesychia is an undisturbed *nous* and a *heart* with peace, freed from *thoughts*, *passions*, and from influences of the environment. It is dwelling in God. Hesychia is the way by which man achieves *theosis*. External stillness can help one achieve hesychia.

Hieromonk (ἱερομόναχος)

A hieromonk is a monk who has been ordained to the priesthood.

Holy Mountain (τὸ Ἅγιον Ὄρος)

See *Athos*.

Icon (εἰκών)

An icon is a two-dimensional sacred depiction of Christ, of His saints, or of a holy event. Icons are to be venerated, not worshipped, as worship is due to God alone. As St. Basil the Great has stated, the reverence given to icons is transferred to their prototype, that is, to the one portrayed.

Illumination (φώτισις)

Closely connected with *noetic prayer*, illumination of the *nous* occurs when the *heart* is purified from the *passions*, the nous returns within the heart, and *the prayer* operates unceasingly. At this stage, one weeps tears of *repentance* daily.

Imagination (φαντασία)

The imagination is one of the lower psychical faculties of man, operating in a realm between reason and sense. Although the imagination can be used by the *nous* to create beneficial *contemplations*, it is also the chief instrument evil spirits use to create *fantasies* of worldly or sinful things which distract one from prayer and lead one to wrong thinking, wrong feeling, and wrong doing.

Inner voice (ἐνδιάθετος λόγος)

St. Nikodemos the Hagiorite explains the "inner voice" or "inner reason" in this manner:

"Once you have brought your *nous* into the *heart*, it should not just stay there, looking and doing nothing, but should find reason, that is, the inner voice of the heart through which we think, compose essays, make judgments, analyze, and read whole books silently, without saying a single word with the mouth.

"After the nous has found this inner voice, do not let it say anything else except this short, *single-phrased* prayer: 'Lord Jesus Christ, Son of God, have mercy on me.' But this is not enough. It is also necessary to activate the soul's will so that you say this prayer with all your will and power and love. To put it more clearly, let your inner voice say only *the prayer*, let your nous pay attention through its spiritual vision and hearing to the words of the prayer alone and especially to the meaning of the words, without imagining any forms, shapes, or any other perceptible or intelligible thing, internal or external, even if it is something good. . . . Let all your will cleave to the same words of the prayer with love, so that the nous, the inner voice, and the will—these three parts of your soul—will be one, and the one three, for in this way man, who is an image of the Holy Trinity, is united with the Prototype, as St. Gregory Palamas, that great practicer and teacher of *noetic prayer* and *watchfulness*, has said."

—*A Handbook of Spiritual Counsel*,
St. Nikodemos of the Holy Mountain, pp. 117-118 (Gk. ed.)

Intellect (διάνοια)

The word "διάνοια" means the reason of man, that is, his discursive, conceptualizing, and logical faculty of conscious thinking and cogitation. It draws conclusions and formulates concepts from information obtained either by revelation or by the senses.

Jesus prayer (εὐχὴ Ἰησοῦ)

The Jesus prayer is a short prayer which is continually repeated, usually consisting of the words "Lord Jesus Christ, have mercy on me."

Knowledge (γνῶσις)

Through the process of *theosis*, man attains to a knowledge of a higher order than any human knowledge and beyond any other natural knowledge. It is neither an intellectual speculation about God nor knowledge about God, but it stems from personal experience of God, first through undistracted prayer accompanied by peace and love of God or joyous *mourning*, and later by means of *theoria* of His Uncreated Light.

Meditation (μελέτη)

The term "meditation," as used by the Holy Fathers, indicates a thoughtful reflection or pondering upon a certain aspect of the faith, e.g., the Incarnation, God's mercy, the Crucifixion, the Transfiguration, one's sinfulness, etc. This is quite different from what is known as "Eastern meditation," which is the use of various psychosomatic techniques intended to bring about self-identification with a "supreme being" (or so-called "deity"), an "impersonal reality," or even nothingness. On the other hand, for an Orthodox Christian, meditation brings about humility, gratitude, and love, and is a preparation for prayer, which is a personal experience of the one, true, living God.

Metanoia (μετάνοια)

In its primary sense, "μετάνοια" (pronounced "meh-tah'-nee-ah") means *repentance*, literally, "a change of mind." However, it can also mean the specific act of making the sign of the cross, followed by a bow either down to the ground or to the waist. It is a gesture of reverence, worship, respect, or repentance. A typical *prayer rule* includes a number of metanoias done while saying the *Jesus prayer*. Some translators use the word "prostration" for this term.

Mourning (πένθος)

The elder uses the word "mourning" to mean godly mourning. Godly mourning is caused by grace and gives rise to repentance and sometimes tears. Godly mourning, as well as "joyous sadness" (χαρμολύπη), has a positive effect on the soul, bringing it peace and a determination to struggle harder to live a Christian way of life. But merely human mourning is a destructive sorrow that leads one to despair and causes psychological and psychosomatic abnormalities.

Noetic (νοερός, νοητός)
Belonging to, characteristic of, or perceptible to the *nous*.

Noetic Prayer (νοερὰ προσευχή)
Noetic prayer is prayer done with the *nous* without distraction within the *heart*. Another name for it is *"prayer of the heart."* It is contrasted with the prayer of the *intellect* which is done within the reason.

Nous (νοῦς)
The English word that best conveys the meaning of the Greek word "νοῦς" is the word "mind." The Fathers use this term with several other meanings, too. They mainly refer to the nous as the soul (the "spiritual nature" of a man—St. Isaac the Syrian) and the *heart* (or "the essence of the soul"—vid. *Philokalia*, Vol. II, p. 109, 73). More specifically, it constitutes the innermost aspect of the heart (St. Diadochos §§79, 88). However, they also refer to it as the "eye of the soul" (St. John of Damascus, *The Orthodox Faith*, FC Vol. 37, p. 236) or "the organ of theoria" (*Makarian Homilies*) which "is engaged in pure prayer" (St. Isaac the Syrian). They call the energy of the nous "a power of the soul" (St. Gregory Palamas, *On the Holy Spirit*, 2, 9) "consisting of thoughts and conceptual images" (St. Gregory Palamas, *On the Hesychasts*, p. 410, 3). However, the nous is more commonly known as the energy of the soul, whereas the heart is known as the essence of the soul.

Panagia (Παναγία)
This title of the Virgin Mary means "the All-holy one."

Papa- (Παπᾶς)
This prefix is added to the names of people who are priests.

Pascha (Πάσχα)

Pascha literally means "passover." It is the celebration of the Lord's Resurrection, known in Western Christianity as Easter.

Passion (πάθος)

A passion is a spiritual disease that dominates that soul. When one repeatedly falls into a certain sin, it becomes second nature—a passion—for him to keep falling into this sin. Thus, one who misuses the God-given powers of the soul of desire and anger, or one who continually succumbs to temptations of lust, hate, malice, or jealousy, or one who succumbs to pride and vainglory acquires those passions. It is primarily through obedience to an experienced elder that one is cleansed or healed of the passions and reaches *dispassion*.

Passionate (ἐμπαθής)

The word "passionate" in this text is not used in any of the secular senses of the word, but is used to describe someone or something subject to the *passions*.

Patristic (πατερικός)

This adjective is used to describe something of, or relating to, the Holy Fathers of the Church.

Praxis (πρᾶξις)

Praxis is the practice of the virtues, in contrast with *theoria*. It refers to the external aspect of the ascetical life (namely, *purification, fasting, vigils, metanoias*, etc., and in general the keeping of the commandments) and is an indispensable prerequisite of theoria.

The prayer (ἡ εὐχή)

The *Jesus prayer*, "Lord Jesus Christ, have mercy on me," is usually referred to as simply "the prayer."

Prayer of the heart (καρδιακὴ προσευχή)

Prayer of the heart is the highest form of prayer, in which the *nous* is kept in the *heart* by the grace of the Holy Spirit and prays there without distraction. Beyond this form of prayer is *theoria*.

Prayer rope (κομποσχοίνι)

A prayer rope is a cord with many knots (usually thirty-three or one hundred) which is used in prayer to help the *nous* concentrate. At each knot, one prayer (usually the *Jesus prayer*) is said.

Prayer rule (κανών)

A prayer rule consists of the prayers and *metanoias* which one does daily, under the guidance of one's spiritual father.

Predisposition (πρόληψις)

Predisposition is "the involuntary presence of former sins in the memory," according to St. Mark the Ascetic. This state is caused by repeated sinful acts, which predispose a person to yield to particular temptations. Even though in principle he retains free choice and can reject provocations from the demons, in practice the force of habit makes it progressively harder for him to resist.

Proskomidi (προσκομιδή)

The proskomidi is the service of preparation for the Divine Liturgy, in which the portion to be used for the Eucharist is cut out of the *prosphoron*, and during which the living and the dead are commemorated.

Prosphoron (πρόσφορον)

A prosphoron (plural: prosphora) is a round loaf of bread specially prepared to be used in the *Proskomidi* in preparation for the Divine Liturgy.

Purification (κάθαρσις)

In patristic theology, purification refers to three states: (1) the rejection of all *thoughts* from the *heart*, (2) the ascetical effort by which the three powers of the soul are turned towards God, thereby moving in accordance with and above nature, and (3) the ascetical method by which man overcomes selfish love and achieves unselfish love.

Rebuttal (ἀντιλογία)

Rebuttal is the repulsing of a demonic thought at the moment of *assault*. See also *consent*.

Repentance (μετάνοια)

The Greek word for "repentance" does not mean merely regret or contrition, but it literally means a "change of mind" through which one directs his entire life towards God. See also *metanoia*.

Restoration (ἀποκατάστασις)

The term "restoration" is used by the Holy Fathers to denote the reinstating into paradise of man, which is to occur after the Last Judgment. The term was misused by Origen, who claimed that the restoration applies to all men, as well as to the fallen angels, i.e., the demons. See also Acts 3:21.

Schema (σχῆμα)

The schema, usually called the "great schema" or "angelic schema," is the habit of a monk of the highest level of monasticism. It is called the "angelic schema" because its bearer strives to live angelically in purity and devotion to God alone.

Single-phrased (μονολόγιστος)

This is an adjective used by St. John of the Ladder and other Church Fathers to describe the *Jesus prayer* because of its short form.

Skete (σκήτη)

A skete is a small monastic village, usually consisting of a central church and several "cells." Cells are monastic houses, each with its own *synodia* and usually with its own chapel.

Synodia (συνοδία)

A synodia (pronounced "seen-oh-dee'-ah") is a group of monks living together, consisting of an elder and his *disciples*. This word is often translated as "brotherhood."

Theoria (θεωρία)

Theoria is the "vision of the spirit" or "a non-sensible revelation of the *nous*" (St. Isaac the Syrian) through which one attains spiritual *knowledge*. That is, through theoria, the Holy Spirit grants one understanding of the mysteries of God and creation which are hidden to the rational human *intellect*. Knowledge stemming from theoria is revelation from above. Theoria is not intellectual work, but an operation of the Holy Spirit which opens the eyes of the soul to behold mysteries. The Church Fathers often contrast it with *praxis,* which is an indispensable prerequisite of theoria. In the first stage of theoria, *the prayer* is said without distraction and with a sense of the presence of God with love, peace, *mourning*, etc. In the next stage, the nous proceeds to feel what Adam felt in Paradise before the Fall, and it sees spiritually how all nature glorifies God. Furthermore, it sees His omnipotence, omniscience, and providence therein. St. Maximos the Confessor calls this "perceiving the inner essences or principles of created beings" (*Philokalia,* Vol. II, p. 69). In the final stage of theoria, one beholds God Himself in the Uncreated Light. (Evagrios the Solitary, *On Prayer, Philokalia,* Vol. I, p. 61). See also *contemplation.*

Theosis (θέωσις)

Connected with the *theoria* of the Uncreated Light, theosis, (or "divinization") is a participation in the uncreated grace of God. At this stage of perfection, one has reached *dispassion*. Through the cooperation of God with man, theosis is attained through the action of the transfigurative grace of God.

Theotokos (Θεοτόκος)

This is a title for the Virgin Mary, the Mother of God. Literally, it means "God-birthgiver." This title was approved by the Third Ecumenical Synod.

Thoughts (λογισμοί)

In the *patristic* sense, "thoughts" refers not merely to thoughts in the ordinary sense, but also to evil thoughts provoked by the demons. Only with *watchfulness* can we prevent the demons' *assaults* of thoughts from developing into sins.

Toll-houses (τελώνια)

When a person dies, angels come to take his soul to the throne of God to be judged. At various "toll-houses," demons as "tax collectors" try to stop the soul's ascent, accusing it of sins, while the angels defend it, presenting its good works. If the soul's unconfessed sins outweigh its good works on the scales of God's judgment, then He permits the demons to cast it into Hades before it even reaches the throne of God. Of course, the toll-houses are not material but spiritual. They were revealed in *theoria* to many saints, who then used material imagery to describe the spiritual reality.*

Tonsure (κουρά)

A tonsure is the rite in which a novice becomes a monk or nun. It is called a tonsure because during the rite, some of the novice's hair is cut.

Typikon (τυπικόν)

The "typikon" can mean (a) a brotherhood's system of rules regulating the life of a monk in general, or (b) the set of rubrics governing the order of liturgical services.

---

* Although some modern theologians question the teaching concerning the toll-houses, there can be no doubt about its veracity in view of its extensive support in Scripture, the service books, iconography, and the writings of dozens of saints, including St. Athanasios the Great, St. Basil the Great, St. Ephraim the Syrian, St. Makarios the Great, St. John Chrysostom, St. Cyril of Alexandria, St. John of the Ladder, St. Maximos the Confessor, St. John of Damascus, St. Ignatius Brianchaninov, St. Theophan the Recluse, St. Nikolai Velimirovic, St. John Maximovitch, and St. Paisios of the Holy Mountain. See *The Departure of the Soul According to the Teaching of the Orthodox Church* (St. Anthony's Monastery: Florence, AZ, 2017) and www.thedepartureofthesoul.org.

Watchful Fathers (Νηπτικοὶ Πατέρες)

The Watchful Fathers, or Neptic Fathers, are the Church Fathers who wrote about *watchfulness*.

Watchfulness (νῆψις)

Watchfulness is unceasing attentiveness, alertness, or vigilance whereby one keeps watch over one's inward *thoughts* and *fantasies* so that they do not enter the *heart*; it is only the *nous* which must be within the heart.

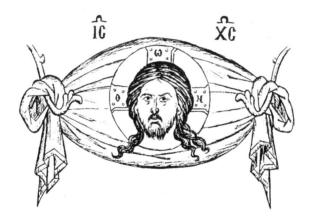

Index

(numbers in bold are glossary entries)

Glory be to God
for all things.